BUILDING AND INTERPRETING POSSESSION SENTENCES

Neil Myler

The MIT Press
Cambridge, Massachusetts
London, England

This book was set in Computer Modern by the author.

Printed and bound in the United States of America.

Library of Congress Cataloging-in-Publication Data

Names: Myler, Neil, author.

Title: Building and interpreting possession sentences / Neil Myler.

Description: Cambridge, MA : The MIT Press, [2016] | Includes bibliographical references and index.
Identifiers: LCCN 2016002505 | ISBN 9780262034913 (hardcover : alk. paper)
Subjects: LCSH: Grammar, Comparative and general–Possessives. | Grammar, Comparative and general–Syntax. | English language–Sentences. | Semantics, Comparative.
Classification: LCC P299.P67 M95 2016 | DDC 415–dc23 LC record available at https://lccn.loc.gov/2016002505

10 9 8 7 6 5 4 3 2 1

To all Mylers and Bryces, but most especially to the memory of my grandfather and namesake, Neil Bryce. I would have loved to have had the chance to explain this work to him, and I like to think that he would have enjoyed hearing about it. Sometimes I flatter myself, and I think I got it from him.

Contents

Acknowledgments

This book is a substantially rewritten and reorganized version of my 2014 doctoral dissertation of the same title. It therefore owes a great deal to my mentors and colleagues from my graduate institution, New York University; also to three anonymous reviewers, and to a team of very helpful (and very patient) people at the MIT Press.

I was extremely fortunate to have an advisor who is simultaneously a visionary and an unbelievably kind and forgiving human being. Alec Marantz was the reason I applied to NYU, but I had no idea how good an instinct that was until I actually got there. I'll never be able to thank him enough for his guidance and support over my years there, and since.

As for my internal committee members, it was an immense privilege to have Stephanie Harves, Richard Kayne, and Anna Szabolcsi involved in a project on predicative possession. For want of a better organizing principle, let me discuss them alphabetically.

Without Stephanie Harves I would never have figured out what this book had to be about. Back in Fall 2009 (my first semester at NYU) and then again in Fall 2011, she co-taught two seminars directly relevant to the HAVE/BE question with Richard Kayne, both of which played a role in me realizing what I had to do. Stephanie has a unique ability to cut through the most forbidding paper to extract its central insight. This skill is basically obligatory when it comes to navigating the literature on possession, and so I am extremely lucky that she was (along with Richie) among my first instructors in this domain. Who knows what would have happened otherwise. On top of everything else, she is a magnificent collaborator, a masterful teacher (there's nothing like being a TA for Stephanie), and an excellent friend.

Richard Kayne has done so much in my cause since I met him in 2009. He co-taught the seminar on *having, being, wanting, and needing* that got me started on possession, and his other classes were always immensely inspiring and productive for me. These days a lot of people who know of me do so via my work on English dialect syntax. But none of that was part of my identity until Richie encouraged me to make it so. This is all part of a pattern that has run throughout Richie's career: he knows the importance of encouraging native speakers to investigate their own varieties, and the field of comparative syntax in general (and I in particular) would never have been able to make the strides that it has without his guidance. He always asks exactly the right question, and even the briefest interactions with him yield a flood of new insights and directions. He has exhibited more patience than I deserve with respect to the projects he has advised me on. Thanking him adequately would require literary skill beyond my reach.

Anna Szabolcsi was my first true formal semantics teacher (what a privilege it is to be allowed to say that). She always went above and beyond the call of duty, helping to prepare me for Semantics I before I even officially arrived at NYU, and continuing to help me and other semantic neophytes after we arrived, inside and outside normal class times. I would never dare to call myself a semanticist, but insofar as I can communicate with them, Anna deserves a lot of the credit. She always pushed me to lay out the "rules of the game" in everything I do, much to the benefit of this project.

Pieter Muysken has been a hero of mine since I first became interested in the Quechua family back in 2006, when I came across the Cajamarca variety. It was on a wing and a prayer that I sent an email to him, asking if he would be the external examiner on my dissertation. To my enduring amazement, he agreed within two minutes of me sending the email. He has been similarly rapid and helpful ever since.

Moving outside my committee, but just barely, I owe so much to Gillian Gallagher. I say "just barely" outside my committee, because Gillian's role in making this book happen would count as extraordinary for even a committee chair. By taking me to Bolivia with her as a research assistant, and then acting as PI for my NSF DDRIG grant application, she made my Quechua fieldwork possible. She even went as far as giving me the laptop I wrote the dissertation version of this book on, when my old one started to break down towards the end of my second qualifying paper. (The laptop in question, Josephine, was also used to write Gillian's dissertation. Now Josephine has retired in peace, safe in the knowledge that she has contributed more to Quechua studies than perhaps any other MacBook Air). Gillian is also great fun to be around, and she's been a fantastic source of personal and professional advice at crucial times.

NYU has marvelous faculty in every subfield, and I was very lucky to be able to learn from them. Maria Gouskova's Phonology II course was a massive eye-opener for me, and having her as the chair of my second qualifying paper was a wonderful experience. Chris Barker is a remarkable semantics teacher, and I shudder to think what might have happened to my trajectory were it not for his willingness to make time for me throughout Semantics II and his Fragments seminar. Chris Collins ran some of the richest and most productive seminars during my time at NYU, and his Field Methods course was as important to my development as it was exhilarating. Paul Postal, though officially retired by the time I arrived, still found time to come in for a day of meetings with me, Salvador Mascarenhas, and Jim Wood. He and Chris Collins also provided Stephanie and me with a tremendous amount of helpful discussion of our *have yet to* project. I would also like to thank Mark Baltin for teaching us Syntax I, and Greg Guy for leading such a fun and thought-provoking Sociolinguistics course.

"When I find myself in the company of scientists," W.H. Auden once remarked, "I feel like a shabby curate who has strayed by mistake into a drawing-room full of dukes." My awe for NYU's phonologists and semanticists would have made me feel much the same way, if it weren't for the fact they were always so helpful and welcoming towards me when I took their courses or showed up to their group meetings. So thank you, Frans Adriaans, Chris Barker, Lucas Champollion, Lisa Davidson, Gillian Gallagher, Maria Gouskova, Philippe Schlenker, and all the semantics and phonology graduate students, for creating this atmosphere. Thanks also to Kathryn Pruitt, for allowing me to be a part-time auditor of her fantastic Harmonic Serialism seminar.

I am the eldest of three siblings, and I often used to wonder what it would be like to have a big brother. Knowing Jim Wood has answered my question. Jim has been unflaggingly supportive and inspiring, both as a friend and as an intellectual ally. Insofar as this book achieves anything at all, it is climbing up a staircase that Jim installed with much time and effort before I turned up. Any fair-minded observer of both our work will know what my debt to him is. If the opportunity ever arises to repay it, I will not hesitate.

I want to thank Tricia Irwin, Inna Livitz, and Jim Wood for all those syntax pub-nights back in the day. They took place at a crucial time for me intellectually, and I benefited massively from them on a number of levels. I'd also like to thank Itamar Kastner–if Alec is George Best, then Itamar is NYU's Ryan Giggs.

To my NYU cohortmates, it's hard to know what to say. I'll never forget those group outings in our early years (although the outings that ended up at The Continental are harder to recall, for some mysterious reason). So thanks Meera Saeed Al Kaabi, Carina Bauman (my favorite CB–and that's saying something), Sangjin Hwang, Sang-Im Lee, Tim Leffel (for SYNC, and helping me clean up on more than one occasion), Kim Leiken, Sean Martin, Tim Mathes, Luiza Newlin-Lukowicz, Emily Nguyen, and Mike Solomon.

Outside of NYU, there are a huge number of linguists whose input has been very important to me–so many that I'm doomed to miss some of them out. Thank you David Adger, Artemis Alexiadou, Sam Al Khatib, Peter Alrenga, Karlos Arregi, Jon Barnes, John Beavers, Rajesh Bhatt, Bronwyn Bjorkman, Jonathan Bobaljik, Hagit Borer, Ruth Brillman, Guglielmo Cinque, Eve Clark, Jessica Coon, Elizabeth Cowper, Marcel den Dikken, David Embick, Michael Yoshitaka Erlewine, Carlos Fasola, Janet Dean Fodor, Robert Frank, Vera Gribanova, Bill Haddican, Paul Hagstrom, Daniel Harbour, Heidi Harley, Anders Holmberg, Larry Horn, Sabine Iatridou,

Gianina Iordachioaia, Daniel Ezra Johnson, Kyle Johnson, Stephanie Kakadelis, Laura Kalin, Lena Karvovskaya, Chris Kennedy, Isa Kerem Bayirli, Brooke Larson, Rich Larson, Beth Levin, Ted Levin, Tom Leu, Terje Lohndal, Chris Lucas, Victor Manfredi, Gretchen McCulloch, Tom McFadden, Moreno Mitrovic, Iain Mobbs, Carol Neidle, Andrew Nevins, Corbin Neuhauser, Teresa O' Neill, Cathy O'Connor, Roumi Pancheva, Marcel Pitteroff, Maire Noonan, Orin Percus, David Pesetsky, Omer Preminger, Norvin Richards, John Rickford, Ian Roberts, Liliana Sánchez, Beatrice Santorini, Florian Schäfer, Halldór Ármann Sigurðsson, Pete Smith, Gary Thoms, Christina Tortora, Lisa Travis, Coppe van Urk, George Walkden, Tom Wasow, Jeffrey Watumull, and Rafaella Zanuttini.

I've been lucky to have a number of fantastic collaborators, and our work together has in many cases fed directly into important parts of this book–so thank you Karlos Arregi, Stephanie Harves, Daniel Erker, Josef Fruehwald, Einar Freyr Sigurðsson, Andrew Nevins, Jim Wood, and Bert Vaux.

For nine years since the happy accident that brought me to Cajamarca, I have been hugely fortunate in receiving the kindness and help of many Quechua speakers. It all started with Dolores Ayay Chilón and Marcelino Intor Chalán in Cajamarca. Once I got to NYU, Odi González helped me both inside and outside classes with his native Cuzco Quechua. For this book, I have had the opportunity to work on Cochabamba Quechua in Bolivia and on Santiago del Estero Quechua in Argentina. My profound thanks go to María Cardoza, Gladys Camacho Rios, and Cristina Puente Arista (in Cochabamba) and Dario Acosta, Rosinda Barreta, Casilda Chazarreta, Estela Chazarreta, Guillermo Chazarreta, Manuela Jimenez, Raquel Gomez, Teodosia González, Agustino Grano, Haydee Palavecino, and Aurella Quita (in Santiago) for sharing their languages with me. Gladys Camacho Rios deserves special mention for helping both me and Gillian so much with the coordination of our fieldwork, and for working so intensely with me during her stay at NYU in Fall 2013. Lelia Albarracín was my first point of contact when I began exploring the possibility of doing fieldwork in Santiago del Estero, and I thank her for all she did to make that possible. I would also like to thank Héctor Andreani for all his friendship, hospitality, and help finding speakers–without Héctor, my time in Santiago del Estero would have been nowhere near as successful and enjoyable as it was. I'd also like to acknowledge a number of linguists working on Quechua for responding to questions about the dialects on which they are experts, including David Coombs-Lynch, Heidi Carlson de Coombs, Paul Heggarty, Pieter Muysken (again), Liliana Sánchez (again), and David Weber.

My fieldwork was supported by NSF Doctoral Dissertation Research Improvement Grant BCS-1324839. I am extremely grateful to the committee for their faith in this project.

To my old mentors in Cambridge, I will forever be grateful. Theresa Biberauer made me into a linguist. Even all these years after I wrote the "Additional Acknowledgments" to my MPhil thesis, I still haven't figured out how to thank her properly. Now that the fighting chance she gave me has been converted, it will be even more difficult to do so. Ian Roberts supervised that thesis, and I benefited enormously from our discussions, from his teaching, and from his curry recommendations. Bert Vaux arrived at Cambridge about halfway through my undergraduate degree, and his impact on me was enormous. He introduced me to Distributed Morphology, and encouraged me to do graduate school in the United States. Adam Ledgeway taught me almost everything I knew about Romance syntax before I got to the states, and he supervised my undergraduate dissertation on Romance clitic placement, which I ended up using as a writing sample for my NYU application.

The process of working my dissertation into a book took place mostly at my new institution, Boston University. Thanks to all my new colleagues for making my transition to the other side of the desk so smooth–Byron Ahn (now of Princeton), Pete Alrenga, Sudha Arunachalam, Jon Barnes, Charles Chang, Daniel Erker, Paul Hagstrom, Carol Neidle, and Sasha Nikolaev. I'd especially like to thank Byron Ahn and Danny Erker for many stimulating Dugoutings in my first year, without which the collaboration between Danny and me could not have happened. I'd also like to thank my students at BU, especially the participants in my Spring 2015 class on *Having and Being*, for energizing discussion of some of the material in this book.

It's been a pleasure to work with Marcy Ross, Marc Lowenthal, and their team at MIT Press to bring this book to fruition. Special thanks also to Amy Hendrickson, without whose LATEX help I would never have finished.

My family and friends in England have always been with me, even when I'm half the world away. I've missed too many weddings (and too many funerals) since I crossed the Atlantic, but the times I have managed to get back have been wonderful beyond words. My mother, Sharon Myler, has nurtured and encouraged my academic side for as long as I can remember, as well as every other side of me, of course (I recall the first time she took me to Ormskirk library, to look at what the encyclopedias had to say about deep sea life, which for some reason I was obsessed with as a very young child. I wanted to learn all the Latin names for the creatures we were looking at. That should have been a sign of what was to come, I suppose). My father, Joseph Myler, has always been in my corner. He used to say to me, "the more you work in school now, the less you'll have to work as a grown-up." In terms of hours spent at my desk, my career choice has not vindicated him. But that's hardly his fault. And I would argue he was still partly right, because my job is also my hobby.

On paper, my brother Mike looks like a very different person from me. But we laugh at the same stupid things ("I'm going to punch your face [!!!!!] ... in the face"). Also, when I've asked him for judgments on things related to my English dialect syntax projects, he's proven to be such a metalinguistically insightful informant that I reckon he could have been a linguist (not that he would have wanted to be). My sister Fay is hilarious and wise, and she reads with a voracity that I've never been able to match. All of them have supported me through thick and thin, and made me who I am. Thanks to Nan and Gran for all the tea, and the teas, and the chats. Thanks to Gina for her fun outlook and her support. I'd also like to thank Roger Hewstone for making my mother so happy, and for only being slightly annoying when Liverpool are doing well and United are doing badly. Thanks also to my unofficial American family–Diane, Dave, Kelly, and Bailey (where's your toy?), for welcoming me into their home in the holidays, giving me somewhere to work when I needed it, and supporting me in uncountable ways over the last half-decade or so. I look forward to the day, in the not-too-distant future, when they'll become my official American family.

Finally, I want to thank Robin Marcus for her love.

1 Introduction

1.1 The Domain of Inquiry

A major question for linguistic theory is: how does the structure of sentences relate to their meanings? A subquestion concerns *argument realization*: what are the constraints on the relationship between the meanings of predicates and the syntactic status of their arguments (i.e., their subjects, objects, etc.)? While this latter question has been asked and answered in a number of different ways, the field is broadly agreed that there is a good deal of regularity in the way in which lexical semantics and syntax are related, so that thematic roles (the different participant roles in an event, such as agent, theme, goal, etc.) are predictably associated with particular syntactic positions (see Levin and Rappoport Hovav 2005 for a summary). To give three simple examples, (i) the agent of a transitive verb is invariably more syntactically "prominent" than the theme argument of the same verb across languages; (ii) many languages show evidence for two syntactically distinct types of intransitive verbs, which divide precisely on the question of whether their subject is an agent or a theme (the so-called unergative/unaccusative distinction); and (iii) the set of verbs in a given language that undergo the so-called *(anti-)causative* alternation (*John opened the door* vs. *the door opened*) will always be a subset of the change-of-state verbs (although which subset varies from language to language). A question that arises from these observations is the following: what is the nature of the association between syntactic positions and thematic roles, such that it gives rise to these regularities? In other words, what is the place of thematic roles in the architecture of the grammar?

This book is fundamentally about this latter question. One contemporary viewpoint takes thematic roles to be formal features present in the syntax, analogous to phi-features and abstract Case features, which must be checked via (internal or external) Merge in the course of the derivation (the movement theory of control of Hornstein 1999 et seq. relies on such a view). A different view, visible in work by Heim and Kratzer (1998), Schäfer (2008), Marantz (2009a, 2009b, 2013a), Wood (2012, 2015), Bruening (2013), and many others, takes it that thematic roles are not syntactic entities at all, but are rather determined post-syntactically, in the semantic component. From the perspective of Distributed Morphology (Halle and Marantz 1993), this latter view gives rise to some intriguing expectations concerning parallels with phenomena at the PF interface. First, we expect that the denotations associated with certain terminal nodes could vary depending on the surrounding syntactic structure, just as the PF realizations of terminal nodes can vary in a manner determined by the syntactic context (i.e. we should find conditioned *allosemy* at the LF interface, analogous to conditioned allomorphy at PF).

Secondly, just as there are zero morphemes at the PF interface (i.e., terminal nodes that are effectively ignored by the phonological component), we expect to find that terminal nodes can be *semantically zero* in certain circumstances, effectively being ignored by the semantic component. I will provide novel grounds for taking this second view to be correct, by showing that it permits new and promising solutions to long-standing puzzles in a complex empirical domain.

The empirical domain in question is the syntax and semantics of predicative possession cross-linguistically. This is a vast area of study, and its rich puzzles have vexed linguists from many traditions, including Indo-Europeanists (Buck 1949; Benveniste 1959; Allen 1964), Classicists (Kahn 1966), typologists (Heine 1997; Stassen 2009), formal semanticists (Beavers, Ponvert, and Wechsler 2009; Gutiérrez-Rexach 2012; Koontz-Garboden and Francez 2009; Partee 1999; Partee and Borschev 2001/2004, 2002; Sæbø 2009), cognitive grammarians (Langacker 1987; Brugman 1988), and generative syntacticians (Bach 1967; Belvin 1996; Bjorkman 2011; Emonds 1976; Freeze 1992; Harley 1995, 1997, 1998, 2002; Iatridou 1995; Jung 2011; Kayne 1993; Kim 2010, 2012; Levinson 2011; Lyons 1968; Mahajan 1994; Pylkkänen 1998; Szabolcsi 1981, 1994; several others).

My purpose in adding another study to this long (and not even nearly exhaustive) list is to show how recent work on the syntax/semantics interface in the generative tradition can be extended to shed light on two major puzzles in the syntax and semantics of predicative possession. The two puzzles I have in mind are what I call the *too-many-meanings* puzzle and the *too-many-(surface)-structures* puzzle. The nomenclature is new,[1] but the puzzles themselves are not. Indeed, it is my belief that all of the studies mentioned in the previous paragraph are fundamentally about at least one of these puzzles, and some attempt to address both. Alongside the intrinsic interest of the puzzles themselves, I hope to show that addressing them yields new insights into the theory of argument structure, and in particular into the place of thematic roles in the architecture of the grammar. I will now introduce each puzzle in turn.

The too-many-meanings puzzle springs from the observation that, in any given language, the construction used to express archetypal possessive meanings (like personal ownership of some object) is also often used for a myriad of other notions as well. These other notions commonly include, but need not be limited to: kinship relations, the relation between a person and his/her body parts, the relation between wholes and their subparts, the relation between a disease-sufferer and his/her illness,

1. Though it echoes the name of the *too-many-solutions* problem associated with Optimality Theoretic phonology (Steriade 2001/2009).

and the relation between an attribute and its holder. For example, the English verb *have* can be used to express all of these relations (and, as is well-known, many others as well–see Brugman 1988 and Belvin 1996 for especially thorough discussions; also Chapter 4 of this work, which is devoted principally to English *have*).[2]

(1)   John has a Playstation 3.   (Ownership)

(2)   John has a sister.   (Kinship)

(3)   John has blue eyes.   (Body Part)

(4)   This table has four sturdy legs.   (Part-Whole)

(5)   John has a cold.   (Disease)

(6)   John has a great deal of resilience.   (Attribute)

The too-many-meanings puzzle can thus be characterized as a problem for the theory of lexical semantics: how can one structure involving one particular verb (in this case, the English verb *have*, although the puzzle arises in some form or another in every language) be associated with so many different meanings? As we will see in Chapter 2, two main lines of attack have been taken on this question (as well as approaches that are to some extent a mixture of the two). I will introduce both briefly here.

One is to take the position that there is such a thing as a single "possession" relation which the lexical item *have* (and its cross-linguistic brethren) expresses, and that this possession relation has an extremely vague meaning, such that it is compatible with all of these notions. This vague meaning is often said to be something like "control" (Hagège 1993) or being in the subject's "sphere of influence"

---

2. Acknowledgement of facts like these goes back at least as far as Aristotle, who writes, with respect to Ancient Greek, the following at the end of his *Categories*: "The term 'to have' is used in various senses. In the first place it is used with reference to habit or disposition or any other quality, for we are said to 'have' a piece of knowledge or a virtue. Then, again, it has reference to quantity, as, for instance, in the case of a man's height; for he is said to 'have' a height of three or four cubits. It is used, moreover, with regard to apparel, a man being said to 'have' a coat or tunic; or in respect of something which we have on a part of ourselves, as a ring on the hand: or in respect of something which is a part of us, as hand or foot. The term refers also to content, as in the case of a vessel and wheat, or of a jar and wine; a jar is said to 'have' wine, and a corn-measure wheat. The expression in such cases has reference to content. Or it refers to that which has been acquired; we are said to 'have' a house or a field. A man is also said to 'have' a wife, and a wife a husband, and this appears to be the most remote meaning of the term, for by the use of it we mean simply that the husband lives with the wife. Other senses of the word might perhaps be found, but the most ordinary ones have all been enumerated."
Aristotle addresses analogous issues that arise with the Ancient Greek BE verb in his *Metaphysics* Book 5, part 7.

(Langacker 1987) (see Heine 1997, 3-10 for discussion of these and many other attempts to establish a core meaning for the possession relation).

The second line of attack is to deny that there is a single possession relation at all. One can imagine two ways of implementing this idea, both of which have instantiations in the literature. It could be that *have* is lexically ambiguous–in its most extreme form, this approach would involve saying that six different lexical entries for *have* are on show in examples (1)-(6). This would be unsatisfying for obvious reasons (both as a description of English and as a cross-linguistic claim, given the fact that some subset of these notions often "go together" in other languages). For this reason, existing implementations of this idea try to collapse at least some of these diverse relations together, before positing perhaps two or three lexical entries for *have*. Examples of this approach in action include Partee (1999), Tham (2004, 2006), Beavers, Ponvert, and Wechsler (2009), and Gutiérrez-Rexach (2012). A second way of implementing the idea that there is no single possession relation is to say that predicative possession sentences are structurally ambiguous– *have* itself contributes no semantic roles to the structure, and is perhaps even meaningless; the real semantic work is being done by additional, silent elements. On this approach, it is variation in the content of this silent matter that accounts for the plethora of interpretations that we see in (1)-(6). Perhaps the earliest version of this approach in the generative literature is Bach (1967); more recent versions include Iatridou (1995), Belvin (1996), Ritter and Rosen (1997) and, insofar as one of the two meanings they assign to *have* is basically an identity function over relations, Partee (1999) and Beavers et al. (2009). The approach advocated here will be of this kind, although many of its important details will be different from those of its antecedents.

The too-many-meanings puzzle is to be set against the too-many-(surface)-structures puzzle, which in some ways is its exact opposite. While the too-many-meanings puzzle asks "How can one possession structure have so many different meanings in a given language?", the too-many-(surface)-structures puzzle asks "How can it be that the same set of possessive meanings is realized on the surface in so many syntactically different ways across languages?"

To see the problem, consider the surface differences between simple possession sentences in English, Icelandic, Cochabamba (Bolivian) Quechua, Russian and Hungarian.

(7)   I have a book.

(8)   Ég er með bók.   (Icelandic)
      I   am with book.ACC

      'I have a book.'

(9)   Noqa libru-yoq ka-ni.   (Cochabamba Quechua)
      I   book-YOQ be-1SUBJ

      'I have a book.'

(10) u menja est'   kniga.   (Russian)
      At me.GEN be$_{exist}$.3SUBJ book

      'I have a book.'

(11) Nekem van   könyvem.   (Hungarian)
      I.DAT be$_{exist}$.3SUBJ book.3POSS.NOM

      'I have a book.'

The nature of the puzzle should be clear: although these sentences are translations of each other, they seem to differ radically in argument structure, at least on the surface.

We can see that English employs a transitive verb *have* here; judging by the "Predicative Possession" chapter of the online version of the World Atlas of Language Structures (Stassen 2013), around a quarter of the world's languages have a transitive possession verb (63 languages out of 240 surveyed, which equates to just over 26%). The fact that this pattern is relatively rare has been remarked upon by many (see especially Benveniste 1959, 1966; Bach 1967; Kayne 1993), and we will return to this issue. Languages that pattern with English in this respect are often referred to as HAVE languages,[3] and I will continue to refer to them in this way (Harves and Kayne 2012; Jung 2011; Isačenko 1974). The other languages in (7)-(11) instead use a construction based around the intransitive verb BE. Icelandic, although closely related to English, expresses possession of portable possessees (and some other "possessive" relations) using a copular construction in which the possessee appears as the complement of a preposition corresponding to English *with*.[4]

---

3. Following common practice, I will use *italics* when discussing a morpheme in a particular language, and SMALL CAPS to refer to a correspondence class of morphemes across languages. Hence, *have* refers to the English verb, and HAVE refers to transitive verbs of the relevant sort across languages.

4. As discussed by Levinson (2011), Wood (2009), and Irie (1997), Icelandic has two additional possession constructions involving the transitive verbs *eiga* and *hafa* (the latter cognate to English

As noted in footnote 4, Icelandic also has predicative possession constructions that employ a transitive verb (in fact, there are two such verbs in Icelandic), and so Icelandic would still usually be classified as a HAVE language.

Far more common are languages with no such transitive verb at all, as seems to be the case in Cochabamba Quechua, Hungarian, and Russian. Languages of this sort are often referred to collectively as BE languages, and counterposed as a group to the HAVE languages for the purposes of discussing parametric variation (Freeze 1992; Kayne 1993; Mahajan 1994; Pylkkänen 1998; Harley 2002; Bjorkman 2011). However, an important part of the too-many-(surface)-structures puzzle is the fact that variation within the BE languages is also apparently formidable. Although superficially similar to the Icelandic construction, the Cochabamba Quechua[5] construction in (9) is in fact somewhat different. The possessee in this construction is marked by a suffix -yoq. While some have assumed that -yoq is an adpositional element (e.g. Sánchez 1996, 21), in Chapter 6 I show that it is a nominal suffix that converts possessees into predicate nominals.[6] Hence, the -yoq construction is a copular BE construction of a rather different kind than that found in Icelandic. The Russian and Hungarian examples can be set apart from the Icelandic and Quechua ones along another dimension of variation: Russian and Hungarian employ existential BE constructions rather than copular BE constructions. But the variation does not end there, because the status of the possessor appears to differ: it is apparently embedded in a locative PP in Russian, but is marked dative in Hungarian, just as possessors in the specifiers of possessed DPs are in that language.[7]

The too-many-(surface)-structures problem is a challenge both for the theory of argument structure and for comparative syntax more generally. Just like in the case of the too-many-meanings puzzle, there are two main sorts of reaction to it that we can imagine (and just as in that case, a range of mixed positions are also possible). One way to proceed is to take the surface variation exhibited in (7)-(11) at face value, and develop some theory of the interaction of syntax and semantics

---

have). See Chapter 4 of the present work, and Myler, E.F. Sigurðsson and Wood (2014), for discussion.

5. All Cochabamba Quechua examples cited without attribution are from the author's fieldnotes.

6. Some version of this analysis seems to be the majority view on -*yoq* in the descriptive literature on Quechua languages. See Chapter 6 for discussion.

7. Famously, Szabolcsi (1981, 1983, 1994) argued that the Hungarian construction is simply an existential construction containing a possessed DP, of which the possessor has "run away from home" out of that DP and into its surface position. From this analysis, the dative case marking on the possessor follows.

that explains how such diverse structures come out with truth-conditionally identical meanings. Outside of the generative tradition, Heine (1997) has attempted to develop such a theory from a functional-typological perspective, by bringing together Cognitive Grammar (Langacker 1987) and the theory of grammaticalization. Within the generative tradition, taking the surface variation at face value has traditionally been eschewed, since developing a theory of the syntax/semantics interface that achieves the desired the result from this starting point has often been taken to require an unacceptable weakening of the theory of Theta-role assignment. In particular, it seems to require a radical departure from the Uniformity of Theta Assignment Hypothesis, which has been widely adopted since it was proposed by Baker (1988, 46).[8]

(12)   *The Uniformity of Theta Assignment Hypothesis (UTAH)*
         Identical thematic relationships between items are represented by identical structural relationships between those items at the level of D-structure.

Accordingly, a number of generative syntacticians have tried to reduce the surface variation exemplified in (7)-(11) to a single underlying structure, or perhaps a couple of underlying structures. For instance, Freeze (1992) collapses possessives, existentials, and locatives, arguing for a single underlying structure for at least English (7) and Russian (10).[9] The alternation between HAVE and BE is syntactic in nature: a transitive HAVE verb arises only if an adposition incorporates into BE during the course of the derivation. Kayne (1993), in a celebrated paper, pursues the same idea in a different way. He proposes that possessors are universally merged inside the possessed DP,where the appropriate possessive Theta-role(s) are assigned.

---

8. Numerous reformulations of UTAH have been put forward since it was first proposed, including a relativized version that requires only that relative structural prominence correlate with position on a Theta-role hierarchy (Larson's 1990 RUTAH), but all have in common the idea that there is some predictable and universal relationship between particular structural positions and particular thematic roles. Since the advent of the Minimalist Program and the concomitant abandonment of D-structure as an independent level of representation, the formulation "at the level of D-structure" has been updated by some authors so that it refers instead to each thematic role being associated with a single consistent structural configuration (Baker 1997; Collins 2005).

9. One might expect such an approach to extend to Hungarian too, since (11) is clearly an existential construction. Nonetheless, the apparent absence of an overt locative in the Hungarian construction (and others like it in K'ekchi') leads Freeze (1992, 591) to put such constructions outside of his Locative-Existential-HAVE paradigm, assigning them a different structure closer to that adopted by Kayne (1993). As for the other languages in (7)-(11), Levinson (2011) argues that Freeze's approach does not have a ready account for the Icelandic *vera með* construction in (8) (see also Chapter 7 of this book). I will show in Chapter 6 that the same can be said of the Quechua *-yoq* construction and phenomena like it. Chapter 5 contains numerous arguments that HAVE constructions of the English sort should not be collapsed with existentials either.

In Hungarian, the surface structure results from extracting the possessor from the DP, as Szabolcsi (1981) proposed. English and other HAVE languages have a similar derivation, but require an additional step in order to allow the possessor to be extracted. Leaving the technical details until Chapter 2, this additional step involves incorporating a certain DP-internal adpositional element into BE, which causes BE to be spelled out as HAVE. Like Freeze's, Kayne's analysis makes the explicit claim that HAVE and BE are variants of the same element, and that which of these variants surfaces is determined by syntactic factors. This claim is supported by the fact that HAVE and BE in their perfect auxiliary uses alternate within certain languages, and when this happens the conditioning factors are syntactic in nature, as Kayne shows extensively (e.g. the argument structure of the main verb in French, Italian, German and Dutch; the phi-features of the subject or the presence of object clitic climbing in some dialects of Italy). In addition, both the Freeze and the Kayne analyses treat HAVE as more complex than BE, since HAVE arises as a result of incorporating an additional element into BE. The added complexity that these accounts attribute to HAVE is an attractive property, since it gives us the beginnings of an explanation for the relative typological rarity of HAVE languages. It also opens the door to the possibility that the difference between HAVE languages and BE languages is parametric in nature, and raises an intriguing challenge for comparative syntax: that of uncovering which other syntactic properties, if any, correlate with the HAVE/BE difference, and of explaining such correlations. A flurry of work has responded to this challenge since then in various ways, albeit with no consensus emerging as of yet (Hoekstra 1994; Mahajan 1994; Pylkkänen 1998; Harley 2002; Boneh and Sichel 2010; Bjorkman 2011; Jung 2011; Levinson 2011, amongst many others). Some of this work retreats at least somewhat from the position that all of the variation in possession constructions is to be reduced to a single underlying structure. For instance, Boneh and Sichel (2010) motivate three separate underlying structures for three different BE-based possession constructions in Palestinian Arabic, and Levinson's (2011) paper postulates a difference between English and Icelandic in the first-merge position of the possessor. Even in these proposals, however, the difference between HAVE and BE is argued to be one of incorporation.

   In this book, I will follow the Freeze/Kayne tradition in taking seriously the idea that the variation between HAVE and BE is syntactically interesting. Nevertheless, a point that I will repeatedly stress is that the too-many-(surface)-structures problem is not just about HAVE languages versus BE languages–it is about, at the very least, HAVE languages versus COPULAR BE + predicate nominal/adjective languages versus COPULAR BE + WITH languages versus EXISTENTIAL BE + DP languages. In other words, there are many ways of being a BE-based possession construction, and I hope to convince the reader that examining them closely reveals differences at least as intriguing and challenging as those between BE and HAVE, much as Boneh and Sichel (2010) found for Palestinian Arabic. As such, my approach to the too-many-(surface)-structures puzzle leans much further towards taking the surface variation seen in (7)-(11) at face value than it does towards reducing it. Indeed, I shall be proposing that each of the constructions in (7)-(11) corresponds to a different way of introducing the possessor argument into the structure. The issues at stake here, and the nature of the arguments to be made, are reminiscent of the classic debate surrounding so-called dative shift, exemplified in (13).[10]

(13)   a.   I gave a book to John.

       b.   I gave John a book.

There has been much discussion over whether the base positions/first-merge positions of the theme and goal in these two constructions are the same (in which case the surface forms differ because of movement and/or deletion transformations) or distinct (see, amongst others, Anagnostopoulou 2003; Baker 1997; Den Dikken 1995; Kayne 1984; Larson 1988; Oehrle 1976; Pesetsky 1995; Pylkkänen 2002/2008; for various perspectives). The arguments have turned partly on semantics and partly on (morpho)syntax. The semantic arguments have to do with whether the two constructions are, in fact, semantically identical to the extent that we would want to say that the same Theta-roles are involved in each case. The (morpho)syntactic arguments have turned on the question of whether differences in behavior between the two internal arguments indicate underlying hierarchical differences between the two that cannot be reduced to movement differences. Just as many have concluded for the dative alternation,[11] I believe that arguments of both sorts can be found to indicate that the different possession constructions found cross-linguistically cannot be related to a single underlying structure (or even just a couple of them).

---

10. Thanks to Alec Marantz (pers. comm.) for pointing out the parallel here.

11. Richard Kayne reminds me (pers. comm.) that heavy DP shift of the goal argument out of a Double Object Construction requires the surfacing of the preposition *to*, which might speak in favor of a transformational relationship between DOCs and *to*-datives after all.

   (i)   The noise gave me a head-ache.

   (ii)   * The noise gave a head-ache to me.

   (iii)   The noise gave a head-ache to everyone within a sixty-mile radius.

For an analysis of this pattern which seeks to reconcile it with a non-transformational approach to the dative alternation, see Bruening (2010).

While the line taken here will entail a departure from the letter of the UTAH,[12] I will argue that this proposal does not require an unacceptable weakening of Theta-theory. In fact, given a particular implementation of a widespread view of the meanings of BE/HAVE (namely, that they are semantically vacuous at least as far as Theta-roles are concerned), the possibility that thematically identical constructions might have different argument structures turns out to be a logical consequence of restrictive proposals already made in work by Schäfer (2008) and especially Wood (2012, 2014a, 2015), which itself extends proposals in Kratzer (1996) and Marantz (2009a,b). This view turns out to have a number of advantages. It will yield a coherent solution to the too-many-meanings puzzle. It will explain the availability of non-possessive uses of possession constructions (e.g. causative, locative, and experiencer *have* in English), all of which are treated in Chapter 4 in terms of the normal action of argument-introducing heads like Kratzer's (1996) Voice. It will also yield an explanation for the relative rarity of HAVE. In a nutshell, HAVE in this book is taken to be the form that BE takes when something is merged in the specifier of a Voice head bearing phi-features–in other words, HAVE is the transitive form of BE. Since there are many ways of merging a possessor into the structure that lead to BE (anywhere below VoiceP or in the specifier of unergative Voice), but only one way to merge a possessor into the structure that yields HAVE (into the specifier of a transitive VoiceP), HAVE's rarity no longer looks anomalous.

In this section, I have introduced the two problems that I regard as key to the question of how possession sentences are built and interpreted across languages: the too-many-meanings puzzle and the too-many-(surface)-structures puzzle. I briefly surveyed the kinds of approach that have been taken to these puzzles in the previous literature (more in-depth discussion of earlier approaches is the goal of Chapter 2). I also hinted at the solutions to these puzzles that will be defended in this book. For the too-many-meanings puzzle, I will take the position that HAVE and BE themselves do not contribute to the meaning of possession sentences, and the various thematic roles involved in predicative possession sentences will be argued to come from elsewhere (sometimes from various syntactically distinct positions inside the possessed DP, sometimes from outside the DP–for instance, Kratzer's Voice head).

---

12. As I show later on in this chapter, some such departure is conceptually inevitable in any case once thematic roles are no longer thought of as being assigned by verbs to their arguments syntactically, but rather to be ways of semantically relating individuals to events and states read off from the output of syntax, as in much recent work on argument structure (e.g. Alexiadou, Anagnostopoulou, and Schäfer 2014; Baker 1997, 122-127; Borer 2005a,b, 2013; Bruening 2013; Kastner 2016; Marantz 2009a,b, 2013a; Schäfer 2008; Ramchand 2008; Wood 2010, 2012, 2013, 2014a, 2015).

The too-many-(surface)-structures puzzle will be addressed by providing arguments that the surface variation points to real differences in argument structure, and showing that a restrictive theory of the syntax/semantics interface exists which can account for how such different syntaxes can be assigned truth-conditionally identical meanings. In the ensuing sections, I introduce the properties of this theory of the syntax/semantics interface, and of the architecture of the grammar in general, in some detail in section 1.2 (drawing on Kratzer 1996; Marantz 2009a,b; Schäfer 2008; and important innovations in Wood 2012, 2014a, 2015). I then proceed to introduce the major claims of the book in section 1.3, before sketching how they solve the puzzles posed by predicative possession in section 1.4. The structure of the book is summarized in section 1.5.

1.2   The Architecture of the Grammar

Grammar consists of subsystems that appear to deal with representations of rather different sorts. Morphophonology deals in sound (or sign), semantics in denotations and their composition, and syntax in categories and constituents. Yet, different as they are, these representations interact with each other in a complex fashion to give rise to the language faculty. A theory of the architecture of the grammar is a theory of what each component of the grammar consists of, how they fit together, and how their interaction gives rise to natural language as we find it.

This work takes as its background the Minimalist Program for syntactic theory (Chomsky 1995, 2000, 2001), supplemented with the architectural assumptions of Distributed Morphology (DM; Halle and Marantz 1993 et seq.). In this system, syntax is responsible for constructing all complex expressions–including phrases and morphologically complex words–and both morphophonology and semantics are independently "read off" from the output of syntax. The result is the familiar Y-model (or T-model) of the grammar, but one which explicitly denies the existence of a generative lexicon in the sense of a separate component for constructing words. This is known as the Single Engine Hypothesis (Embick and Noyer 2007), or alternatively by the slogan *syntactic hierarchical structure all the way down* (Halle and Marantz 1993, 1994).

(14) *Architecture of the Grammar*

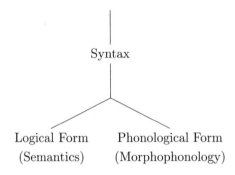

Syntax manipulates only abstract terminal nodes consisting of bundles of formal features. A consequence of this view on the PF side of the grammar is that the morphophonological forms of terminal nodes are not present in the syntax. The traditional notion of a lexical item as a bundle of syntactic and morphophonological features therefore dissolves. Syntactic terminals are not linked to their morphophonological forms by being bundled with them in the lexicon. Instead, they are related by rule after the syntactic derivation is complete. This hypothesis is known as Late Insertion (Halle and Marantz 1993). Taken together, Late Insertion and the Single Engine Hypothesis form the core of the DM architecture. The consequences of Late Insertion on the PF side of the grammar have been the subject of much productive investigation since the early 1990s. As a result of such work, many strong typological generalizations concerning the nature of allomorphy and its conditioning have been revealed, and much has been learned about what the translation from syntax to morphophonology must look like in order to account for them (see especially Bobaljik 2000, 2012; Embick 2010; Wolf 2008; see below for more discussion). Rather less work has investigated the question of whether Late Insertion holds in an analogous way on the LF side, and what its consequences are if so, but see Alexiadou, Anagnostopoulou, and Schäfer (2014), Borer (2013), Kastner (2016), Marantz (1997, 2009a,b), Schäfer (2008, 2012), and Wood (2010, 2012, 2014a, 2015). The present work is directly concerned with this latter issue.

In an architecture like (14), the general question arises of how much information relevant at PF or LF is also present in the syntax itself, and how much is present only at those interfaces. That is, what features are subject to Late Insertion, as opposed to being present in the syntactic derivation? Here the phenomena we call 'morphology' have a special role to play, especially with respect to features that are clearly relevant at LF but whose presence in the syntax is open to doubt. The architecture in (14) predicts that any feature in the syntax can potentially have an influence at both PF and LF. In other words, if a given feature is present in the syntax, we should be able to detect it in the form of an overt morpheme somewhere in some language. If overt realizations of a given feature are not attested anywhere, then we can begin to suspect that that feature is not in the syntax at all (see also Wood 2015, 7-8 for application of such reasoning).

In the remainder of this section, I examine each of the components of (14) in turn, introducing assumptions that the rest of the book will take as background.

1.2.1   Syntax

The syntactic component puts elements together via a single operation known as Merge (Chomsky 1994, 1995). Merge takes two syntactic elements α and β, and forms the set containing them: $\{\alpha,\beta\}$. On standard assumptions, one of the elements so combined will *project*, giving its label to the whole.[13] The result of projecting α can be represented in a tree structure as in (15), or via the notation $\{\alpha,\{\alpha,\beta\}\}$. I will continue to use the more familiar tree diagrams, and/or equivalent labelled bracketings, throughout this work.

(15)

$$\alpha$$
$$\alpha \quad \beta$$

The elements combined by Merge may be simple morphemes drawn from the lexicon (known as a lexical item, or a head), or may themselves be complex objects created by Merge, such as (15). Hence, a head γ can be merged with the structure in (15) to yield $\{\gamma,\{\alpha,\{\alpha,\beta\}\}\}$. Assuming γ projects, we will have $\{\gamma,\{\gamma,\{\alpha,\{\alpha,\beta\}\}\}\}$, or equivalently:

(16)

---

13. I will leave open how the system determines which head projects its label–see Chomsky (2013) for much discussion. There is some controversy over whether labelling is part of merge or a separate operation (see Chomsky 2013; Hornstein 2009), and some have questioned whether labelling is a necessary part of the syntactic computation at all (Collins 2002). The present work does not rely on any particular approach to labeling, and the particular implementation in the text is adopted for concreteness only.

Since γ in (16) was drawn from the lexicon rather than from inside the constituent it merged with, (16) is an example of what is called External Merge. If a syntactic object is merged with an element drawn not from the lexicon, but rather from inside itself, we have Internal Merge, also known as movement. This is illustrated in (17), in which β has been copied and merged with the complex object γ. It is often assumed that Internally Merged elements never project, and this is reflected in (17) by the fact that γ has projected. This assumption has been questioned (Donati 2006), but this debate is of no consequence here.

(17)

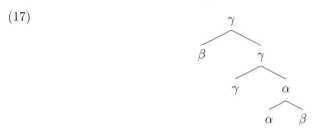

The structure produced by Internal Merge in (17) contains two occurrences of the element β. In this circumstance, the PF component generally realizes only one of the occurrences, and usually only the hierarchically highest one. Syntactically present occurrences which are left unrealized by the PF component are indicated by strikethrough notation, thus:

(18)

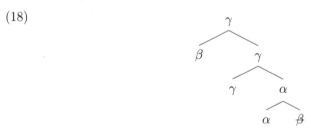

Merge eliminates many of the primitives of the X-bar theory of phrase structure, including the notion of the single bar-level as a non-maximal, non-minimal projection. It also reduces the notions of complement and specifier to purely relational notions defined in terms of Merge–the complement of a head X is the first syntactic object to Merge with it, and the specifier of a head X is the second syntactic object to merge with it.[14] Nevertheless, I will continue to make use of the terms bar-level, specifier, and complement as useful expository devices, and as labels on trees to aid

14. Even this relational notion of specifier has come under scrutiny recently, with several proposals to eliminate specifiers from syntax emerging in recent years (Chomsky 2013; Lohndal 2012, 2014;

discussion of structures in the text. Hence, a tree like (18) will often be labelled as follows in the coming discussion:

(19)

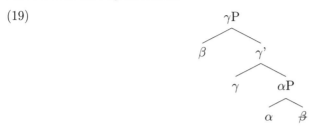

To summarize, (Internal and External) Merge applies recursively to create nested hierarchical structures made up of heads (terminal nodes), some of which project to give their label to a larger syntactic object. It is these structures that the interpretive components of grammar (PF and LF) convert into sound/sign and meaning. At PF, Vocabulary Insertion relates terminal nodes to their underlying morphophonological representations (Vocabulary Items). At LF, as we will see below, I will assume that an analogous process occurs to relate terminal nodes to their denotations (following Marantz 2009a,b; Wood 2015; and many others). More detail on these interpretive components is provided in later subsections. I assume that syntactic structures are sent to PF and to LF in chunks known as *phases*. The sending of a piece of syntactic structure to the interfaces is known as Spell Out, and it is triggered by particular functional items known as *phase heads*, discussed in more detail below.

While Merge is the only operation in Universal Grammar that creates hierarchical structure, on its own it does not determine whether a particular syntactic structure is viable in a particular language. This is determined by the lexical items themselves–the heads and their properties. Heads come in various sorts, determined by the formal features they bear. As well as a categorial feature, which determines the label assigned to the phrase when a given head projects, heads can have a range of selectional features which determine their distribution. These features impose certain needs on the heads that carry them, and the meeting of those needs guarantees a well-formed syntactic structure. Failure to meet those needs will cause the structure to be ill-formed. A plausible conjecture, which I will follow in this work, is that all parametric variation amongst languages is to be reduced to variation in the featural needs of functional heads (Baker 2008 refers to this as the Borer-Chomsky Conjecture–see Borer 1984; Chomsky 1995).

Starke 2004). In this book, I will frequently make reference to particular functional heads requiring or lacking specifiers as a possible parameter of variation. I will leave open the question of whether these analyses will ultimately be recastable in a specifierless system.

The heads whose needs will be of greatest importance to our discussion will be those responsible for introducing arguments and the eventualities they participate in. As we will see below, there appears to be a family of such heads. These heads nonetheless have many things in common with each other,[15] amongst them susceptibility to the following sorts of requirement (from Wood 2015, 15, his (16)):[16]

(20)   *Syntactic Properties of Heads*

    a.   **C-selection**: a head may be specified to select the category of its complement.

    b.   **Case-selection**: a head may specify a particular case on its complement or specifier.

    c.   **Specifier requirement**: a head may be specified to take a specifier or not.

Parametric variation in the existence of specifier requirements on particular heads will turn out to play an especially important role in understanding the typology of possession sentences.

Heads may also carry certain unvalued formal features that can be valued by the features of other constituents. A prominent example of such features are the so-called phi-features, which include at least person, number, and gender. The presence of such a bundle of unvalued phi features on a head (a Probe) will trigger the application of the operation Agree, which will provide a value for those features by copying them from some other constituent (the Goal), under conditions defined as in (21) (Chomsky 2000, 2001, 2008). Agree plays an important role in legitimizing the presence of nominal constituents in the structure; it is standardly assumed that DPs must enter into an Agree relation in order to be licensed.

(21)   *Agree*

    α can agree with β iff:

    a. α carries at least one unvalued and uninterpretable feature and β carries a matching interpretable and valued feature.

    b. α c-commands β.

---

15. Indeed, these argument-introducing heads have so much in common, and their differences appear to be so predictable from their structural context of occurrence, that Wood (2015, 16-17) conjectures that they will ultimately prove to be reducible to a single head. See Wood and Marantz (2015/to appear) for further development of this idea.

16. Heads outside of the thematic domain may also have requirements of these kinds, of course, but I highlight their relevance for argument-introducers because of the centrality of such heads in this book.

    c. β is the closest goal to α.

    d. β bears an unvalued uninterpretable feature of its own.

In the original version of the Agree proposal, Agree is necessary partly because of the need for DPs to be licensed and partly because the presence of unvalued uninterpretable features in the output of syntax leads to an ill-formed representation at the interfaces. This view has been challenged by Preminger (2011), who argues that Agree is an obligatory operation independent of valuation considerations–whether the phi features get valued is not what matters, what matters is that the operation itself is attempted during the derivation. Other proposals have been made to allow Agree to hold between a Probe and a Goal that c-commands it, either as a parametric variant of downward Agree (Baker 2008), as a cyclically-determined second option after downward Agree has been attempted (Béjar and Rezac 2009), or across the board (Zeijlstra 2012–though see Preminger 2013 for a reply to this last proposal). Other amendments to Agree have been suggested to allow it to target more than one Goal simultaneously (Multiple Agree–see Hiraiwa 2001, 2005; Nevins 2011). The original formulation of Agree also stipulated that unvalued features are invariably uninterpretable at the semantic interface, and that valued features were invariably interpretable. This too has been challenged, by Pesetsky and Torrego (2004), who propose that all logically possible combinations of (un)valued and (un)interpretable are viable and attested. I will take no position on these amendments here, since they will not play a role in the discussion to come.

Heads may additionally bear EPP features, which can be satisfied by Internal or External Merge of some phrase in their specifier. In some languages, EPP features are parasitic on a phi-feature bundle, so that only a phrase that values a head's unvalued phi set can move to satisfy the EPP requirement.[17]

1.2.1.1   Clause Structure and the Thematic Domain

Recent work on the structure of the clause has converged on the conclusion that it consists of at least three domains. The lowest of these is the thematic domain, where

---

17. This dependency between phi-agreement and movement reverses a dependency that was assumed under earlier proposals concerning the syntactic properties of agreement, according to which agreement between a head X and a phrase YP was parasitic on YP's moving into X's specifier (the Spec-Head view of agreement–see Chomsky 1986, 1995; Kayne 1985/2000, 1989/2000; Koopman 2006). I believe that the balance of evidence points towards downward Agree being empirically necessary. However, as Kayne (2000, vii) notes, various challenges remain with respect to phenomena in which agreement shows up only under movement and not without it, such as past participle agreement in certain Romance languages. For an attempt to meet this challenge (focussing on Romance past-participle agreement), see D'Alessandro and Roberts (2008).

predicate-argument structure is expressed. Next there is an inflectional domain, associated with at least tense and aspect. Finally, there is a left-periphery associated with clause typing and with certain informational structural notions. Agreement on the existence and the relative hierarchical positions of these domains is widespread. The main points of contemporary disagreement focus on the richness and universality of the projections found in these domains–see Cinque (1999, 2006); Julien (2002); Svenonius and Ramchand (2014); Rizzi (1997); and the papers collected in van Craenenbroeck (2009) for various perspectives.

(22)   *The Structure of the Clause*

<pre>
                    CP/The Left Periphery
                       /   \
                   C   ....
                    TP/The Inflectional Domain
                          /   \
                      T   ...
                      VoiceP/The Thematic Domain
                             /   \
                        Voice   ...
                               ◁——
                                ...
</pre>

Our focus in this book will be on the thematic domain, and I will not weigh in on the discussion of the structure of higher domains. The heads that make up the thematic domain, and the principles that regulate their combination, will be the major players in the discussion to come. I will proceed to introduce them in some detail now.

The theory assumed here falls under the bracket of *constructivist* approaches, which take it that argument structures are independent from the verbs that appear in them. That is, argument structures are not *projected* by verbs. Rather, event structures are realized in syntax via the combination of heads that denote more basic predicates (see Baker 1997, 122-127; Borer 2005a, 2005b; Hale and Keyser 1993, 2002; Kratzer 1996; Ramchand 2008; as well as much earlier work in the theory of Generative Semantics–Dowty 1979; Postal 1970; Ross 1972). Roots, understood as being independent from the grammatical categories "verb", "noun", etc., may impose restrictions on the structures they appear in (whether because of incompatibility with their lexical semantics or for purely formal reasons). However, roots themselves do not "project" these structures (see Marantz 2013a for recent discussion of constructivist vs. projectionist approaches to argument structure).

The minimal structure that can be present in the thematic domain is a Voice head (possibly with specifier) selecting a vP (which may or may not take a complement).[18]

(23)   *Basic Verb Phrase Structure*

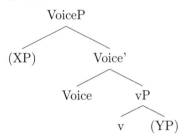

Semantically, v usually introduces an eventuality of some kind. Voice (taken from Kratzer 1996) is responsible for introducing an external argument in its specifier (when it has one); the interpretation that Voice assigns to this argument is dependent on the content of the vP, in a manner that will be discussed in section 1.2.3. The Voice head is additionally taken to define a phase (Chomsky 2001), in that its complement constitutes a chunk which is sent to interpretation at the PF and LF interfaces.

Although v introduces an eventuality variable (usually), the lexical semantics associated with the sort of eventuality expressed by the verb phrase comes not from v, but from an acategorial root in the structure (Pesetsky 1995; Marantz 1997). Roots in this system are therefore a sort of modifier: in the context of verb phrases, they may be event modifiers (in which case they are adjoined to v), or they may modify the result state of an element in v's complement (in which case they will be adjoined to that element instead; see below). A case of a root adjoined to v as an event modifier is given in (24).

---

18. Below I will suggest that VoiceP itself is radically absent in one subtype of unaccusative structure (following Alexiadou, Anagnostopoulou, and Schäfer 2014). Perhaps no verb realizes (23) with both spec-VoiceP and the complement of v missing. Even plausible candidates for zero place predicates (like weather verbs) seem doubtful, given the quasi-argumental status of their "expletive" arguments. See Krejci (2014) for recent discussion, and arguments that even weather verbs have a thematic argument.

(24)   John ate the cake.

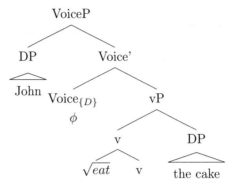

The configuration in (24) is what will be referred to as a transitive configuration, by virtue of the fact that Voice introduces an external argument (the notation {D} on Voice signifies a specifier requirement–see Embick 2004; Schäfer 2008; Wood 2012, 2015) and carries a bundle of phi-features with which it can license the DP complement of v. In a nominative-accusative language, the DP so licensed will surface in accusative case.[19]

If VoiceP takes a specifier, and v takes no complement, we have what is referred to as an unergative configuration.[20] The v head will usually introduce an activity, which is semantically modified by the root. In such a confirguration, Voice demands a specifier, but it carries no phi-features. Semantically, v in this circumstance will usually denote an activity, which will be modified by the root.[21]

---

19. It matters little here whether accusative case assignment is guaranteed by virtue of the Agree relation between Voice and the internal argument (Chomsky 2001; Pesetsky and Torrego 2011), or is instead calculated configurationally on the basis of the presence of c-commanding DP (Marantz 1991/2000).

20. The view on unergatives embodied by (25) is controversial, since there is a subtradition (associated most prominently with Hale and Keyser 1993) that takes unergatives to be hidden transitives with an incorporated direct object. See Marantz (2009a,b), Preminger (2009), and Rimell (2012) for arguments of various sorts against this position.

21. See below for more on the semantics of v. The semantics of the roots of verbs will not play much of a role in this book, but for concreteness I illustrate one way of implementing the semantic intuition mentioned in the text:

  (i) $[\![\sqrt{dance}]\!] = \lambda f_{\langle s,t \rangle}.\lambda e_s.f(e) \wedge dance(e)$

  (ii) $[\![v]\!] = \lambda e_s.activity(e)$

  (iii) $[\![vP]\!] = \lambda e_s.activity(e) \wedge dance(e)$ (from (i) and (ii) by Functional Application)

(25)   John danced.

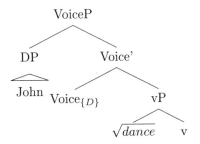

    Structures in which VoiceP lacks a specifier, or is absent altogether, are referred
to collectively as *unaccusative* structures. Unaccusative structures come in multiple
kinds, corresponding to different options for the internal structure of vP's complement (see Irwin 2012). In one variety of unaccusative structure, vP's complement
is a DP. In such structures, the root's semantic contribution is often to name the
state of the DP complement of v. I will assume, following Marantz (2009a,b) and
Wood (2015, 28-29), that this semantic fact is manifested syntactically by having
the root adjoined to the DP complement of v underlyingly. Following Alexiadou,
Anagnostopoulou, and Schäfer (2014), I will assume that there are two structures
for this subtype of unaccusative, often dubbed *anticausatives*. One involves VoiceP
being present, but having its specifier filled by some expletive element. This is the
structure for marked anticausatives, such as the Spanish example in (26) (inspired
by the analysis of the *-st* morpheme in Wood 2013, 2014a, 2015). Another structure involves VoiceP being radically absent–this is the structure for unmarked anticausatives, as seen in (27).[22] The root in (27) happens to be an externally-caused
change-of-state predicate, which are famous for participating in the so-called anti-
causitive alternation (Levin and Rappoport Hovav 2005:2). In the present system,
this is derived by allowing this root to occur also in a structure in which Voice
introduces an external argument, as shown in the structure in (28).

---

22. Alexiadou, Anagnostopoulou, Alexiadou, and Schäfer (2014, 97-114) argue against an imagin-
able alternative that involves saying that unmarked anticausatives involve a silent expletive Voice
with no specifier, on the basis that (i) such a head would be difficult to acquire, and (ii) this system
does not allow for an easy statement of the distribution of non-active Voice in Greek, whereas
the system in the text allows one to state that non-active Voice is simply the realization of Voice
when it lacks a specifier (cf. Embick 2004).

(26)   El florero se rompió. (Spanish)
          the vase   SE broke

          'The vase broke.'

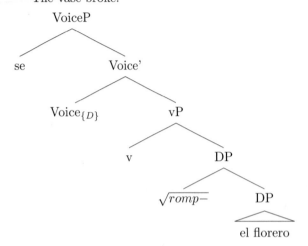

(27)   The vase broke.

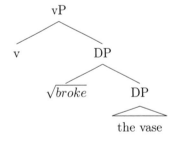

(28)   John broke the vase.

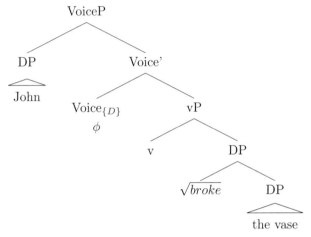

The second subcase of an unaccusative structure comes about when v's complement is some sort of small clause. I will take small clauses universally to be headed
by a Pred head (Adger and Ramchand 2003; Baker 2003; Balusu 2014; Bowers 1993;
Citko 2008). An example is provided in (29).

(29)   John came to the pub.

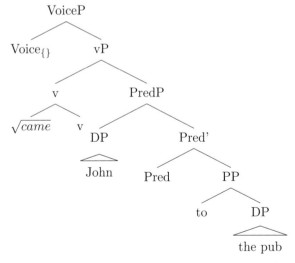

One reason that I adopt the PredP hypothesis in the present context, beyond
the arguments in the cited works, is that it appears that the morphophonological
component sometimes treats small clauses as a natural class for the determination

of allomorphy. The analysis of Icelandic HAVE verbs in Chapter 4 is such a case. This is most straightforwardly accounted for if small clauses share some functional structure regardless of the category of their lexical head, and the PredP hypothesis claims precisely this.

So far, all of the configurations depicted have included a root somewhere in the structure. One might ask whether it is ever possible for a rootless structure to be generated. The answer to this question is yes–this is precisely what light-verb constructions are in the present system.

(30)   *Definition of a Light-Verb Construction*

         A light-verb construction is one that contains a v but no root.

The idea in (30) captures the intuition that the light-verb in a phrase like *John did a dance* contributes only event structure, and no conceptual semantics, to the interpretation of the whole sentence. The morpheme *do* in such a sentence is a realization of v, whose only semantic contribution is to bring in an eventuality variable. The direct object supplies the content of the event, in this way playing a role analogous to the role played by the root in unergative structures like *John danced.*[23]

These most basic verb-phrase types can be augmented by other argument introducers–in particular, so-called applicative heads (Marantz 1993; Pylkkänen 2002/2008). Applicative heads come in at least two varieties, named after their positions in the structure. Low Applicatives (henceforth Low Appl) are the complement of v. They take a DP in both the specifier and the complement position, and introduce a relation between the two DPs. Within the present framework, the standard analysis of a double object construction involves a Low Appl head, as shown in (31). As well as Low Appl, some languages (apparently not including English, though see Chapter 4) have access to a High Appl head. This head takes vP as its complement and introduces a DP in its specifier. Semantically, High Appl relates the individual (supplied by DP) in its specifier to the eventuality (supplied by vP) in its complement in a variety of different ways cross-linguistically. Benefactive and/or malefactive roles are commonly-discussed subcases of High Appl roles, although applied arguments with many other roles are well-attested (including instruments, locations, and others). An example from Cochabamba Quechua is given in (32), and a structure using English morphemes is given in (33).

---

23. Analogous, but crucially not identical–in particular, the aspectual properties of *John did a dance* are drastically different than is the case with *John danced*, a difference plausibly relatable to the presence of the determiner in *a dance*. See Marantz (2009a,b).

(31)   John sent Bill the letter.

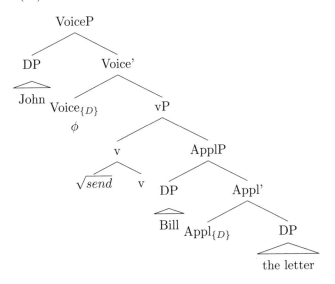

(32)   Noqa Juan-paq phawa-pu-∅-rqa-ni.   (Cochabamba)
          I   Juan-BEN run-APPL-3OBJ-PAST-1SUBJ

          'I ran for Juan (in his honor/so that he wouldn't have to.)'

(33)   *I ran John.

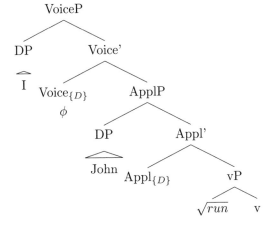

Certain DP-internal heads, responsible for introducing possession relations, will also play an important role in this book. However, I postpone discussion of these until section 1.4, where their role in the account will be clearer.

Before ending this subsection, I will briefly introduce some assumptions about the structures of copular predications, since these will play a central role in the discussion of possession sentences. I assume that all copular constructions, both existential and predicative, involve minimally a VoiceP in which v takes a PredP complement. A predicate locative construction with a PP predicate, for instance, will look as follows. I take BE to be a light-verb (I will take the position, in fact, that it is the lightest possible verb in that it makes no event structural or thematic contribution of its own), hence the lack of a lexical root in (34).[24] Predicate adjective structures can apparently vary within and across languages with respect to the first-merge position of the subject. That is, sometimes they appear to involve merging the subject of the predication in spec-PredP, yielding an unaccusative structure, but sometimes they involve an unergative structure, with the subject in spec-VoiceP (see Cinque 1990a; Irwin 2012, 40-41). These two possibilities are depicted in turn in (35) and (36) (the examples are taken in slightly adapted from Irwin's discussion). Note that adjectives in this system, analogously to verbs, consist of an acategorial root and a categorizing morpheme (for adjectives, such morphemes are labeled a). Categorizing morphemes may be null or overt. In (36), a is realized as the suffix *-ly*. Similar considerations will apply to nouns (where the categorizer is notated n).

---

24. In a number of languages, the "copula" is identical in form to a pronoun of some kind, and one might wonder how this can be reconciled with my assumption that BE is a v head. I think that languages with pronominal copulas should in fact be reanalyzed as having a silent verbal copula, with the pronoun being a realization of some other category. As evidence for this, I note that Citko (2008, 262-263) shows that Polish allows a "pronominal copula" to co-occur with a verbal one.

    (i)   Jan **jest** moim najlepszym przyjacielem.
              Jan is   my   best   friend

           'Jan is my best friend.'

    (ii)   Jan **to**   mój najlepszy przyjaciel.
              Jan PRON my   best   friend

           'Jan is my best friend.'

    (iii) Jan **to**   **jest** mój najlepszy przyjaciel.
              Jan PRON is   my   best   friend

           'Jan is my best friend.'

I will leave open what category the pronoun is realizing. See Citko (2008) for arguments that it realizes (the phi-features on) T in Polish.

(34)   John is in the garden.

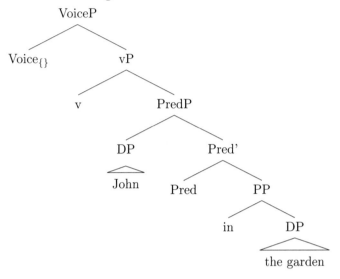

(35)   Only some of his poems are known. (unaccusative)

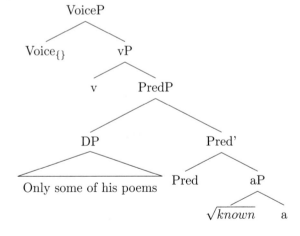

(36)   Many hippies are friendly. (unergative)

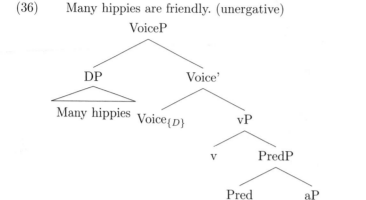

Cinque (1990a) identified evidence for a distinction in Italian between unergative and unaccusative adjectives using standard tests for unaccusativity in the language, such as cliticization of the partitive clitic *ne* (which is usually possible only from underlying object positions; see Burzio 1986, 20-21; though cf. Bentley 2006). The basic pattern for unaccusative and unergative verbs is shown in (37) and (38).

(37)   *Ne Cliticization in Italian: unaccusative*

    a.   [Molti esperti]$_i$ arriveranno   t$_i$.

        Many experts   arrive.3PL.FUT t

        'Many experts will arrive'.

    b.   Ne$_i$ arriveranno   [molti t$_i$].

        of.them arrive.3PL.FUT [many t   ]

        'Many of them will arrive.'

(38)   *Ne Cliticization in Italian: unergative*

    a.   Molti esperti telefoneranno.

        Many experts telephone.3PL.FUT

        'Many experts will telephone'.

    b.   *Ne$_i$ telefoneranno   [molti t$_i$].

        of.them telephone.3PL.FUT [many t   ]

        'Many of them will telephone.'

Turning to adjectives, we see that Italian *note* '(well)-known' patterns as an unaccusative, whereas *simpatici* 'friendly' patterns as an unergative.

(39)   *An Unaccusative Adjective*: 'note'

Ne$_i$ sono note   solo [alcune t$_i$] (delle sue poesie).
of.them are   well.known only [some   t] (of.the his poems)

'Only some of them (i.e. his poems) are well-known.'

(40)   *An Unergative Adjective*: 'simpatici'

*Ne$_i$ sono simpatici [molti t$_i$] (dei   figli dei   fiori).
of.them are   friendly   [many t$_i$] of.the sons of.the flowers

'Many of them (i.e. hippies) are friendly.'

I will not attempt to explain these differences among adjectives here; at this stage, I can only acknowledge that the differences exist, and show how this fact can be accommodated within the present approach. The question is further complicated by cross-linguistic variation. Harves (2002) notes that the ability to surface in the genitive of negation has been acknowledged as a diagnostic for unaccusative subjects in Russian since Pesetsky (1982). However, in Russian all adjectives pattern as unergatives in forbidding their subjects from taking genitive of negation, including the translational equivalents of those adjectives that are clearly unaccusative in Italian, and ones formed on the basis of Russian verbs that are unaccusative (Harves 2002, 252-255).

Predicate nominals, on the other hand, do not vary cross-linguistically in the way adjectives do with respect to the unaccusative/unergative distinction. Instead, they appear to be reliably unergative (Burzio 1986; Harves 2002; Higginbotham 1985; Irwin 2012; Williams 1980, 1994). This fact cries out for explanation, but it will not receive one here. I will simply acknowledge this as a fact, and show what this means for the syntactic representation of such sentences in the present theory.

(41)   John is a doctor.

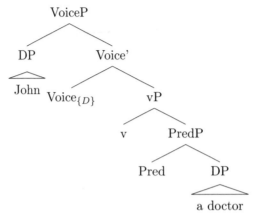

Finally, I turn to existential sentences. I will follow Hazout (2004), Williams (1994), and Tremblay (1991) in taking existential sentences to involve a small clause embedded under the copular verb, with an expletive as the subject of that small clause. A structure of this sort is displayed in (42).

(42)   There is no tea.

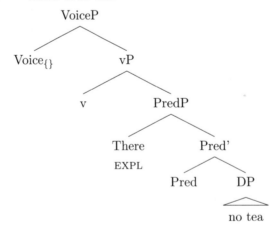

On the present approach, the difference between existential BE and predicative copular BE will not be attributed to the copular verb itself, even in languages that have morphologically distinct copulas in this domain (see Francez 2007, 2009 for a similar approach; also Roy 2013; Welch 2012). Instead, I will argue that the same meaningless BE verb is involved in each case, and that the existential semantics in a structure like (42) comes from elsewhere–in particular, from the so-called exple-tive. In languages that distinguish the existential copula from the predicative one morphologically, this will be accounted for as a case of conditioned allomorphy, in which the surface form of BE is sensitive to the content of PredP, its complement. The main argument for this position (as opposed to a position that makes exis-tential and predicative BE syntactically distinct verbs that make different semantic contributions themselves) is that languages with complex copula systems of this sort frequently exhibit *morphological neutralization* of this system in certain cir-cumstances (Clark 1978; Chapter 3 of the present work). This strongly suggests that predicative copular BE and its existential counterpart cannot be entirely dis-tinct elements, but instead must be realizations of the same element in different environments.

This concludes the discussion of the internal structure of the thematic domain, and of the syntactic component of the grammar. We have seen that the syntax combines bundles of formal features (heads) via a single combinatorial operation, Merge. Heads have syntactic features that determine their distribution. Some of these features impose "needs" on the heads themselves, and the failure to meet these needs renders a derivation illicit. Syntactic variation is reducible to variation in the feature content of functional heads (Borer 1984; Chomsky 1995). The output of the syntactic component forms the input to the other two components. Upon the completion of a phase, a chunk of syntactic structure is sent simultaneously to the PF component and the LF component. The purpose of these components is to convert an abstract syntactic representation into something that is usable by language-external systems; i.e, something pronounceable (or signable) in the case of the PF component, and something meaningful in the case of the LF component.

1.2.2   PF (The Morphophonological Component)

The morphophonological component takes as its input a chunk of syntactic struc-ture made up of abstract terminal nodes hierarchically arranged, and outputs a linearly-ordered, phonologically interpreted string, which can be uttered or signed. The translation from one sort of representation to the other does not occur all at once, but rather in a series of steps. Research in the Distributed Morphology framework over the last two decades (Arregi and Nevins 2012; Bobaljik 2000, 2012; Embick 2010; Halle and Marantz 1993) has done much to clarify the nature of these steps and their ordering, by investigating the possible interactions amongst various morphosyntactic and morphophonological phenomena.

Here, I will focus the discussion on Vocabulary Insertion, the process that translates terminal nodes into their underlying phonological forms, and Impoverishment, a process that deletes features on terminal nodes prior to Vocabulary Insertion under certain circumstances. I will not discuss how structures are linearized and at what point in the derivation linearization takes place (see for various perspectives Arregi and Nevins 2012; Embick 2010; Kayne 1994, 2008/2010, 2010a). I will also lay aside the question of whether any other post-syntactic operations beyond Vocabulary Insertion and Impoverishment are needed (i.e., there will be no discussion of Lowering, Local Dislocation, Morphological Metathesis, or other operations–for discussion of the issues surrounding these, see the references in the previous two paragraphs, as well as Embick and Noyer 2001; Kayne 2010a; Myler 2009). Nor will there be any discussion of possible feature-insertion processes (see Harbour 2003).

1.2.2.1   Vocabulary Insertion

Consider the following structure, which will be the output of syntax in a derivation corresponding to *the boy will devour the cake* (to simplify the exposition, I will ignore the fact that Voice defines a phase).

(43)   The boy will devour the cake.

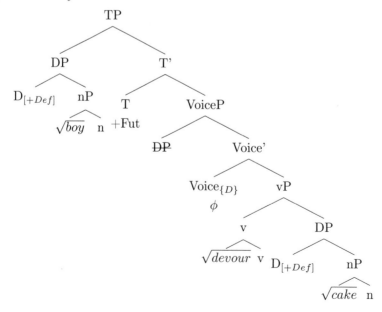

The structure in (43) reflects the fact that the phonological forms of terminal nodes are not present in the syntax. Terminal nodes are related to their phonological forms by rule–namely, by the process known as Vocabulary Insertion. The PF component has access to a repository of underlying phonological forms of morphemes, called Vocabulary Items. Vocabulary Items consist of the underlying phonological form itself, and a specification of the abstract features for which they can be inserted. As we will see below, they may also carry a conditioning environment that restricts their contexts for insertion. The Vocabulary Items relevant to spelling out the structure in (43) are listed in (44).

Once Vocabulary Insertion is complete, phonology proper begins, mapping underlying forms to surface representations. I will take no position on the nature of phonology proper here (see Embick 2010; McCarthy 2002, 2007, 2008; Vaux 2008; Wolf 2008 for discussion of relevant issues).[25]

(44)   *Vocabulary Items for (43)*

    a. $\sqrt{cake} \Leftrightarrow$ /kejk/

    b.   n $\Leftrightarrow \emptyset$

    c. $D_{[+def]} \Leftrightarrow$ /ðə/

    d. $\sqrt{devour} \Leftrightarrow$ /dəvaʊɹ/

    e.   v $\Leftrightarrow \emptyset$

    f.   Voice $\Leftrightarrow \emptyset$

    g. $T_{[+Fut]} \Leftrightarrow$ /wɪl/

    h. $\sqrt{boy} \Leftrightarrow$ /bɔj/

It turns out that Vocabulary Insertion does not apply to all terminal nodes simultaneously. Instead, it appears to take place from the most deeply embedded terminal node outwards, one by one. Hence, setting aside the subject, the rules in (44) will apply from (44a) through to (44g) in that order, since this tracks depth of embedding. The evidence that Vocabulary Insertion proceeds in this way cannot be found in a relatively trivial example like (43), but it becomes clear when examples involving conditioned allomorphy are considered. It is to such cases that we turn now.

---

25. Following Harley (2014), I take it that roots are represented in the syntax, and undergo Late Insertion at both interfaces, just like function morphemes.

1.2.2.2   Conditioned Allomorphy

Allomorphy arises when there is more than one Vocabulary Item eligible for insertion at a particular terminal node. Although cases of so-called *free variation* in allomorphy may occur, more usually the choice of allomorph is forced by aspects of the
structure surrounding the terminal node in question. This is known as *conditioned
allomorphy*. Investigation of the sorts of features that can condition allomorphy,
and the locality restrictions on such conditioning, has been an important and fruit-
ful source of evidence in the development of the theory of the architecture of the
grammar assumed here (Bobaljik 2000, 2012; Embick 2010; Merchant 2015; Paster
2006; Wolf 2008).

Conditioned allomorphy comes in two main sorts: morphosyntactically conditioned allomorphy and phonologically conditioned allomorphy. Morphosyntactically
conditioned allomorphy is sensitive to the morphosyntactic features of adjacent terminal nodes. A canonical example is the allomorphy of the verb *go* in English, which
surfaces as *went* in the past tense, but as *go* elsewhere. The Vocabulary Items that
account for this state of affairs are given in (45).[26]

(45)   *The Allomorphy of 'go'*

    a. $\sqrt{go} \Leftrightarrow$ /wɛnt/ / ___ +Past

    b. $\sqrt{go} \Leftrightarrow$ /goʊ/

The Vocabulary Items in (45) are eligible to spell out the very same terminal node,
namely the root $\sqrt{go}$. However, the allomorph *went* is additionally restricted by a
conditioning environment requiring an adjacent past-tense feature. The allomorph
go is not restricted in this way. While *go* is therefore technically compatible with
the past tense environment also, it is always beaten by *went* to be inserted in this
circumstance, because *went* has a more specific conditioning environment.

It is clear that morphosyntactically conditioned allomorphy is subject to strict
locality restrictions, although there is disagreement over how local conditioning
must be. A standard claim in the Distributed Morphology literature has been that
only structurally adjacent nodes may condition each other (Embick 2010; Bobaljik
and Harley 2013). However, Merchant (2015) points out some examples that appear

---

26. An alternative to the decomposition assumed in (45a) would be to take the root allomorph to
be /wɛn/, with /-t/ a realization of the +Past feature. For the purposes of this demonstration,
nothing hinges on this choice. Gregory Guy informs me (pers. comm.) that the /-t/ in *went*
undergoes variable -t/-d deletion at a rate that suggests that no morpheme boundary intervenes
between the /t/ and the /n/ in *went*. This could be taken as evidence against factoring out the
/t/ as a realization of past tense.

to require a somewhat more permissive notion of locality, one that allows conditioning by a contiguous span of heads in an extended projection. This area of inquiry, although important, will not have much of a bearing on the matters discussed in the main part of this book.

A familiar example of phonologically conditioned allomorphy can be found in the English indefinite article, which has the forms *a* and *an*, depending on whether the following word begins with a consonant or vowel.

(46)   a.   a cake, *an cake

       b.   *a egg, an egg

The Vocabulary Items that account for this situation are similar in format to those we have previously seen, except that the conditioning environment contains phonological information, rather than morphosyntactic information.[27]

(47)   *Allomorphy of the English Indefinite Article*

       a. $D_{[-Def]} \Leftrightarrow$ /ən/ / ___ V

       b. $D_{[-Def]} \Leftrightarrow$ /ə/ / ___ C

The rules in (47) provide a clear case where it becomes crucial that Vocabulary Insertion proceeds from the most deeply embedded constituent outwards. Consider the structure of a DP that comes to be spelled out as *an egg*.

(48)   an egg

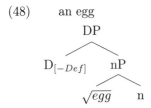

In order for (47a) to apply as desired, it is necessary for the phonological form of $\sqrt{egg}$ to be present in the representation before the D head undergoes Vocabulary Insertion; otherwise, the crucial conditioning information will not be available. The desired result follows if Vocabulary Insertion proceeds from the most deeply embedded constituent outwards. Even more compellingly, it turns out that the directionality of conditioning in (47) is not an isolated case. Phonologically conditioned allomorphy is always "inwardly" sensitive, and never "outwardly" sensitive.

---

27. I am vastly oversimplifying the underlying forms of the indefinite article here (cf. Pak 2014). Note also that I make the assumption that *a/an* realizes the D head only to simplify the exposition. To take the indefinite article to be a D head, and hence on a par with the definite article, is almost certainly incorrect–see Kayne (1994, 2009), Leu (2012, 2015, 116-120), and Perlmutter (1970).

For instance, one sees cases in which the phonological forms of roots condition the choice of allomorph in suffixes and prefixes, but never the other way around. Similarly, the phonological shapes of "inner" morphemes can condition allomorphy of "outer" ones, but the opposite is not attested (Bobaljik 2000; Paster 2006).[28] This is strong support for the idea that Vocabulary Insertion occurs cyclically from the most deeply embedded terminal node outwards.

1.2.2.3   Impoverishment

Impoverishment is a notion introduced in Bonet (1991), and refers to the deletion of certain features from the output of syntax in the PF component, prior to Vocabulary Insertion. Impoverishment can lead to the neutralization of certain morphosyntactic contrasts that are clearly syntactically relevant, and that may be distinguished elsewhere in the morphological system of the language. The result of Impoverishment is often characterized as a *retreat to the general case*–that is, a particular context that would normally call for a more highly specified allomorph is instead realized with a more general allomorph.

As a simple illustration of Impoverishment, consider first the forms of the English verb BE in the present tense in standard varieties of English (this discussion is based partly on Halle 1997, and partly on Harley 2008, 251-253).

(49)   *The Present Tense of 'be'*

    a.   I **am** here.

    b.   You **are** here.

    c.   S/he **is** here.

    d.   We **are** here.

    e.   Y'all **are** here.

    f.   They **are** here.

We see that *am* and *is* are reserved for extremely specific contexts: 1st person singular and 3rd person singular respectively. The form *are*, on the other hand, is found across the board in the plural forms, and in the 2nd person singular.[29] It therefore seems plausible to let *are* be the *elsewhere* form of present tense *be*,

---

28. Alleged counter-examples to these generalizations are occasionally reported, but the cases I have seen are uncompelling. See, for instance, Wolf (2011) for an apparent case from Armenian, and Arregi, Myler, and Vaux (2013) for a reply.

29. Kayne (1985/2000) has suggested that *you* is inherently plural. If so, then there is no need to refer to 2nd person singular as a separate case. I will abstract away from this here.

and further specify the other allomorphs so that they are only inserted in the environment of their particular person features (which I will assume to be hosted on T).

(50)   *Allomorphs of 'be'*

    a. $v_{BE} \Leftrightarrow$ æm / ___ {1st person, singular, +Pres}

    b. $v_{BE} \Leftrightarrow$ ɪz / ___ {3rd person, singular, +Pres}

    c. $v_{BE} \Leftrightarrow$ aɹ / ___ {+Pres}

In cases where more than one allomorph is eligible to be inserted into a given node, the competition is regulated by the Subset Principle.

(51)   *The Subset Principle* (Halle 1997, 128, his (7))

The phonological exponent of a Vocabulary Item is inserted into a morpheme in the terminal string if the item matches all or a subset of the grammatical features specified in the terminal morpheme. Insertion does not take place if the Vocabulary Item contains features not present in the morpheme. Where several Vocabulary Items meet the conditions for insertion, the item matching the greatest number of the features specified in the terminal morpheme must be chosen.

The rules in (50), in combination with the Subset Principle, capture the pattern in (49). However, there turns out to be an environment in English where *are* is grammatical as the realization of 1st person singular present tense *be*, at least for some speakers. This environment obtains only when (i) the negative clitic *n't* is present, and (ii) T-to-C movement has taken place. Both factors must be present in order for *are* to be grammatical: one alone does not suffice.

(52)   a.   Aren't I invited?

       b.   Not only aren't I invited, I'm not even allowed near the building.

       c.   * Are I invited?

       d.   * I aren't invited.

The appearance of *are* for *am* is a retreat to the general case, in that *are* is a less specified allomorph than the expected *am*. The generalization here can be captured in terms of an Impoverishment rule deleting the 1st person and singular features from T in the relevant environment, as follows:

(53)   {1st, singular} $\Rightarrow \emptyset$ / v_{BE} ___Neg-C

This will leave the T node bearing only a [+Pres] feature when Vocabulary Insertion begins, so that *am* will be overspecified. The only rule in (50) eligible to apply will be the one that inserts *are*.

Impoverishment rules are language-specific by nature, but there are universal markedness-driven tendencies in their operation. That is, Impoverishment tends to take place in environments where several marked features are in play.

1.2.2.4   A Note on the Notion "Word"

Conspicuously absent from the foregoing discussion has been any morphosyntactic correlate of the notion "word." The atoms of syntactic representation, and the targets of Vocabulary Insertion, are terminal nodes (heads). As the reader will have noticed, however, heads may be realized by free morphemes or bound ones. Therefore, the theory of grammar presented here makes no room for the traditional notion of word, defined as a unit which is atomic from the point of view of syntax and which also forms a particular phonologically relevant domain (the *phonological word*). It is thus radically incompatible with the lexicalist hypothesis, which asserts the existence of such a unit.

Evidence that phonological wordhood and syntactic atomicity are orthogonal to each other is not difficult to come by, especially in morphologically complex languages, where phonological words often are not even syntactic constituents (cf. Weber 1983; also comments by Meyers 1990; also Haspelmath 2011, who cites related insights going as far back as Bloomfield 1933, 182-183; Hockett 1958, 58; and Pike 1967, 399ff). To see this, consider the translational equivalent in Cochabamba Quechua of a PP like *with that little boy*.

(54)   Chay huch'uy wayna-wan (Cochabamba Quechua)
        That little   boy-with

        'with that little boy'

The correspondent of English *with* in Cochabamba Quechua is the suffix *-wan*, which is part of the same phonological word as the head noun *wayna* 'boy', as shown by the fact that it counts for the calculation of word stress (which is assigned to the penultimate syllable). Despite forming a phonological word together, however, *wayna* and *-wan* are demonstrably not a constituent in (54). Instead, the DP *chay huch'uy wayna* 'that little boy' forms a constituent to the exclusion of *-wan* just as *that little boy* forms a constituent to the exclusion of *with* in English. This can be shown, in Quechua as well as English, via the pronoun replacement test:

(55)   Pay-wan   (Cochabamba Quechua)
         S/he-with

         'with him/her'

Now, a linguist determined to save the lexicalist hypothesis in the face of data like
(54) and (55) might be happy to concede that *-wan* is a syntactically independent
element on these grounds, and go on to claim that *-wan* is a clitic rather than an
affix, and hence irrelevant to an evaluation of the lexicalist hypothesis. But here
we encounter a problem: *-wan* and other postpositional elements in Quechua show
no phonological properties that would distinguish them from anything we would
want to call an affix in Quechua. They count for the calculation of word stress, and
they can both cause and undergo word-bound phonological processes (such as vowel
lowering in the environment of a uvular consonant, post-nasal voicing in dialects
that have it, etc.). Indeed, a class of elements that are clearly not constituent with
adjacent elements but are fully integrated into them prosodically has been known
about since at least Zec (1993) and Selkirk (1995)–Selkirk refers to them as Internal
Clitics. It seems to me that the existence of such elements has deadly consequences
for the testability of the lexicalist hypothesis.

In the rest of this book, and especially in Chapters 3 and 6, I will present trees in
which constituency and phonological wordhood are mismatched without comment.
I will take the phonological word to be a domain constructed in the morphophonological component somehow, but the details of how phonological words arise need
not concern us here (see Myler in press; Trommer 2008 for algorithms compatible with the present approach). The more relevant point is that, whatever else
phonological words are, they are not the atoms of syntax.

1.2.2.5   A Note on "Spanning" and Constituent Spell-Out

In the foregoing I have assumed that Vocabulary Insertion is into terminal nodes
only, as is standard within Distributed Morphology. I will continue to make this
assumption throughout the present work, although nothing I will have to say pre-
cludes the possibility, advocated in the theory known as Nanosyntax (Caha 2009;
Starke 2009; Svenonius 2012), that spell-out of larger elements is possible. Within
Nanosyntax, two versions of this claim have arisen. One claims that Vocabulary
Items may realize whole phrases, so long as they are a constituent (Caha 2009;
Starke 2009). A different view, put forward in Svenonius (2012), does not require
constituency, but permits Vocabulary Items to realize a *span* (defined as a struc-
turally contiguous set of terminal nodes on the same extended projection). The

debate between the terminal-nodes-only view of spell-out and these other views will revolve around cross-linguistic generalizations regarding suppletion and the proper characterization of blocking effects (see Embick and Marantz 2008 for much germane discussion of the latter). Neither of these issues will be at the forefront of this investigation, however, so I will say no more about this debate here.

This concludes the discussion of the morphophonological component (PF), which is responsible for converting the abstract hierarchical structures produced by syntax into a phonological representation. In this component, the output of syntax may be adjusted by feature-deleting Impoverishment rules, before undergoing Vocabulary Insertion (which relates terminal nodes to their underlying phonological forms) cyclically from the most deeply embedded constituent outwards. The output of Vocabulary Insertion is the input to phonology proper.

1.2.3   LF (The Semantic Component)

The other interpretive component that works on the output of syntax is Logical Form. Analogous to what we have seen on the PF side, the semantic component of the grammar must translate the hierarchical arrangement of abstract feature bundles produced by syntax into a rather different sort of representation. Following Wood (2015, 21-31), I will take this to mean that the need for such a translation is serviced by a form of Late Insertion at the LF interface. The conversion of a syntactic representation into a semantic one will therefore take place in a manner analogous to what is found in the derivation to Phonological Form. Terminal nodes will not come pre-packaged with their denotations–instead, they will be related to them by rule, just as with Vocabulary Insertion at PF. Just as at PF, it will sometimes be the case that more than one denotation is eligible for insertion into a given terminal node, with the choice being determined by aspects of the surrounding structure. This situation will be termed *conditioned allosemy*, and the denotations competing for insertion at a given terminal will be known as its *allosemes*. Just as some syntactic nodes are realized as zero at PF, effectively being ignored by the phonological component, so too will it be possible for terminals to be *semantically zero*, or expletive, therefore being ignored by the semantic component. Then, once denotations have been selected, a small set of composition rules will combine the denotations of terminals together. If there is no way for the structure to compose semantically, this will result in ill-formedness.

Here, I will provide an inventory of the composition rules assumed, followed by a discussion of the denotations available to the functional heads in the thematic domain introduced in section 1.2.1.

The composition rules assumed in this book will be the same as those in Wood (2015). The two most important composition rules in the present context will be Functional Application and Event Identification.

Firstly, we have Functional Application, which is defined by Heim and Kratzer (1998, 44) as follows:

(56)   *Functional Application*

If α is a branching node, $\{\beta,\gamma\}$ is the set of α's daughters, and $[\![\beta]\!]$ is a function whose domain contains $[\![\gamma]\!]$, then $[\![\alpha]\!] = [\![\beta]\!]([\![\gamma]\!])$.

The next rule, Event Identification, plays an important role in how the semantic contribution of argument-introducing heads is integrated into the composition. It is defined by Kratzer (1996, 122) as in (57).

(57)   *Event Identification*

If α is a branching node, $\{\beta,\gamma\}$ is the set of α's daughters, where $[\![\beta]\!]$ is in $D_{<e,<s,t>>}$ and $[\![\gamma]\!]$ is in $D_{<s,t>}$, then $[\![\alpha]\!]=\lambda x_e.\lambda e_s.[\![\beta]\!](x)(e)\wedge[\![\gamma]\!](e)$.

A further rule is Function Composition, which, in Wood's felicitous phrase , "applies when the sister of A is one argument away from being the type A is looking for" (Wood 2015, 36). It is more formally defined as follows (this definition is taken from Wood 2015, 26).

(58)   *Function Composition*

If α is a branching node, $\{\beta,\gamma\}$ is the set of α's daughters, where $[\![\beta]\!]$ is in $D_{<b,c>}$ and $[\![\gamma]\!]$ is in $D_{<a,b>}$, then $[\![\alpha]\!]=\lambda x_a.[\![\beta([\![\gamma(x)]\!])]\!]$

A final rule, which will not play much of a role in the present book, is Predicate Conjunction. This takes two functions of the same semantic type, conjoins them, and identifies their arguments pointwise. As Wood (2015, 23-24) notes, Predicate Conjunction and Event Identification could be collapsed into one, given their obvious similarity, but I will follow him in keeping Event Identification separate (since it is familiar in that form to many).

(59)   *Predicate Conjunction*

If α is a branching node, $\{\beta,\gamma\}$ is the set of α's daughters, and $[\![\beta]\!]$ and $[\![\gamma]\!]$ are both in D_f, f a semantic type which takes n arguments, then $[\![\alpha]\!]=\lambda(a_1,...,a_n).[\![\beta]\!](a_1,...,a_n)\wedge[\![\gamma]\!](a_1,...,a_n)$.

With this inventory of composition rules in hand, we will turn to the denotations of the syntactic pieces that make up the thematic domain of the clause. We will begin with the categorizing head v.

In this book, I will assume that there are two syntactically distinct varieties of v: substantive v, and meaningless copula v. Substantive v is the more familiar version from previous literature on argument structure. It has the following allosemes.

(60)   *Allosemes of Substantive* v (Wood 2015:28)

    a. $[\![v]\!] \Leftrightarrow \lambda e_s.\text{activity}(e)$

    b. $[\![v]\!] \Leftrightarrow \lambda e_s.\text{state}(e)$

    c. $[\![v]\!] \Leftrightarrow \lambda P_{<s,t>}.\lambda e_s.\exists e'_s.\text{activity}(e)\wedge\text{CAUS}(e,e')$
         $\wedge P(e')/\underline{\quad}(\text{eventuality})$

The first two allosemes can be chosen so long as the conditioning environment for the 3rd is not met. The choice among the first two is free up to compatibility with the lexical semantics of the root. The alloseme in (60c) is the *causative* alloseme, and is chosen just in case the complement of v denotes an eventuality (Marantz 2009a,b).

On the other hand, copula v (which, depending on the surrounding structure, will be spelled out as a form of HAVE or BE at PF) will simply be taken not to contribute anything to the thematic interpretation, following a long tradition (Bach 1967; Lyons 1968; Partee 1999; Roy 2013). Its sole purpose is to act as a syntactic scaffold to link fundamentally non-verbal forms of predication to functional heads in the verbal extended projection (such as tense, aspect, and clause typing). In itself, this view does not entail that copula v is totally meaningless. What I have to say here is perfectly compatible with, for instance, Rothstein's (1999) idea that BE is a sort of verbal classifier which converts mass-states (e.g. adjectival denotations) into countable eventualities. Nevertheless, for simplicity I will make the assumption that copula v is a type-neutral identity function in this work:

(61)   *Copula* v

     $[\![v]\!] \Leftrightarrow \lambda x.x$

Next, we turn to Voice, which introduces the external argument. The way in which Voice integrates the external argument into the event structure provided by vP is entirely predictable from the denotation of that vP complement. If vP denotes a set of dynamic events, then Voice relates the external argument to it as an agent. If vP denotes a set of states, then the external argument is interpreted as the holder of that state. These options are captured by the first two allosemes listed in (62). If vP denotes something other than a predicate of eventualities, or if the eventuality in its complement does not conceptually entail an agent or causer, then the third option will be chosen–this is *expletive Voice*, which simply passes the denotation of its complement up the tree (Kastner 2016; Schäfer 2008; Wood 2015). I take expletive Voice to be a type-neutral identity function, rather than an identity function over event predicates (as Wood 2015 does); this amendment allows Voice to push relations up the tree, a possibility that will come to play an important role in the account of the typology of possession sentences.

(62)   *Rules for the Interpretation of Voice* (Adapted from Wood 2015, 30)

    a. $[\![\text{Voice}]\!] \Leftrightarrow \lambda x_e.\lambda e_s.\text{Agent}(x,e)$ / ___(agentive, dynamic event)

    b. $[\![\text{Voice}]\!] \Leftrightarrow \lambda x_e.\lambda e_s.\text{Holder}(x,e)$ / ___(stative eventuality)

    c. $[\![\text{Voice}]\!] \Leftrightarrow \lambda x.x$ / ___(elsewhere)

In the coming discussion, Applicative heads will play an important role, especially high Appl heads. In Pylkkännen (2008), high Appl is assigned the following denotation when it introduces a beneficiary argument (the denotation will be analogous for other sorts of high Appl, with beneficiary exchanged for the relevant role).

(63)   *High Appl According to Pylkkännen* (2008:12)

    $[\![\text{Appl}]\!] \Leftrightarrow \lambda x_e.\lambda e_s.\text{Beneficiary}(x,e)$

However, in Chapter 3, I will argue (following a suggestion from David Embick, pers. comm.) that there is evidence that high Appl itself is always semantically vacuous, at least in Quechua, and perhaps in all languages that have it. The meaning traditionally attributed to high Appl is, I will suggest, actually contributed by the oblique marking on the argument in Appl's specifier.

The Pred head has been identified in earlier work as the locus of the stage level/individual level distinction. Since these different meanings of the Pred head are sometimes spelled out in different ways (see Citko 2008, Balusu 2014),[30] this must be a syntactic distinction between two Pred heads, rather than a case of conditioned allosemy of one Pred head. I follow Balusu (2014), Adger and Ramchand (2003),

---

30. For example, Balusu (2014) points out contrasts of the following sort in Telugu, and argues that the morpheme -*gaa* is the spell-out of the stage-level Pred head. The individual level Pred head is instead silent, on Balusu's analysis.

    (i)   naaku koopam-gaa undi. (Telugu)
          I.DAT anger-gaa   BE

          'I am angry.'

    (ii)   naaku koopam undi. (Telugu)
          I.DAT anger   BE

          'I am an angry person.'

and Markman (2008) in assigning the different Pred heads the following semantics. The idea is that Stage Level Pred introduces an eventuality variable, which
can be modulated by tense and aspect, whereas Individual Level Pred does not, so
that tense and aspect instead modulate the lifetime of the individual of whom the
property holds. Individual Level Pred is therefore expletive in our technical sense,
and hence will be the only one usable if the complement of Pred denotes something
other than a predicate.

(64)   *Stage Level Pred* (Adapted from Balusu 2014)

         $[\![\text{Pred}_{stage}]\!] \Leftrightarrow \lambda P_{<e,t>}.\lambda x_e.\lambda e_s.\text{holds}(P,e) \wedge \text{Holder}(x,e)$

(65)   *Individual Level Pred* (Adapted from Balusu 2014)

         $[\![\text{Pred}_{indiv}]\!] \Leftrightarrow \lambda x.x$

Finally, I introduce my assumptions regarding the main locus of meaning in existential constructions. It is commonly assumed that existential BE is a fundamentally
different animal than predicative copular BE. However, the fact that the paradigms
of these verbs frequently merge in marked environments in languages that distinguish them (Clark 1978; Chapters 2 and 3 of the present work) is redolent of
Impoverishment. If these two BE's are relatable via Impoverishment, it follows that
they must be versions of the same thing, and it also follows that it is wrong to
make the two BEs separate verbs with different meanings. Instead, I attribute the
special semantics of an existential to a separate syntactic piece, and have the morphological distinctness of existential BE as a case of allomorphy, conditioned by the
presence of this other piece. This is consistent with Francez's (2009) argument that
the existential semantics of existential constructions is not provided by the copula
itself. The crucial other piece, I suggest, is the so-called expletive present (sometimes silently, sometimes overtly) in the structure of such sentences. It is not the
purpose of the present work to propose a sophisticated semantics for existentials
(see Francez 2007, 2009; McCloskey 2014 for recent discussion). For simplicity, I
will assume that the expletive introduces simple existential closure, as follows (this
is basically Williams' 1994 analysis of the semantic contribution of the expletive):[31]

(66)   *EXPL in Existentials*

         $[\![\text{EXPL}]\!] \Leftrightarrow \lambda f_{<e,<s,t>>}.\lambda e_s.\exists x_e.f(x)(e)$

---

31. I believe that my analyses elsewhere in this book can be recast in terms of Francez's approach
to the semantics of existentials. I do not do this in the main text because it would greatly complicate the exposition. However, see the appendix for sample recastings of some analyses from
chapter 3 in terms of Francez's system.

This concludes the discussion of the semantic component, and also the discussion of the architecture of the grammar in general. In the architecture assumed here, syntax is the only generative engine, and PF and LF are interpretive components, in that they translate the output of syntax into a different kind of representation. I have taken the position, following Wood (2015), Marantz (1997, 2009a,b), and Halle and Marantz (1993), that this translation procedure takes the form of Late Insertion at both interfaces. In the morphophonological component, there is Late Insertion of the underlying phonological forms of morphemes. In the semantic component, there is Late Insertion of the denotations associated with these morphemes. At both interfaces, there is potential competition amongst ways of realizing terminal nodes, leading to allomorphy at PF and allosemy at LF. Both interfaces also have their own versions of zero realizations, in which a certain terminal node is effectively ignored by the component in question. At PF, such nodes are known as silent elements. At LF, such nodes are interpreted as type-neutral identity functions.

1.3   Consequences and Major Claims

With this picture of the architecture of the grammar now in place, I am in a position to sketch my main proposal. I argued at the beginning of this chapter that much of the literature on predicative possession is grappling with two main puzzles, which I dubbed the too-many-meanings puzzle and the too-many-(surface)-structures puzzle.

(67)   *The Too-Many-Meanings Puzzle*

        How can one possession structure have so many different meanings in a given language?

(68)   *The Too-Many-(Surface)-Structures Puzzle*

        How can it be that the same set of possessive meanings is realized on the surface in so many syntactically different ways across languages?

The major claim of the book is that the following theoretical postulates suffice to solve both of these puzzles, given certain other widely agreed-upon aspects of the syntax and semantics of DPs and of copular verbs.

(69)   *Theoretical Claims*

    a.   Thematic roles are not syntactic features; instead they are (parts of) the meanings of functional heads, relevant only in the semantic component.

    b.   Functional heads can vary within and across languages with respect to whether they require a specifier or not.

    c.   Heads can be semantically null or contentful at the LF interface (that is, they may or may not introduce additional entailments of their own), just as they can be phonologically covert or overt at the PF interface.

Neither (69a) nor (69b) imply any new theoretical mechanisms; (69c) is perhaps more controversial, but it is a natural consequence of the sort of theory of the architecture of the grammar entertained here, and its implications have been studied extensively for the case of argument-introducing heads by Alexiadou, Anagnostopoulou, and Schäfer (2014); Schäfer (2008); and Wood (2015). Claim (69a) is one of the standard ways of eliminating the Theta Criterion in the context of the Minimalist Program (see Heim and Kratzer 1998, 53-58 for one articulation of the idea; Baker 1997, 121-122 for another).[32] Claim (69b) has been a staple of the comparative syntax literature for a long time–one need only think of the standard account of the difference between languages that have V2 and those that lack it (partly a matter of whether spec-CP must be filled; see Den Besten 1983 et seq.), or of Minimalist analyses of the EPP (formulated in terms of the presence or absence of a specifier requirement for T; see Chomsky 1995, 55, 232; Alexiadou and Anagnostopoulou 1998). Nevertheless, the combination of the claims in (69) yields a certain independence between the notions "syntactic argument of head X", and "semantic

---

32. The other major way of eliminating the Theta Criterion, of course, is to assimilate thematic roles to other formal features in the syntactic derivation (Hornstein 1999 et seq). On morphological grounds, this move seems unlikely to be correct. Thematic roles never seem to be realized morphologically in the way that case and phi are. A language in which thematic roles were morphologically realized independently of case would, for instance, have active/passive alternations of the following sort (where AG and TH represent suffixes spelling out the thematic roles themselves).

    (i)   The man-AG-NOM ate the cake-TH-ACC.

    (ii)   The cake-TH-NOM was eaten by the man-AG-OBL.

Languages of this kind are not attested.
Recall that the Movement Theory of Control exploits the idea that thematic roles are formal features in order to motivate movement into theta positions. While the architecture of grammar assumed here is not inherently incompatible with movement into theta positions, it would require that some other motivation for such movement be found.

argument of head X", as discussed by Wood (2015). This is so because a meaningful head X might occur in a derivation, and yet fail to take a specifier in the syntax. If this occurs, then a DP merged higher up in the structure might end up "going in" as the missing argument of the function contributed by X, despite that DP not being in XP's specifier. This possibility, which I will refer to as *delayed gratification*,[33] is depicted in (70). In (70), the DP is *syntactically* an argument of Y, since it is merged in spec-YP; yet *semantically* it is an argument of head X. Of course, if XP did happen to take a specifier in the syntactic derivation, the composition would have had the same result but would have occurred in a more familiar fashion. I refer to this more familiar situation, in which a thematic role is satiated by an argument in the specifier of the head that introduced it, as *instant gratification*. This is depicted in (71).

(70)   *Delayed Gratification*

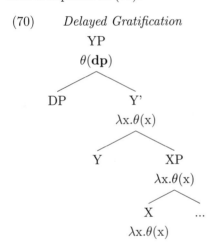

<hr />

33. Hale and Keyser (2002:24) independently invented the term "delayed gratification" for a notion which is related to the mechanism under discussion here, but rather different in nature. In Hale and Keyser's work, delayed gratification refers to delaying the syntactic requirement of a given head for a specifier, and satisfying that syntactic requirement by having the next head up project a specifier instead. I will assume that such proxy satisfaction of a syntactic requirement is impossible (independent of Agree). I will thus reserve the term "delayed gratification" for the notion discussed in the text, whereby the semantic argument of a head happens not to have been merged in the specifier of that head, but is instead introduced higher in the structure.

(71)   *Instant Gratification*

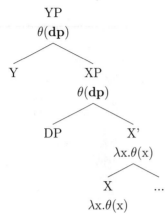

Mechanisms very like delayed gratification have been a feature of LFG (Alsina 1996; Bresnan 2001), HPSG (Sag, Wasow, and Bender 2003), and other non-movement-based theories (Jacobson 1990) for some time, where they are used to analyze raising and control constructions in frameworks where movement chains and silent pronominals are, for one reason or another, eschewed. One might therefore wonder whether delayed gratification is redundant with raising and control. However, in the context of a theory in which agreement, case, and scope relations are calculated over configurations, delayed gratification has very different morphosyntactic consequences than raising or control. All these differences follow from the fact that delayed gratification implies the absence of any syntactic representation of the argument in the lower thematic position, whereas raising and control imply the presence of such. Compare (72) with (73).

(72)   *Delayed Gratification*

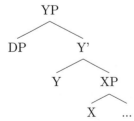

(73)   *Raising and Control*

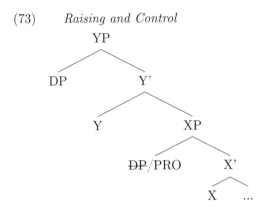

In (73), there is a syntactically present occurrence of a DP in spec-XP, which could, in principle, trigger agreement, cause an intervention effect for another moving DP, or act as a scope position (in the case of raising) for the moved DP under reconstruction. None of these possibilities arise in (72). Hence, delayed gratification makes different predictions than raising and control, and indeed there is evidence that all three are necessary. The existence of raising and control per se is hardly controversial (although debate continues as to whether one will ultimately be reducible to the other). Wood (2013, 2014a, 2015) provides ample evidence for the necessity of delayed gratification from multiple separate domains in Icelandic. In Chapter 3, all three of DP-movement, control, and delayed gratification will be crucial in the analysis of the alternation between what I call the BE construction and the BE-APPL construction in Cochabamba Quechua. In Chapters 4 and 5, I will argue that delayed gratification, rather than raising or control, is involved in deriving the interpretation of several different types of HAVE sentence.

1.4   Building and Interpreting Possession Sentences: The Solution in a Nutshell

Having introduced delayed gratification and shown how its existence follows from the claims in (69), I will now show that its existence yields instant answers to both the too-many-meanings puzzle and the too-many-(surface)-structures puzzle, once we adopt four long-standing and well-motivated claims concerning the syntactic and semantic properties of copulas and of possession relations.

(74)   *Syntax and Semantics of Possession Relations and Copulas*

    a. Possession is fundamentally a relationship between two DPs–the posses-
sor and the possessee. (Szabolcsi 1981, 1994; Kayne 1993; Partee 1999).

    b. To link such a relation to tense, clause type, etc., one needs a copula: a
dummy verb.

    c. Copulas exist to "sentencify" fundamentally non-sentence meanings
(Pustet 2003; Tham 2013).

    d. The copula is realized as HAVE if the rest of the structure is transitive
(Hoekstra 1994); it will be realized as BE otherwise.

As mentioned, all of (74a)-(74d) have appeared in many guises in previous literature, and I believe them to have been abundantly vindicated in that literature (see
Chapter 2 for details). My contribution is to show that putting them together with
(69) yields novel and promising solutions to both of the puzzles that have made
predicative possession such a vexed topic.

First, however, we need to flesh out (74a) by making some explicit assumptions
about how possession relations are introduced inside DP. I will assume that inalienable relations of various sorts are introduced by the noun root itself; the type of
relation depends on the meaning of the root. This is illustrated for the case of a
body-part noun in (77), on the next page. Alienable possession relations are introduced by a family of Poss heads inside DP. The role of Poss is essentially to relation-
alize nPs that are not themselves inherently relational (Barker 1995). A structure
including this head is given in (78), two pages below. The cross-linguistic morphological evidence for Poss turns out to be very strong indeed. In some languages,
such as the Kampan languages of the Arawakan family, North Carib languages, and
many others, alienable possession is expressed in a more morphosyntactically complex way than inalienable possession (see Nichols 1988, 1992). Alienable possession
in such languages requires an additional suffix: an overt Poss.

(75)   *Inalienable Possession in Kampan Languages (Michael 2012, his (16a))*

    No-gito
    1SG-head
    'My head'

(76)   *Alienable Possession in Kampan Languages (based on Michael 2012, (7))*

    No-biha-ne
    1SG-bow-POSS
    'My bow'

(77)   *Root Introduces an Inalienable Possession Relation*

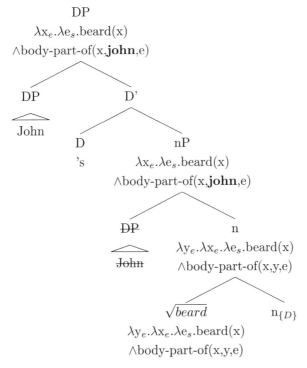

An excursus is necessary at this point on the definition of the notion *inalienable*. It is well known that there is a vast amount of variation amongst languages that mark inalienability with regard to which roots "count" as inalienably possessed. Nevertheless, it is clear that lexical semantics at least to some degree "hems in" the set of roots that are allowed to be inalienable in principle. This situation is exactly analogous to what we find with the (anti)causative alternation cross-linguistically. There too, there is a clear lexical semantic generalization about the predicates that can alternate in principle (externally-caused change-of-state verbs; see Levin and Rappoport Hovav 2005, 2). And there, too, there is cross-linguistic variation in terms of the verbs that actually do alternate in a given language (Haspelmath 1993). For the anticausative alternation, Schäfer (2008) and Wood (2015) suggest that, in order to participate in the alternation, two conditions must be met: (i) the root must be semantically compatible with encoding a change of state, and (ii) the root must permit itself to be merged in structures where Voice has a thematic specifier and in ones where it does not. Condition (ii) is a matter of language-specific selectional restrictions on roots, hence the cross-linguistic variation.

(78)   *Poss Head can Introduce an Alienable Relation*

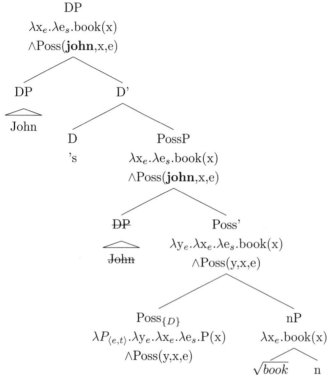

We can say something analogous about the variation in inalienable possession. In order for a given root to be compatible with inalienable morphosyntax, it must both (i) be capable of introducing its own relation semantically, and (ii) must carry an instruction for nP to merge with a DP (i.e., it must bear a {D} feature). If (ii) is not met, then even a relational noun will have its possessors introduced in the specifier of an expletive PossP, and will thus not be treated as inalienable in morphosyntactic terms. This proposal immediately explains two generalizations about inalienable possession identified by Nichols (1988, 1992). The first is that inalienable possession "involves a tighter structural bond between possessee and possessor" (Heine 1997, 172, citing Nichols 1992, 117)–this follows because inalienable possession involves merging the possessor directly with nP, whereas alienable possession involves the additional mediation of the Poss head. The second is that inalienably possessed nouns in languages that have them are usually a closed class, whereas alienably-marked nouns are an open class (Heine 1997, 172, citing Nichols 1988, 562). This follows because inalienably possessed nouns on the present approach are those that stipulate as a lexical property that they can only combine with n if it takes a complement. In the absence of such a selectional restriction on the root, having the possessor be introduced in spec-PossP comes for free.

Returning to the details of the structures in (77) and (78), note that, unlike Barker (1995), I assume that any possession relation is between two individuals and a state. That is, the possessee (either by itself as in (77) or by combining with Poss as in (78)) contributes an eventuality variable. This assumption will not play much of a role until Chapter 4, but since it will ultimately prove essential to achieving a unified analysis of main verb HAVE in that chapter, it deserves some justification here.[34]

One piece of evidence for the existence of such an eventuality variable is that some languages have morphemes that modify the temporal properties of the possession state. For example, Aikhenvald and Dixon (2012, 20-21) point out that there is a distinction in the DPs of most North Carib languages between past and non-past possession; i.e. "what I had before and what I have now."

(79)   *Past vs. Non-Past Inalienable Possession in Macushi* (Abbott 1991:86-7)

    a.   u-ye
           1SG-tooth
           'my tooth'

    b.   u-ye-rî'pi
           1SG-tooth-former.possession
           'my former tooth'

(80)   *Past vs. Non-Past Alienable Possession in Machushi* (Abbott 1991:86-87)

    a.   u-wa'ka-ri
           1SG-axe-POSS
           'my axe'

    b.   u-wa'ka-ri-rî'pi
           1SG-axe-POSS-former.possession
           'my former axe'

Notice in passing that the affix order in (80b) is exactly as one would expect on the analysis in (78): Poss introduces the eventuality variable in the possession relation, and the temporal morpheme modifies that variable, hence the temporal suffix follows the Poss suffix.

---

34. I would like to thank an anonymous reviewer for urging more explicit motivation for this idea, and for pointing out the relevance of Larson (1998) in developing such.

Evidence for my position can be detected even in English, with respect to modifiers like *former*: *my former tooth* can mean something which is still a tooth, but which is no longer a tooth in my body. If Larson (1998) is correct that modifiers like *former* modify an eventuality, then this is evidence for the presence of an eventuality variable in possession relations.[35]

Other languages exhibit different sorts of temporal modification of this eventuality variable. Aikhenvald and Dixon state that "a number of languages distinguish items owned by someone on a temporary basis–for instance, borrowed–from those owned permanently" (2012:21). West Greenlandic, Dyirbal, and Martuthunira are all cited in this connection. I conclude that there is ample reason to believe that possession relations introduced inside DP are associated with their own eventuality variable.

Since possession relations are introduced inside DP in the way shown in (77) and (78), we need to bring a copular verb into the picture if we want to build sentences about possession relations. Only then will it be possible to introduce aspect, tense, and clause-typing heads, which will allow us to link these relations to these aspects of sentential meaning (that is, "sentencify" them). There are a variety of ways in which Natural Language can introduce such a verb, but *all of them will (in principle) work just as well regardless of where inside DP the relation was introduced.* This is enough to solve the too-many-meanings puzzle.

(81)   *Solution to the Too-Many-Meanings Puzzle*

   Possession constructions can mean so many things because they involve sentencifying a meaning that comes from inside DP. There are many subtypes of such meaning, and they do not form a semantic natural class. These meanings pattern together because they are a *syntactic* natural class: they are all introduced by syntactic heads inside DP.

What of the too-many-(surface)-structures puzzle? To answer this question, we need to consider some ways in which a copula can be introduced in order to sentencify a possessive meaning born in DP. One way of doing this, employed by many natural languages, is simply to build a possessed DP and combine it with an existential copula. This is the strategy employed by such languages as Hungarian, as in (82). A schematic structure for languages exhibiting this pattern is given in (84)

---

35. The judgments are somewhat unclear for alienable possession in English: a reviewer reports not being able to find an analogous reading for *my former Playstation*, but such a reading is available to me. Perhaps there is variation amongst speakers' grammars in whether or not *former* can merge above PossP in English.

overleaf. Here and throughout the discussion to come, I will ignore the contribution of indefinite determiners; see the discussion of Partee (1999) in Chapter 2 for a possible treatment of their meaning compatible with the present approach.

(82)   Nekem van könyvem.   [Existential BE + Possessive DP]
       I.DAT   is   book.1POSS.NOM

       'I have a book.' (lit: 'there is a book of mine') (Hungarian; see Szabolcsi 1981)

In (84), the possessor thematic role introduced by Poss is satiated by the DP in Poss's specifier. This is what I earlier referred to as instant gratification of the possessor thematic role.[36] Presumably, Poss in Hungarian demands a specifier whenever it is used in the derivation. We know, however, that functional heads can vary cross-linguistically with respect to whether they may (or must) take a specifier (recall the standard analyses of V2 and of the EPP property discussed above). It follows from this familiar feature of the mircro-parametric approach that other languages might allow (or even require) Poss to lack a specifier. In such a language, it will be possible to build a structure of the sort seen in (83). This structure includes the Poss head, but Poss does not take a specifier.

(83)   *The Consequences of Leaving Poss Specifierless*

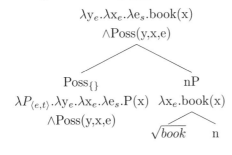

36. The possessor subsequently moves out of the possessee DP in Hungarian. What is crucial here is where the possessor is first brought into the structure. The point I am making here still goes through on Den Dikken's (1999) analysis involving the full DP possessor binding a resumptive pronoun. See Chapter 2 for detailed discussion of both of these approaches to possession in Hungarian.

(84)   *Possessed DP + Existential Verb*

vP

$\lambda e_s.\exists x_e.\text{book}(x)$
$\wedge\text{Poss}(\textbf{speaker},x,e)$

be$_{exist}$ PredP

$\lambda x.x$ $\lambda e_s.\exists x_e.\text{book}(x)$
$\wedge\text{Poss}(\textbf{speaker},x,e)$

EXPL   Pred'

$\lambda f_{<e,<s,t>>}.\lambda e_s.\exists x_e.f(x)(e)$ $\lambda x_e.\lambda e_s.\text{book}(x)$
$\wedge\text{Poss}(\textbf{speaker},x,e)$

Pred   DP

$\lambda x.x$ $\lambda x_e.\lambda e_s.\text{book}(x)$
$\wedge\text{Poss}(\textbf{speaker},x,e)$

DP   D'

I   D   PossP

$\lambda x_e.\lambda e_s.\text{book}(x)$
$\wedge\text{Poss}(\textbf{speaker},x,e)$

DP   Poss'

I $\lambda y_e.\lambda x_e.\lambda e_s.\text{book}(x)$
$\wedge\text{Poss}(y,x,e)$

Poss$_{\{D\}}$ nP

$\lambda P_{\langle e,t\rangle}.\lambda y_e.\lambda x_e.\lambda e_s.P(x)$ $\lambda x_e.\text{book}(x)$
$\wedge\text{Poss}(y,x,e)$

$\sqrt{book}$ n

The DP in (83) denotes a relation; it still needs its possessor. If we embed (83) in some kind of copula construction (any kind will do as far as Universal Grammar is concerned, so long as all the semantics comes together successfully), and introduce the possessor somewhere higher up, the result will be a viable possession sentence. The possessor role will be satiated under what I have called *delayed gratification*.

As an example, we might embed (83) under an existential copula and introduce the possessor in a locative PP adjoined to vP. This will give us a plausible structure for a language like Russian.

(85)   u   menja   est' kniga. [Existential BE + Locative PP Possessor]
       At me.GEN is   book

       'I have a book.' (lit: 'at me is a book')   (Russian)

A schematic structure for languages of this sort is given in (87). Crucially, the denotation of vP in (87) is identical to the one in Hungarian, despite the difference in the first-merge position of the possessor. Note that EXPL composes with its complement in (87) via Function Composition, rather than via Functional Application as in the case of the Hungarian derivation. Here is how this works in detail. Pred' is one argument away from being of the right type to compose with EXPL: Pred' is of type $\langle e, \langle e, \langle s, t \rangle \rangle \rangle$, whereas EXPL requires its first argument to be of type $\langle e, \langle s, t \rangle \rangle$. By Function Composition, the interpretation of PredP is as shown in the first line of (86), and lambda conversion proceeds as indicated.

(86)   *Interpretation of PredP in (87): Full Derivation*

$\lambda y_e.(\lambda f_{<e,<s,t>>}.\lambda e_s.\exists x_e.f(x)(e)(\lambda y_e.\lambda x_e.\lambda e_s.\text{book}(x) \wedge \text{Poss}(y,x,e)y))$

$= \lambda y_e.(\lambda f_{<e,<s,t>>}.\lambda e_s.\exists x_e.f(x)(e)(\lambda x_e.\lambda e_s.\text{book}(x) \wedge \text{Poss}(y,x,e)))$

$= \lambda y_e.\lambda e_s.\exists x_e.(\lambda x_e.\lambda e_s.\text{book}(x) \wedge \text{Poss}(y,x,e)(x)(e))$

$= \lambda y_e.\lambda e_s.\exists x_e.\text{book}(x) \wedge \text{Poss}(y,x,e)$

(87)   *Existential BE + Locative PP Possessor*

$$vP$$
$$\lambda e_s.\exists x_e.book(x)$$
$$\wedge Poss(\textbf{speaker},x,e)$$

PP

At me

$$vP$$
$$\lambda y_e.\lambda e_s.\exists x_e.book(x)$$
$$\wedge Poss(y,x,e)$$

$$be_{exist}$$
$$\lambda x.x$$

$$PredP$$
$$\lambda y_e.\lambda e_s.\exists x_e.book(x)$$
$$\wedge Poss(y,x,e)$$

EXPL
$$\lambda f_{<e,<s,t>>}.\lambda e_s.\exists x_e.f(x)(e)$$

$$Pred'$$
$$\lambda y_e.\lambda x_e.\lambda e_s.book(x)$$
$$\wedge Poss(y,x,e)$$

Pred
$$\lambda x.x$$

$$DP$$
$$\lambda y_e.\lambda x_e.\lambda e_s.book(x)$$
$$\wedge Poss(y,x,e)$$

D

$$PossP$$
$$\lambda y_e.\lambda x_e.\lambda e_s.book(x)$$
$$\wedge Poss(y,x,e)$$

$$Poss_{\{\}}$$
$$\lambda P_{\langle e,t\rangle}.\lambda y_e.\lambda x_e.\lambda e_s.P(x)$$
$$\wedge Poss(y,x,e)$$

$$nP$$
$$\lambda x_e.book(x)$$

$$\sqrt{book}$$ n

As I will argue in Chapters 6 and 7, other options beyond the ones exemplified by Hungarian and Russian include embedding a DP substructure like (83) under a PP headed by a WITH preposition (one of the options employed by Icelandic), or embedding it under a derivational little-a or little-n morpheme, which takes a relation as its first argument semantically and yields a predicate which can then be predicated of the possessor. Constructions of this last sort have been referred to as Predicativization by Stassen (2009), and I will argue that they include the Quechua -*yoq* construction in (9), and the English -*ed* of *Sarah is brown-eyed* (see Nevins and Myler 2014, submitted).

Finally, if gratification is delayed until the highest position in the thematic domain (VoiceP as Kratzer 1996 calls it), the result will be a configuration like (90).[37] This, I propose, is what gives rise to a HAVE construction.

(88)   John has a book.

The relationship between HAVE and BE in this framework can then be schematized as follows:

(89)   a.   v $\Leftrightarrow$ HAVE / ___Voice$_{\{D\},\phi}$

       b.   v $\Leftrightarrow$ BE / elsewhere

An advantage of this suggestion, as mentioned earlier, is that it provides an explanation for the relative cross-linguistic rarity of HAVE compared to BE. There are many ways of merging a possessor into the structure that lead to BE (anywhere below VoiceP or in the specifier of unergative Voice), but only one way of merging a possessor into the structure that yields HAVE (into the specifier of a transitive VoiceP). Hence, HAVE's rarity comes about because fewer combinatorial possibilities for verb phrases allowed by UG lead to HAVE than lead to BE.

---

37. I assume that the open variable corresponding to the direct object *a book* in this configuration is existentially closed at the VoiceP level, in the spirit of Diesing (1992). An alternative might be to assume, partly following Partee (1999) and Wood and Marantz (2015/forthcoming), that the indefinite determiner existentially closes only the variable corresponding to the possessee.

(90)   *A Transitive Possession Construction*

VoiceP
$\lambda x_e.\lambda e_s.\text{book}(x)$
$\wedge\text{Poss}(\mathbf{john},x,e)$

DP   Voice'
                $\lambda y_e.\lambda x_e.\lambda e_s.\text{book}(x)$
John $\wedge\text{Poss}(y,x,e)$

Voice$_{\{D\}}$ vP
ϕ $\lambda y_e.\lambda x_e.\lambda e_s.\text{book}(x)$
$\lambda x.x$ $\wedge\text{Poss}(y,x,e)$

v   DP
$\lambda x.x$ $\lambda y_e.\lambda x_e.\lambda e_s.\text{book}(x)$
$\wedge\text{Poss}(y,x,e)$

D   PossP
$\lambda y_e.\lambda x_e.\lambda e_s.\text{book}(x)$
$\wedge\text{Poss}(y,x,e)$

Poss$_{\{\}}$ nP
$\lambda P_{\langle e,t\rangle}.\lambda y_e.\lambda x_e.\lambda e_s.P(x)$ $\lambda x_e.\text{book}(x)$
$\wedge\text{Poss}(y,x,e)$

$\sqrt{book}$ n

An additional advantage of this approach to HAVE is that it makes a strong morphological prediction: it ought to be possible to find a language with a transitive possession construction, where the verb is made up of the BE verb plus a transitivity suffix. In other words, it ought to be possible to spell out Voice and v separately from each other in a structure like (90). This prediction is correct, as shown by the following data from the Sino-Tibetan language Qiang (LaPolla and Huang 2003, 98; cited in Stassen 2009, 226, his example (51b)), and from the Quechua language Huallaga Quechua (Weber 1989, 164, his (582)).

(91)   *HAVE as BE + Transitivity in Qiang*

Khumtsi tutʂ-ɣʒə-zi   ʒi-ʒ.
Khumtsi younger.brother-four-class be$_{exist}$-CAUS
'Khumtsi has four younger brothers.'

(92)   *HAVE as BE + Transitivity in Huallaga Quechua*

Mana papa-ta   ka-chi-:-na-chu.
Not   potato-ACC be-CAUS-1SUBJ-NOW-NEG
'I don't have any potatoes now.'

The foregoing, it should be clear, essentially solves the too-many-(surface)-structures puzzle, as summed up in (93).

(93)   *Solution to the Too-Many-(Surface)-Structures Puzzle*

Possession sentences involve a meaningless v head. Since it lacks a root and introduces no eventuality variable, this head makes no semantic demands on the surrounding structure. This means that syntax alone gets to decide where the possessor is introduced. Possession relations originate inside a DP (embedded) in the complement of this v. Since the possession relation originates low, Universal Grammar can choose from any position in the VoiceP as the first-merge position of the possessor.

This approach makes the correct prediction (its correctness is pointed out independently by Tham 2013) that *the typology of BE-based possession constructions allows the full gamut of copular predication types.* In other words, it seems that, if a given syntactic structure is possible in a predicative or existential copular construction, there will be some language whose possession sentences have that structure. Another correct prediction is that the extra structure involved in introducing a possessor under delayed gratification need not be semantically innocent. This is already known from studies of other aspects of argument structure. For example, Alexiadou, Anagnostopoulou, and Schäfer (2014) and Schäfer (2012) give a delayed gratification analysis of causer PPs in Greek anticausatives, showing that the semantic contributions of two different P heads that can be involved in such structures force different interpretations of the ontological type of causer involved. Hence, in the domain of possession sentences, such extra material might narrow down the set of possession relations that the construction as a whole can express. This is wholly unexpected if all possession constructions are related transformationally to a single underlying structure, as in Freeze (1992), but it is predicted to be attested on the present approach. Existence proofs of the correctness of this prediction are given in

Chapter 3 and in Chapter 7. To anticipate the discussion in Chapter 7, Levinson (2011) and Irie (1997) point out that the Icelandic *vera með* 'be with' construction is restricted to temporary possession, body-part possession, and disease possession. It seems, then, that the lexical semantic contribution of *með* 'with' restricts the construction to possessees that accompany the possessor.

(94)   Ég er með bók.   [Copular BE Verb + Possessee in WITH]
       I   am with book.ACC

       'I have a book.' (lit: 'I am with a book')   (Icelandic; Levinson 2011)

Let us summarize how the theory outlined here solves the too-many-(surface)-structures puzzle. I assume that the positions in which the relevant Theta-roles are introduced do not vary, but there is variation in (i) whether delayed gratification is allowed at all and (ii) if so, in what position the relevant Theta-role is eventually saturated. This in turn is conditioned by fundamentally morphosyntactic factors; namely, which argument-introducers require a filled specifier, under what circumstances they require one, and whether expletive elements like Icelandic *-st* (see Wood 2013, 2015) are available to satisfy the syntactic requirement for a specifier without absorbing a Theta-role. If delayed gratification is allowed to the extent that the relevant Theta-role is eventually assigned to spec-VoiceP in a transitive structure, we have a HAVE construction/language. If the Theta-role is assigned in its base position, or gratification is delayed until some position lower than vP (this might be spec-PredP, spec-ApplP, or some other position), or if the structure is an unergative one involving a predicate nominal or predicate adjective, then we have a BE construction/language. The differences between different sorts of BE construction depend on what sort of complement BE is taking, and on precisely where in the structure the possessor is introduced. The present theory of variation in predicative possession constructions is thus syntactic and *parametric* in nature, inkeeping with the tradition started by Freeze (1992) and Kayne (1993). The present account also shares with the Freeze/Kayne tradition the idea that HAVE=BE+X, although for me X=Voice$_{\{D\},\phi}$, rather than an adpositional element, and for me no special incorporation operation need be involved beyond ordinary short verb movement.[38]

---

38. This difference might seem like a radical one because of the consequences it has for the sorts of structures assumed for HAVE sentences in the present approach compared with those in Freeze (1992) and Kayne (1993). It is important to note, though, that if it turns out to be correct that the set of argument-introducers is to be unified in the manner entertained by Wood (2015) and Wood and Marantz (2015/to appear), then Voice=Appl$p$. In that case, at an abstract level my hypothesis about the relation between HAVE and BE will be the same as that of the Freeze/Kayne tradition, although the predictions of the two approaches concerning the argument structures of possession sentences will remain extremely different.

However, it departs sharply from Freeze (1992) and Kayne (1993) in arguing that a good amount of the variation in the surface structure of possession sentences reflects real differences in their underlying argument structure. Much of the rest of this book will amount to a sustained defense of this departure.

The solution to the too-many-(surface)-structures puzzle in (93) makes rather different predictions about what the typology of possession sentences should look like than the Freeze/Kayne tradition. The strongest version of this tradition would imply assigning a single underlying argument structure for all possession sentences, and deriving all of the surface variants by movement. My approach gives rise to two expectations that are incompatible with this strong interpretation of the Freeze/Kayne tradition, as follows:

(95)   *Predictions of the Present Approach*

  a. Possession constructions can vary in the place in the structure where the possessor is introduced.

  b. The different ways of building possession sentences permitted by (a.) could have somewhat different (albeit potentially overlapping) meanings, depending on the semantic contributions of the pieces that make them up.

1.5 Excursus: Why *John is a doctor* $\neq$ *John has a doctor*

Following a long tradition, I have taken the position that neither HAVE nor BE make any meaning contribution of their own. If this is true, however, then the question arises why HAVE and BE are not interchangeable (see Brugman 1988): in particular, why aren't the sentences in (96) equivalent in meaning? Breaking the problem down into two parts, (i) why can't (96a) have a relational HAVE meaning, and (ii) why can't (96b) be interpreted like a predicate nominal sentence?

(96) a. John is a doctor.

  b. John has a doctor.

Question (i) is answered on my approach by how a structure with the meaning of (96b) is built in a language like English. The structure in question is as in (97). The v head in such a structure must be spelled out as *have* rather than *be*, since it occurs in the environment of transitive, external-argument-introducing Voice. Hence, there is simply no way for the grammar to output *John is a doctor* as the realization of a structure which means (96b).

(97)   John has a doctor.

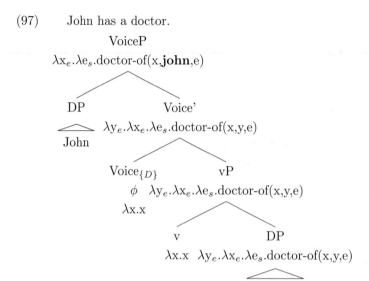

The answer to question (ii) is somewhat more involved, since it is not immediately obvious what goes wrong if v takes a predicate nominal as its complement, and the subject of that predicate is introduced in the specifier of a transitive Voice head. This structure would look as in (98), and ought to yield (96b) with the meaning of *John is a doctor*. Clearly, this is an undesirable result.

(98)

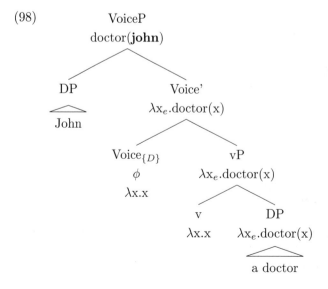

There is no way to rule out such an instance of delayed gratification via the semantics; nothing should go wrong compositionally in (98). Luckily, however, there seems to be a clear morphosyntactic rationale for the badness of this derivation. Recall that HAVE is spelled out only in the environment of transitive Voice, which is distinguished from other instantiations of Voice in that it carries phi-features that license some DP embedded in VoiceP's complement. There is good reason to believe that predicate nominals are not eligible to be licensed by Voice in this way, however, and this explains why we always get BE and not HAVE in copula sentences containing a predicate nominal. Predicate nominals are associated with special morphological cases in some languages, which are not typical of the structural case assigned to direct objects in general (e.g., instrumental in some Slavic, nominative in many other languages). Hence, there is good reason to believe that predicate nominals are licensed in some special way, *before* Voice is able to probe them. This would make predicate nominals incompatible with transitive Voice, forcing v to be spelled out as BE rather than HAVE.[39]

1.6   Structure of this Book

The remainder of this book is structured as follows. In Chapter 2, I provide a review of previous approaches to the too-many-meanings puzzle and the too-many-(surface)-structures puzzle, taking in literature from Greenbergian typology, comparative syntax in the Principles and Parameters tradition, and formal semantics. The focus will be on what this literature has to teach us about the extent of these puzzles, what the right solutions to these puzzles must look like, and how my own proposals relate to earlier approaches. Chapter 3 presents a series of case studies from the domain of BE-based possession constructions in an effort to show that the predictions in (95) are correct. The data come mostly from novel fieldwork on two closely related Quechua dialects: Cochabamba Quechua, a Bolivian variety, and Santiago del Estero Quechua, an Argentine variety. Both dialects have a range

---

39. An alternative approach would be to say that predicate nominals do not need to be licensed. Predicate nominals, unlike true direct objects, seem to be unable to introduce new discourse referents (see (i), and Błaszczak 2007, 191). Many have proposed a link between referentiality and the need to be licensed. If there is such a link, then (i) might mean that predicate nominals always yield BE rather than HAVE for that reason.

(i)   John is a student and *that student is a genius.

(ii)   John has a student and that student is a genius.

(iii)   John is teaching a student and that student is a genius.

of morphosyntactically distinguishable possession constructions, making them an ideal test-bed for my purposes. An added point of comparative syntactic interest comes from the fact that Santiago del Estero Quechua is a HAVE language, whereas Cochabamba Quechua is not. I tentatively propose that the existence of a certain subtype of psych construction correlates with this difference across the Quechua family. In Chapter 4, I turn away from the domain of BE and towards HAVE, showing that the present approach yields a unified analysis of much of the English main verb *have* paradigm. I also address certain ways in which English *have* differs from HAVE in other languages, as well as how the analysis deals with languages that exhibit more than one HAVE verb (here drawing on joint work on Icelandic with Einar Freyr Sigurðsson and Jim Wood). Chapter 5 examines the broader consequences of this approach to HAVE by comparing it explicitly with the approaches of Freeze (1992) and Kayne (1993). I demonstrate that my approach makes different predictions than the Freeze/Kayne tradition with respect to (i) the nature of definiteness effects in HAVE sentences, and (ii) the sort of argument structures that HAVE-sentences should display. In both cases, my approach makes the correct predictions. The next two chapters extend the account to two other types of possession sentence not adequately dealt with by the Freeze/Kayne tradition. In Chapter 6, I examine the phenomenon which Stassen (2009) has dubbed *Predicativization*, via a close study of the so-called -*yoq* construction in Quechua languages. Drawing on joint work with Andrew Nevins, I compare this construction to other instances of Predicativization from English, German, Dutch, and Hungarian, thus providing the first generative treatment of the parametric variation in this domain. Chapter 7 discusses how my approach handles possession sentences built around BE and a preposition WITH, focusing on a comparison between the WITH-Possessive of Icelandic and those of certain Bantu languages; again, the discussion of Icelandic will rely heavily on joint work carried out with Einar Freyr Sigurðsson and Jim Wood. Finally, Chapter 8 summarizes the main arguments and outlines some open questions.

2   Previous Approaches to Predicative Possession: A Guide for the Perplexed

This chapter has the goal of summarizing previous approaches to the puzzles posed by predicative possession. This goal is worthwhile in itself. The literature on this topic is as complex as it is diverse, and it can be extremely forbidding for the uninitiated. It is my hope, therefore, that this chapter will prove useful to those who are just beginning to grapple with this topic, even if read independently from the rest of the book. Although it is written with a general audience of morphosyntacticians and semanticists in mind, this chapter should nevertheless have plenty to offer people with a long-standing interest in the topic of possession. In particular, the chapter provides a uniquely detailed and up-to-date appreciation of much of the recent work in this area, both generative and functional-typological. Finally, the chapter aims to help all readers of this work to understand how my proposals relate to the vast array of other work on predicative possession. It is worth mentioning that, although the chapter is long, it can safely be skipped without impeding comprehension of the rest of this book.

Allow me to preface this discussion with the following caveat. Anyone looking for a comprehensive summary of research on predicative possession is looking for a work which (i) is several volumes in length, and (ii) does not yet exist anywhere, to my knowledge. Heine (1997, 209), before embarking on his review of previous approaches to predicative possession, makes the following remark: "possession has been a popular topic in linguistics, and to do justice to all the studies that have been devoted to this topic in the course of this century would require a separate book-length treatment." Eighteen years have passed between the publication of Heine's book and my writing these words, and in that time a great deal of important research on this topic has taken place. Prioritization will therefore be even more of the essence for me than it was for Heine. It is for this reason that, with the exception of a few works from the 1970s and 1980s that are especially important background to my own proposals, I will concentrate in this chapter on work from the beginning of the 1990s onwards. For more detailed review of work before this time, I can recommend relevant sections of Heine's book (1997, 209-239), as well as Belvin (1996, 221-235) and Jung (2011, 37-72).

The discussion is organized along the lines of the two main puzzles outlined in Chapter 1, in the following way.

Section 2.1 sets out the scale of the puzzles involved by examining the findings of four typological works on predicative possession: Clark (1978), Heine (1997), Stassen (2009), and Tham (2013).

Next, we turn in section 2.2 to what might be thought of as the "standard" generative approach to the too-many-(surface)-structures puzzle from the 1990s onwards. This is the tradition started by Freeze (1992) and Kayne (1993), building on foundational insights of Anna Szabolcsi's work (1981, 1983, 1994). Almost all subsequent generative studies on predicative possession (including this book) either build upon or react against this tradition, which takes the position that the vast surface diversity in possession constructions is to be derived via movement from one or two underlyingly identical structures.

In section 2.3 we look at some of these extensions and reactions to the Freeze/Kayne/Szabolcsi position. We will concentrate particularly on the ways in which different authors have dealt with the question of how HAVE and BE are related to each other, and we will evaluate the proposals that have been made concerning which other syntactic properties interact parametrically with the HAVE/BE difference.

Subsequently, we turn away from the too-many-(surface)-structures puzzle and on to the too-many-meanings puzzle. In Section 2.4 we will compare two major approaches to the meaning of HAVE/BE in possessive and other contexts: one which says that these verbs have a core meaning that happens to be vague, and another which says that these verbs are not meaningful in and of themselves.

Section 2.5 is a general conclusion. There I argue that the balance of evidence favors (i) a less reductionist approach to the too-many-(surface)-structures puzzle than originally envisaged by Freeze (1992) and Kayne (1993); and (ii) an approach to the too-many-meanings puzzle which takes as its starting point the idea that HAVE and BE are not meaningful in themselves. I will point out that many of the most important recent advances towards solving the too-many-(surface)-structures puzzle have taken place in isolation from considerations bearing on the too-many-meanings puzzle, and similarly *vice versa* for work on the too-many-meanings puzzle, which often does not face up to the comparative syntactic challenges that have vexed morphosyntacticians. It is my hope that this chapter will facilitate work that attempts to address both puzzles at once, and that the book as a whole constitutes a successful exemplar of such work.

2.1   The Scale of the Puzzles: Typological Work

2.1.1   Clark (1970/1978)

While other linguists (including Lyons 1968; Verhaar 1967) had pointed out morphosyntactic parallelisms between locative sentences, existential sentences, and possessive sentences, the credit for first thoroughly demonstrating the typological robustness of these parallelisms falls to Clark (1970), and her (1978) paper that superseded it. I will concentrate here on her (1978) paper, which is based around a survey of a core of thirty languages (supplemented by data on around five others). The languages surveyed are from a wide variety of locations, including Europe, East Asia, Africa, the Indian subcontinent, and North America; however, European and Indian languages are far better represented than other groups. Clark (1978, 87) surveys these languages with respect to the following construction types, which she unites under the umbrella term *locationals*.[1]

(1)   *"Locationals": Constructions Surveyed by Clark (1978)*

a.	There is a book on the table.	(Existential construction)
b.	The book is on the table.	(Locative construction)
c.	Tom has a book.	(Possessive$_1$ construction)
d.	The book is Tom's.	(Possessive$_2$ construction)

Beyond reaffirming the observation that these constructions tend to be built out of the same morphosyntactic pieces across languages, Clark proposes a number of interesting generalizations concerning them. Amongst the generalizations identified are patterns of copula syncretism (in languages where the copular verb has more than one morphological form depending on the type of sentence at issue) and interactions among definiteness, animacy, and word order. The latter generalizations of Clark's are of particular interest, since versions of them are independently[2] identified by Freeze (1992), and used as the basis of his influential generative analysis of the so-called Locative Paradigm. I will also review the generalizations concerning copula syncretism in considerable detail; while these have not been as influential on the generative literature on possession hitherto, they provide interesting clues to the syntax of copular constructions when viewed from a Distributed Morphology perspective (see Bobaljik 2012; Caha 2009 for case studies in how syncretism patterns can be reflective of aspects of syntactic structure). Because the syntax of different kinds of copular construction (especially the distinction between existential constructions and predicative copular constructions) is so crucial to the account of predicative possession defended in this book, Clark's generalizations in this area are of special interest.

---

1. I note here that the possessive$_1$ constructions examined by Clark are of the HAVE type and of the existential BE type; none of them are of the WITH-Possessive type or of the Predicativization type.

2. Since Freeze (1992) does not cite Clark's work, I must assume he happened upon roughly the same generalizations independently.

I begin with Clark's discussion of word order in existential constructions as compared with locative constructions. First, I introduce some of Clark's (1978:92) notational conventions: Loc refers to the locative argument in such a sentence, Nom (short for nominal) refers to what we would pre-theoretically refer to as the subject argument in the constructions, pro-loc refers to a (potentially cliticized) pronominal form of the Loc argument, and V refers to the copular verb. If there is no overt copula in a given construction in a given language, this is indicated by leaving V out of the schema. Clark's sample reveals a stark difference between existential and locative constructions with respect to the ordering of Loc and Nom, as can be seen by comparing (2) with (3)).[3] In the existential construction, a sizeable majority of the languages surveyed (twenty-seven out of forty, or just under 68%) have (at least a pronominal double of) the Loc argument preceding the Nom argument, with Nom-Loc being a minority order in existentials. The locative construction, on the other hand, is just the opposite: thirty-five out of forty languages in Clark's survey (about 88%) have Nom preceding Loc, with a small minority showing the opposite order.

(2)   *Word Order in Existential Constructions in Clark (1978, 92)*

a.	Loc Nom V	13 languages
b.	Loc V Nom	10 languages
c.	Loc Nom	1 language
d.	pro-loc V Nom Loc	3 languages
e.	V Nom Loc	4 languages
f.	Nom V Loc	6 languages
g.	Nom Loc V	3 languages

---

3. In this and some other tables from Clark's paper, the total number of languages adds up to a number greater than thirty. This is sometimes because Clark includes data from languages beyond her core sample of thirty; sometimes because some of the languages exhibit more than one grammatical option, and are thus counted more than once; and sometimes because of a combination of these two reasons. In the particular case of my (2) and (3), Clark's data are based on a sample of thirty-five languages, of which five are counted twice because they exhibit two grammatical orders.

(3)   *Word Order in Locative Constructions in Clark (1978, 92-93)*

    a.   Nom V Loc   18 languages

    b.   Nom Loc V   14 languages

    c.   Nom Loc   3 languages

    d.   Loc Nom V   3 languages

    e.   Loc V Nom   1 language

    f.   Loc Nom   1 language

Clark (1978, 91-92) relates these preferences to the discourse functions of existential constructions vs. those of locative constructions. She suggests (91) that "[e]xistential constructions are usually used to introduce new information, and they normally therefore contain indefinite nominals." This contrasts with locative constructions, which often provide information about the location of an entity which is already given in the discourse, and in which the subject nominal is therefore generally definite. With these discourse functions in mind, Clark (1978, 119) proposes that the following Discourse Rule, which is supposed to be operative in all sentences (not just existentials, locatives, and possessives), accounts for the above word order generalizations:

(4)   *Clark's (1978, 119) Discourse Rule I*

    +Definite nominals precede −Definite nominals.

Turning to possessive constructions, recall that Clark discusses two types, which she refers to by the names possessive$_1$ and possessive$_2$. These are exemplified by the following cases, repeated from (1c) and (1d).

(5)   *Subtypes of Possession Construction Discussed by Clark*

    a.   Tom has a book.   (Possessive$_1$ construction)

    b.   The book is Tom's.   (Possessive$_2$ construction)

Clark (1978, 89) explicitly analogizes these constructions to the previous pair, arguing that "the possessor in the two possessive constructions is simply an animate place." She notes (89-90) that, at least in English, possessive$_1$ is closely allied to the existential construction (since both involve an instantiation of Loc preceding the verb[4]), whereas possessive$_2$ is analogous to the locative construction, in which the Loc argument follows the verb. Clark is quick to point out, however, that the

---

4. Clark takes the *there* of English existentials to be a pronominal form of the Loc argument.

cross-linguistic word-order facts do not straightforwardly bear out the relation of possessive$_1$ to existentials and of possessive$_2$ to locatives, since "the two possessive constructions do not usually show regular word-order alternations according to the definiteness of the Nom" (1978, 94).[5] Instead, the overriding word-order effect in both possessive$_1$ and possessive$_2$ is that Loc (i.e., the possessor, shortened to Pr in the following data) practically always precedes Nom (the possessee, which Clark abbreviates to Pd). Clark shows this by presenting data from thirty-three languages.

(6)   *Word Order in Possessive Constructions (Clark 1978, 94)*

a.	Pr V Pd	15 languages
b.	Pr Pd V	13 languages
c.	V Pr Pd	3 languages
d.	Pr Pd	3 languages
e.	Pd V Pr	5 languages

As we can see, thirty-four out of thirty-nine[6] languages have Pr preceding Pd (87%). To account for this effect of animacy in possessive constructions, Clark proposes a second Discourse Rule:

(7)   *Clark's (1978, 119) Discourse Rule II*

+Animate nominals precede −Animate nominals.

Clark is at pains to emphasize that, despite the fact that she terms (4) and (7) Rules, "this is not intended to imply that they are without exception in the language sample. In fact, language-particular constraints may over-ride these general discourse rules" (1978, 120). This caveat is an important one to bear in mind, because it means that Discourse Rules I and II should not be translated wholesale into deterministic triggers of grammatical operations in a derivational generative framework. As we shall see, Freeze (1992) develops a system in which animacy and definiteness trigger movement operations that give rise to the surface differences amongst existentials, locatives, and possessives from a single underlying structure. The fact that these alleged triggers are only tendentially associated with these different surface forms, as explicitly acknowledged by Clark, will thus turn out to be a major sticking point for Freeze's approach.

---

5. We shall see later, however, that possessive$_1$ and existentials match up very well with respect to copula suppletion, as do possessive$_2$ and locatives.

6. In this case, six of the surveyed languages are counted twice because they exhibit more than one grammatical option.

At this point we will turn away from word order and examine Clark's findings on copula suppletion, which are highly relevant to the present work in particular. Clark notes that copular verbs in both existentials and locatives are "often irregular" (1978, 101), and discusses a number of different factors that turn out to condition such suppletion. Tense is often relevant (as it is in Cochabamba Quechua, discussed in Chapter 3). As Clark observes: "The past and future tenses frequently take on a different aspectual status, being glossed as 'become' or 'happen' rather than 'be'" (1978, 101). She adds that "the future is sometimes excluded from occurring in the existential construction even though it occurs in the other three locationals." Unusual interactions with negation are also regularly found, as Clark states (1978, 101): "the verbs in these constructions may also be set apart from regular verb paradigms in some languages by having a special negative verb form in place of the usual negative-marker-plus-verb for negation." Clark (1978, 105, 108) found seventeen languages with such a special negative copula. These sorts of suppletion are triggered by features of what modern generative work identifies as the inflectional domain above VoiceP. This is a familiar sort of suppletion, the possibility of which is readily analyzed in a Distributed Morphology framework (see Bobaljik 2000, 2012; Embick 2010; Halle and Marantz 1993, and many others for discussion). While the frequency of such suppletion with BE and HAVE verbs is notable and deserving of investigation, I will make no attempt to explain its pervasiveness, nor will I make much use of this sort of suppletion to elucidate the structure of BE and HAVE sentences in what follows (see instead Becker 2004; Postma 1993 for much germane discussion). I will note in passing, however, an intriguing generalization of Clark's concerning the effects of negative suppletion.

As Clark puts it "[t]he negative verb form sometimes appears in both existential and locative constructions, even if two different verbs are used in the positive, e.g. KHALKHA, PANJABI" (1978, 105). In other words, in a subset of languages in which existential and predicative copulas are morphologically distinguishable, the distinction collapses under negation in some languages. It turns out that certain marked tense forms can also sometimes cause such a morphological distinction in the copula system to collapse: we will see in Chapter 3 that the distinction between the existential and predicative copula in Cochabamba Quechua disappears in the past and future tenses. Such syncretism in the presence of marked inflectional feature values has the character of a retreat to the general case, of the sort usually treated in Distributed Morphology in terms of Impoverishment (see section 1.2.2 of the present work for discussion of Impoverishment; also Bonet 1991; Halle 1997; Halle and Marantz 1993). The fact that existential and predicative copular verbs can apparently be linked by Impoverishment in this way has an important implication:

we ought not to analyze existential and predicative copulas as being manifestations of two totally different syntactic flavors of v, even in languages where the two types of copula are morphologically distinct. Instead, as proposed in this book, we must treat them as manifestations of the same v, which come to have somewhat different formal features in the course of the syntactic derivation. Only then can we make sense of the fact that their paradigms can be rendered syncretic by Impoverishment.

My main focus, however, will not be on suppletion triggered by features of the IP domain. Instead, I will focus on the types of copula suppletion which are conditioned by features that have been identified as corresponding to heads within VoiceP in contemporary generative syntactic theory. The rationale for this choice of focus is that the latter sort of suppletion, unlike inflectionally-conditioned suppletion, can give us direct clues regarding the main topic of this book: the argument structure of possession sentences and related constructions.

Clark's discussion of such suppletion (1978, 105-109) yields a series of generalizations that can be summarized in (8). I repeat the English examples of each construction in (9) for ease of reference.[7]

(8)   *Generalizations on Copula Suppletion from Clark (1978)*

    a.   Some languages use a single BE verb for all four of locative, existential, possessive$_1$, and possessive$_2$.

    b.   Where possessive$_1$ and possessive$_2$ use a different verb, possessive$_1$ patterns with existentials, and possessive$_2$ patterns with locatives and other predicative copular constructions.

    c.   Existentials and possessive$_2$ are never marked with the same BE verb to the exclusion of the others.

    d.   Locatives and possessive$_1$ are never marked with the same BE verb to the exclusion of the others.

    e.   Existentials and locatives sometimes share a BE verb to the exclusion of copula constructions with a nominal predicate.

---

7. In addition to the generalizations in (8), Clark (1978, 118) mentions a syncretism type where the existential and locative pattern together in taking one BE verb, and possessive$_1$ and possessive$_2$ pattern together in taking another. This syncretism pattern, if real, would cause problems for the perspective on copula suppletion which I am about to outline in the text. Luckily, however, the examples that Clark gives of this pattern turn out not to survive scrutiny. There are only two languages that are argued to instantiate this type of syncretism. In one of them, Japanese, the conditioning factor for the allomorphy in question turns out to be animacy, not argument structure (see Tsujioka 2002, 12). In the other, Yoruba, there appears to be a tone difference between the possessive$_1$ and possessive$_2$ forms.

       f.   There are languages in which the locative copula may or must be silent (especially in the present tense), but where the existential must be overt in all tenses. There are no languages with the opposite pattern (see also Stassen 1997; 2009).

(9)   *"Locationals": Constructions Surveyed by Clark (1978)*

     a.   There is a book on the table.   (Existential construction)

     b.   The book is on the table.   (Locative construction)

     c.   Tom has a book.   (Possessive$_1$ construction)

     d.   The book is Tom's.   (Possessive$_2$ construction)

Since morphophonology is an interpretation of the syntactic structure, we can use information concerning which patterns of syncretism are attested and which are not attested to make inferences about what syntactic structures are different from each other, and in what ways they are different or similar. The copular verb in these four constructions is clearly similar enough in each case that it can be marked in the same way, as (8a) states. We saw earlier that such copula syncretism is sometimes conditioned by Impoverishment, so that a stronger inference is possible: the copulas in these constructions are instantiations of the same v, and the allomorphy of this v is potentially conditioned by the nature of its complement. The patterns in (8b)-(8e) indicate that the structure of this complement is identical in some crucial respect in the cases of existentials and possessive$_1$, and is identical in some crucially different respect between locatives and possessive$_2$. Nevertheless, as (8e) indicates, existential and locative structures have at least one thing in common which they do not share with predicate nominal constructions.

The syntax for existential and copular constructions sketched in Chapter 1 of this work (and elaborated in more detail for Quechua in Chapter 3) provides ready accounts for these patterns. Recall that, on this view, both types of construction involve the same semantically vacuous v taking a small clause complement of some kind. Only the nature of that small clause is different. In existential structures, the DP "pivot" is the predicate of the small clause, and the subject is a PP (spelled out as *there* in English), as shown in (10) (following Hazout 2004; Tremblay 1991; Williams 1994; and many others). In locational copula structures, the small clause predicate is a PP, and the subject is a DP. This is shown in (11).

(10)   *Schematic Structure of an Existential* (there is a book)

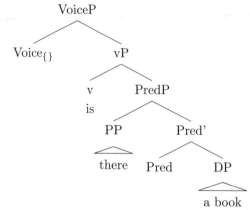

(11)   *Schematic Structure of a Locative* (a book is there)

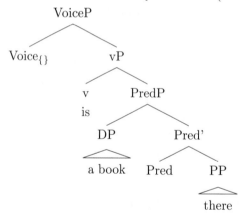

The fact that possessive₁ patterns with existentials and possessive₂ patterns with locatives (as stated in (8b)) then suggests that possessive₁ structures are built like (10), whereas possessive₂ structures are built like (11). The allomorphy of the copula is potentially sensitive to whether PredP has a PP as its subject or not; where this is the factor that conditions the choice of allomorph, we see the pattern described by (8b). An alternative is for the copula to be sensitive only to whether or not its complement contains a PP, with no sensitivity as to the position of this PP in the small clause structure; in languages with this property, locatives and existentials will be marked differently from other sorts of copula predication. This is precisely the pattern in (8e). On the other hand, the only way for existentials and possessive₂ to be marked identically is if (i) the copula is sensitive only to the presence of a PP somewhere in the PredP, or if (ii) the copula exhibits no conditioned allomorphy at all. But both scenarios (i) and (ii) entail that the same copula allomorph would be used for locatives and possessive$_1$ also. Thus, existentials and possessive$_2$ can never be syncretic to the exclusion of the other two: constraint (8c) is explained. Similar reasoning applies *mutatis mutandis* to explain observation (8d).[8] It is less immediately clear what to make of observation (8f), however: why should existential copulas be less readily silent than predicative ones? I will leave this important issue aside here, pending a better theoretical understanding of the factors that condition silence (see Leu 2008, 5-9 for a clear statement of the issues).

In summary, Clark (1978) is to be credited with showing the cross-linguistic robustness of the similarities amongst existential, locative, and possessive sentences. She also identified different tendencies in word order amongst the constructions, formalized in her Discourse Rules I and II. These rules, which link linear precedence to animacy and definiteness, are by no means exceptionless, although they do pick out important tendencies that are reflected in other types of constructions also. Therefore, Discourse Rules I and II should not be converted directly into the triggers of grammatical operations in a deterministic generative account. Furthermore, Clark points out a number of generalizations concerning patterns of syncretism in the suppletive allomorphy of locative and existential copulas. Viewed through the lens of Distributed Morphology, these generalizations turn out to provide important confirming evidence that BE is the spell out of a single syntactic flavor of little v, one that varies allomorphically depending on the content of its complement in many languages. The cross-linguistic constraints on the attested syncretisms are also a crucial source of evidence as to the structure of BE's complement in different constructions. These are important steps forward in the search for a solution to the too-many-(surface)-structures puzzle.

---

8. Let me again raise the caveat that Clark only discusses languages where possessive$_1$ is based around existential BE, and does not discuss WITH-Possessive or Predicativization types of BE possessive construction. These sorts of construction would count as instantiations of possessive$_1$ by Clark's criteria, but on my approach these latter constructions would be expected to pattern with predicative copular constructions. It seems that my own approach makes the right cut: the *-yoq* construction of Quechua, which is of the Predicativization type, occurs with the predicative allomorph of the copula rather than the existential one. See Chapter 6 for an analysis of Predicativization.

2.1.2   Heine (1997)

Heine (1997) is a major typological study on possession that aims to explain the syntactic variation in predicative possession constructions using notions from cognitive grammar and grammaticalization theory. Unlike Stassen's later (2009) study, it does not limit itself to alienable possession, and there is a concerted effort to address the too-many-meanings puzzle as well as the too-many-(surface)-structures puzzle.[9] The book also contains a very informative overview of previous attempts to deal with these puzzles (although Heine does not, of course, use the names I have been using for the puzzles in question). Heine's book is particularly useful in identifying ways in which semantically distinct subtypes of relation can differ in their surface morphosyntax. This information can in turn be used, just as I used it in my fieldwork on Cochabamba Quechua and Santiago del Estero Quechua, as a guide to what to look out for when investigating semantic distinctions among possession constructions within a language where this topic has not been worked on in depth before. Here I will discuss the distinctions made by Heine, and what they should be taken to indicate under my approach.

As is well known, many languages make a morphosyntactic distinction between alienable possession relations and inalienable relations. These distinctions are usually visible in attributive possession only, although they do sometimes manifest themselves in predicative possession too. One of Heine's most useful contributions is his (1997, 10) documentation of the set of relations that are frequently marked as inalienable across the world's languages, and his cataloguing of the vast (but by no means arbitrary) variation in what "counts" as inalienable cross-linguistically. Heine's list of relations commonly classed as inalienable is as follows:[10]

---

9. There is a trade-off here, since Stassen (2009)'s focus on one subtype of possession allows him to include data on a much larger collection of languages than does Heine (1997). Stassen surveys 420 languages, versus Heine's 234 (counting the entries in Heine's Index of Languages, minus the names of language families and proto-languages).

10. Heine (1997, 10) cites Lichtenberk (1985:105) for observation (12e), and Tsunoda (1996, 578) for observation (12g).

(12)   *Heine (1997, 10; 18): Common Inalienable-Marked Relations*

    a.   Kinship roles

    b.   Body-parts

    c.   Relational spatial concepts like 'top', 'bottom', 'interior', etc.

    d.   Parts of other items, like 'branch', 'handle', etc.

    e.   Physical and mental states, like 'strength' and 'fear', etc.

    f.   Nominalizations, where the 'possessee' is a verbal noun, for example 'his singing' , 'the planting of bananas'.

    g.   Clothes that are being worn (as opposed to hanging in a wardrobe somewhere).

The fact that some subset of the relations in (12) turns up with special inalienable marking in many unrelated languages suggests that there are real lexical semantic constraints on the sorts of relation that can be so marked in principle. However, the precise set of nouns that any given language chooses to mark as inalienable turns out to be subject to a surprising degree of variation. Here is a handful of cases illustrating this variation, as cited by Heine (1997, 11-12).

(13)   *Cross-Linguistic Variation in Inalienability (Heine 1997, 11-12)*

    a.   Paamese and Tinrin: kinship, body parts, and spatial relations count as inalienable.

    b.   Many Australian languages: body parts are inalienable, kinship relations are not.

    c.   Ewe: kinship and spatial relations are inalienable, body parts are not.

    d.   Most Athabaskan: kinship and body parts are inalienable, spatial relations are not.

    e.   Saker: body parts, part-whole relations, and most kinship relations are inalienable, but 'husband', 'wife', and 'child' are not (Z'graggen 1965, 124).

    f.   The word for 'wife' is inalienable in Fijian, but alienable in the closely-related language Lenakel (Lynch 1973, 15).

For a discussion of how such variation can be analyzed within the framework of this book, see Section 1.4 of Chapter 1.

Before moving on to Heine's discussion of the syntactic variation in predicative possession, I introduce the taxonomy of semantic subtypes of possession relation that Heine presupposes, which he adopts from Miller and Johnson-Laird (1976,

565). This taxonomy is important, because it turns out that Heine is able to identify differences among the distinct syntactic subtypes of possession construction with respect to which of these possession relations they can express. The existence of such differences, which are copiously exemplified below and in the other chapters of this work, pose a problem for attempts to reduce the syntactic variation in predicative possession constructions to a single underlying argument structure.

(14)   *A Semantic Taxonomy of Possession Relations (Heine 1997, 34-35; Miller and Johnson-Laird 1976, 565)*

   a.   Physical Possession: The possessor and the possessee are physically associated with each other at reference time, as in *do you have a pen (on you)?*

   b.   Temporary Possession: The possessor can dispose of the possessee for a limited time, but s/he cannot claim ownership to it.

   c.   Permanent Possession: The possessee is the property of the possessor.

   d.   Inalienable Possession: The possessee is conceived of typically as being inseparable from the possessor.

   e.   Abstract Possession: The possessee is a concept that is not visible or tangible, like a disease, a feeling, or some other psychological state.

   f.   Inanimate Inalienable Possession: The possessee is a subpart of the possessor, which is inanimate.

   g.   Inanimate Alienable Possession: The possessee is located relative to the inanimate possessor, as in *the stadium has two pubs next to it.* (This type of possession is referred to as locative HAVE in Chapter 4).

I will leave aside for now the question of how appropriate the terminology in (14) is, and the important question of the extent to which the categories in (14) map on to grammatically significant generalizations–my own position on this is sketched in Chapter 1, and the details are filled in through Chapters 3, 4, 6, and 7. Instead I will turn directly to the syntactic taxonomy of predicative possesion that Heine identifies. Heine identifies seven of what he calls *event schemas* (1997, 46), which "account for the majority of possessive constructions in the languages of the world." The names of these schemas, along with formulaic descriptions of them, are given in (15) (adapted from Heine 1997, 47, table 2.1).[11]

11. Heine's table includes an 8th schema, the Equation schema, which corresponds to *belong*-type verbs and sentences like *the book is mine* rather than the HAVE/BE domain with which I am

(15)   *Heine's (1997, 47) Event Schemas for Predicative Possession*

Formula	Label of event schema
X takes Y	Action
Y is located at X	Location
X is with Y	Companion
X's Y exists	Genitive
Y exists for/to X	Goal
Y exists from X	Source
As for X, Y exists	Topic

Some explication is in order. What Heine calls the Action schema corresponds to the major historical source of transitive HAVE verbs, which tend to be etymologically derived from verbs meaning 'take', 'grab', or 'hold'. The Companion schema corresponds to what I have been calling WITH-Possessive constructions, following the terminology of Stassen (2009) to be discussed in the next section. The other five schemas correspond to different types of existential BE construction in my discussion: Location, Genitive, Goal, Source, and Topic. The Goal and Source schemas correspond in some cases to what I call BE-APPL constructions elsewhere in this work (the BE-APPL construction of Cochabamba Quechua analyzed in Chapter 3 would count as an instance of the Goal schema in Heine's taxonomy). Taking an approach inspired by Cognitive Linguistics, Heine suggests that these different schemas are cognitively distinct ways of conceptualizing eventualities which come to overlap in meaning with the domain of possession via a process of grammaticalization.

Heine surveys a range of languages in order to motivate the set of schemas in (15). As he does so, he uncovers semantic differences that correlate systematically with the morphosyntactic differences gathered in (15). Some of these are summarized below. For Heine, these differences amount to evidence that the grammaticalization processes that transform the event schemas in (15) into predicative possessive constructions do not always go to completion. In the present approach (which is by no means at odds with the idea that grammaticalization as discussed in the historical linguistics literature has a part to play), these differences receive a synchronic explanation: they reflect the fact that these possession constructions are built out of slightly different pieces made available by Universal Grammar, which

---

principally concerned. Although deserving of attention, *belong* and its cross-linguistic brethren are not the focus of this book, and so I leave this schema out of consideration here. As Stassen (2009, 30) notes, there is often no or very little information about *belong*-like verbs in descriptive grammars, which creates a practical difficulty in discussing their comparative syntax given the present state of knowledge.

means that they may be interpreted in overlapping but not necessarily identical ways depending on the exact semantic contribution of those pieces.

(16)   *Event Schemas: Semantic Generalizations (Heine 1997, 92-3)*

  a. The Location schema is most likely to be associated with physical and temporary possession.

  b. The [Genitive, Goal, and Topic schemas] are more likely to be associated with permanent and inalienable possession.

  c. The Companion schema is claimed to be more likely to express physical and temporary or, more generally, alienable possession rather than inalienable possession (Kilian-Hatz and Stolz 1992, 4).

  d. The [Genitive, Goal, and Topic schemas] are very seldom recruited for the expression of physical possession.

While Heine's generalizations in (16) are probabilistic in nature, and therefore should not be translated directly into a generative account for familiar reasons, we will see in the next section that Stassen (2009) is able to strengthen some related generalizations to the point of exceptionlessness.

In summary, Heine (1997) is an important work for its clear laying out of the empirical challenges posed by the vast amount of surface variation in predicative possession constructions. The fact that it identifies some tendential differences in the semantics of these constructions provides a preliminary indication that it might be necessary to attribute some underlying differences in argument structure to these different surface syntaxes.

Before closing, let us reflect on how Heine himself reacts to these empirical challenges at the end of his book: "any attempt at setting up one single universal structure of predicative possession, to account for all the morphosyntactic variation to be found in the languages of the world, is doomed to failure" (Heine 1997, 239). To an extent, the present approach agrees with Heine on this. But I would hasten to add that there is still a structural core which is common to all predicative possession constructions (built, as I have said in Chapter 1, on the same structural core as is found in attributive possession), and the existence of this structural core plays a crucial role in explaining the constraints on the initially baffling array of variation that we see in this domain. Heine's conclusion, therefore, is overstated. Stassen, at the end of his book on the typology of predicative possession, agrees that "Heine's assessment of the situation may just be too pessimistic" (2009, 724). It is to Stassen's work that we turn now.

2.1.3   Stassen (2009)

Stassen (2009, 36) employs a sample of 420 languages, drawn from every major language family (including several isolates) and linguistic area, although "the languages of Eurasia are slightly over-represented." Stassen defines the domain of his inquiry as follows (2009, 35, his (56)):

(17)   *Domain Definition*
       The domain of inquiry consists of positive sentences which encode predicative alienable possession, such that:

       a.   the noun that represents the possessor is topical, and

       b.   the noun phrase that represents the possessee is not modified or quantified.

The first restriction mentioned in this definition is that only positive sentences are considered, so that special negative forms of copulas (discussed earlier in the section on Clark (1978)) are not included. Secondly, only alienable relations are considered. Restriction (17a) is designed to exclude *belong*-type verbs and sentences like *this book is mine*. Via (17b), Stassen excludes sentences with modified or quantified possessors from his survey. Many languages require constructions like "Mary's nails are long" and "John's houses are many" to be used instead of the equivalents of "Mary has long nails" and "John has many houses," which in some languages are ungrammatical. The exclusion of modified and quantified possessees from the domain of inquiry is designed to avoid the complexities raised by this fact.[12]

Stassen presents a typology organized around four basic types of possession construction, which differ principally in "the encoding of the possessor and the possessee in terms of their grammatical function" (2009, 48). The four basic types recognized by Stassen (introduced 48-69) are listed in (18) and will be discussed in more detail below:

---

12. Such restrictions on adjectival modification will not be addressed in this book either. An interesting generalization is that constraints of this sort seem to be restricted to a subset of existential BE-based possession constructions (for instance, in Japanese (Tsujioka 2002) and in Russian (Inna Livitz (pers. comm.)). I know of no HAVE or WITH-Possessive language that has this property. Discovering the reason for such restrictions will require a deeper appreciation of the syntax and semantics of adjectives than I can provide in this book.

(18)   *Stassen's Four Basic Possession Construction Types*

    a.   Locational Possessive

    b.   WITH-Possessive

    c.   Topic Possessive

    d.   HAVE-Possessive

However, this is not the complete picture of the typology Stassen ultimately discusses. Chapter 3 of his book is called "Non-Standard Variants," which means constructions that look vaguely like one of Stassen's four basic types, but fail to fit in for some reason. His Chapters 4-6 discuss certain other variants that also fall outside of his main taxonomy. Stassen argues that all of these "non-standard" types can be accounted for by diachronic drift away from the core types, and therefore do not require an expansion of his taxonomy. This might be defensible as an organizing principle for Stassen's purposes, but it has the consequence that his taxonomy fails to make several distinctions that are important at the synchronic level. For a generative linguist concerned with building a parametric theory of morphosyntactic variation, it would therefore be a mistake to try to assimilate Stassen's typology as presented. Instead, we must go beyond this and supply a coherent synchronic picture of what the non-standard types are. My own view of how to do this is set out in Chapter 1. For now, I will discuss Stassen's own taxonomy, pointing out the places in which it fails to cut nature at its joints. I will discuss the Locational Possessive (18a) and the Topic Possessive (18c) together, since they turn out to be closely aligned, and then proceed to the WITH-Possessive and the HAVE-Possessive.

The first construction in Stassen's taxonomy is called the Locational Possessive and is defined as follows (2009, 49-50, his (11)). An example of this construction from Japanese is given in (19) (Stassen 2009, 51, his (20); I have slightly adjusted the glosses to reflect the conventions of the present work).

(19)   *Japanese* (Martin 1975, 647)

    Otooto   ni   naihu ga   aru.

    younger.brother DAT knife NOM be$_{exist}$-PRES

    'Younger Brother has a knife.'

(20)   *Definition of the Locational Possessive*

    a.   The construction contains a locative/existential predicate, in the form of a verb with the rough meaning of 'to be'.

    b.   The POSSESSEE NP (PE) is constructed as the GRAMMATICAL SUBJECT of the predicate. As such, it takes all the morphosyntactic 'privileges' that the language allows for grammatical subjects. For example, if the language allows subject-agreement on verbs, the PE will be the determining factor in that agreement. Likewise, if the language has a case system, the PE will be in the case form that is employed for intransitive subjects in general.

    c.   The POSSESSOR NP (PR) is constructed in some OBLIQUE, ADVERBIAL CASE FORM. As such, the PR may be marked by any formal device that the language employs to encode adverbial relations in general, such as case affixes or adpositions.

The Locational Possessive is perhaps the most widely discussed type of BE construction in the generative literature on predicative possession. Many of the constructions discussed for several different languages by Freeze (1992), for Japanese by Tsujioka (2002), for Palestinian Arabic by Boneh and Sichel (2010), and for Russian by Jung (2011) would count as instances of it under Stassen's definition. The fact that this construction is so well-studied compared to certain other types of BE-based possession construction is perhaps to be attributed to how wide-spread it is: the Locational Possessive is "the most frequent encoding option encountered in [Stassen's] sample" (Stassen 2009, 50), and it is the predominant form found "in Eurasia and Northern Africa, as well as in Polynesia and the northern part of South America" (Stassen 2009, 54).

The Topic Possessive, on the other hand, is defined as follows (Stassen 2009, 58, his (58)):

(21)   *Definition of the Topic Possessive*

    a.   The construction contains a locative/existential predicate, in the form of a verb with the rough meaning of 'to be'.

    b.   The POSSESSEE NP (PE) is constructed as the GRAMMATICAL SUBJECT of the predicate.

    c.   The POSSESSOR NP (PR) is constructed as the SENTENCE TOPIC of the sentence.

An example of this construction from Mandarin is given in (22) (Stassen 2009, 59, his (59)). As will be obvious already, the Topic Possessive and the Locational

Possessive have almost everything in common, the only difference coming in the morphological marking and presumed syntactic position of the possessor.

(22)   *Mandarin* (Li and Thompson 1981, 513)

Tā   yŏu   sān-ge   háizi
S/he be$_{exist}$ three-CLASS child
'S/he has three children.'

Alongside the standard variants of the Locational Possessive and Topic Possessive, Stassen recognizes three non-standard variants of them. The first of these (Stassen 2009, 79) is what Stassen refers to as *zero encoding*, but this simply means that the copula is silent, and there doesn't seem to be much reason to take this as a syntactically separate type from the present perspective.

A more interesting non-standard variant in the context of the present discussion is the so-called Adnominal Possessive (Stassen 2009, 107). This construction, which is called the Genitive Possessive in earlier typological work[13] (Locker 1954, 502; Clark 1978, 115; Heine 1997, 58), consists of a possessed DP and an existential verb.[14] The following is an example from Nepali (Stassen 2009, 108, his (2)).

(23)   *Nepali–Indo-European, Indic* (Clark 1966, 82; 91)

   a.   Mero eutā kitāp mātrey cha.
        I-GEN one book only   be.3SG.PRES
        'I have only one book.'

   b.   Ram-ko   pasal
        Ram-GEN shop
        'Ram's shop.'

Since languages vary in terms of whether or not they have overt genitive case marking, languages with Adnominal Possessives inevitably vary themselves in terms of whether their Possessors bear such morphology in the Adnominal Possessive construction. But instead of taking this variation as independent morphological vagaries over fundamentally the same sort of syntactic relationships, Stassen (2009, 113) treats marked and unmarked forms of the Adnominal Possessors as being of

---

13. Stassen's (2009, 110-111) rationale for renaming the construction the Adnominal Possessive is that not all languages that have it display an independent genitive case.

14. The BE construction of Cochabamba Quechua, discussed in Chapter 3, is an instantiation of such a case, as is the Hungarian case discussed in Szabolcsi's (1981, 1983, 1994) work. However, for reasons we will get to presently, Stassen himself would be forced to analyze them as Locational Possessives.

entirely different syntactic category; as he puts it: "I will regard the marked Adnominal Possessive as a variant of the Locational Possessive. Likewise, I will subsume
the unmarked variant of the Adnominal Possessive under the general heading of the
Topic Possessive." Stassen's rationale for this partition is that Locational Possessives are like Marked Adnominal Possessives in terms of marking but are different
in constituency. On the other hand, Topic Possessives and Unmarked Adnominal
Possessives are united in their lack of marking, but differ in their constituency in the
same way as the previous pair do. This is shown schematically as follows (Stassen
2009, 113, his (21) and (22)).

(24)   Locational Possessive   [PR-LOC] [PE] [BE]
       Marked Adnominal Possessive   [PR-LOC PE] [BE]

(25)   Topic Possessive   [PR] [PE] [BE]
       Unmarked Adnominal Possessive   [PR PE] [BE]

Stassen's reasoning seems plausible, until one considers that he is referring to
surface constituency, and not anything amounting to underlying argument structure (i.e., the first-merge positions of the arguments involved, in modern minimalist
terms). As the following quotation of Stassen's makes clear, this would force him to
conclude that the BE construction of Quechua (see Chapter 3) and the Hungarian
construction discussed by Szabolsci are Locational Possessives rather than Adnominal ones, despite the clear morphosyntactic evidence that the possessor is Adnominal at the beginning of the derivation ("[in] the case of the unmarked Adnominal
Possessive, a refutation of constituent status for the PR+PE combination immediately reduced the construction to an instance of the Topic Possessive" (2009, 114).
Here we have a clear case where Stassen's commitment to surface generalizations
above all others actively impedes his ability to categorize the phenomena correctly.
Even on his own terms, this division creates methodological problems for Stassen,
as he acknowledges when he writes the following:

[A] major practical problem in determining the degree of configurationality of
a language in general, and the configurationality of the PR+PE construction
in particular, is that such an endeavour presupposes a detailed knowledge
about the applicability–or, as the case may be, the inapplicability–of a number of syntactic devices, such as 'scrambling' and other 'movement' rules.
For most of the languages in my sample, such knowledge is not available at
the moment. Therefore, I have had no other option than to be very hesi-
tant in my conclusions about the non-configurational status of the PR+PE
combination in the predicative possession construction in a given language.

In practice, I consider the constituent status of such a combination to be refuted in cases in which the classic criteria for constituency–such as contiguity and inseparability–are clearly not met. In all other cases, I will assume that there is in fact constituency between the two noun phrases involved. It is, of course, possible that, for at least some languages, this attitude may be somewhat over-cautious. Thus, for example, it is well-known that the variants of Quechua allow for quite a bit of 'scrambling', so that it is conceivable that further research will show that the (marked) possessor NP and the possessee NP in their predicative possession construction do not form a constituent after all. (Stassen 2009, 114-115)

Stassen's hypothetical example could not have been better chosen: as I will show in Chapter 3, the possessor and the possessee of the BE construction in Cochabamba Quechua do not form a constituent on the surface. But the broader lesson here is that this lack of surface constituency does not reduce the importance of the evidence that the possessor is first-merged inside the possessee DP in that construction. Stassen's approach to the classification of these constructions must be rejected, because it assigns such evidence no relevance at all.

The argument that Stassen's taxonomy fails to make the right cuts here can be made even stronger by considering his discussion of Topic-Locational hybrids (Stassen 2009, 96). These are constructions in which the possessor appears once in a topic position, and once as a bound pronoun inside a locative PP. The following is an example of such a construction from Classical Arabic (Stassen 2009, 97, his (119)).

(26)   *Classical Arabic* (Comrie 1989, 224)

Zayd-un kaana-t la-hu   xubzatu-n.
Z.-NOM was-F   to-him loaf-NOM.INDEF
'Zayd had a loaf.'

In my view, Topic Possessives should not be seen as a separate class of possessive construction from the point of view of argument structure. Instead, I suggest that what Stassen calls Topic Possessives are variants of his Adnominal Possessive in which, for some language-internal reason, the Possessor is obligatorily topicalized. Similarly, his Topic-Locational hybrids are, I submit, instances of his Locational Possessive in which the Possessor appears as a hanging topic (Cinque 1990b). The category of "Topic Possessive" therefore dissolves. As further confirmation that this is the right way of looking at things, consider the following comment of Stassen's concerning the "hybridism" exhibited in cases like (26): "In principle, all sorts of hybrid constructions are conceivable. However, it turns out that, in practice, hybrid possession encoding is limited to cases in which features of the Locational Possessive and the Topic Possessive are found to interact" (2009, 96). It would seem that the correct reaction to this situation is to conclude that there is no such thing as a "hybrid construction" (whatever this would mean), and that the appearance of hybridity in this case springs from the fact that Topic Possessives do not constitute a separate sort of argument structure configuration, but are instead derived from other (genuinely different) constructions via topicalization.

It remains to address the other "non-standard" variants of the Topic Possessive and Locational Possessive that Stassen discusses. One such variant is known as the Conjunctional Possessive, which Stassen (2009, 94) ultimately argues is a variant of the Topic Possessive (correctly, I believe, but with the added caveat that Topic Possessives are themselves to be assimilated to Locational Possessives and Adnominal Possessives). Here is an example of this initially bizarre-looking construction (Stassen 2009, 92, his (111)).

(27)   *Canela-Krâho* (Popjes and Popjes 1986, 135)

Capi mā̱ catoc.
Capi and gun
'Capi has a gun.'

To see that the *mā̱* morpheme in (27) is indeed a co-ordinator, consider the following example (Stassen 2009, 93, his (113)).

(28)   *Canela-Krâho* (Popjes and Popjes 1986, 147)

A-te   po   curan mā̱ Capi apu   cuku.
You-PAST deer kill   and Capi CONT eat
'You killed a deer and Capi ate it.'

Stassen (2009, 94-95) argues that the Conjunctional Possessive can be better understood with relation to an even rarer non-standard variant; namely, what he calls the Clausal Possessive. As Stassen puts it, "[t]he defining feature of these Clausal Possessives is that the construction consists of two clauses, instead of the usual single sentence" (2009, 95). An example from the Sino-Tibetan language Daflā̱ is given in (29).

(29)   *Daflā* (Grierson 1909, 603)

Lok nyi ak da-tla   ka anyiga da-tleya.
One man one be-CONV.PAST son two   be-3DU.PAST

'A man had two sons.' (lit. 'there being a man, there were two sons.')

I believe Stassen (2009, 100-101) is correct to state that Clausal Possessives are
a variant of the Topic Possessive, where the possessor is made topical by putting
it in an adverbial clause of some kind. I also agree with him that Conjunctional
Possessives are to be thought of in the same way, except with an overt conjunction
tying the two clauses involved together. The Canela-Krâho example in (27) can then
be understood as involving two clauses, the first of which introduces the possessor
as a topic, and the second of which asserts the possession relation. These two clauses
are conjoined by *mā*. In each clause, the main verb is apparently silent.

This concludes the discussion of Stassen's categories of Locational Possessive and
Topic Possessive.

The next construction to discuss is what Stassen calls the WITH-Possessive, a
name which was chosen, according to Stassen (2009, 54), "after some hesitation."
This construction is defined as follows (Stassen 2009, 54, his (40)). As Stassen (2009,
55) points out, the WITH-Possessive is the opposite of the Locational Possessive in
terms of the grammatical functions assigned to the possessor and the possessee.

(30)   *Definition of the WITH-Possessive*

   a.   The construction contains a locative/existential predicate in the form
        of a verb with the rough meaning of 'to be.'

   b.   The Possessor NP (PR) is constructed as the 'grammatical subject'
        of the predicate.

   c.   The Possessee NP (PE) is constructed in some oblique, adverbial case
        form.

A familiar instance of the WITH-Possessive is provided by the Icelandic construction recently discussed by Levinson (2011) and discussed in Chapter 7 of the present
work. An example given by Stassen is the following, from Hixkaryana (Stassen 2009,
56, his (46)).

(31)   *Hixkaryana* (Derbyshire 1979, 110)

    Apaytara hyawo naha   biryekomo.
    chicken   with   be.3SG.PRES boy
    'The boy has chickens.'

Notice however that (30c) says nothing about the type of oblique marking that the possessee must carry in order to qualify as a WITH-Possessive for Stassen's purposes. It is to this that Stassen's hesitation over the name is to be attributed. As he himself puts it "there are quite a few instances of the WITH-Possessive in which the marker of the PE does not–or at least not synchronically–function as a marker of comitativity. Thus, the label 'WITH-Possessive' is something of a misnomer" (Stassen 2009, 55). Just as with the Locational and Topic Possessives, then, there turn out to be a number of non-standard variants of the WITH-Possessive that a full synchronic typology would need to analyze somewhat differently. One of the most important of these is what Stassen calls *Predicativization*, to which we turn now.

For Stassen (2009, 137), Predicativization is a diachronic process by which a possessee phrase "comes to be reanalyzed as the predicate of a possessive construction that has the possessor as its subject." Hence, Stassen does not treat this as a separate major type of possession construction, instead treating it as a diachronic offshoot of (mostly) WITH-Possessives. Synchronically, however, Predicativization turns out to have rather different properties than WITH-Possessives of the Icelandic sort do.

Stassen recognizes two variants of Predicativization, a *copular variant* and a *flexional variant*. The flexional variant involves combining verbal inflection directly with the possessee itself, sometimes with the mediation of a verbal derivational morpheme or an affixal adposition. An example is given in (32) (Stassen 2009, 140, his (10)):[15]

(32)   *Tundra Yukaghir–Yukaghir* (Maslova 2003, 70)

    Mārqa-n lāme-n'-ηi
    one-ATTR dog-COM-3PL-INTR
    'They have one dog.'

The copular variant of Predicativization consists of a predicative copula construction in which the predicate is formed by marking the possessee with a nominalizing or adjectivalizing morpheme. Such constructions are found in many parts of the

---

15. The morpheme glossed ATTR is an attributive marker.

world, including in Altaic languages (Stassen 2009, 145-147), many Australian languages (Stassen 2009, 154; see also Dixon 1976), the Quechua family (see Chapter 6), and in certain corners of some European languages, including English (as in *John is blue-eyed, John is slow-witted*). Adjectival cases seem to be somewhat more prevalent than nominal ones, although see Chapter 6 for evidence that the *-yoq* construction of Quechua is a case of Predicativization that is nominal for at least some speakers. In addition, there is a cross-linguistic correlation between the morphosyntactic behavior of adjectives and whether a given language has the flexional or copular variant of predicativization. As Stassen puts it "these predicativized possessee phrases are to be seen as essentially 'property-indicating' or ADJECTIVAL, and [...] their morphosyntactic behavior can be predicted from the way in which the language at issue constructs items like 'big', 'bad', or 'beautiful' in predicate function" (Stassen 2009, 137). In particular, Stassen proposes the following universals (Stassen 2009, 141, his (15)):

(33)   *Universals of Predicativization*

    a.   If a language has a predicativized WITH-Possessive of the copular variant, its predicative adjectives are nouny.

    b.   If a language has a predicativized WITH-Possessive of the flexional variant, its predicative adjectives are verby.

Hence, there is no doubt that synchronic Predicativization has rather different properties than Icelandic-style WITH-Possessives, in that the possessee phrase in the former is of some category other than PP. We will see in Chapter 6 that there are semantic differences too. Predicativization exhibits across-the-board definiteness effects, which are absent from true WITH-Possessives. Additionally, depending on other structural factors explored in Chapter 6, Predicativization is sometimes restricted to inalienable possession, whereas such restrictions are unknown in true WITH-Possessives as far as I know.

The final major category of possession sentence recognized by Stassen is the HAVE-Possessive, defined in (34) (Stassen 2009, 62, his (83)).

(34)   *Definition of the HAVE-Possessive*

    a.   The construction contains a transitive predicate.

    b.   The POSSESSOR NP is constructed as the SUBJECT/AGENT.

    c.   The POSSESSEE NP is constructed as the DIRECT OBJECT/PATIENT.

Stassen makes the point that HAVE-Possessives are by no means limited to Europe, and are instead found all over the world. He identifies a number of interesting generalizations concerning properties that HAVE-Possessives have cross-linguistically. On the diachronic side, he notes (2009, 63) quoting Givón (1984, 103): "Most commonly a 'have' verb arises out of the semantic bleaching of active possession verbs such as 'get', 'grab', 'seize', 'take', 'obtain', etc."

More crucially for our purposes, Stassen (2009, 63, his (85)) identifies what appears to be an exceptionless generalization about the semantics of HAVE-Possessives that separates them from existential BE-based possession constructions like the Locational Possessive and the Topic Possessive.

(35)   *The Universal of HAVE-Possessives*

         If a language employs a HAVE-Possessive for the encoding of alienable possession, it will employ a HAVE-Possessive for the encoding of temporary possession.

Insofar as generalizations like (35) can be discovered, and insofar as they hold for certain subtypes of possession construction but not others, we have evidence that it is impossible to relate all possession constructions to a single underlying structure via movement. Thus, typological generalizations like (35) provide valuable evidence concerning what the right solution to the too-many-(surface)-structures puzzle must look like.

This concludes the discussion of Stassen's major types of possession construction and the so-called non-standard variants thereof, as well as the taxonomy's associated problems. We have seen that many of these problems result from the fact that Stassen builds his typology around perceived diachronic relationships amongst constructions, which sometimes leaves the taxonomy with no room for certain distinctions that are demonstrably important at the synchronic level. This issue also has unfortunate consequences for Stassen's attempt to discuss generalizations about what other syntactic properties co-vary with differences in possession constructions cross-linguistically, as we shall now see.

2.1.3.1   Stassen's Proposals on What Covaries with Variation in Possession Constructions

A long-standing point of interest for generative syntacticians working on predicative possession has been the question of whether any other syntactic properties in language covary with the different types of possession construction. Such covariation could provide valuable clues to the cause of the vast variation in possession constructions, as well as opening the door to the possibility of developing powerful parametric theories to explain such covariation between possession and other areas of syntax. It is therefore highly relevant here that Stassen (2009, 274) proposes such correlations with respect to all four of his major types of possession construction. Unfortunately, however, Stassen himself is able to find a number of robust counter-examples to his generalizations. This matters little for Stassen, because the tendencies he identifies are still statistically rather striking. It does, however, mean that the correlations cannot and should not be recast straightforwardly in a parametric account. We shall also see that the manner in which he counts counter-examples for one of his correlations (having to do with the morphosyntax of adverbial clauses) means that the situation is certainly worse than Stassen paints it, at least from the point of view of trying to convert the correlations into comparative syntactic universals of the sort that are the bread and butter of parametric approaches. It is for this reason that I have not attempted to assimilate the following generalizations to the approach developed in the other chapters of this work. Before presenting the generalizations, some terminology is needed. *Balancing* languages are those in which adverbial clauses contain an amount of functional material equivalent to main clauses. *Deranking* languages are those in which adverbial clauses have reduced functional material compared to main clauses. Relevant to Stassen's universals are adverbial clauses which encode *simultaneous D(ifferent) S(ubject)* sequences–that is, adverbial clauses where the subject is different from the matrix subject, but where the eventuality in the adverbial clause holds at the same time as that in the main clause. *Split* languages are ones where there is a morphological distinction between a locative/existential copular verb and a copular verb used with nominal predicates. *Share* languages are ones in which the same copula is used with locative and nominal predicates. The universals themselves are stated as follows (Stassen 2009, 274, his (52)).

(36)   *The Universals of Predicative Possession Encoding*

   a. If a language has a Locational Possessive, it has deranking of simultaneous DS-sequences.

   b. If a language has a WITH-Possessive, it has deranking of simultaneous DS-sequences.

   c. If a language has a (standard) Topic Possessive, it has balanced simultaneous DS-sequences, and it is a split-language.

   d. If a language has a HAVE-Possessive, it has balanced simultaneous DS-sequences, and it is a share-language.

Stassen himself is at pains to emphasize that "none of these statements will be shown to be one hundred per cent correct" (2009, 275). Sticking to the generalizations under (36d), counter-examples cited by Stassen himself to the generalization that HAVE languages never have split copula systems include Touareg (658), Spanish (570), Wolof, Fulani, and a number of other West Atlantic languages (680-1), and the Kru language Grebo (685-6).[16] There are also counter-examples to the generalization that HAVE languages are exclusively balancing: Stassen (2009, 672) cites Maasai. In fact, the balancing/deranking parameter will be even more difficult to defend from the point of view of a generative theory of syntactic variation, because such a view would require a given language to be exclusively deranking or balancing in order to yield a strong prediction that a certain predicative possession construction will be available or unavailable. In fact, however, Stassen only counts a language as a counter-example if it makes predominant use of the unexpected type of adverbial clause. This means that there can be no doubt that the number of counter-examples in the sense relevant to generative work will be a lot higher. Nevertheless, Stassen does attempt to offer a synchronic theory of predicative possessive encoding designed to account for the generalizations in (36). It is to this theory that we turn now.

2.1.3.2   Stassen's Proposed Explanation for His Universals of Predicative Possession Encoding

Although Stassen's taxonomy itself is based partly on synchrony and partly on diachrony, in the final chapter of his book he offers a model of predicative possessive encoding that aims to account for the attested typology (and Stassen's generalizations in (36)) in synchronic terms. The account is rooted in a theory of the architecture of the grammar, which brings it close enough in spirit to the theory expounded in this book that they can be fruitfully compared.

For Stassen (2009, 702, his Figure 3.1), the grammar is organized as shown in (37). The components inside the box constitute the parts of grammar which are linguistic in the strict sense; components outside the box represent interfaces with other cognitive domains. The grammatical entities that constitute *Underlying Structure* are quasi-logical representations of meaning, which are converted into Surface Structures by various deletion, insertion, and transposition operations. Stassen's architecture, then, is fundamentally that of Generative Semantics (Katz and Fodor 1963; Katz and Postal 1964; much subsequent work).

---

16. To these we can add Santiago del Estero Quechua, a HAVE language with a split copula system, discussed in Chapter 3.

(37)   *The Architecture of the Grammar According to Stassen (2009)*
        Cognitive Structure ('Thought')

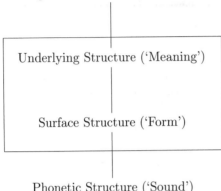

        Phonetic Structure ('Sound')

With this grammatical architecture as background, Stassen proposes that "the observed typological facts about predicative alienable possession can be explained if we assume that the formal encoding of this domain is a mapping of AN UNDERLYING STRUCTURE WHICH CONSISTS OF A SIMULTANEOUS SEQUENCE OF TWO EXISTENTIAL PREDICATIONS" (2009, 705). The sort of representation Stassen has in mind here is in (38), which he says can alternatively be represented as in (39).

(38)   ∃(a) & ∃(b)

(39)   [PR BE] [PE BE]

The idea is that predicative possession sentences are fundamentally propositions that assert that "two objects, namely the PR and the PE, 'are there', or are in the same space, at the same time." (Stassen 2009, 705). I will note immediately that there is no clear sense in which (38) should give rise to a possessive meaning–such a meaning is not an automatic consequence of conjoining two existential sentences (cf. *there are two bedrooms and there's a small kitchen*). Stassen offers nothing that addresses this basic objection, as far as I can see. Laying this aside for now, Stassen goes on to claim that the ordering of the sentence containing the possessor before that containing the possessee is a universal one, and derives the fact that the possessor is topical in predicative possession sentences. Variation in predicative possession constructions then results from various distortions of the Underlying Structure in (39), which can take place in a given language on the way to Surface Structure. Stassen claims that leaving (39) as it is yields a Clausal Possessive of the Ixtlan Zapotec sort. Deleting both BE verbs and realizing an overt conjunction between the two yields the so-called Conjunctional Possessive found in Canela-Krāho. Stassen's four major types of possession construction can then be thought of as different end-points in a parametric decision tree, which is reproduced in (40) (Stassen 2009, 723, his Figure 13.3).

(40)   *Stassen's Parametric Decision Tree*

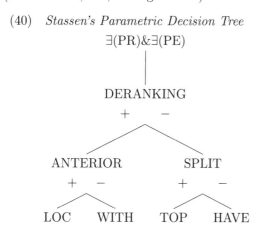

The first decision in the tree is whether the language has Deranking or not. If it does, then the next step is to decide whether copula deletion and oblique marking take place in the PR clause (in which case the language is +Anterior) or in the PE clause (in which case the language is −Anterior). Deleting the BE of the PR clause and marking the PR as oblique yields a Locational Possessive. Deriving WITH-Possessives involves the exact opposite procedure: the BE in the PE clause is deleted and oblique marking is given to the PE. The possibility of such oblique case marking in a reduced clause relies upon the availability of Deranking in a language, and this is why Locational Possessive languages and WITH-Possessive languages have Deranking (Stassen 2009, 708). In contrast, Topic Possessives for Stassen have BE deletion in the PR clause (as do Locational Possessives), but no oblique marking ensues, because Topic Possessive languages do not generally allow Deranking. The difference between Topic Possessives and HAVE-Possessives then comes down to the nature of the copula system: Topic Possessive languages are associated with split copula systems, which means that there is never any possible ambiguity between predicative possession constructions (which will use the existential/locative copula) and predicate nominal constructions (which will instead use the distinct, predicative copula). HAVE-Possessives arise when a language that lacks Deranking also lacks a split copula system. This creates the possibility that predicate nominal constructions and predicative possession constructions could be perfectly ambiguous. HAVE-Possessives, Stassen submits, are a way of avoiding this ambiguity by "giv[ing]

up the whole thing" (Stassen 2009, 721) and using a transitive verb instead of a BE verb. There are two problems with this general picture, however. The first is the fact that both the Deranking generalization and the Split Copula generalization are robustly counter-exemplified, as we have already seen. The second is that the chart only has room for the standard variants of Stassen's four major possessive constructions. As Stassen himself puts it "non-standard variants are not accounted for" (2009, 724). This means that there are several serious gaps in Stassen's attempt to explain the typology as revealed by his own investigation. To conclude, Stassen (2009) is to be commended for bringing together data from a number of languages that illustrate the scale of the too-many-(surface)-structures puzzle. However, we have seen that the typology of possession constructions set up by Stassen fails to carve up the phenomena in appropriate ways at several points, and that his laudable attempts to link this typology to other syntactic phenomena are unsatisfactory in a number of respects. In the next section, we look at recent work by Tham (2013), which has much in common with the present proposal.

2.1.4   Tham (2013)

While Tham (2013) does not bring together a new typological sample, I discuss it briefly here because its proposed solution to the too-many-(surface)-structures puzzle is very similar in spirit to my own. Moreover, Tham's proposed typology avoids many of the organizational and explanatory problems that were identified for Stassen's (2009) approach in the previous section.

Tham's (2013) major insight is that possessive predication is fundamentally non-verbal in nature, and is therefore to be thought of as a special case of nonverbal predication (that is, predication that is mediated by a copular verb in English and similar languages). She notes that this immediately explains why predicative possession constructions vary so much in their surface syntax (as revealed by Heine 1997, Stassen 2009 and others): possession constructions are able to exploit all of the variation available in predicative copula constructions more generally. Tham extends this typology not only to the HAVE/BE domain, but also to the domain of BELONG-type verbs, which are not addressed in the present work.[17]

My own approach is similar, although it makes a more specific suggestion regarding the way in which possession relations are non-verbal: namely, that they are

---

17. Tham (2013, 1) refers to HAVE/BE constructions as "indefinite" possession and BELONG-type constructions as "definite" possession. For reasons discussed already in the section on Clark (1978) and in the section on Freeze (1992) below, these labels need to be taken with a grain of salt.

introduced by DP-internal functional heads. Tham, on the other hand, makes no particular proposal regarding where possessive meanings come from, and how possession constructions come to have the meanings they do given the way they are put together. Nor does she discuss non-possessive uses of possessive constructions (such as the various types of ECM HAVE sentences discussed in Chapter 4 of this work). Nevertheless, the fact that I have been unable to cover BELONG constructions in this book may prove to be a disadvantage in the long run, if indeed it proves desirable to relate the BELONG paradigm to the HAVE/BE paradigm.

2.2   The Too-Many-(Surface)-Structures Puzzle: The Freeze/Kayne Tradition

In the early 1990s, work by Freeze (1992) and Kayne (1993) proposed what was to become the standard solution to the too-many-(surface)-structures puzzle within generative syntax. Although they differ importantly in a number of details, these papers are fundamentally similar in the solution to this puzzle they adopt: both argue that the initially bewildering array of surface syntaxes associated with possession sentences cross-linguistically are a red-herring. The surface variation between BE and HAVE structures is to be accounted for by movement operating on a single D-structure. The relationship between BE and HAVE for both authors is also transformational in nature: HAVE is produced via the incorporation of an adpositional element into BE; in BE constructions, this same adpositional element instead surfaces as an adposition or a case marker on one of the arguments. This tradition has been immensely influential, and has triggered a vast literature looking at the comparative syntax of HAVE and BE, much of which seeks to identify the parameter(s) that are relevant to having HAVE and lacking it. This comparative literature is the topic of section 2.3. In this section, I give a brief introduction to the Freeze/Kayne tradition itself. Detailed comparisons between this tradition and my own approach are reserved until Chapter 5. Section 2.2.1 reviews papers from Szabolcsi (1981, 1983, 1994), which were important inspirations for the Freeze/Kayne approach. Section 2.2.2 reviews Freeze (1992). Kayne (1993) is the subject of Section 2.2.3. Section 2.2.4 is a conclusion, summarizing what I take to be the core of the Freeze/Kayne tradition.

2.2.1   The Foundations: Szabolcsi (1981, 1983, 1994)

Szabolcsi (1981, 1983, 1994) is a series of works discussing the internal structure of the DP in Hungarian, with particular focus on the structure of possessed DPs. Szabolcsi (1981) explicitly analogizes the structure of the Hungarian noun phrase to the structure of the sentence in configurational languages like English, and makes a seminal proposal about the structure of possession sentences in Hungarian: namely, that they involve a possessed DP embedded under an existential verb, with obligatory extraction of the possessor from inside the possessed DP. It is this idea of possessor extraction that the Freeze/Kayne tradition extends to the broader typology of possession sentences. Szabolcsi (1983), which is described as "a revised version of parts of Szabolcsi (1981[...])" (Szabolcsi 1983, 89), does not discuss possession sentences directly. However, it does contain some important refinements of the description and analysis of the Hungarian DP that appears in Szabolcsi (1981), and so brief discussion of it is included here. Szabolcsi (1994) updates the analysis and contains important new reflections on what forces possessor extraction in Hungarian possession sentences. In this section, I will focus on the key analytical insights that are shared by all three of Szabolcsi (1981, 1983, 1994), and the data used to motivate them, rather than on tracing the evolution of the details of the approach.

The core insight of Szabolcsi (1981, 1983, 1994) is that the Hungarian noun phrase shares two important properties with sentences: it has (i) an inflectional node associated with an A-position that introduces the possessor, much like the subject position associated with sentences; and (ii) a left-peripheral A-bar position that can serve as an escape hatch for further movement, much like the left-peripheral COMP/spec-CP position associated with sentences.

The evidence for (i) comes partly from the morphology associated with the presence of a possessor inside a DP, and partly from the way in which the surface position of the possessor within DP interacts with its case-marking. Consider the examples in (41) (from Szabolcsi 1981, 263, her (5); Szabolcsi credits Mel'čuk 1973 with motivating the morphological segmentation embodied in (41)):

(41)   *Possessed DPs: Hungarian*

    a.   Az én-∅   kar-ja-i-m
           the I-NOM arm-POSS-PL-1SG

           'my arms'

    b.   Az te-∅   kar-ja-i-d
        the you-NOM arm-POSS-PL-2SG

        'thine arms'

    c.   (A) Péter-∅   kar-ja-i-∅
        the Peter-NOM arm-POSS-PL-3SG

        'Peter's arms'

Focus first on the nominal morphology on the possessee in each of the examples
in (41). The possessee in all three cases is itself plural, and this is reflected by the
morpheme -*i*. However, this morpheme is accompanied by a POSS morpheme to its
left and an agreement morpheme to its right. This agreement morpheme reflects the
phi-features of the possessor. The possessor itself surfaces to the right of the definite
article, and carries the (zero-marked) nominative case. Intriguingly, the word-order
and the case-marking pattern seen here alternate with another pattern, displayed
in (42). Here, the possessor precedes the definite article rather than following it,
and it is marked with dative case instead of nominative (examples from Szabolcsi
1981, 265, her (9)).[18]

(42)   *Possessed DPs with Dative Possessor: Hungarian*

    a.   én-nek-e-m   a kar-ja-i-m
        I-DAT-POSS-1SG the arm-POSS-PL-1SG

        'my arms'

    b.   te-nek-e-d   a kar-ja-i-d
        you-DAT-POSS-2SG the arm-POSS-PL-2SG

        'thine arms'

    c.   Péter-nek a kar-ja-i-∅
        Peter-DAT the arm-POSS-PL-3SG

        'Peter's arms'

Szabolcsi (1981, 1983, 1994) proposes that this confluence of word-order and
case-marking facts is to be accounted for as follows: the Hungarian DP contains
an A-position below the position of the definite article, associated with nominative
case, where the possessor is introduced. The possessor may, but need not, move into
an A-bar position higher than the definite article. This position, which is identified

---

18. Notice that dative pronouns in Hungarian themselves have the internal structure of a possessed
DP. I will not address this here.

with spec-DP in Szabolcsi (1994, 198), is associated with dative case.[19] This basic
idea is formalized in a variety of ways across Szabolcsi (1981, 1983, 1994). In (43)
below, I depict a version of the structure for example (41a) based partly on Szabolcsi
(1994, 192).[20] In (44) on the next page, I depict an analogous structure for (42a).

(43)   *Hungarian: Nominative Possessor*

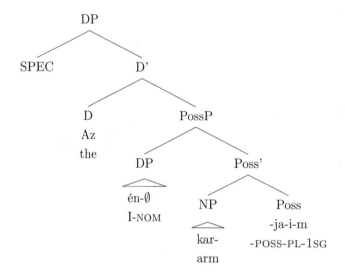

There are two pieces of independent evidence that the word order in (42) involves
movement to a left-peripheral A-bar position, as depicted in (44). The first concerns
possessors that are operator-like. It turns out that these must be dative, and must
move into the pre-article position, consonant with the idea that this position is an
A-bar position (example from Szabolcsi 1981, 268, her (15)). This is demonstrated
in (45).

19. We will see that this position serves as an escape hatch for further possessor movement. For
this reason, it is called KOMP by Szabolcsi (1981, 267; 1983, 92), partly to evoke the label COMP
(the then-current name for what is now referred to as spec-CP, itself assumed to be an escape
hatch for movement out of the clause), and partly to evoke the Hungarian word for 'ferry'.

20. Szabolcsi's (1994, 196) does not decompose the possessive morphology in this way. Her reasons
for not adopting an analysis like (44) have partly to do with scopal facts: it turns out that quantified
possessors can never scope under the determiner associated with the possessee. The representation
in (44) does not automatically predict this fact, since one might expect reconstruction of the
possessor into its lower position to be possible. A second reason why Szabolcsi does not adopt this
analysis has to do with complications with thematic role assignment, but such complications do
not arise on the approach to thematic roles embraced here.

(44)   *Hungarian: Dative Possessor*

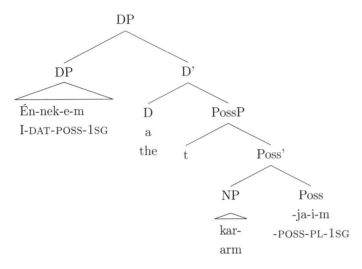

(45)   *Hungarian: Wh-Possessors must Move*

    a.   * (A) ki-∅   kar-ja-∅
            The who-NOM arm-POSS-3SG

            'Whose arm'

    b.   Ki-nek   a   kar-ja-∅
            Who-DAT the arm-POSS-3SG

            'Whose arm'

The second argument for the status of dative possessors as being in a left-peripheral A-bar position comes from the fact that dative possessors can be reordered with respect to the possessee DP and moved away from it, whereas nominative possessors are immobile. This generalization, which is illustrated in (46a) and (46b) (based respectively on Szabolcsi 1981, 264, her (8b) and Szabolcsi 1981, 265, her (10b)), follows if dative possessors are indeed in the left periphery of DP, and therefore extractable from it (on the assumption that spec-DP acts as an escape hatch).

(46)   *Hungarian: Only Dative Possessors may be Extracted*

    a.   * Péter-∅$_i$ hosszú-ak [t$_i$ a   kar-ja-i-∅].
            Peter-NOM long-PL   [t the arm-POSS-PL-3SG]

            'It is Peter whose arms are long.'

  b.   Péter-nek$_i$ hosszú-ak [t$_i$ a   kar-ja-i-∅].
       Peter-DAT long-PL   [t the arm-POSS-PL-3SG]
       'It is Peter whose arms are long.'

Most interesting for our purposes is the relationship between these facts and the
form of Hungarian possession sentences. An example of such a sentence is given in
(47a) (from Szabolcsi 1981, 276, her (43)). The similarity with attributive possession
is striking, as can be seen by comparing (47a) with (47b).

(47)   *Hungarian: Predicative vs. Attributive Possession*

  a.   Péter-nek van kar-ja-∅.
       Peter-DAT BE   arm-POSS-3SG
       'Peter has an arm.'

  b.   Péter-nek a   kar-ja-∅.
       Peter-DAT the arm-POSS-3SG
       'Peter's arm'

Notice that the possession sentence in (47a) involves a dative possessor and a
possessee marked with possessive morphology, just like the possessed DP in (47b)
does. As Szabolcsi notes, the presence of this morphology is entirely unexpected if
the possessee and the possessor are taken to be separate arguments of the BE-verb
van, since "agreement between co-arguments seems unattested in human languages"
(1981, 276).[21] She thus proposes that Hungarian predicative possession sentences
involve embedding a possessed DP underneath the existential verb *van*, and then
extracting the possessor from that DP. Given the assumptions independently needed
to account for possessed DPs in the language, this accounts simultaneously for the
possessive inflection on the possessee and the dative marking on the possessor in
(47a).

     There is, however, an interesting conceptual wrinkle in this elegant account,
which is discussed at length in both Szabolcsi (1981, 276-282) and Szabolcsi (1994,
224-231). Namely, possessor extraction appears to be *obligatory* in the predicative possession construction, whereas normally it is optional. To see this, consider
the following cases. The examples in (48) (adapted from Szabolcsi 1981, 276, her
(46)) show that, in sentences other than possesssion sentences, it is possible for the

---

21. As discussed in Szabolcsi (1994, 224), Steele (1990) proposed a revision of the theory of agreement to permit agreement between co-arguments on the basis of Luiseño predicative possession
constructions, which are rather similar to those of Hungarian. Szabolcsi's proposal has the advantage of making such a revision (which would at any rate be somewhat suspicious in being necessary
for predicative possession only) unnecessary.

possessor and possessee to surface as a constituent either after the verb (with the possessor in nominative as in (48a), or in dative, as in (48b)), or in the preverbal focus position with the possessor in dative, as in (48c).

(48)   a.   hosszú [(a) Péter-∅   kar-ja-∅   ]
            long   [the Peter-NOM arm-POSS-3SG]
            'Peter's arm is long.'

        b.   hosszú [Péter-nek$_i$ a   t$_i$ kar-ja-∅   ]
            long   [Peter-DAT the t arm-POSS-3SG]
            'Peter's arm is long.'

        c.   [Péter-nek$_i$ a   t$_i$ kar-ja-∅   ]$_j$ hosszú t$_j$
            [Peter-DAT the t arm-POSS-3SG] long   t
            'It's Peter's arm that is long.'

If we now turn to a sentence expressing predicative possession with *van*, we find that none of these options are viable: as shown in (49) (based on Szabolcsi 1981, 277, her (47)), no method of keeping the possessor and the possessee in constituency together yields a grammatical sentence. This is disturbing, because it appears to cast a shadow of suspicion on the idea that the possessor begins the derivation inside the possessed DP.

(49)   a.   * van [Péter-∅   kar-ja-∅   ]
            BE   [Peter-NOM arm-POSS-3SG]
            'Peter has an arm.'

        b.   * van [Péter-nek$_i$ t$_i$ kar-ja-∅   ]
            BE   [Peter-DAT t arm-POSS-3SG]
            'Peter has an arm.'

        c.   * [Péter-nek$_i$ t$_i$ kar-ja-∅   ]$_j$ van t$_j$
            [Peter-DAT t arm-POSS-3SG] BE t
            'Peter has an arm.'

Though (49) presents an interesting problem, I agree with Szabolcsi that it does not, on its own, threaten the idea that the possessor is introduced inside the possessed DP in Hungarian possession sentences, especially given the obligatory possessor agreement on the possessee. As Szabolcsi puts it, the apparent obligatoriness of possessor extraction in such sentences is "unusual, though much less shocking than [the alternative of saying that the possessor and possessee are co-arguments of *van* which for some reason must agree with each other]: what we seem to be dealing with is the obligatoriness of an otherwise standard process, rather than the occurrence of a wholly non-standard process" (1994, 225).

Nevertheless, one wants to understand why this possessor extraction is obligatory. The question is made all the more urgent by the fact that this pattern is not restricted to Hungarian–as we will see in Chapter 3, the very similar BE construction of Cochabamba Quechua is also characterized by possessor extraction. Szabolcsi (1981) and Szabolcsi (1994) give partial answers to this question that differ in their details but are united in tying the necessity of possessor extraction to the definiteness effect in existential sentences (Milsark 1977). In what follows, I will focus on the discussion in Szabolcsi (1994).[22]

Szabolcsi (1994, 225) begins by pointing out a fact about possessed DPs in English. Such DPs invariably have a specific reading when a definite possessor is prenominal, but may have a non-specific reading when such a possessor is postnominal (these examples appear as Szabolcsi's (116) and (117)).

(50)   I haven't read Chomsky's poem.

(51)   I haven't read a poem of Chomsky's.

Example (50) can be felicitously uttered only if Chomsky has, in fact, written at least one poem. Example (51), on the other hand, comes with no such commitment, and can be used even if the speaker is unconvinced that any Chomsky-authored poems exist. Relatedly, (52) means that everyone read a particular poem by Chomsky, whereas (53) allows the Chomsky-authored poems to vary with the readers (these examples are Szabolcsi's (118) and (119), respectively from Szabolcsi 1994, 225 and Szabolcsi 1994, 226).

(52)   Everyone has read Chomsky's poem.

(53)   Everyone has read a poem of Chomsky's.

---

22. Briefly, the account given in Szabolcsi (1981) is as follows: (a) *van* (and other verbs subject to definiteness effects) c-selects for a null non-specific article (Szabolcsi 1981, 279, her (55)); (b) a surface filter (found in Szabolcsi 1981, 278, her (53)) bans any overt manifestation of a possessor inside a DP containing an Article Phrase with lexical content. These two together will force possessor extraction or deletion when a possessed DP is embedded under *van*, explaining the badness of (49). One issue for this approach is the fact that c-selection for a particular article of the type assumed in (a) is otherwise unheard of. Secondly, the surface filter in (b) is not only *ad hoc*, but turns out to be descriptively inaccurate, since it predicts that dative possessors can never surface in constituency with the possessee in the presence of an article of the relevant type. While Szabolcsi (1981, 277) claims that this is correct, the judgments presented there (in Szabolcsi 1981's (50) and (51)) turn out to have been too restrictive, and they are corrected in Szabolcsi (1983). I would like to thank Anna Szabolcsi (pers. comm.) for discussion of these matters.

The generalization is that prenominal definite possessors inside a possessed DP force a specific reading of the possessee. If we turn again to Hungarian, it turns out that a related, but not identical, generalization holds there (Szabocsi 1994, 226, her (120)):[23]

(54)   a.   When the possessor is inside DP (in the nominative or in the dative), DP is specific (potentially also definite).

       b.   For DP to be non-specific, it must have the possessor extracted (in addition to not containing any specific determiner, of course).

Examples (55)-(57) establish the validity of (54). In (55) (from Szabolcsi 1994, 226, her (121)),[24] we see a nominative possessor (which, recall, is possible only if the possessor remains inside the possessed DP), and the only available interpretation is specific.

(55)   Nem olvas-t-ad   [Chomsky-$\emptyset$ vers-é-$\emptyset$-t.]
       not   read-PAST-2SG [Chomsky-NOM poem-POSS-3SG-ACC]
       'You haven't read Chomsky's poem.'

The same is true if a dative possessor is used but does not exit the possessed DP. In (56) (Szabolcsi 1994, 226, her (122)), the fact that the possessor is inside the possessed DP is established by placing the possessor-possessee string in the preverbal focus position, which is able to accommodate exactly one constituent of the clause. As the translation indicates, only the specific reading for this DP is available (Szabolcsi 1994, 226 notes that this example is somewhat archaic).

(56)   (Csak) [Chomsky-nak$_i$ t$_i$ vers-é-$\emptyset$-t   ] nem
       only   [Chomsky-DAT   t poem-POSS-3SG-ACC] not
       olvas-t-ad.
       read-PAST-DEF.2SG
       'It is (only) Chomsky's poem that you haven't read.'

However, if a dative possessor is clearly extracted from the possessed DP, then a non-specific reading becomes possible. In fact, the non-specific reading is the preferred one, although a specific reading is available with a somewhat marked, archaic flavor.

---

23. The discussion of split DPs in Cuzco Quechua in Hastings (2003, 2004) indicates that Quechua languages are subject to much the same generalization as (54).

24. Here and below I adapt the glossing conventions of Szabolcsi (1994) so that they match those of Szabolcsi (1981). The only major difference concerns zero morphemes, which are depicted less often in Szabolcsi (1994).

(57)   Chomsky-nak$_i$ nem olvas-t-ad   [t$_i$ t$_i$ vers-é-∅-t.   ]
        Chomsky-DAT not read-PAST-DEF.2SG [t t poem-POSS-3SG-ACC]

        'You haven't read any poem of Chomsky's.'
        ? 'You haven't read Chomsky's poem.' (archaic)

Hence, it seems that Hungarian and English (and Quechua; see Chapter 3, and footnote 23 of the present chapter) share the property that a prenominal possessor forces a specific reading upon the possessed DP. The two languages vitiate this effect in different ways. English can vitiate this specificity effect by placing the possessor after the possessee and inserting *of* before the possessor. Hungarian does not have this option, but can achieve the same effect by extracting the possessor from the possessed DP.[25]

This contains the seed of a solution to the puzzle with which we started; namely, why is possessor extraction apparently obligatory in Hungarian possession sentences, whereas usually such extraction from possessed DPs is optional? First, recall that Hungarian possession sentences are essentially existential sentences, as can be seen by comparing (58) and (59) (Szabolcsi 1994, 227, her (109) and (125)). Existential sentences inherently require a non-specific indefinite complement (Milsark 1977).

(58)   Mari-nak van-nak kalap-ja-i-∅.
        Mari-DAT BE-3PL hat-POSS-PL-3SG

        'Mari has hats.'

(59)   Van-nak kalap-ok.
        BE-3PL   hat-PL

        'There are hats.'

Conjoining this fact with the conclusion that prenominal possessors in Hungarian induce specificity unless they are extracted from the possessed DP, the necessity of such extraction in possession sentences can be understood as follows (Szabolcsi 1994, 227-228, her (126)).

---

25. As Alec Marantz points out to me, these two ways of vitiating specificity might be unifiable under Kayne's (1993/2000) approach to *of*, which involves extraction of the possessor into *of*'s specifier in the first step.

(60)   The HAVE-sentence in Hungarian is an existential sentence with a [+Poss]
         nominative argument. Given that (1) the existential verb requires a non-
         specific indefinite argument and (2) a [+Poss] DP has a non-specific indef-
         inite interpretation only if its possessor is extracted, possessor extraction
         in the HAVE-sentence is obligatory.

The key insight behind (60) is intuitively satisfying, and it moreover makes a
cross-linguistic prediction, not noted by Szabolcsi, which on initial evidence seems
to be correct. The prediction is this: if we can find a language which is like Hungarian
in having an existential BE-based possession construction, but unlike Hungarian in
that prenominal possessors do not force a specific reading of their possessed DP,
then we expect the BE-based possession construction in that language to allow the
possessor to stay inside the possessed DP. This is because such a language will
be able to get away with leaving the possessor "at home" without violating the
existential verb's requirement for a non-specific indefinite argument.

It turns out that certain Austronesian languages of Taiwan are of the relevant
sort (for general discussion of predicative possession in Formosan languages, see
Zeitoun, Huang, Yeh, and Chang 1999). Here I will discuss data from Isbukun
Bunun. For this data and much helpful discussion thereof, I am indebted to K.C.
Lin (pers. comm.), who has done extensive fieldwork on Isbukun Bunun.

Data showing that Isbukun Bunun has possessed DPs with prenominal possessors,
and that it allows such DPs to receive a non-specific indefinite interpretation, are
given in (61).

(61)   M-aun a   'inak   'uvaz mas bunbun.
         AV-eat NOM 1Sg.GEN child OBL banana

         'A child/children of mine eat banana(s).' (specific reading also possible)

The next step is to look at how possession sentences work in Isbukun Bunun. It
turns out that the language has two constructions that are relevant here. The first,
which is directly comparable to the Hungarian construction discussed by Szabolcsi,
is exemplified in (62). This construction, which I will call the BE construction,
consists of an existential BE verb, followed by the possessor in genitive case, followed
by the possessee. As shown in (62b), the possessor must be marked for genitive in
this construction.

(62)   *BE Construction: Isbukun Bunun (Formosan, Taiwan)*

   a.   'Aiza   'inak   'uvaz.
         BE$_{exist}$ I.GEN child

         'I have a child.'

b. *'Aiza   saikin 'uvaz.
    BE$_{exist}$ I.NOM child
    'I have a child.'

The second construction is somewhat different from the Hungarian construction, but we shall presently see that its properties are nonetheless extremely relevant here. This construction involves the same existential BE verb root, but with the addition of a morpheme glossed LV for *locative voice*. Furthermore, in this BE-LV construction the possessor may no longer surface in genitive case, and must instead surface in the nominative, as can be seen by comparing (63a) and (63b). Thus, the case pattern in the BE-LV construction is the exact opposite of the pattern found in the BE construction, as a comparison between (63) and (62) makes clear.

(63)   *BE-LV Construction: Isbukun Bunun (Formosan, Taiwan)*

    a. *'Aiza-an   'inak 'uvaz.
        BE$_{exist}$-LV I.GEN child
        'I have a child.'

    b. 'Aiza-an   saikin 'uvaz.
        BE$_{exist}$-LV I.NOM child
        'I have a child.'

It turns out that, unlike in the Hungarian construction, it is impossible for clausal material such as adverbs to intervene between the possessor and the possessee in the Isbukun Bunun BE construction (see (64a)). This is evidence that the possessor does indeed stay at home in this construction, just as Szabolcsi's (60) leads us to expect given that prenominal possessors in the language do not force a specific or definite interpretation on their containing DP. Striking confirmation of this comes from contrasting the BE construction with the BE-LV construction: in the latter, the possessor behaves like a clausal argument not only in taking nominative case, but also in allowing adverbs to intervene between the possessor and the possessee.

(64)   *Adverb Placement in Isbukun Bunun Possession Sentences*

    a. *'Aiza   'inak **laupaku** 'uvaz.
        BE$_{exist}$ I.GEN now   child
        'I have a child now.'

    b. 'Aiza-an   saikin **laupaku** 'uvaz.
        BE$_{exist}$-LV I.NOM now   child
        'I have a child now.'

Szabolcsi's hypothesis that the need for possessor extraction in the Hungarian construction is driven by the specificity effect induced by prenominal possessors therefore receives significant independent support from the Isbukun Bunun data. There remains, however, an important question: why, exactly, should movement of the possessor in Hungarian (and Quechua) eliminate the specificity effect? Why, for example, does the trace or copy of the moved possessor not itself induce such an effect? Szabolcsi (1994, 230-231) is forced to leave this question open, and so, for the time being, am I.

Before closing, it is important to note that Szabolcsi's analysis of the Hungarian possession construction is not uncontested, and that Den Dikken (1999) has offered strong arguments for diverging from some of its details. In particular, he shows that full DP possessors in Hungarian possession sentences trigger possessive agreement in a manner reminiscent of pronominal DP-internal possessors. This suggests that Hungarian possession sentences involve the dative possessor binding a silent pronoun inside the possessee DP, rather than being moved from that position.[26] This argument seems convincing for Hungarian, but it is important to note that it does not threaten Szabolcsi's more general point that possession sentences are built on top of possessed DPs, nor the idea that the semantics of the possession relation come from a functional head inside DP (this point is reinforced by the data from Isbukun Bunun, where the underlying structure originally suggested by Szabolcsi for Hungarian actually surfaces).

To conclude, Szabolcsi's (1981, 1983, 1994) analysis of possessed DPs and possession sentences in Hungarian motivated two ideas that form the foundation of the Freeze/Kayne approach to the typology of predicative possession. The first is that possessors are introduced in a particular structural position within DP, but may be moved from that position. The second is that possession sentences can be built on top of possessed DPs by embedding such a DP under an existential verb–in Hungarian, this additionally requires that the possessor be extracted, for (somewhat mysterious) reasons having to do with the semantic requirement of the existential verb for a non-specific DP. In the next two subsections, we will see how Freeze (1992) and Kayne (1993) built on these foundational ideas.

26. As Anna Szabolcsi points out to me, however, (pers. comm.), it remains a mystery on this approach why the resumptives in question can never be overt.

2.2.2   The Locative Paradigm: Freeze (1992) and P Incorporation

2.2.2.1   Freeze (1992): The Fundamentals

Freeze (1992) is a paper whose stated goal is to unify the analysis of predicate locatives, existentials, and possession sentences, examining data from a range of different languages (Freeze does not discuss auxiliary uses of HAVE and BE, which is a major focus of Kayne (1993)). Freeze's main claim is that these three types of expression, embodied in English (65) and Russian (66), "are all derived from a single and maximally simple abstract syntactic structure (D-structure)" (Freeze 1992, 553; the examples are respectively Freeze's (1) and (2)).

(65)   a.   **Predicate locative:** The book is on the bench.

     b.   **Existential:** There is a book on the bench.

     c.   **HAVE:** Lupe has a book.

(66)   *Russian*

     a.   Kniga   byla na stole.
          Book.NOM.FEM was on table.LOC

          'The book was on the table.' (Predicate locative)

     b.   Na stole   byla kniga.
          On table.LOC was book.NOM.FEM

          'There was a book on the table.' (Existential)

     c.   U menja   byla sestra.
          At me.GEN was sister.NOM.FEM

          'I had a sister.' (HAVE)

In particular, the unified D-structure that he proposes for such sentences is as follows (Freeze 1992, 558; based on his (7)).[27]

---

27. See Langacker (1968, 68) for an earlier proposal on the D-structure of possession sentences in French, which has much in common with Freeze's proposal.

(67)   *The D-structure of Predicate Locatives, Existentials and Possession Sentences* (Freeze 1992)

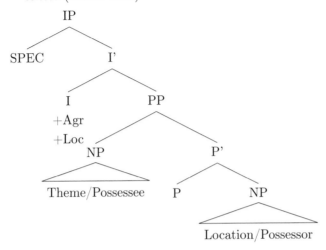

All three construction-types have a PP predicate as their argument-structural core, with the Location/Possessor occurring as the complement of the adposition in question, and the Theme/Possessee occurring as its specifier. The copula is held to be a realization of the I (inflection) node carrying a [+Agr] and a [+Loc] feature (this [+Loc] feature is what crucially distinguishes the locative/existential copula from the predicative copula that occurs with NP and AP predicates). This I node, which is spelled out either as HAVE or as some variant of BE depending on what else occurs during the derivation, takes the PP as its complement directly.[28] Note that Freeze's theory entails that all of the thematic roles associated with these constructions are assigned inside the PP predicate. Freeze (1992) therefore falls within the camp of theories that treat HAVE and BE as thematically inert.

Existentials and predicate locatives differ from each other only in terms of which argument moves to spec-IP (the subject position). In predicate locatives, the theme argument moves into this position, as shown in (68). In existentials the P' node that dominates the preposition and the Location argument moves to this position instead, as shown in (69). The trees in (68) and (69) are based on Freeze's (9) (Freeze 1992, 559).

---

28. Given that the copula is a realization of the I node, one wonders how Freeze's approach would extend to cases where *have* and *be* occur in past participle form embedded under the perfect auxiliary, as in *I have been here for some time* and *I have never had any such problems*. Freeze is silent on this issue, however.

(68)   *Predicate Locative: Theme Moves to Spec-IP*

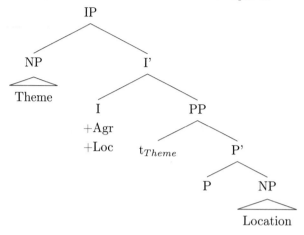

(69)   *Existential: P' Containing Location Moves to Spec-IP*

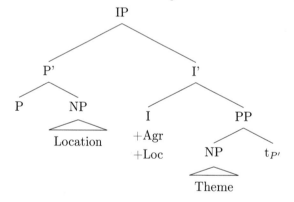

The choice between these two movement options is claimed to be determined by the definiteness of the theme: if the theme is definite, it moves to subject possession. If the theme is indefinite, then the derivation in (69) ensues, and the P' containing the Location argument moves to the subject position instead.[29]

29. In the case of existentials, something more must be said to account for (i) expletive subjects in English and other languages, and (ii) the locative clitic pronouns that surface in such sentences in many languages, including many prominent Romance languages. There is also a third question concerning how to account for copula allomorphy in languages that distinguish existential/locative BE from predicative BE, and in cases where the locative copula patterns allomorphically with the predicative copula and against the existential one. Freeze presents answers to each of these questions. Since these questions are orthogonal to the main thrust of Freeze's paper but are nonetheless highly relevant to the present investigation, I postpone discussion of them until Chapter 5.

The case and agreement properties of these constructions are accounted for as follows. In the case of the predicate locative, the assignment of these features is straightforward, and proceeds as standard in the Government and Binding framework assumed by Freeze. The movement of the theme to spec-IP in (68) allows the theme to receive Nominative Case, and also triggers Spec-Head Agreement, so that the phi-features of the theme are copied onto the I node. The location argument instead receives inherent Case from P. In the existential also, the location is similarly licensed by inherent Case from the P. Case assignment to the theme in the existential construction is somewhat more involved. In (69), I assigns Nominative Case to the theme under government. Ordinarily, government of the theme by I would be blocked by the fact that the theme rests in the specifier of a PP, which is a barrier to government (Chomsky 1986, 10). However, the movement of P' to spec-IP in (69) leaves PP without a head, thereby voiding its barrierhood and allowing Case-assignment to take place. Freeze assumes that, as a result of this Case assigment, I is able to agree with the theme argument despite the lack of a Spec-Head relation between the two. Freeze notes the apparent problem that in many languages the copula fails to display such agreement overtly in existentials, but attributes it to language-particular idiosyncrasies (1992, 562).

Turning to possession sentences, Freeze (1992, 576-580) argues that such sentences are closely allied to existentials as opposed to predicate locatives. His evidence here is of a similar sort to that of Lyons (1968), who is cited by Freeze, and for a much larger sample of languages by Clark (1970/1978), who is not cited by him— namely, that there are many languages (such as Russian) where the copula used in possession sentences is the same one as is used in existentials, and that there are many languages in which the order Location-Theme in the existential is mirrored by the order Possessor-Possessee in a possession sentence. Hence, possession sentences in BE languages simply *are* existential sentences, the only difference residing in the [+/− Human] feature of the Location (which can, in some such languages, lead to a special adposition being chosen in possession sentences–an example would be the Russian preposition *u*).[30]

HAVE-Possessives in languages that have them are like existentials in that the Location(=Possessor) moves to subject position rather than the Theme(=Possessee). They differ only in the behavior of the adposition: in HAVE sentences, this adposition head-moves to the I-node, incorporating into it. This

---

30. No mention is made by Freeze of what Stassen calls Predicativization, which, as we have seen, involves a predicative rather than a locative/existential copula in languages where these are distinguished morphologically. It follows that Predicativization must fall outside of Freeze's Locative Paradigm.

I+P combination is spelled out as HAVE (Freeze 1992:588; the tree below is based on his (80)).

(70)   *HAVE: Possessor Moves to Spec-IP; P Incorporates into I*

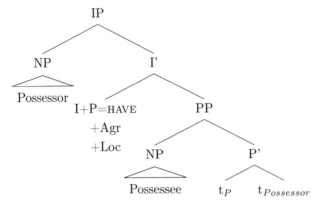

It is left open how Case assignment takes place in a structure like (70). Freeze (1992, 588) suggests two possibilities: either the I+P complex assigns Case to the possessor, with the possessee receiving a default Case (Freeze notes that default Case "is often accusative"); or the possessor is Case-licensed by P before movement, and the I+P complex assigns Case to the Theme. The resolution of Agreement in HAVE sentences is not discussed at all.

So-called WITH-Possessives receive a similar analysis to the HAVE-Possessive, the only claimed difference being that I and P come together via a process of "reanalysis," whose exact nature is left vague.[31] As a result of such reanalysis, it is predicted that such strings as *está com* 'be with' in the Portuguese WITH construction in (71) form a constituent, rather than the string *com fome* 'with hunger' (Freeze 1992, 587; his (76a)).

---

31. What Freeze has in mind cannot be identical in nature to the V+P reanalysis processes that were then standard in analyses of preposition stranding (see Hornstein and Weinberg (1981) for an example of such a reanalysis proposal; also Baltin and Postal (1996) for more extensive references and a critique of reanalysis proposals in general). This is because the standard sort of reanalysis required adjacency between V+P in order for it to occur. However, to deal with WITH-Possessives in SVO languages like Portuguese and Icelandic, Freeze's reanalysis process must be capable of applying without linear adjacency (since it must unite I and P across the intervening Possessee argument). Given this, it is not clear how exactly Freeze's reanalysis process would differ from the head-movement operation implicated in the derivation he proposes for HAVE sentences.

(71)   *Portuguese WITH-Possessive*

O   menino está com fome.
The child   is   with hunger
'The child is hungry.'

In support for the idea that such structures involve BE and WITH being reanalyzed as a constituent, Freeze cites the fact that the following interrogative sentence is bad, compatible with the idea that *com fome* is not a constituent, and therefore ineligible to be moved (Freeze 1992, 587; fn 25, his (i)).

(72)   *Com que   está o   menino?
       With what is   the child
       'With what is the child?' = 'What does the child have?'

See Levinson (2011) and Chapter 5 of this work for a critique of Freeze's attempt to assimilate WITH-Possessives to his Locative Paradigm.

There is a subtype of possession sentence cross-linguistically that Freeze is forced to assign a different D-structure, separate from the rest of his Locative Paradigm. The construction in question is precisely that discussed by Szabolcsi (1981, 1994) for Hungarian, termed the Adnominal Possessive by Stassen (2009), and referred to as THEME-SUBJECT 'HAVE' by Freeze (1992, 589). Henceforth, I will use Stassen's term. Freeze (1992, 590; fn 27, his (i)) cites the following example from Szabolcsi (1981, 276; her (43)).[32]

(73)   Péter-nek van kar-ja-∅.   (Hungarian)
       Peter-DAT BE arm-POSS-3SG
       'Peter has an arm.'

The problem, as Freeze puts it, is that such structures "cannot derive from the universal locative D-structure in [Freeze's (7), my (67) above–NJM], largely because there is no preposition and thus no PP predicate" (1992, 589). Freeze (1992, 589) still claims some relationship between the Adnominal Possessives and the Locative Paradigm based on the idea that "a possessor is widely acknowledged to be a location semantically,"[33] and on the intuition that "the genitive marking of a possessor and

---

32. Freeze (1992, 590) claims that his analysis differs from Szabolcsi's in that "she does not mention predicative locatives or existentials." This is untrue for existentials, since Szabolcsi extensively discusses the role of the verb *van* as an existential copula in the course of explaining the necessity of possessor extraction in Hungarian possession sentences, as discussed in section 2.2.1.

33. The idea that locations and possessors are semantically identical is far from innocuous, and is not adopted in this book. Tham (2004), discussed in detail later in this chapter, is an extended argument that possessors and locations must be distinguished both semantically and syntactically.

the P of a P-marked locative subject are equivalent." Nevertheless, the D-structure
Freeze assigns to the Adnominal Possessive differs from the one associated with
the Locative Paradigm in terms of where the Possessor itself is introduced. In
Adnominal Possessives, the Possessor is introduced in Spec-NP, rather than in the
complement of a PP as in the Locative Paradigm. This D-structure is schematized
in (74) below, which is a simplified version of Freeze's (1992, 590) tree in his (82),
adjusted to have initial rather than final specifiers. Note that, aside from the lack
of a PP in (74), this D-structure also differs from the one Freeze assigns to the
Locative Paradigm in terms of *the relative hierarchical positions of the Possessor
and the Possessee*. In the Adnominal Possessive, the Possessor c-commands the
Possessee at D-structure; in the Locative Paradigm it is the other way around.

(74)   *The D-structure of Adnominal Possessives* (Freeze 1992)

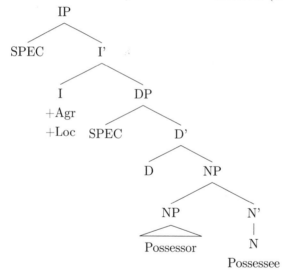

In summary, Freeze's (1992) account unifies Locatives, Existentials, and three
types of possession sentence (HAVE-Possessives, WITH-Possessives, and ones based
around existential BE plus a PP possessor). HAVE and BE are taken to be two realizations of the same locative/existential copula, with HAVE differing structurally from
BE only in having an adposition incorporated into it. The fact that this account
attributes greater structural complexity to HAVE than to BE is attractive, because it
potentially forms the basis of an understanding for why HAVE constructions are so
much rarer than BE-based possession constructions across languages. The Adnominal Possessive is assigned a different D-structure, and so is not unified with the
other subtypes of sentence completely, although it is built out of some of the same

pieces as the other constructions (including an existential/locative copula, represented in Freeze's account by an I node carrying a [+Loc] feature). Another major subtype of possession construction recognized in this book (and in Stassen 2009) but not discussed by Freeze is Predicativization. This type of construction, since it involves predicative BE rather than locative/existential BE, would presumably fall outside of Freeze's Locative Paradigm also.

2.2.3   A Modular Approach to BE vs. HAVE: Kayne (1993)

2.2.3.1   Kayne (1993): The Fundamentals

Kayne (1993) (which was reprinted in 2000; all citations are from the reprinted version) is a paper that attempts to relate HAVE and BE to one another in a manner similar to Freeze (1992). However, the paper goes beyond Freeze (1992) by attempting to provide a unified account of HAVE and BE that encompasses both possessive and aspectual uses of these forms, with a particular focus on various types of HAVE/BE alternation in Romance auxiliary systems. In seeking such a unification, Kayne (1993/2000, 107) takes inspiration from a suggestion of Benveniste (1966, §15) that the development of HAVE and BE as auxiliaries in the history of Indo-European languages should be considered as parallel to their development as verbs of possession.[34]

This paper has been immensely influential on subsequent discussions of predicative possession and of auxiliary selection. The possession-related literature that has built on or reacted against this paper is discussed more extensively later in this chapter, particularly in section 2.3. Since the issue of auxiliary uses of HAVE and BE is not treated in any depth in this book, I do not review any of the vast amount of work on auxiliary selection that has emerged in the wake of Kayne (1993/2000). However, see Bentley (2006), Bjorkman (2011), Coon and Preminger (2012), D'Alessandro (2012), D'Alessandro and Ledgeway (2010), D'Alessandro and Roberts (2010), Ledgeway (2000), Loporcaro (2007), Sorace (2004), Steddy and van Urk (2013), and references cited there for various perspectives.

---

34. It is worthwhile to emphasize that Kayne does not imply that Benveniste himself was making any claim about the HAVE/BE relation at the level of the synchronic grammar. Moreover, Iatridou (1995, 199-200) and Belvin (1996, 221) both stress that Benveniste was merely noting the cross-linguistic and semantic correspondence between the two, and making the diachronic observation that HAVE constructions systematically replaced earlier BE constructions over time in the auxiliary systems of many Indo-European languages, much as they did in the possession sentences of many languages in the family.

Although the main focus of the paper is HAVE and BE in their auxiliary uses, and more precisely on the morphosyntactic conditioning factors that produce HAVE/BE alternations in (Romance) auxiliary selection, Kayne (1993/2000:107) notes that an understanding of the structure of possession sentences is a prerequisite if the auxiliary uses of these verbs are to be unified with their main verb uses. To this end, he proposes the following as the D-structure underlying possession sentences in BE languages of the Hungarian type and HAVE languages of the English type, roughly following Szabolcsi (1981) (Kayne 1993/2000, 110; his (7)).

(75)   *D-Structure for Possession Sentences, Kayne (1993/2000)*

      ...BE $[_{DP}$ Spec D/P $[_{AgrP}$ DP$_{poss}$ $[_{Agr'}$ Agr QP/NP $]$ $]$ $]$

The element notated D/P is a *prepositional determiner* (analogous to a prepositional complementizer), which is capable of assigning an oblique Case to its specifier in some languages. Languages in which D/P has this capability include Hungarian, and this is Kayne's account of the dative case assigned to possessors in spec-DP as investigated by Szabolcsi (1981, 1983). In other languages, D/P does not have the ability to assign an oblique Case in this way. One such language is English. This means that, in a language like English, the possessor in a possession sentence must raise to a higher position to be licensed, namely, the subject position.[35]

This results in a representation like (76), from Kayne (1993/2000, 110, his (9)).

(76)   *Schematic S-Structure for Possession, Kayne (1993/2000)*

      ...DP$_{possessor}$ BE $[_{DP}$ t$_{possessor}$ D/P $[_{AgrP}$ t$_{possessor}$ $[_{Agr'}$ Agr QP/NP $]$ $]$ $]$

However, since Spec DP is an A-bar position, (76) is apparently ruled out by the constraint against Improper Movement, which bans movement from an A-bar position into an A position. Kayne proposes that this problem is eliminated via incorporation (in the sense of Baker 1988) of the D/P head into BE. Kayne (1993/2000:111) suggests that this incorporation, "in the spirit of Baker's (1988) Government Transparency Corollary," allows D/P to inherit the A-position status of BE, thus voiding

---

35. Case-licensing of a possessor in an ordinary possessed DP in English works somewhat differently. In Kayne's (1993/2000, 109) approach, DP-internal possessors are licensed by Agr (which is spelled out as the so-called genitive morpheme (*'s*)) in conjunction with a D head. This D head must be silent if definite (so that *John's sister* is syntactically *THE John's sister*). If indefinite, it is spelled out as *of* and attracts the possessee NP/QP into its specifier, yielding *a sister of John's* from the D-structure in (i).

(i)   ...$[_{DP}$ SPEC of$_{D/P}$ $[_{AgrP}$ John 's$_{AgrS}$ $[_{QP}$ a sister $]$ $]$ $]$

spec-D/P's A-bar status and allowing the movement depicted in (76) to proceed. The complex head formed by incorporating D/P into BE is realized as HAVE (in this, Kayne is in agreement with Freeze (1992)).[36]

For HAVE and BE in their aspectual auxiliary uses, Kayne proposes a structure that is the same as (75) except for the category of the phrase embedded under D/P– whereas for possession sentences this structure consists of an Agr head embedding an NP/QP, in aspectual uses D/P embeds a verbal substructure. The exact content of this verbal substructure varies from language to language in a manner that accounts for part of the cross-Romance variation in auxiliary alternations, but a schematic version of the D-structure for the perfect aspect is provided in (77) (from Kayne 1993/2000, 111; his (14)).

(77)   *Schematic D-Structure for the Perfect, Kayne (1993/2000)*

         ...BE $[_{DP}$ SPEC D/P ... $[_{VP}$ DP$_{Subj}$ [V DP$_{Obj}$]]]

The core of Kayne's proposal for HAVE/BE alternations in the perfect aspect is the same as for possession sentences: the specifier of the D/P head is an A-bar position. The subject requires Case, and must raise to an A-position above BE to receive it. However, this would require successive cyclic movement via spec-D/P, thereby triggering a violation of the Improper Movement constraint. Therefore, the subject should be stuck inside the DP headed by D/P, and the derivation should crash as a result of the subject violating the Case Filter. The way around this problem is the same as it was in Kayne's account of possession sentences: the A-bar status of spec-D/P must be voided somehow if the derivation is to converge. One way to achieve this is for D/P to incorporate into BE, yielding HAVE. In some languages, this is the only means of voiding the A-bar status of spec-D/P, so that all verbs take HAVE as the perfect auxiliary in all of their forms. Such languages include Spanish and English.

However, other languages have alternative ways of voiding the A-bar status of spec-D/P, which do not require this head to incorporate into BE, so that BE can surface as such rather than being spelled out as HAVE. In some languages, these alternative means are always available; such languages will have BE as the perfect

---

36. The main point of difference between Kayne (1993/2000) and Freeze (1992) is in the category of the phrase embedded under BE: for Freeze (1992) it is a PP, for Kayne it is a DP. Additionally, the possessee c-commands the possessor in the D-structure Freeze assigns to the Locative Paradigm, whereas the opposite holds in Kayne's account. However, the D-Structure that Freeze (1992) assigns to Adnominal Possessives (his *theme-subject* possession sentences), which Freeze puts outside his Locative Paradigm and does not connect to transitive HAVE constructions, is almost identical to the D-Structure that Kayne (1993/2000) proposes.

auxiliary across the board. On the other hand, in some languages these alternative means may be only selectively available, with their availability in a given derivation being contingent on a variety of syntactic factors, as we shall see. Languages which have such selectively-available means of avoiding incorporation of D/P into BE will exhibit HAVE/BE alternations.

One such means, for example, is available for languages in which D/P embeds a verbal substructure large enough to contain AgrS, depicted as (78) below (Kayne 1993/2000, 116; his (38)).

(78)   *Perfect Aspect with "Large" Verbal Substructure*

    ...BE $[_{DP}$ SPEC D/P [AgrS AgrO VP]]

Kayne proposes that AgrS may incorporate into D/P, so long as AgrS is activated by a DP landing in its specifier. Since AgrS is itself an A-related projection, this incorporation is sufficient to void the A-bar status of spec-D/P. The DP subject can then move into the matrix subject position above BE without the D/P having to incorporate into BE, and so the perfect auxiliary in this scenario will surface as BE rather than HAVE.

This proposal allows Kayne to account for dialects in which the HAVE/BE alternation is sensitive to the phi-features of the subject. There are many subtypes of such dialects, which vary in terms of which combinations of person/number features on the subject require BE and which require HAVE, although the most common system is one in which 1st and 2nd person subjects take BE and 3rd person subjects take HAVE (Kayne 1993/2000, 116, 118). An example of such a system, presented by D'Alessandro (2012, 5; her (2)) for the Ariellese dialect, is provided in (79). This micro-variation can be captured on Kayne's approach in terms of a parameter on AgrS with respect to which sets of phi-features are able to activate it. In the most common system (exemplified in (79)), AgrS will be specified so that only 1st and 2nd person DPs will be able to activate it, and 3rd person DPs will be unable to.

(79)   *Person-Conditioned Perfect Auxiliary Selection in Ariellese*

Person/Number	Singular	Plural
1st	(Ji) **so** magnatə I **am** eaten	(Nu) **seme** magnitə We **are** eaten
2nd	(Tu) **si** magnatə You **are** eaten	(Vu) **sete** magnitə You.pl **are** eaten
3rd	(Essə) **a** magnatə s/he **has** eaten	(Jissə) **a** magnitə They **have** eaten

Hence, if the subject is 1st or 2nd person, AgrS is activated and incorporates into
D/P, eliminating its A-bar status and allowing subject extraction. Since D/P does
not need to incorporate into BE, BE surfaces as such. If the subject is 3rd person,
on the other hand, it will not be eligible to activate AgrS, meaning that it will not
be possible to void spec-D/P's A-bar status by incorporating AgrS into D/P. Such
a derivation can converge only if D/P incorporates into BE, and this is why 3rd
person subjects take HAVE in dialects like Ariellese. Systems with different person
sensitivity patterns can be captured by varying which feature combinations are
eligible to activate AgrS.

Kayne is able to extend this basic system to account for varieties in which the
HAVE/BE alternation is sensitive to whether object clitic climbing has taken place
(clitic climbing forces HAVE in some dialects; see Kayne 1993/2000, 116-117), varieties in which the alternation is sensitive to tense (119-120), and also more familiar
varieties in which the alternation is sensitive to the unaccusative vs. unergative/-
transitive distinction (120-121).

To summarize, then, Kayne (1993/2000) proposes a theory of the argument structure of possession sentences in which predicative possession is built "on top of"
attributive possession, in the sense that such sentences involve embedding a possessed DP under a copula. In this, he builds on insights from Szabolcsi (1981),
extending this idea to the wider typology of possession sentences. HAVE and BE are
taken to be two sides of the same coin, with HAVE being more complex than BE in
that it involves the incorporation of an adpositional element into BE, in the spirit of
Freeze (1992). Since Kayne's approach is like Freeze's in attributing greater structural complexity to HAVE than to BE, it inherits an apparent advantage of Freeze's
approach: this added complexity could play a role in explaining why HAVE is so much
rarer than BE. In addition, Kayne (1993/2000) goes a step further than Freeze in
bringing aspectual auxiliary uses of HAVE and BE into a unified theory of the syntax of these verbs. This unified account also provided a framework for investigating
HAVE/BE alternations in auxiliary systems, setting the agenda for later work on
this topic.

2.3   Extensions and Reactions to the Freeze/Kayne Tradition

The aim of this section is to review a small part of the enormous literature that has
extended and/or reacted to the claims originating from the works of Freeze (1992),
Kayne (1993), and Szabolcsi (1981, 1983, 1994). The focus will be on three themes:

(i) parametric variation and its interaction with the domain of predicative possession; (ii) evidence that the theory must accommodate more than one underlying
syntactic source for possession sentences; and (iii) the nature of the relationship
between HAVE and BE.

Section 2.3.1 deals with theme (i) by examining proposed comparative syntactic
correlations between being a HAVE/BE language and other syntactic properties.
The generative literature in this area makes key use of the Freeze/Kayne idea that
HAVE is the result of incorporating an adposition into BE. Theme (ii) is dealt with in
section 2.3.2 via a close examination of a recent study by Boneh and Sichel (2010)
of predicative possession in Palestinian Arabic, which leads to the conclusion that
any solution to the too-many-(surface)-structures puzzle must address not only
the HAVE/BE question, but also the question of how the various subtypes of BE
construction are related to each other. In sections 2.3.3 and 2.3.4, theme (iii) is
explored by examining proposals that dispute the view that HAVE and BE are to
be related to each other via P Incorporation. Section 2.3.3 briefly discusses one
possible counterproposal to the P Incorporation view–namely, the idea that HAVE
is a lexical transitive verb which may simply be missing from a language's lexicon,
and which is not related in any grammatical way to BE. This idea, which I will
show to be untenable, has recently been advocated by Błaszczak (2007). Section
2.3.4 looks at what I take to be a more promising way of relating HAVE and BE–this
is the view, put forward by Hoekstra (1994), Isačenko (1974, 60), and Jung (2011),
that HAVE is nothing other than the transitive form of BE.

2.3.1   Principles and Parameters and the HAVE/BE Question

By tying the HAVE/BE difference to a syntactic operation (P Incorporation), the
Freeze/Kayne tradition opened the door to a new research program in comparative syntax. Could it be that certain other features of the grammar of a language
might interfere with P Incorporation, or even force it to take place? If so, then we
might expect to find correlations between having HAVE and having certain other
morphosyntactic properties. The search was on to identify such correlations, and
to explain them using the theoretical tools of the Principles and Parameters framework.[37] The rest of this section reviews three attempts to pursue this question.

---

37. Some years before the Principles & Parameters framework coalesced, Isačenko (1974:64-76)
made a series of proposals about what correlates with being a HAVE language vs. being a BE
language. Amongst these proposals were antecedents of the ideas regarding psych constructions
put forward by Noonan (1993) and Harley (1995, 1998) below. For space reasons, I do not review
Isačenko's proposals themselves here.

2.3.1.1 Mahajan (1994)

Perhaps the most ambitious attempt to identify and explain a comparative syntactic correlation between the HAVE/BE issue and other syntactic properties is Mahajan (1994). This paper proposes that ergativity, head directionality, and prevalence of oblique subject constructions are tied to each other and to the HAVE/BE question. In particular, the precise correlations argued for are as follows (Mahajan 1994, 2; his I-IV):

(80)   *Mahajan's Proposed Correlations*

   I.   SVO languages are never ergative. Ergativity is found only in verb final and verb initial languages.

   II.   Ergative languages are very often split ergative.

   III. Ergative languages usually lack a verb corresponding to Romance and Germanic HAVE. The auxiliary (wherever applicable) in ergative constructions is BE.

   IV.   Ergative languages usually have a proliferation of oblique (non-nominative) subject constructions in addition to the ergative construction itself.

Mahajan's (1994, 2) major claim is that all of the correlations in (80) are related to basic word order: ergativity, lacking HAVE, and having many types of oblique subject are properties of languages where the verb is initial or final. As we will now see, however, there are severe empirical problems for the parts of this claim that pertain most directly to possession sentences.

The first two correlations are of some interest still even after more evidence has accrued. Correlation I is remarkably robust, as far as I know, although the World Atlas of Language Structures (WALS) claims one potential counter-example (namely the Arauan language Paumarí), which merits further investigation. The prevalence of split ergativity is cited by Mahajan (1994, 9) as being parallel to the prevalence of HAVE/BE splits in auxiliary systems, which are triggered by many of the same conditioning factors, as has been widely remarked upon. While these generalizations are striking, they are not directly relevant to the domain of possession sentences, and I will leave them aside here.

Correlations III and IV are much more relevant to our concerns; III is a direct claim about HAVE and BE, and IV deals with oblique subjects, which are commonly found not only in possession sentences but also in psych constructions (which are closely aligned with the domain of possession in many ways). Unfortunately, these generalizations (and their relationship to Mahajan's claim about the relevance of word order) also turn out to be much less convincing than the previous pair.

As reflected in its formulation, Correlation III is not absolute, with Basque being a prominent example of an ergative HAVE language noted by Mahajan (1994, 12, fn 2); WALS furthermore yields West Greenlandic, Lakhota, and Guaraní as ergative languages which have HAVE.[38] Moreover, Mahajan's claim that word-order is the key issue predicts that only SVO languages should have HAVE, and this prediction is even more robustly counterexemplified. It is falsified on the SOV side by many West Germanic languages (as Mahajan 1994, 9-10 acknowledges), by Santiago del Estero Quechua (spoken in Argentina and discussed in Chapter 3), and by up to nineteen other languages of the twenty-one listed by WALS as having SOV order and a transitive HAVE verb.[39] VSO languages with HAVE, which are also problematic for Mahajan's prediction, include some dialects of Breton (see Jouitteau and Rezac 2008), as well as three languages named by WALS (Lillooet, Maasai, and Krongo).

No typological database allows me to evaluate correlation IV straightforwardly, but it should be noted that nominative-accusative languages with a number of different kinds of oblique subjects are also in existence (Finnish, Icelandic, and Russian spring to mind; as do many languages of the Quechua family; for discussion of oblique subjects in Quechua, see Cole 1982; Hermon 1985, 2001; Jake 1985; Muysken 1977; Willgohs and Farrell 2009).

While it might seem redundant to review Mahajan's analysis of the correlations in (80) given these fatal empirical problems, I will introduce some of its details in order to give an "in-principle" demonstration of the sort of reasoning involved in extending a theory of the HAVE/BE question to make broader comparative syntactic predictions.

Mahajan (1994, 4) takes Kayne (1993) as background, but argues that the ability of the adpositional element to incorporate into BE is contingent on linear adjacency between the verb and the adposition. In an SOV language, the object will inevitably intervene, as shown in (81), so that incorporation cannot take place and it is impossible to derive HAVE. As (82) shows, on the other hand, no such problem arises in an

---

38. WALS additionally names Georgian and Abkhaz, but both of these languages (see Hewitt 1989, 96 for Abkhaz and Lomashvili 2011 for Georgian) have constructions in which the possessor is dative and the possessee is absolutive, suggesting a non-transitive structure (perhaps a BE-APPL structure along the lines I argue to exist in Cochabamba Quechua in Chapter 3). These are not HAVE languages, therefore, but a particular type of BE language.

39. Georgian and Abkhaz are included in the WALS list, but should be excluded for reasons discussed in the previous footnote.

SVO language.[40] Similarly, the movement of the verb to a higher clausal position in VSO languages is argued to render incorporation impossible.

(81) *Incorporation Impossible: SOV*

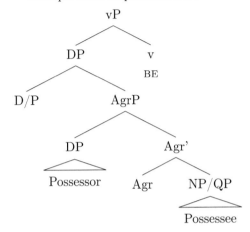

(82) *Incorporation Possible: SVO*

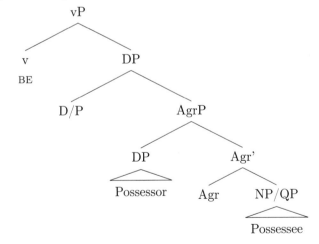

40. The trees in (81) and (82) follow the published version of Kayne (1993/2000), which assumes that the adpositional element is in D/P. Mahajan himself reverts of an earlier version of Kayne (1993/2000) in which the adposition takes the possessor as its complement, and that PP is generated in Spec-AgrP. This difference is not relevant here, although it is worth noting that this earlier formulation raises the question of how the P is able to incorporate at all, given that it would be moving from inside a complex specifier.

Thus, the idea was that word-order properties of a language can prevent the formation of HAVE by interfering with the P Incorporation operation that derives it. While flawed for a number of empirical and conceptual[41] reasons, Mahajan (1994) thus represents an ambitious early attempt to identify and explain comparative syntactic correlations between the sorts of possession sentence that a language has and its other syntactic properties.

2.3.1.2   Harley (1995, 2002)

In her (1995) dissertation and her (2002) paper, Harley suggests a rather different correlation than Mahajan's–namely, that the pieces out of which possession sentences are built are a subset of those used to build ditransitives, and that therefore the relative hierarchical relations between the two internal arguments in the ditransitives of a language can be predicted from the structure of its possession sentences, and vice versa. Harley (1995, 201-208; 2002, 50-53) further suggests, partly following Noonan (1993), that the structure of psych verbs is parasitic on the structure of possession sentences, so that correlations between the structure of possession sentences and the structure of psych-constructions are also predicted.

Specifically, Harley (2002, 23-24, adapted from her (33)) proposes that all possession sentences involve one of the following two structures. The structure in (84) is also what underlies predicate locatives such as *Mary is in the garden.*

(83)   *Possession in HAVE Languages and Certain BE Languages*

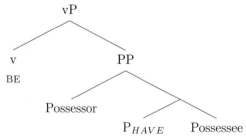

41. One conceptual problem concerns the fact that Mahajan (1994) relies on linear adjacency to constrain a syntactic operation, whereas movement is usually conditioned only by structural factors. Mahajan (1994, 1) suggests that the analysis might be translatable into more structural terms if head-final orders are all derived by movement as required by the Linear Correspondence Axiom (Kayne 1994), for then the requisite phrasal movement might bleed incorporation. However, even this would not be enough to make the desired prediction follow: one would still have to rule out a derivation in which D/P incorporation applies before the possessed DP moves past the verb.

(84)   *Predicate Locatives and Locational Possession Structures*

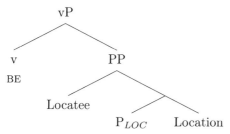

Except for the fact that it implicitly denies that the possessor is assigned its possessive thematic role inside the possessed DP,[42] the structure in (83) has much in common with the structure advocated by Kayne (1993/2000): the possessor c-commands the possessee underlyingly, and an adpositional element mediates between them. The structure in (84), on the other hand, is almost identical to the structure assumed to underly the locatives, possessives, and existentials in Freeze (1992). Hence, Harley's theory is one in which there are (at least) two D-structures for possession sentences. The main differences between the two stem from the fact that a different adposition is used in each case: in (83), the adposition (labelled P_{HAVE}) is one that takes a Possessor as its specifier and a Possessee as its complement; (84) instead contains a Locative adposition P_{LOC}, which has the opposite argument structure. Crucially, P_{HAVE} in (83) can incorporate into BE to yield HAVE, but whether it does or not varies from language to language. In other words, (83) can also surface as a BE construction, just as (84) can. This is important because it means that BE languages are not treated as a natural class: one sort of BE language is closely allied to the class of HAVE languages, but the other is not.[43] As we shall see, this has implications for the predictions that the theory makes about ditransitives, to which we now turn.

Harley (2002, 24) suggests that Universal Grammar allows ditransitives to be built in two ways, by merging a causative light-verb with either a PP headed by P_{HAVE} or one headed by P_{LOC}. Both of these options are available in Engiish, and this is what produces the dative alternation.

---

42. Harley (2002, 27, fn 10) sets aside languages like Hungarian and similar languages, so it is not clear how the analysis would extend to languages in which predicative possession is very clearly built on top of attributive possession.

43. Harley (1995, 2002) does not discuss what would happen if P_{LOC} in (84) incorporated into BE, but one could imagine treating BELONG-type verbs in this way.

(85)   *Ditransitive Structure with* P_{HAVE}: *Double Object*
        'Mary gave John a book.'

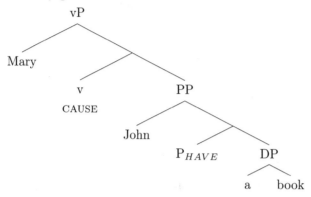

(86)   *Ditransitive Structure with* P_{LOC}: *To-Dative*
        'Mary gave a book to John.'

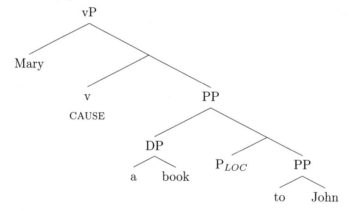

According to this picture, ditransitives contain a substructure that is also contained in possession sentences–all that differs between the two is the light-verb which embeds this substructure. If so, then the (un)availability of a crucial part of this substructure should influence both types of construction simultaneously; we predict correlations between the sorts of possession sentence a language allows and the structure of its ditransitives. Harley (2002, 24-24) assumes that P_{LOC} is available in all languages, since all languages have predicate locatives of some kind. However, languages vary as to whether they also have P_{HAVE}.[44] If a given

_____

44. This leads to a prediction regarding ditransitives cross-linguistically: all languages should have at least a *to*-dative-like ditransitive in which the Theme c-commands the Goal, and some

language does have P_{HAVE}, then it will have possession sentences in which the Possessor clearly c-commands the Possessee (whether of the HAVE type or of the BE type), and it will also have the Double Object Construction, in which the Goal c-commands the Theme. If a language lacks P_{HAVE}, it will use a locative structure like (84) for possession sentences (i.e., a subtype of BE construction in which the Possessee c-commands the Possessor underlyingly), and its ditransitives will all be of the *to*-dative type in (86).

Taking inspiration from Noonan (1993), Harley goes on to suggest that the availability of stative transitive psych verbs is also parasitic on the availability of P_{HAVE}. Noonan (1993) had noted that Irish lacks transitive psych verbs like *fear, know,* and *love,* and that the translational equivalents of these verbs are identical in appearance to Irish possession sentences, which are of the Locational Possessive type (examples from Harley 2002:52, her (74) and (75); citing Noonan 1993).

(87)   *Irish Psych Constructions*

    a.   Tá gaeilge ag Fliodhais.
            BE Irish   at Fliodhais
            'Fliodhais knows Irish.'

    b.   Tá eagla roimh an bpúca ag Ailill.
            BE fear before the Puca at Ailill
            'Ailill fears the Puca.'

    c.   Tá meas ar Meadhbh ag Ailill.
            BE respect on Meadhbh at Ailill
            'Ailill respects Meadhbh.'

(88)   *Irish Possession Sentence*

        Tá peann ag Máire.
        BE pen   at Mary
        'Mary has a pen.'

Noonan (1993) suggested that the parity in (87) and (88) gives a clue as to why Irish lacks transitive psych verbs: perhaps transitive psych verbs can only exist

---

languages might also have a Double Object Construction in which the Goal c-commands the Theme. However, there should be no language which has a Double Object Construction to the exclusion of the *to*-dative. I do not know if this prediction is borne out. Richard Kayne (pers. comm.) points out to me that *to*-datives are extremely limited in Icelandic relative to the DOC variant–it is not clear whether this situation is expected on Harley's account. I would additionally like to thank Jim Wood and E.F. Sigurðsson for discussion of Icelandic ditransitives.

if a language also has HAVE.[45] Taking up this suggestion and translating it into her own approach, Harley (2002:53-54) proposes that transitive psych verbs involve incorporation of a psych noun into P_{HAVE}, with subsequent incorporation of the complex head into BE. An example of such a derivation is given in (89) (the correct word order will be produced by movement of the subject into spec-TP, not depicted in the tree).

(89)   *Transitive Psych Verb*
        'Calvin fears the weirdos from another planet.'

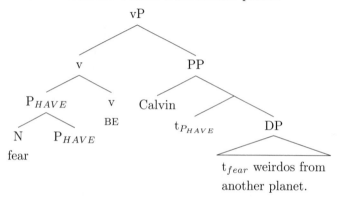

The prediction made is as follows: if P_{HAVE} is absent from a given language, transitive psych verbs will also be absent from that language, there will be no Double Object Constructions in which the Goal c-commands the Theme, and possession

---

45. This suggestion has been investigated very thoroughly for the particular case of the psych verb NEED by Harves and Kayne (2012), with promising results. Halpert and Diercks (2014) have since presented convincing cases of BE languages with a transitive NEED verb. Intriguingly, all of Halpert and Diercks' counter-examples are from WITH-Possessive languages, and Halpert and Diercks propose an explanation of this fact that preserves the spirit of Harves and Kayne's proposal. Antonov and Jacques (2014) also challenge Harves and Kayne's conclusions. Many of their arguments do not go through, however. Some of the languages they examine are Bantu languages, and are subject to Halpert and Diercks' counter-analysis. Antonov and Jacques' contention that the Quechua verb *munay* 'to want' is actually a transitive NEED verb is seriously flawed. While *munay* can be used to translate Spanish *necesitar* in some of its uses, it certainly cannot be taken to be a NEED verb in any general sense. For example, it has no "obligation" reading when combined with an infinitive:

(i)   T'anta-ta mikhu-y-ta muna-ni.
       bread-ACC eat-INF-ACC want-1SUBJ
       'I want to eat bread.' NOT: 'I need to eat bread.'

The other counter-examples cited by Antonov and Jacques (2014), from Estonian and two different dialects of Arabic, seem more robust.

sentences will have a structure based around that of predicate locatives. If P_{HAVE} is present, then transitive psych verbs are expected to be present, ditransitives will be available in which the Goal c-commands the Theme, and the possession sentences will exhibit either a transitive verb HAVE, or will involve a BE construction in which the Possessor c-commands the Possesee underlyingly. Harley (2002, 28-40; 50-56) discusses a number of languages in which these correlations appear to pan out, including English, French, Italian, Irish, Japanese, and Hiaki.

There are two theoretical issues and one empirical issue that go against these proposals, however.

The first theoretical issue concerns the status of HAVE languages and those BE languages that have the P_{HAVE} adposition. Such languages differ from each other only in terms of whether P_{HAVE} incorporates into BE–if it does, then we get a HAVE language; if it does not, the result is BE. While this is clear, what is less clear is why this incorporation difference correlates infallibly with a Case-assignment difference. Apparently, whenever P_{HAVE} incorporates, it assigns Accusative to its complement, but if it fails to incorporate, it sometimes (i.e., in a Locative Possessive language) assigns some oblique Case to its specifier. This correlation is crucial to deriving the case-marking properties that divide HAVE languages from BE languages, but it does not seem to follow from anything in the approach. A second theoretical issue concerns the structure of transitive psych verbs exemplified in (89). By invoking incorporation here, Harley (1995, 2002) is analogizing transitive psych constructions to phenomena found in languages with Noun Incorporation. However, there are no phenomena in such languages that look like overt cases of a noun head incorporating into an adposition which in turn incorporates into the verb (Marantz 2013b, class lectures).

On the empirical side, there is at least one language which is like Irish in lacking transitive psych verbs, but for which there appears to be evidence that the Possessor c-commands the Theme in possession sentences. This language is Scottish Gaelic, as recently discussed by Adger and Ramchand (2006). The similarity of Scottish Gaelic's psych constructions to its possession sentences is exemplified in (90) (Adger and Ramchand 2006, 3; their (10) and (9)).

(90)   *Scottish Gaelic: Psych and Possession*

a.   Tha   gaol agam   ort.
       BE.PRES love at+me on+you
       'I love you.'

b.   Tha   peann aig Dàibhidh.
      BE.PRES pen   at David
      'David has a pen.'

It turns out, though, that Possessors c-command Possessees in Scottish Gaelic, leading to the expectation that P_{HAVE} should be available to license transitive psych constructions in the language. The key evidence comes from the binding of reflexives. Example (91) shows that a Possessor can bind a reflexive embedded inside the Possessee.

(91)   *Possessors Can Bind Reflexives in Scottish Gaelic*

       Tha   dealbh dheth-fhèin aig Dàibhidh.
       BE.PRES picture of-him-self at David
       'David has a picture of himself.'

Crucially, for at least some speakers it is not possible for the Location in a predicate locative construction to bind into the Theme, showing that the structural position of a Possessor really does differ from that of a Location for those speakers.

(92)   *Locations Cannot Bind Reflexives in Scottish Gaelic*

       * Tha   dealbh dheth-fhèin aig/anns a' pheile.
         BE.PRES picture of-it-self   at/in   the pail
         'lit. A picture of itself is in the pail.'

The predicted correlation thus does not seem to be upheld in the domain of psych constructions, judging by the available Scottish Gaelic evidence (Adger and Ramchand 2006 do not discuss ditransitives).

Despite these theoretical and empirical issues, the arguments elsewhere in this book vindicate Harley's (1995, 2002) proposal that there is more than one underlying argument structure available for BE languages. While the validity of the precise correlations she predicts must remain an open question, there is little doubt that possession sentences and ditransitives (and, for that matter, possession sentences and psych constructions) are built out of the same pieces in at least some languages.

2.3.1.3   Conclusion

This subsection has reviewed three proposals that aimed to extend the Freeze/Kayne tradition so as to explore potential comparative syntactic correlations between the structures found in possession sentences and the other syntactic properties of a language. These proposals all make crucial use of the notion of P Incorporation in the way they are formulated. The conclusion was that no consensus as to the existence of such correlations has yet been established, since none of the parametric proposals that have so far been made have been entirely successful in their details. Nevertheless, the relationship between possession sentences, ditransitives, and psych constructions as pursued by Harley (1995, 2002) (partly following earlier insights by Noonan 1993 with respect to psych constructions) remains a potentially promising avenue, even though the relationships between these domains are more complicated than Harley envisaged.

This concludes the discussion of literature on the interaction of parametric variation with the HAVE/BE question. In the next section, I discuss recent literature that bears on the question of how many different argument structures underlie possession sentences, and in particular on the question of whether the class of BE constructions is uniform. As anticipated in the discussion of the Freeze/Kayne tradition in section 2.2, and in the section on Harley (1995, 2002) above, there is now considerable evidence that the formidable surface variation in BE constructions is reflective of real underlying differences in argument structure.

2.3.2   Acknowledging the Multiplicity of BE Constructions

Boneh and Sichel (2010) have recently offered evidence that BE-based possession constructions differ amongst themselves in argument structure. In particular, their results indicate that BE constructions must be able to differ both in the "pieces" that are involved in constructing possession relations, and in the structural position where possessors are introduced. While they depart from the strongest version of the Freeze/Kayne tradition in this respect, they retain the assumption that HAVE constructions are to be derived via incorporation of an adposition into BE. Here I will suggest that their conclusions regarding BE constructions are correct, but that their arguments for a P Incorporation analysis of HAVE are no more convincing than those of Freeze (1992) or Kayne (1993).[46]

Boneh and Sichel (2010) provide evidence that Palestinian Arabic has three syntactically distinguishable BE-based possession constructions. All of the postulated structures have uses in subtypes of copular sentence with no semantic relationship to possession. As Boneh and Sichel (2010, 29) note, there is therefore "no theoretical

---

46. Much the same can be said of Levinson's (2011) discussion of the WITH-Possessives in Icelandic and its relationship to HAVE-Possessives in other Germanic languages. However, since WITH-Possessives are discussed at length in Chapter 7, I postpone discussion of Levinson (2011) until then.

harm" in their conclusion that possession can be associated with so many different argument structures–these structures must be taken to be permitted by Universal Grammar in any case.

The structures in question are associated with somewhat different (albeit overlapping) subtypes of possession relation. One structure involves the copula taking a possessed DP complement, from which the possessor may or may not extract (cf. Szabolcsi's 1981, 1983, 1994 discussions of Hungarian). This structure is associated with a range of meanings, all of which fall within the domain of inalienable possession, including "for humans [...] kinship, social relations, and body parts, and for non-humans [...] inherent relations between inanimate objects, such as Parts of Wholes" (2010, 9).[47] An example of this construction and its associated syntactic structure are given in (93) (based on Boneh and Sichel 2010, 31; their (65c)).[48] A second structure has a meaning which Boneh and Sichel (2010, 2) dub Location. It has the syntax of a standard predicate locative small clause, which Boneh and Sichel take to involve a Rel head selecting a locative PP complement, as depicted in (94). The third structure involves BE taking an ApplP complement–this structure conveys alienable possession, as well as a subset of the inalienable relations (including kinship for all speakers, and body parts for some speakers, according to Boneh and Sichel 2010, 4). This structure is given in (95).

The syntactic distinction between (93) and (94) treats the inalienable possession structure as a Hungarian-style existential construction, whereas Location possession is treated as a predicate locative structure. Boneh and Sichel (2010, 12) give evidence from subject agreement that this is correct.

47. I will use the term inalienable possession as an umbrella term for the meanings that this construction has. Boneh and Sichel (2010) use Part Whole as their umbrella term, but this causes confusion when it becomes necessary to distinguish part-whole from other inalienable relations.

48. The correct surface order in (93) is derived by movement of the PP containing the possessor to spec-IP, not depicted here. Similar comments apply to (94).

(93)   *Inalienable Possession in Palestinian Arabic*

Kaan   la-əš-šajara ʕruʔ   ktar.
WAS.3SG.MASC to-the-tree branches many
'The tree had many branches.'

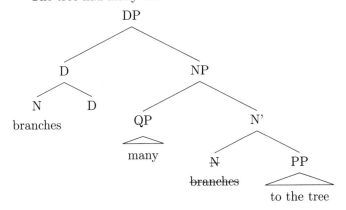

(94)   *Location in Palestinian Arabic*

Kaan   jamb əṣ-ṣabra   wardaat.
WAS.3SG.MASC beside the-cactus flowers
'Beside the cactus were flowers.'

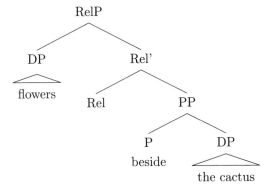

(95)   *Alienable/Inalienable Possession in Palestinian Arabic*

ʕind mona tlat   ʔalaam.
at   Mona three pens
'Mona has three pens.'

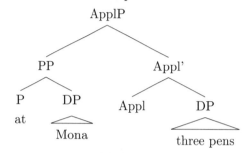

Agreement with immediately post-verbal subjects in non-existential sentences (including predicate locatives) is required in Palestinian Arabic. In existential constructions, on the other hand, the copula must surface in a default 3rd singular masculine form, and cannot display full agreement with the pivot, even if it is immediately postverbal (see Boneh and Sichel 2010, 11-18 for an analysis of the agreement pattern itself). If we now turn to the possession constructions, we find that the Inalienable Possession construction patterns with existentials, whereas the Location construction patterns with predicate locatives.

(96)   *Inalienable Possession Patterns with Existentials*

a.   Kaan   xams ʕruʔ   la-əš-šajara.
     WAS.3SG.MASC five   branches to-the-tree
     'The tree had five branches.'

b. ??Kaan-u   xams ʕruʔ   la-əš-šajara.
     WERE-3PL five   branches to-the-tree
     'The tree had five branches.'

(97)   *Location Possessive Patterns with Predicate Locatives*

a.   *Kaan   tlat ʕšuuš ʕind əš-šajara.
     WAS.3SG.MASC three nests at   the-tree
     'Three nests were near the tree.'

b.   Kaan-u   tlat ʕšuuš ʕind əš-šajara.
     WERE-3PL three nests at   the-tree
     'Three nests were near the tree.'

This is strong evidence that the Inalienable Possession construction and the Location construction must be distinguished syntactically along the lines suggested by Boneh and Sichel. These authors also provide evidence of a different sort that the Inalienable Possession construction cannot be assimilated to an applicative syntax, thereby motivating the distinct analyses of the Inalienable Possession construction and the Alienable/Inalienable Possession construction seen in (93) vs. (95). This evidence comes from the behavior of topicalization.[49] It turns out that the possessor in the Alienable/Inalienble structure cannot be topicalized, whereas the possessor in the Inalienable Construction can. The data are given in (98) and (99). The (a) examples show non-topicalized instances of the construction. The (b) examples display topicalization, which in Palestinian Arabic involves fronting of the topicalized constituent and the insertion of the expletive *fiih* immediately after the verb.

(98)   *Inalienable Possession Construction: Topicalization Possible*

    a.   Kaan   la-mona ʕijreen ṭuwal.
         WAS.3SG.MASC to-Mona legs   long

         'Mona had long legs.'

    b.   La-mona kaan   fiih   ʕijreen ṭuwal.
         to-Mona WAS.3SG.MASC EXPL legs   long

         'Mona had long legs.'

(99)   *Alienable/Inalienable Possession Construction: Topicalization Impossible*

    a.   Kaan ʕind   mona tlat ulaad.
         at   Mona three kids

         'Mona had three kids.' (inalienable)
         'Mona had three kids in her company.' (locative)

    b. # ʕind mona kaan   fiih   tlat   ulaad.
         at   Mona WAS.3SG.MASC EXPL three kids

         *'Mona had three kids.' (inalienable)
         'Mona had three kids in her company.' (locative)

As can be seen, topicalization destroys the inalienable reading of (99)–a locative reading of (99b) is still possible, since (99a) is structurally ambiguous, but the absence of the inalienable reading indicates that topicalization of a PP from spec-ApplP is not permitted. There is no such constraint on the Inalienable Possession

49. Boneh and Sichel (2010, 30-32) offer an additional argument against an Appl analysis for the Inalienable Possession construction based on possible word orders and possible omission of the copula when an expletive is present–this is not discussed here for reasons of space.

construction, however, as shown by the grammaticality of (98b). Therefore, the
Inalienable Possession construction cannot be assimilated to an applicative analy-
sis. Conjoining this fact with their earlier finding that the Inalienable Possession
construction must also be distinguished from the Location construction, Boneh and
Sichel (2010) conclude that all three constructions must receive different analyses.
Predicative Possession in Palestinian Arabic thus serves as an existence proof that
BE-based possession constructions can have different underlying argument struc-
tures.

Having established this point, Boneh and Sichel (2010, 33-37) go on to examine how this analysis might extend to languages with a transitive verb HAVE, such
as English. They note that English *have* effectively neutralizes distinctions which
are manifest in the surface syntax in Palestinian Arabic, since (100a) expresses
meanings covered by the Alienable/Inalienable Possession construction in Palestinian Arabic, (100b) is in the remit of the Inalienable Possession construction, and
(100c) would be expressed by the Location Possessive in Palestinian Arabic (Boneh
and Sichel 2010, 34; their (72)).

(100)   a.   Mary has (Paul's) books (on the/her shelf).

        b.   The tree has many branches.

        c.   The tree has many nests *(in it/near it/beside it).

They suggest that this situation is compatible with an approach of the sort in
Freeze (1992) or Kayne (1993), if it is assumed that the surface realization of *have*
is not sensitive to the sort of element which incorporates into BE. In other words,
the sentences in (100) would involve a similar underlying syntax to their Palestinian
Arabic counterparts, except with incorporation of the relevant P, Rel or Appl head
into BE, all yielding HAVE. Boneh and Sichel (2010, 36) go on to claim a potential
advantage of their approach in being able to explain the apparently obligatory PP in
English locative *have* sentences (see (100c)). They propose that the PP is necessary
in order to identify the silent P which has incorporated into BE.

While I am in full agreement with Boneh and Sichel's arguments for the multiplic-
ity of BE constructions, I would make the following objections to their incorporation-
based treatment of HAVE. First, note that the analysis is like other analyses in the
Freeze/Kayne tradition in predicting that HAVE-constructions are unaccusative–a
prediction that is highly problematic, as discussed in Chapter 5. Boneh and Sichel
do not discuss an alternative analysis according to which HAVE is the transitive
form of BE, of the sort advocated in the present work. But there is no sense in
which such an analysis would be incompatible with the spirit of Boneh and Sichel's
own conclusions. Moreover, it is clear that such an analysis of HAVE does no more

theoretical harm than do their conclusions with respect to BE: transitive VoicePs
are clearly part of Universal Grammar in any case. Finally, there is a problem with
their idea that the overt PP in locative *have* sentences is obligatory because of the
need to identify an incorporated P head. The problem is that locative *have* sentences can also be licensed by a small clause headed by a verb, which presumably
would not help with the identification of an incorporated P (see Chapter 4 for a
more successful account of the need for this small clause).

(101)   The tree has two buildings *(flanking it).

I conclude that Boneh and Sichel's (2010) discussion of the BE domain in Palestinian Arabic offers strong support for the sort of solution to the too-many-(surface)-
structures puzzle advocated in this book. This means that the ambition of Freeze
(1992) to reduce the domain of predicative possession to a single underlying structure must be forsworn. While these authors attempt to retain some version of the P
Incorporation approach to deriving HAVE, I have argued that they do not succeed
in making a convincing case for doing so. This calls for a different way of conceiving
of the relationship between BE and HAVE. In the next two sections, I briefly look at
two types of proposal that attempt to fill this need.

2.3.3   Severing HAVE from BE: Błaszczak (2007)

There are many possible ways to react to the perceived failure of P Incorporation as
an approach to the relationship between HAVE and BE. One way is to retain the core
insight that BE and HAVE are realizations of the same fundamental category, but
abandon the assumption of P Incorporation in favor of some other implementation.
Another route is to conclude that a decompositional approach to the HAVE/BE
question was on the wrong track to begin with, and to instead adopt the assumption
that HAVE is a completely separate entity from BE. HAVE would then be nothing
other than an entry in the lexicon, one which languages can either have or lack.
Błaszczak (2007) has recently argued for precisely this view.

Błaszczak (2007, 325) makes a novel criticism of the Freeze/Kayne tradition. She
points out the following prediction: given that HAVE is produced via the incorporation of P into BE, we expect that HAVE should never appear to have a PP subject on
the surface. In other words, we expect the following pattern of surface possibilities
(Błaszczak 2007, 325, her (4.22)).

(102)   a.   "NP" HAVE NP

        b.   PP BE NP

        c.   *PP HAVE NP

Błaszczak (2007) goes on to show that prediction (102c) is falsified by existential sentences in several Slavic languages. In Polish, for example, negative existential sentences show exactly this pattern in the present tense (Błaszczak 2007, 325, her (4.23c)).

(103)   *PP HAVE NP in Polish*

        W samochodzie nie **ma** silnika.

        in car.LOC   NEG has motor.GEN

        'There is no engine in the car.'

Although the data are interesting, one can legitimately question whether (102c) really is predicted to be out by the Freeze/Kayne tradition. Here is one way in which the prediction might fail to go through. There is a widespread consensus in the literature that PPs have at least one adpositional functional head in their extended projection (Van Riemsdijk 1990; Rooryck 1996; Koopman 1997; Svenonius 2003, 2007, 2010; Gehrke 2008; Den Dikken 2003, 2010; many others), and much of this literature argues for a highly articulated adpositional functional sequence. If it is one of these higher heads that incorporates into BE to yield HAVE, then (102c) becomes a possible surface form. Hence, while there are many legitimate criticisms of the Freeze/Kayne tradition (see especially Chapter 5), (102) is not among them.

Błaszczak (2007, 223-324) levels an even more fundamental criticism, one that potentially threatens any approach that postulates a syntactically-mediated relationship between BE and HAVE. Błaszczak gives an updated implementation of the Freeze/Kayne approach, in which P Incorporation is motivated by an uninterpretable P feature [uP] on v itself. She goes on to claim that this analysis "would amount to saying that there are–cross-linguistically–two different BEs: (i) a BE without [uP], and (ii) a BE with [uP]. But if so, why not simply assume that there are two different verbs, BE and HAVE, that languages might have at their disposal?" (324). This criticism is off the mark, for there is a very big difference between postulating a functional head that varies in its featural content on the one hand, and postulating two syntactically distinct heads on the other hand. In the case of a single head whose feature content varies, one expects a very particular morphological profile–namely, it might be possible for the morphology to "neutralize" the distinction between the two variants via Impoverishment in certain languages. In the case of two entirely distinct heads, no such neutralization is predicted to be possible.

The question is, what is the cross-linguistic morphological profile of the HAVE/BE relation?

As is well-known, cases of the paradigms of HAVE and BE being neutralized in the presence of certain marked feature values are attested in certain languages. Since they are triggered by marked features, these neutralizations are plausibly caused by Impoverishment. Examples include *ain't* in non-standard varieties of English, and the past participle forms of HAVE and BE in Breton (as well as certain other parts of the paradigm; see Press 1986, 139-155). The latter is exemplified in (104).[50]

(104)   HAVE/BE *Neutralization in Breton*

Infinitive	beza 'be'	kaout 'have'
Past Participle	bet	bet

Such patterns are completely unexpected, *unless* HAVE and BE are taken to be variants of the same thing. There is therefore no plausibility to the idea that HAVE and BE are entirely separate verbs which languages may simply have or lack. Moreover, such a theory offers no way of understanding why HAVE constructions are so much rarer than BE constructions (Harves 2009, 7, class handout).

It follows that the correct reaction to the problems with the Freeze/Kayne tradition is to seek some other way of implementing the core insight that HAVE is BE plus something else. In this book, I argue that the relevant "something else" is transitivity–more technically, the presence of an external-argument-introducing Voice head endowed with phi-features with which it can license a DP in its complement. This idea has recent antecedents in Hoekstra (1994) and Jung (2011).[51] The rest of this book, particularly Chapters 4 and 5, defends this tradition in general. In the next section, I will instead discuss the differences between my implementation of this idea and these earlier ones.

2.3.4   Relating HAVE and BE via (In)transitivity

Hoekstra (1994) proposed that the major difference between HAVE and BE languages lies in the distribution of Case assigners. He follows Szabolcsi (1981; 1983) and Kayne (1993) in taking BE languages of the Hungarian type to have a functional head internal to DP capable of assigning Case to the possessor. The possessee in a

---

50. Interesting confirmation for the idea that HAVE is in some way the more complex of the two comes from the fact that the neutralized form in Breton is a form of BE.

51. Isačenko (1974, 60), in discussing the relationship between Russian *byt'* and *imet'*, makes a version of the same suggestion.

BE language can then be licensed by AgrS, receiving Nominative. Suppose, however, that a given language has no functional head internal to DP capable of licensing the possessor on its own. Such a language will require a rather different division of Case-assigning labor if the derivation is to converge. Hoekstra's idea was that, in this eventuality, an AgrO head can be introduced above BE. This will permit a convergent derivation in which the possessor raises to spec-AgrSP for Nominative Case, and the possessee raises to spec-AgrOP, which is associated with Accusative Case. The resulting case-frame will be transitive in form, and the combination of BE and AGRO is realized as HAVE. The D-structure for each kind of language is given in (105) and (106).

(105)   *BE-Language: Hoekstra (1994)*

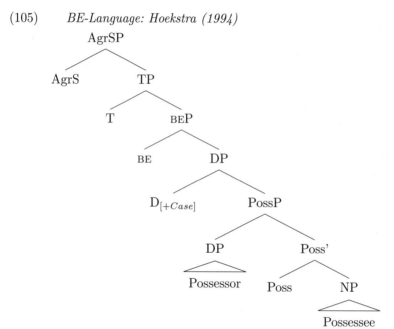

Hoekstra's (1994) reasoning suggests that this AgrO (and therefore HAVE) is a last resort that a language uses only if it lacks the Case resources to make a BE possession construction work. Conceiving of HAVE in this last-resort fashion leads to the expectation that it is rarer than BE–a desirable result, as we have seen.

(106)   *HAVE-Language: Hoekstra (1994)*

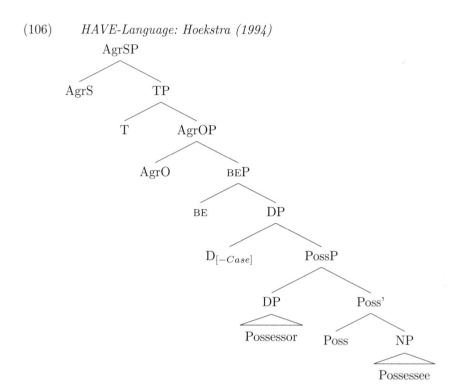

The theory outlined in Jung (2011, 93-95) is more or less an updating of Hoekstra's account to a Probe-Goal approach to Case assignment, which dispenses with bespoke Agr projections. For her, BE is a functional element F with a parameter associated with it–either it is [+Case], and thus able to license an argument on its own, or it is [−Case], in which case it cannot. Jung (2011, 93) proposes that the [+Case] variant of F is realized as HAVE, and that the [−Case] variant is realized as BE. Jung (2011, 94) adopts a similar last-resort-like view of HAVE to Hoekstra's: the [+Case] variant is chosen only if needed.[52]

---

52. Jung (2011, 94) says that this is "perhaps for economy of derivation," although she entertains the idea that "economy may be overridden by other needs in a particular language," giving the example of cases in South and West Slavic languages when HAVE is forced in negative existential sentences (Błaszczak 2007).

(107)   *BE-Language: Jung (2011, 94)*

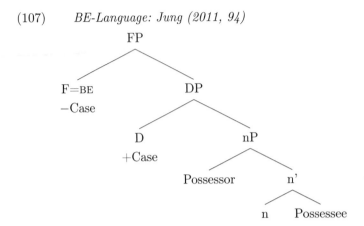

(108)   *HAVE-Language: Jung (2011:94)*

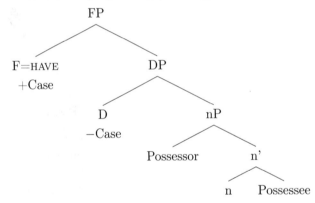

It is my belief that Hoesktra (1994) and Jung (2011) are on the right track when they propose linking HAVE and BE via transitivity. However, there are two emendations to their implementation that I would like to make.

The first is to eliminate the "last resort" part of the reasoning. The idea that HAVE is a last resort turns out not to be necessary in order to understand why HAVE is rarer than BE. As shown in Chapter 1 of the present work, the mere combinatorics of possible verb phrase structures already derives this typological generalization. Furthermore, it is not clear that the notion of last resort can be coherently applied to HAVE as envisaged by Hoekstra (1994) and Jung (2011). Last resort refers to particular syntactic operations that apply in the course of the derivation only if needed. However, the difference between HAVE and BE in these two approaches has to be made at the level of the numeration: for Hoekstra (1994), it will involve the inclusion (or not) of AgrO, and for Jung it will involve a choice of which variant of F to include. There is no clear way of implementing this last resort reasoning at the level of the numeration, as far as I can see.

The second change that must be made is to the argument structure that characterizes HAVE sentences. Despite linking the HAVE/BE difference to transitivity, both Hoekstra (1994) and Jung (2011) assign basically unaccusative structures to HAVE sentences. This is empirically problematic–as I show in Chapter 5, the traditional arguments that HAVE sentences are "underlyingly" unaccusative do not stand up to scrutiny, and there are also positive arguments in favor of assigning HAVE sentences an underlyingly transitive structure. It is for this reason that I propose to implement Hoekstra's (1994) and Jung's (2011) idea as follows:

(109)   *HAVE-Languages on the Present Proposal*

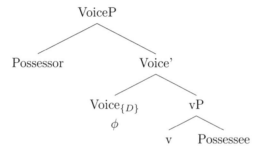

This proposal has the advantage of assimilating HAVE's transitivity to the standard morphosyntactic configuration for transitivity (i.e., the presence of external-argument-introducing Voice with unvalued phi-features), and also avoids the empirical issues with unaccusative analyses of HAVE.

2.3.5   Conclusions: The State of the Art on the Too-Many-(Surface)-Structures Puzzle

This section has discussed some extensions of and reactions against the Freeze/Kayne tradition that have been proposed in the search for a solution to the too-many-(surface)-structures puzzle. Here, I summarize what the discussion has revealed about the state of the art in this area.

The Freeze/Kayne tradition is to be credited with opening up a new domain of comparative syntactic inquiry into what other syntactic properties correlate with the HAVE/BE difference, if any. No consensus answer to this question has emerged as of yet, and existing proposals face a range of empirical and conceptual challenges. Nevertheless, this remains an important area of research, with proposals concerning links between possession and the domains of ditransitives (Harley 2002) and of psych constructions (Harley 1995, 2002; Harves and Kayne 2012; Isačenko 1974; Noonan 1993) looking especially promising. There is, in addition, clear evidence from the patterning of morphological neutralizations that HAVE and BE must be considered realizations of the same category in different environments, as argued by the Freeze/Kayne tradition. We can therefore safely reject any analysis that treats HAVE and BE as entirely distinct lexical verbs that a language can simply have or lack. However, technical and empirical problems beset implementations of the decompositional approach which involve P Incorporation, and I have argued that it is preferable to link HAVE and BE via the notion of syntactic transitivity, along the lines of Hoekstra (1994) and Jung (2011). Also, more recent literature has revealed strong evidence that the domain of BE languages is more complex than the Freeze/Kayne tradition initially supposed. We must recognize that there are a range of different underlying argument structures for BE constructions, and that the variation within the domain of BE is at least as formidable as the variation between HAVE and BE.

This is an interesting result, which has important implications for what a theory of the syntax/semantics interface must look like. On the one hand, such a theory must allow sufficient independence between the syntactic notion of argumenthood and the semantic notion of argumenthood that we can explain how this multitude of underlying argument structures can come out with the same (or at least overlapping) meanings. On the other hand, it must be sufficiently constrained that regularities in argument linking (of the sorts summarized in Levin and Rappaport Hovav 2005) can still be accounted for. An important litmus test for any such theory will be whether it also yields a solution to the other major puzzle posed by possession sentences–what I have been calling the too-many-meanings puzzle. It is to the literature on this puzzle that we turn in the next section.

2.4 Approaches to the Too-Many-Meanings Puzzle

In Chapter 1, we saw that the too-many-meanings puzzle is brought into sharp relief by data of the following sort.

(110) John has a Playstation 3.   (Ownership)

(111) John has a sister.   (Kinship)

(112) John has blue eyes.   (Body Part)

(113) This table has four sturdy legs.   (Part-Whole)

(114) John has a cold.   (Disease)

(115) John has a great deal of resilience.   (Attribute)

The problem becomes all the more acute once "non-possessive" uses of HAVE, including its modal, causative, and experiencer variants, are brought into the picture.

The mystery here lies not merely in the fact that *have* has more than one meaning; there are many verbs that appear to have that property. Rather, the mystery comes from the fact that (some subset of) these meanings are expressed by the same "possession" construction in language after language. It is hard to reconcile this cross-linguistic uniformity with the sheer number and diversity of the meanings involved. What, for instance, do *having a Playstation 3*, *having a sister*, and *having four legs* have in common with one another, such that they are marked in the same way so consistently across languages? This is the essence of the too-many-meanings puzzle. In this section, I review recent work that has contributed to the debate around this question.

Much of the recent work in this area has been carried out by semanticists, and much of it focuses on HAVE verbs in European languages (overwhelmingly English), although we will see that there are exceptions to both of these generalizations. Within this literature, I identify two broad types of solution to the too-many-meanings puzzle. One sub-tradition argues that HAVE does contribute a lexical semantic core of its own, but that this core is very vague, explaining why such a diverse array of meanings (110)-(115) is compatible with it. Another sub-tradition takes it that HAVE itself is meaningless, and that the meaning of a given HAVE sentence is contributed by other elements of the sentence, some of which may be silent. A related question is how many HAVEs there are: do all of the sentences in (110)-(115) involve the same verb, or are there multiple distinct HAVE verbs that just happen to have the same form in English? Below I will argue that there are

empirical and conceptual reasons to favor a unified approach to HAVE, and that this
is easier to achieve if HAVE is taken to be meaningless as opposed to meaningful
but vague. The problem with the latter approach is that it seems to be impossible
to find a meaning for HAVE vague enough to cover (110)-(115) without requiring
either multiple separate lexical entries for HAVE or additional stipulated conditions
designed to capture some of the meanings.

   The section is structured as follows. In 2.4.1, I review various instantiations of
the hypothesis that HAVE has lexical semantic content that is vague. In 2.4.2, I
review work which assigns no lexical semantic content to HAVE–my own proposal is
situated within this tradition, although it exhibits many differences of detail with its
antecedents. Section 2.4.3 is a conclusion in which I argue that the latter tradition
is on the right track, since it is more compatible with a unified analysis of HAVE
itself, and with the idea that HAVE is a grammatically-conditioned variant of BE.

2.4.1   HAVE as Vague but Meaningful

Some work has proposed to address the too-many-meanings puzzle by attributing to
HAVE some core lexical meaning(s) compatible with the array of relations in (110)-
(115). Some of this work, including Belvin (1996) and Belvin and Den Dikken
(1997), aims for a unified analysis of HAVE. Proposals of this sort therefore seek
to identify a single lexical semantic core covering (110)-(115) and beyond. Given
the diversity of these meanings, any such lexical semantic core will necessarily be
of a somewhat vague and abstract character. A weaker version of this tradition,
embodied by Brugman (1988) and Tham (2004), proposes a small handful of lexical
entries for HAVE. This move makes the identification of core meanings for each
of these lexical entries more straightforward than the task of identifying a single
meaning for all of them. However, it yields an account which by its nature is not
capable of accounting for the cross-linguistic consistency of the marking of these
relations in possession sentences.

   The difficulties inherent in trying to uncover a core lexical meaning (or set of
meanings) for HAVE were clear to the first linguists to address the HAVE/BE question
from a generative perspective. Bach (1967) and Lyons (1968, 388-399) were led
to propose that HAVE and BE had no impact on semantics at all, and that the
meanings of sentences containing these elements were derived from elsewhere. In
particular, both argued that HAVE and BE were not present at deep structure,
but were inserted by transformation, and were thus incapable of affecting meaning
under the theoretical assumptions current at the time. My own approach, although
implemented very differently, is in much the same spirit as Bach (1967) and Lyons

(1968), at least as far as the meaning of HAVE is concerned. Proponents of the idea that HAVE must have some contentful lexical meaning have made arguments against these earlier proposals, and it is thus important to see whether these arguments apply to my approach.

  Brugman (1988) offers a series of objections to the idea that HAVE is essentially meaningless, and argues on this basis that it is necessary to attribute some lexical semantics to HAVE itself. It is to her arguments that we turn first. Next, we turn to Belvin (1996). This work argues for a single, vague core meaning for HAVE, in terms of the notion of *zonal inclusion*. The nature of the "inclusion" relation involved in each case is filled in depending on the nature of HAVE's arguments. Finally, we turn to Tham (2004, 2006), who argues that HAVE has three separate meanings.

2.4.1.1 Brugman (1988)

Brugman (1988) is an analysis of the English *have* paradigm couched in the framework of Construction Grammar. Amongst its most notable contributions is a very detailed discussion of the uses of *have* in English, which formed an important empirical basis from which Belvin (1996) was able to distill a number of generalizations that have formed the core of the discussion of the semantics of *have* (and HAVE) ever since (especially in the domain on non-possessive uses of *have*, which was the focus of Belvin (1996)). Brugman (1988, 232) ultimately argues that *have*'s meaning is to be represented in seven separate lexical entries, united in a complex lexical network. She proposes that these distinct senses have an abstract commonality, in that all concern the subject of *have* being "interested" in the material in the complement of *have*, with the particular nature of the "interest" in question being determined at the level of the construction (and therefore modulated by *have*'s complement).

  For space reasons, I will not discuss the details of Brugman's lexical entries here, and nor will I offer a summary of her empirical discussion (since the various subtypes of English *have* are discussed in great detail in Chapter 4). I note, however, that Brugman's approach does not address any of the comparative syntactic questions which a convincing account to the syntax and semantics of possession sentences must address. Instead, I wish to focus here on Brugman's arguments against the idea that HAVE has no meaning (which are cited approvingly by Belvin 1996). It turns out that Brugman's objections apply only to the particular instantiations of this hypothesis that were available at the time, and that the present approach does not run afoul of them.

  Brugman's (1988, 47) first objection concerns an apparent overgeneration of interpretations in the account of Bach (1967, 477), who had implied that *have* and *be* can convey any relation whatsoever, constrained only by "the items they link." Brugman (1988, 47) notes that this cannot literally be true: if a *have* sentence's meaning is constrained only by pragmatically conceivable relations between the subject of *have* and the complement of *have*, then *Susan had the bread* ought to be able to have the meaning *Susan kneaded the bread*. As Brugman shows, however, not even a very rich context can license this meaning for *Susan had the bread*.

Brugman's observation is on point, but it only arises if one relies exclusively on pragmatics to account for the origin of the relations conveyed by sentences involving *have*. My own approach does not do this: for me, the relations come from the meanings of *have*'s complement. These are of a restricted sort, since they come from the compositional semantics of the elements that *have* takes as its complement in a given derivation.

Brugman's (1988, 48-49) second objection is in some ways more obvious in nature, but also more serious. If *have* and *be* are both meaningless, then they are semantically equivalent, which means that they should be interchangeable. Of course, they are not. As discussed in 1.5, my own approach explains this fact in morphosyntactic terms: given that a transitive structure is needed to produce a HAVE construction, the structure that means *John is a doctor* will simply never be spelled out as *John has a doctor*, and similarly *vice versa*.

This subsection has discussed Brugman's (1988) objections to assigning no lexical semantics to HAVE. While these objections were valid for versions of this hypothesis discussed by Brugman, they do not apply to my own approach. Brugman's approach, which involves assigning a complex lexical semantic web of meanings to English *have*, is too language-specific in its formulation to be productively applied to the broader HAVE/BE question. Nevertheless, Brugman is to be credited for identifying a number of interactions between the meaning of *have* sentences and the complement which *have* takes. These observations were the springboard for a number of important insights in the work of Belvin (1996), which is the topic of the next section.

2.4.1.2   Belvin (1996)

Belvin (1996) aims to provide a unified analysis of HAVE grounded in a general theory of the mapping from event conceptualization to linguistic structure. Building on earlier work with A. Arnaiz (Belvin and Arnaiz 1994), Belvin argues that the core meaning of HAVE is an abstract form of *inclusion*. Belvin (1996, 78) does not have in mind the sense of inclusion involved in the relationship between a set and its members. Rather, Belvin refers to zonal inclusion, a notion he defines in terms of *image schemas* in the style of Cognitive Linguistics. Entities are conceived of as having a range of zones associated with them, and the role of HAVE is to assert that a particular zone associated with its subject entity includes the denotatum of HAVE's complement.[53] The nature of the inclusion relation denoted by any given HAVE sentence therefore depends on the nature of HAVE's subject and HAVE's complement. It is this latter insight–that the meanings of HAVE sentences are essentially negotiated between the elements which HAVE links together–that inspired my own approach, which takes HAVE to be a meaningless v head in a transitive configuration. Here, I will review Belvin's approach to this generalization in terms of the notion of zonal inclusion, arguing that the same insight is better captured without attributing such lexical semantic content to HAVE.

Belvin argues that there are four major types of conceptual zone that an entity may be associated with. There is additionally a minor type, the S-Zone, associated only with undifferentiated substances. Their nature is summarized in the following table.

(116)   *Conceptual Zones (Belvin 1996)*

   a.   **Control Zone**: The zone containing entities and eventualities that the entity can willfully influence.

   b.   **Experience Zone**: The zone containing entities and eventualities that the entity can experience.

   c.   **Proximal Zone**: The zone containing entities which are near the entity.

   d.   **Inalienable Zone**: The zone containing attributes and subparts of the entity itself.

   e.   **S-Zone**: The zone occupied by a substance (i.e., an entity with no identifiable subparts).

Not all entities have zones of all these kinds. The number of zones available to a given entity correlates with its degree of animacy. Belvin recognizes four types of entity: *volitional* entities, which have internal mental states and a will of their own; *sentient* entities, which have internal mental states but no will which they can deliberately act upon; *ideal forms*, which are inanimates with distinguishable subparts but no mental states; and *substances*, which are inanimates lacking distinguishable subparts. These types of entity are associated with zones as follows.

---

53. Belvin (1996, 79) credits Langacker (1993) with independently arguing for a similar idea, where HAVE is argued to convey what is within the "dominion" of its subject.

(117)   *Types of Entities and Associated Zones (Belvin 1996, 90)*

    a.   **Volitional**: control, experience, proximal, inalienable

    b.   **Sentient**: experience, proximal, inalienable

    c.   **Ideal Form**: proximal, inalienable

    d.   **Substance**: S-zone

To see how the notion of zonal inclusion accounts for the interpretation of a *have* sentence in English, consider a sentence like (118).

(118)   John has a nose.

For Belvin, this sentence means "zone X associated with John includes a nose." The more precise meaning depends on which of the zones associated with John is chosen. Since John is a volitional entity, the full complement of zones (except the S-zone) is available in principle. If the inalienable zone is chosen, the reading will be that the nose is a subpart or attribute of John–this is the account for the body-part reading that (118) clearly has. On the other hand, if the control zone is chosen, then the interpretation is that John has a nose within his sphere of influence–this is an alienable possession reading in which John has some nose (perhaps a severed one, perhaps not his own) in his control. Similarly, causative *have* sentences like (119) involve the control zone. The idea is that the event of Mary dancing by him was included in the zone containing eventualities that John willfully influenced. Thus, for Belvin, alienable possession and causative HAVE share a semantic commonality: they both involve reference to the control zone.

(119)   John had Mary dance by him.

The way in which Belvin's (1996) account applies to the broader *have* paradigm is rather complex, and it cannot be reviewed in full here. A number of difficulties arise in applying the notion of inclusion to explain *have*'s semantic properties. I will mention two of them here–Belvin's suggested solutions for both of these difficulties are revealing, since they amount to stipulative suspensions of parts of the lexical semantic story he develops for *have*.

The first concerns the sentence in (119). Why can't this sentence be interpreted using John's proximal zone? In other words, why couldn't this sentence be interpreted as a locative *have* sentence with a meaning akin to *Mary danced near John*? Belvin (1996, 85-87) notes this problem, and responds to it by stipulating that "only control and experience zones eventively include events." This stipulation amounts to an admission that the zonal inclusion approach does not directly capture the

relationship between the eventiveness of *have*'s complement and the possible interpretations of *have*'s subject. In contrast, assuming that *have* is meaningless allows
this interaction to fall out from the normal action of argument-introducing heads
in the thematic domain, as I show in Chapter 4.

The second problem I would like to discuss derives directly from the assumption
that *have*'s basic meaning is inclusion. As Belvin himself puts it, "how can an
inherently stative notion like inclusion be transformed into an inherently eventive
notion like 'cause' or 'happen to'?" (1996, 106). This problem arises for causative
and experiencer *have* sentences, as Belvin mentions, but it also applies to eventive
light-verb *have* sentences like *John had a party.*[54] Belvin's solution is as follows: "Let
us suppose that when *have* embeds an eventive complement, each of the inclusion
relations must be temporally individuated. In such a case, the inclusion relations
are no longer appropriately represented as simple zone inclusion, but instead take
on the quality of causal chains" (1996, 108). But this amounts to rewriting the
core meaning of *have* in response to the meaning of *have*'s complement, instead of
deriving the meanings of such sentences from the meanings of their subparts. The
approach developed in this book requires no such rewriting, because it does not
assign *have* a meaning that is inherently stative in the first place.

Despite these and other flaws, Belvin (1996) contains a number of important
insights into the meanings of *have* sentences in English (and, to a lesser degree, in
Spanish) which have been influential in subsequent discussions, and were a particularly important source of inspiration for the approach to HAVE developed in Chapter 4 of the present work. Foremost among these is Belvin's (1996, 29) observation
that the eventive or stative nature of a *have* sentence is inherited from its complement. The validity of this generalization is demonstrated abundantly in Chapter
4; here I will provide just one of Belvin's diagnostics (1996, 32; his (27)). Notice
that causative *have* sentences with eventive complements combine readily with the
progressive, but those where *have* takes a stative complement do not. Hence, the
aspectual status of *have* is inherited from its complement.

(120)   a.   Lou is having Charlie dance.

         b.   Lou is having Charlie wash the dishes.

         c.   *Lou is having Charlie dancing.

         d.   *Lou is having Charlie washing the dishes.

---

54. It is unclear to me whether the zonal inclusion account can be extended to light-verb *have*
sentences at all. Belvin (1996, 93 fn 11) states only that "I have not given much attention to
[them]."

e.   * Lou was having Charlie furious by the time we arrived.

Belvin himself (1996, 140) derives this generalization in a manner which is completely orthogonal to the lexical semantics he assigns to *have*. He argues that verbs have Event features which are specified as eventive or stative for most verbs, but for *have* are not valued in the lexicon. Hence, *have* gains these features in the course of the derivation by attracting them from its complement (under Move-F(eature), the precursor to Agree in Minimalist theorizing–see Chomsky 1995, 261-271). In the absence of specific morphological or syntactic evidence for such features, however, this move is undesirable. This insight of Belvin's is more appropriately captured, I would argue, in the semantics, but this is impossible for Belvin to do given the zonal inclusion semantics that he assigns to *have*. The desired result follows automatically if *have* is meaningless, as I show in Chapter 4.

To conclude this section, Belvin argues for a unified analysis of English *have* which conceives of it as having a very vague lexical semantics of zonal inclusion. In so doing, he identifies a number of important facets of *have*'s meaning, building on earlier work by Brugman (1988). A number of these point to the conclusion that much of the meaning of *have* sentences is negotiated between the subject of *have* and its complement. In light of this, I have argued that even the vague meaning Belvin assigns to *have* is not vague enough to account for the semantics of all *have* sentences without additional stipulations–stipulations which can be done away with if we instead attribute to *have* (and to HAVE cross-linguistically) no meaning at all.

2.4.1.3   Tham (2004, 2006)

Whereas Belvin (1996) seeks a unified analysis for *have*, Shiao-Wei Tham instead argues (in her 2004 dissertation and 2006 paper) for three separate lexical entries for *have* in English. Much of the dissertation is concerned with arguing that possession relations must be distinguished from locative relations, contra Freeze (1992) and a long tradition of "locativist" approaches to possession sentences (Lyons 1968, 388-399). Tham provides a number of novel criticisms of such approaches, including important facts which indicate that possession and location must be distinguished even in languages where they are marked identically. For example, she observes (2004, 22; her (29)) that the locative/possessive ambiguity in a Marathi sentence like (121a) disappears if certain locative proforms are used, as in (121b).

(121)   *Marathi*

    a.   Māzhyā-jawaḷ ek   pustak āhe.
           my.OBL-near   one book   is
           'I have a book.'
           'There is a book near me.'

    b.   Tithe   pustak āhe.
           There$_{LOC}$ book   is
           'There$_{LOC}$ is a book.'

Another observation Tham makes is that "there are languages where the light-verb possessive and existential sentences are surface-identical, but structurally distinct with respect to binding possibilities" (2004, 30). Importantly, Tham is able to show for two such languages (Mandarin and Finnish) that these binding differences are independent of the question of animacy, which undermines Freeze's (1992) claim that possession sentences are effectively existential sentences with an animate location. Examples from Mandarin (Tham 2004, 163; her (233)) are given below. These show that possessors (including inanimate possessors in a part-whole relation) are able to bind the subject-oriented anaphor for all speakers in Mandarin, but some speakers reject similar binding in an existential sentence.[55]

(122)   *Subject-Oriented Anaphor Binding in Mandarin Possession vs. Existentials*

    a.   Zhǔ-wò-fáng$_i$ yǒu zìjǐ$_i$ de   yùshi.
           Master.bedroom HAVE self ASSOC bathroom
           'The master bedroom$_i$ has self$_i$'s bathroom.'

    b.   % Zhǔ-wò-fáng$_i$-lǐ   yǒu zìjǐ$_i$ de   yùshi.
           Master.bedroom-within HAVE self ASSOC bathroom
           'In the master bedroom$_i$ is self$_i$'s bathroom.'

With these parts of Tham's argument, I am very much in agreement. However, there are a number of deficiencies in her three-*have* approach to English possession sentences, for reasons that have to do both with the implications of the analysis as it applies to English and with its implications for the too-many-meanings puzzle and the too-many-(surface)-structures puzzle more generally.

---

55. Here I follow Tham in glossing the Mandarin existential/possessive verb *yǒu* as HAVE, although I remain unconvinced that it is a transitive HAVE verb as opposed to, for instance, an existential form of BE, as assumed by Stassen (2009, 59).

I begin by presenting the three-way distinction that Tham argues for in the
domain of English *have*. Tham distinguishes possessive *have*, focus *have*, and control *have*. She takes a version of Lexical Functional Grammar augmented by an
Optimality Theoretic approach to argument linking as her theoretical background.
For the convenience of the reader, I omit certain irrelevant details from Tham's
lexical entries. In particular, I omit the F-structure contributions from the entries.
I also omit the C-structure part of the entries, since these simply specify that each
of these *haves* is verbal in category. Of the remaining abbreviations, note that SEM
STR gives the semantics of the entry, ARG STR provides a list of the arguments
that the verb must project in the syntax (the variables pick out which arguments
at SEM STR each of these syntactic arguments corresponds to). Finally, I-STR
encodes informational structural effects of the lexical item (this is relevant only for
focus *have* and control *have*). FC in the entry for Control *have* stands for Felicity
Condition, a pragmatic constraint on the construction.

(123)   *Three Lexical Entries for have*: Tham (2004)

    a.   Possessive *have* (Tham 2004, 146; her (209))
        SEM STR $POSS(x,y)$
        ARG STR $<a_x, a_y>$
        $a_y \mapsto NP_{existential}$

    b.   Focus *have* (Tham 2004, 218; her (308))
        SEM STR $R(x,y)$
        ARG STR $<a_x, a_y>$
        I-STR $[_{op} \lambda z.R(x,z)]\ (y)_{focus}$

    c.   Control *have* (Tham 2004, 218; her (309))
        SEM STR $control(x,y)$
        ARG STR $<a_x, a_y>$
        I-STR   FC: some or all of *control(x,y)* is the focus to a salient
        OP in the context.

Entry (123a) is intended to cover *have* as used in ownership sentences, kinship
sentences, body-part sentences, and part-whole relations involving inanimates. Note
that the special condition in the third line of (123a) forces the direct object of this
possessive *have* to be headed by an existential determiner in the sense of Keenan
(1987). This is Tham's account of the definiteness effect exhibited by these *have*
sentences. We will turn to what is meant by Tham's POSS predicate in the SEM
STR of entry (123a) presently.

Examples of what is meant by focus *have* (entry (123b)) and control *have* (entry
(123c)) are given below.

(124)   *Focus Have (Tham 2004, 203; her (282))*

    a.   What can you donate to the drive?

    b.   I have that jacket.

(125)   *Control Have (Tham 2004, 204; her (283))*

    a.   Where's my umbrella?

    b.   Mowgli has it.

The verb *have* in these contexts exhibits no definiteness effects–this is captured in the entries in (123b) and (123c) by the fact that neither of them contains a specification that *have*'s object must be headed by an existential determiner. Tham claims that *have* sentences can denote any pragmatically-induced relation if the direct object is new-information focus. This is captured in the lexical entry of focus *have*, which enforces focus on the direct object (via its I-STR specification) and has the underspecified relation R in its SEM STR. The I-STR of control *have* partially overlaps with that of focus *have*, but allows either argument to be in focus. Only animate subjects can be the external argument of the control relation. Tham exploits this to explain the fact that (125b) is an appropriate answer to (125a), whereas (126) is not.

(126)   # The bathroom has it.

In her (2006, 146) paper, Tham adds a cross-linguistic argument for having focus *have* and control *have* as separate lexical entries: while focus *have* has a correspondent in Mandarin *yǒu* sentences, control *have* does not.

(127)   *Mandarin* yǒu *Has Focus HAVE Uses* (Tham 2006, 146; her (31))

    a.   Sānmáo cā   shénme dōngxi?
            Sanmao wipe what   thing

            'What is Sanmao wiping/polishing?'

    b.   Sānmáo yǒu   nà   xiē   jìngzi.
            Sanmao HAVE that some mirror

            'Sanmao has those mirrors.'

(128)   *Mandarin yǒu Does Not Have Control HAVE Uses* (Tham 2006, 146; her (32))

     a.   Nà   xiē   jìngzi zài   nǎr   ne?

           That some mirror BE.AT where Q.PRT

           'Where are those mirrors?

     b.   # Sānmáo yǒu   (nà   xiē   jìngzi).

           Sanmao HAVE that some mirror

           'Sanmao has those mirrors.'

However, this result is also readily explicable if *yǒu* is an existential BE verb: (127) would then be a case of the list reading (Rando and Napoli 1978), and thus expected to be permitted in an existential context. Since (128) is not such a case, it would be ruled out by the definiteness effect. Hence the contrast in (127) and (128) has no bearing on the number of different *haves* there are in English.

Tham's approach has a number of problematic aspects. Note first of all that, despite setting up three separate lexical entries, Tham's analysis is not intended to cover the whole *have* paradigm. In particular, it does not cover light-verb uses of *have*, nor does it cover the variants of *have* that take small clause complements, such as causative *have*, experiencer *have*, and locative *have*. These would presumably require yet more lexical entries for *have*. Nor does it cover abstract properties such as *John has a great deal of strength*. Tham (2004, 48) defends this omission on the grounds that such sentences "predicate some state or property of an individual or some attribute of that individual," as opposed to "core" cases of possession, which is conceptualized as "a relation between two concrete, independent individuals." While this may be a fair characterization of the semantic difference between sentences like *John has a great deal of strength* and *John has a sister*, one still wants to understand why it is possible to use "possession" sentences to express such relations, especially since such abstract possession is possible in a number of languages beyond English (see the discussion of the Quechua *-yoq* construction in Chapter 6 of the present work, for instance; also Koontz-Garboden and Francez (2014, 2015a, 2015b) on possessed properties in Ulwa).

Secondly, the POSS predicate in Tham's lexical entry for possessive *have* (in my (123a)) merely conceals a key part of the too-many-meanings puzzle, rather than solving it. Recall that this POSS predicate is supposed to range over ownership, kinship relations, body-part relations, and inanimate part-whole relations. Tham (2004:18) claims that these are the core cases of possession, and notes that they have "a privileged status in being the most likely interpretations of constructions typically recognized as being possessive" (2004:26). However, it is not clear what bearing these usage facts have on the proper semantic characterization of these relations.

Tham (2004, 39, her (50) and (51)) does provide some evidence that these relations are a natural class. She notes that the relevant relations are also combinable with verbs like *get* and *lose*, which is not true of certain other possible complements of *have*.[56]

(129)   a.   Mowgli has a sister/a crooked finger/a pen.

     b.   Mowgli got a sister/a crooked finger/a pen.

     c.   Mowgli lost a sister/a crooked finger/a pen.

(130)   a.   Mowgli has an examination.

     b.   ? Mowgli got an examination.

     c.   ? Mowgli lost an examination.

While Tham's intuition that these relations are a natural class is on the right track (and I defend a syntactic understanding of this intuition in Chapter 4), her decision to reflect this in the form of a semantically primitive POSS relation fails to address the basic question of what *having a sister*, *having a crooked finger*, and *having a pen* have in common with one another at the conceptual level in the first place. This is an important omission, and it effectively disqualifies the approach from counting as a solution to the too-many-meanings puzzle.

Finally, the nature of her approach to the multiple uses of *have*, since it relies on positing separate lexical entries with particular lexical semantics, does not feed into a satisfying comparative syntax of the HAVE/BE relation more generally. As we saw in the sections on the literature on the too-many-(surface)-structures puzzle, any theory that treats HAVE and BE as fundamentally separate is unsatisfactory. Unfortunately, Tham's approach appears to fall into this camp, as becomes clear from her analysis of BE languages such as Mandarin and Finnish (in fact, even the syntactico-semantic primitives involved in the analysis of these BE languages are very different in character). This is made even more clear by the way in which Tham characterizes her approach to the HAVE/BE question, which is as follows: "In my

---

56. I note, however, that these same distributional facts hold of abstract properties, which makes Tham's decision to set these relations aside seem all the more unjustified.

   (i)   John has courage.

   (ii)   John got courage.

   (iii)   John lost courage.

analysis, the possessive relations in HAVE and BE sentences have different sources. In HAVE sentences, the verb encodes the possessive relation, whereas in their BE counterparts, it is the case marker on the [possessor] NP that encodes it" (2004, 192).

2.4.1.4   Conclusions

In this section, I have examined three recent versions of the idea that HAVE has its own, vague, lexical semantics. While arguments have been advanced that such a theory is superior in a general way to theories that attribute no lexical semantics to HAVE, most notably by Brugman (1988), I have argued that these objections do not apply to my version of the approach. Moreover, all three of the approaches analyzed in this section have been shown to run into problems caused precisely by the lexical semantics attributed to the verb HAVE. Even if this lexical content is exceptionally vague (as in Belvin 1996), and even if multiple lexical entries for HAVE are given (as in Tham 2004, 2006), this content prevents the account from generalizing straightforwardly to important parts of the *have* paradigm in English. Moreover, none of these proposed solutions to the too-many-meanings puzzle proved to yield a productive way of addressing the too-many-(surface)-structures puzzle, an important desideratum. It is for these reasons that an approach that attributes no lexical semantics to HAVE is to be preferred, and it is into this camp that my own approach falls. In the next section, we turn to various recent versions of this latter hypothesis.

2.4.2   HAVE as Specific but Meaningless

The papers discussed in this section differ mainly in how far they take the hypothesis that the meaning of a HAVE sentence comes from somewhere other than HAVE itself. In particular, they are united in the idea that the possession relation in a relational HAVE sentence comes from within the DP complement of HAVE, and are in some way "passed up the tree" to HAVE's subject.[57] This fundamental insight, which is implemented in somewhat different ways in the papers discussed, originates in a never-published abstract by Landman and Partee (1987), and was eventually published as Partee (1999). The present work extends this insight to the broader

---

57. This contrasts with earlier "meaningless HAVE" proposals in the generative literature like Bach (1967) and Lyons (1968), in which HAVE is absent at deep structure.

typology of possession sentences in a manner that also addresses the too-many-(surface)-structures puzzle, something that most literature in this tradition does not attempt to do.

Starting with Partee (1999), I will discuss the following approaches in quasi-temporal order: Ritter and Rosen (1997), Beavers, Ponvert, and Wechsler (2009), and Sæbø (2009). I should note however that there is other recent work in the same tradition which I cannot discuss in detail here–these include Cowper (1989), Landman (2004), Gutiérrez-Rexach (2012), and Le Bruyn, de Swart and Zwarts (2013).

2.4.2.1   Partee (1999)

A central goal of Partee (1999) (and of the joint work with Fred Landman that ante-ceded it) is to account for the compositional semantics of relational *have* sentences in English, and to explain why they are ill-formed in combination with certain determiners (Partee 1999, 1; her (1) and (2)).

(131)   John has two sisters.

(132)   * John has every sister

Partee was the first to point out that there are close parallelisms between the set of determiners that cause deviance in relational *have* sentences and the ones that trigger the so called *definiteness effect* in existentials (Milsark 1977).[58] These are the determiners that Keenan (1987), who also acknowledged the existence of definiteness effects in relational *have* sentences, termed existential determiners.

The fundamental puzzle posed by (131) and (132), as Partee (1999, 2) sees it, is as follows. The NP complement of relational *have* patterns as if it were an ordinary generalized quantifier which is required to be weak for reasons related to definiteness effects in existential sentences. However, semantically it would seem that the NP (*two sisters* in (131)) denotes a relation, rather than a generalized quantifier, and that the subject of the *have* sentence is interpreted as the subject of that relation. The meaning of the whole sentence would be as in (133), and the meaning of the VP would be (134) (Partee 1999, 3; her (7) and (8)).

(133)   *John has a sister*: $\exists x[\text{sister-of'}(j)(x)]$

(134)   *have a sister*: $\lambda y[\exists x[\text{sister-of'}(y)(x)]\,]$

---

58. As I show in Chapter 5, the definiteness effects in HAVE sentences do not always match up with the ones found in existential sentences, and there are many mismatches both within English and cross-linguistically.

The question is how to reconcile the "relationality" of this meaning with the existence of definiteness effects, which are characteristic of a subtype of generalized quantifier. Partee's solution (dating back to Landman and Partee (1987)) is to give the NP the denotation in (135), and to let relational *have* denote Keenan's *exist* predicate (which holds of every entity in the domain).

(135)   *a sister*: $\lambda P \lambda y [\exists x [\text{sister-of'}(y)(x) \wedge P(x)]]$

(136)   *have*: $\lambda R [R(\text{exist})]$

In the composition of a sentence like *John has a sister*, therefore, the VP meaning is composed by having *a sister* take *have* as its first argument. The result is the following meaning, which then simply takes *John* as its next argument to derive the meaning of the whole.

(137)   *have a sister*: $\lambda y [\exists x [\text{sister-of'}(y)(x) \wedge \text{exist}(x)]]$

The presence of the *exist* predicate in (137) then reduces the definiteness effects of HAVE sentences to Keenan's (1987) explanation for the same effect in existential sentences, according to which strong quantifiers are ungrammatical in such sentences because they yield vacuous meanings (*there is every car = every car is a car that exists*). It also captures the relational nature of *have*'s complement at the same time.

Partee's analysis has the effect of pushing the relation associated with *sister* up the tree to the whole verb phrase, an idea that later literature extended to other types of *have*, on which Partee (1999, 7) takes no position. The approach requires certain technical innovations to account for how determiners are able to combine both with relational nouns on the one hand, and non-relational nouns on the other. She proposes two denotations for *a*, given in (138) (Partee 1999, 3, her (11)), and a general rule which relates normal determiner denotations to their relational counterparts, given in (139) (Partee 1999, 3; her (12)). This proposal is very much in the spirit of the notion of contextual allosemy employed in this book and in much other recent work on argument structure.

(138)   a.   Normal *a*: $\lambda Q \lambda P [\exists x [Q(x) \ \& \ P(x)]]$

         b.   Relational *a*: $\lambda R \lambda P \lambda y [\exists x [R(y)(x) \ \& \ P(x)]]$

(139)   If Det has a normal translation $\lambda Q \lambda P [\Phi(Q,P)]$, i.e. Φ, then its translation as a "relational" Det is $\lambda R \lambda P \lambda y [\Phi(R(y),P)]$.

Similar innovations are required also on my approach, of course, although they are implemented somewhat differently in subsequent chapters, where I move away from the idea that definiteness effects in HAVE sentences should be reduced to those of existential sentences.

While many questions remained about other uses of *have* in English and other languages, not to mention how the analysis of HAVE should relate to that of BE-based possession constructions, Partee and Landman's proposal for relational *have* contains the seed of the idea that is extended to the broader *have* paradigm in subsequent work, including the present one.

2.4.2.2   Ritter and Rosen (1997)

Ritter and Rosen (1997), building on earlier work of theirs (Ritter and Rosen 1993), present an analysis with the following postulates and consequences (Ritter and Rosen 1997, 296).

(140)   *Postulates*

    a.   There is only one verb *have*

    b.   *Have* is a functional item: it has no specific thematic content, and no thematic roles to assign.

    c.   *Have* provides the additional syntactic structure necessary for the insertion of an extra argument, and/or for the modification of event structure.

(141)   *Consequences*

    a.   *Have* lacks the lexical semantic content necessary to provide an interpretation for its subject argument (Ritter and Rosen 1993)

    b.   The subject of *have* must be related to some other constituent in order to get an interpretation.

    c.   The meaning of *have* is determined post-lexically by the nature of the relations it sets up, i.e., by the possible construal of the items related.

With the exception of a few friendly (but important) amendments, including the addition of a detailed compositional account of the semantics involved, the analysis of HAVE presented in Chapter 4 agrees with (140) and (141) entirely.

Ritter and Rosen (1997, 299) depart from the Freeze/Kayne tradition in their conception of the relationship of BE and HAVE–each involves a somewhat different superstructure embedding a small clause or a DP. HAVE is not conceived of as the result of a P incorporating into BE, but rather as the realization of two argument-structural functional heads, whose labels are underspecified. Sample structures (for the case where BE/HAVE embeds a small clause) are presented in (142) and (143). Note that, while the following diagrams (Ritter and Rosen's (4a) and (4b), respectively) depict the subject of HAVE as having raised from the subject position of the small clause, Ritter and Rosen (1997, 298) declare themselves agnostic as to whether the subject is raised or base-generated in spec-F1P.

(142)   *BE for Ritter and Rosen (1997)*

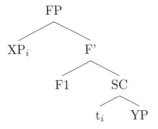

(143)   *HAVE for Ritter and Rosen (1997)*

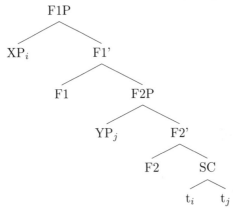

In consequence, languages with possession sentences built around BE and an adposition differ significantly in their structural representation from HAVE languages for Ritter and Rosen (1997, 299). Ritter and Rosen (1997) therefore constitutes an antecedent to my position that BE-based possession constructions have a different underlying argument structure from HAVE constructions, although Ritter and Rosen do not investigate the domain of BE in detail (providing only a sketch of an account of possession sentences in Hebrew).

Since HAVE itself contributes nothing to interpretation, the meaning of a HAVE sentence depends entirely on the elements that F1 and F2 relate in a structure like (143). Ritter and Rosen (1997, 297) claim that there are two main ways in which the subject of HAVE is assigned an interpretation: if the structure as a whole has eventive semantics, then the subject of HAVE is assigned a role in that event–for instance, an agent. If the structure as a whole is non-eventive, then the subject of HAVE can only receive an interpretation if it binds a (possibly covert) pronominal inside the predicate. On this point, the analysis is very similar to that of Belvin (1996). Unlike Belvin's analysis, however, Ritter and Rosen's analysis does not suffer from any of the problems caused by the notion that HAVE denotes an abstract inclusion relation.

Focussing on English *have*, Ritter and Rosen (1997, 302-304) show that the first option for the interpretation of *have*'s subject (whereby it is interpreted as a participant in an event) is instantiated by causative *have* and light-verb *have*, as follows (based on Ritter and Rosen's (8) and (12), respectively; note that ⟨e⟩ is the notation Ritter and Rosen use to indicate an eventive noun). In each of these cases F1's complement contains an element with an eventive denotation, and so *have*'s subject is interpreted as instigating the event in each case.

(144)   John had the students read three articles.

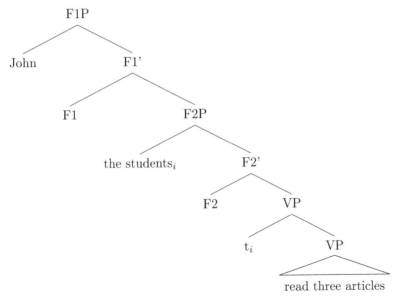

(145)   John had fun.

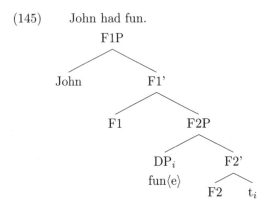

If the complement of F1 does not denote an event, *have*'s subject must instead be interpreted as co-referent with a constituent inside that complement, on Ritter and Rosen's analysis.[59] Cases instantiating this option include locative *have*, relational *have*, temporary possession *have*, and experiencer *have*. The origin of the anaphoric link is different in each case, but the fundamental pattern is the same (Ritter and Rosen 1997, 309-316).

In locative *have* sentences, the link is supplied by a pronoun inside the locative small clause, as shown in (146). Temporary possession sentences are treated in the same manner, except that in this case the small clause can be silent, as seen in (147) (Ritter and Rosen 1997, 315, adapted from their (46a)). For relational *have* and ownership sentences, the link is provided by a silent pronominal internal to the DP itself. Ritter and Rosen assume that the structural position of the pronoun is different in each case, as shown by the structures in (148) and (149). Note that Ritter and Rosen do not give an account of the definiteness effects found in these sorts of *have* sentence–an omission that my own approach seeks to rectify.

---

59. This predicts a perfect correlation between this coreference requirement and stativity–a correlation which is not always borne out, as we will see in Chapter 5.

(146)   The table has a hat on it. (Ritter and Rosen's (27b), adapted)

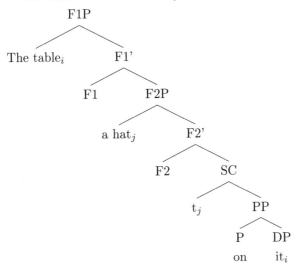

(147)   John has Bill's book.

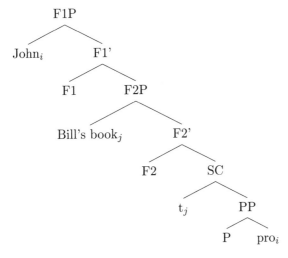

(148)   John has a sister. (Adapted from Ritter and Rosen's (29a))

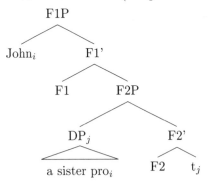

(149)   John has a hat. (Adapted from Ritter and Rosen's (40))

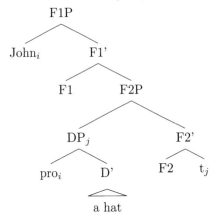

Finally, experiencer *have* involves a similar pronominal relationship, except that the pronoun itself is embedded within an event-denoting constituent (like a VP). Ritter and Rosen (1997, 316) erroneously depart from their earlier work (Ritter and Rosen 1993) in claiming that *have* itself is stative in experiencer *have* constructions. That this is false is shown by the multiple eventivity tests in (151). Note that the pronoun depicted in the tree in (150) may be silent.

(150)   John had the students walk out of class. (From Ritter and Rosen's (48))

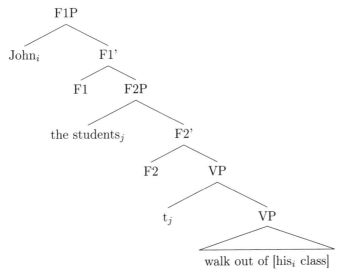

(151)   a.   John is having the students walk out of class (on him).

        b.   John has the students walk out of class (every week). [present tense
              requires generic interpretation]

        c.   What happened was that John had the students walk out of class.

Despite certain problems of detail, then, Ritter and Rosen's move of generalizing
the meaninglessness of *have* enables them to solve a large swath of the too-many-
meanings puzzle.[60] My own approach merely aims to eliminate these problems of
detail, and to embed the Ritter and Rosen-style approach in a broader theory that
also provides an answer to the too-many-(surface)-structures puzzle. Additionally,
I will provide an explicit compositional analysis of the semantics, something not
provided by Ritter and Rosen.

2.4.2.3   Beavers, Ponvert, and Wechsler (2008)

Beavers, Ponvert, and Wechsler (2008) deserves special mention here as an
antecedent of my idea that a certain class of *have* sentences involves a relation

---

60. Ritter and Rosen (1997, 316-320) also tentatively outline an extension of their approach to
auxiliary *have*, but I will not review this here, because my focus is on main verb HAVE.

introduced DP-internally being passed up the tree, without the need for a syntactically present pronominal. They extend this analysis beyond *have* to sentences with
want, *get*, and *give*, but I will focus on their discussion of *have* here.

Their analysis is in part an extension of Partee's approach to sentences like (152a)
to a wider set of possession sentences, seen in (152b)-(152d) (Beavers et al. 2008,
210, their (5)).

(152)   a. John has a sister.

         b. John has a car.

         c. John has the car (for the weekend).

         d. John has the windows (to clean).

Beavers et al. (2008) unite the analysis of *John has a car* with that of *John has
a sister* by adopting Barker's (1995) idea that non-relational nouns can be made
relational via a Poss morpheme–an idea I have also followed in this book. They
point out that this unification is supported by the fact that alienable and inalienable
possessed DPs can be successfully conjoined, as in the following examples (Beavers
et al. 2008, 122, their (43)).

(153)   John has a condo and a generous sister who pays all the bills.

Couching their approach in HPSG, Beavers et al. model their analysis of *have*
after the typical analysis for raising verbs in that framework. Space constraints
prevent me from introducing the HPSG formalism in a comprehensible manner,
so I will instead convey the main intuition behind the account. Essentially, raising
verbs in HPSG are predicates that require an internal argument that is "missing" its
subject syntactically and semantically. They then identify their own subject with
the missing subject of their complement. *Have*, for Beavers et al., is analogous:
its first argument is a possessed DP missing its possessor, and its subject is then
identified as that possessor. This is the same as my analysis for sentences like
(152a) and (152b), although I show in Chapter 4 that the analogy to raising is
on the wrong track for *have*, and that raising must be syntactically distinct from
delayed gratification. Beavers et al. extend the same analysis to cases like (152c)
and (152d), and so do not link the definiteness effects in relational *have* sentences
to the way in which determiners interact with delayed gratification, as I do. Beavers
et al. (2008, 121, fn 11) offer no analysis of the definiteness effect, and why it should
hold for relational *have* and ownership *have* but not for such sentences as (152c)-
(152d). Furthermore, Beavers et al. do not extend the analysis to *have* sentences
beyond the types instantiated in (152).

2.4.2.4   Sæbø (2009)

Sæbø (2009) proposes an analysis in much the same spirit as Ritter and Rosen (1997), but with a more explicit semantic proposal with respect to the interpretation of *have*. His focus is on accounting for *have* sentences of the following sort (2009, 3; his (7)-(9)).

(154)   a.   The beetle had the engine in the rear.

       b.   She has all four grandparents alive.

       c.   Shrek has a donkey for a friend.

Sæbø (2009, 3) identifies two problems posed by these kinds of sentence (he credits Iatridou (1995) with first identifying what Sæbø calls the pertinence problem).

(155)   a.   **Pertinence Problem**
          As it appears, the subject of *have* must bind a variable in the SC.

       b.   **Redundancy Problem**
          Beyond binding some variable in the SC, the subject of *have* seems to have no semantic role to play.

Sæbø (2009, 9) suggests that both of these problems can be solved if *have* is assigned the following denotation (*s* here is the type of states).

(156) $[\![\text{have}]\!] = \lambda \phi_{\langle st \rangle} \lambda \mathrm{x}.\phi$

This denotation takes a set of states as its first argument, and maps it to a function from a set of individuals to the same set of states. The sample derivation in (158) of the sentence *most cars have their engine in the front* shows how this denotation works. *Engine* in this derivation denotes a part-whole relation of which *their* (represented by the index 3) is the "whole." The small clause as a whole denotes the set of states in which the engines of the entities picked out by 3 are "in the front". The role of *have* is to take this denotation and return a new function from a set of individuals to that same set of states. This forces QR of the subject, leaving a trace that goes in for the individual argument introduced by *have*. This same QR operation creates a trace-binder μ_i, whose denotation is the following (Sæbø 2009, 8, his (21)).

(157) $[\![\mu_i]\!] = \lambda \phi \lambda \mathrm{z}.\phi^{f[i \to z]}$

(158)

λs(most cars)(λz.inthefront(engine(z))(s))

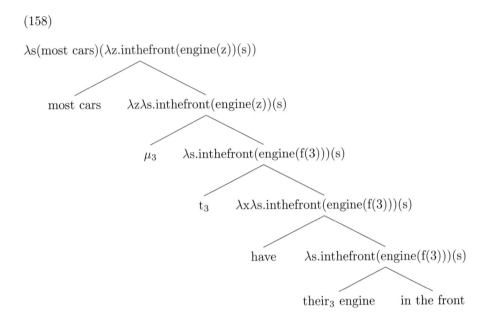

The trace-binder in (157) has the effect of replacing the index 3 with a lambda-abstracted variable. The resulting function is from a set of individuals to a set of states, and the QRed subject can then take that denotation as its argument, yielding the desired meaning for the sentence (note that this requires that the subject of *have* always undergoes QR, so that proper names and definte DPs must be held to have generalized quantifier denotations in order for the account to work).

This simultaneously solves the redundancy problem and the pertinence problem. The redundancy problem is solved because *have* plays a crucial part in ensuring that the subject is integrated into the interpretation (since it absorbs the trace of the subject after QR). The pertinence problem is solved also: in the absence of something for the QRed subject to bind, the sentence would be uninterpretable. The analysis is straightforwardly extended to other *have* cases that clearly have a small clause. Relational *have* sentences like *John has a sister* are also assigned a small-clause analysis, where the small clause predicate is the silent *exist* predicate familiar from the work of Keenan (1987), Partee (1999), and Landman and Partee (1987).[61]

---

61. The account of definiteness effects in such sentences is the same as in these works too, in that it assimilates the definiteness effects in *have* sentences to the ones found in existentials–a problematic move, as discussed in Chapter 5.

Of all the approaches discussed in this section, Sæbø (2009) is perhaps closest to mine in terms of how far it pushes the meaninglessness of *have*–all *have* does in this system is introduce a vacuous lambda abstract, whose only role is to trigger a QR operation that ultimately proves crucial in integrating the subject into the composition. However, since his focus is on the pertinence problem, it is unclear how Sæbø's approach would extend to cases where such a binding relationship is less easy to motivate, as in causative *have* or light-verb *have*.

(159)   a.   John had Bill wash the dishes.

       b.   John had fun.

The analysis developed in Chapter 4 will capture such sentences because it makes *have* more meaningless still: since *have* is a type-neutral identity function, the eventive denotation of *have*'s complement is simply passed up to Voice, which relates the subject to that denotation in the familiar way.

2.4.3   Section Conclusion: The State of the Art on the Too-Many-Meanings Puzzle

This section has compared two major traditions in the previous literature on what I have called the too-many-meanings puzzle. The key division between these two traditions is whether HAVE itself has true lexical semantics of its own. I have argued that attributing even the vaguest lexical semantics to HAVE leads to problems if one is aiming for a unified analysis. Ultimately, more than one lexical entry for HAVE or special stipulated conditions on interpretation turn out to be needed in order to make analyses work when they include the assumption that HAVE has its own lexical semantics. In addition, making HAVE a lexical verb makes it difficult to relate HAVE to BE in a systematic, grammatically-governed way. This is an important deficiency, given that such a relation is well-motivated. All of these problems are eliminated if HAVE is instead taken to be meaningless. The further an analysis pushes the idea that HAVE is meaningless, the more successful it turns out to be.

2.5   Chapter Conclusion: Approaching Predicative Possession

This broad (but nowhere near comprehensive) overview of the literature on the syntax and semantics of possession sentences has led to the following conclusions:

(160)   *Approaching Predicative Possession*

    a.   There is abundant morphosyntactic evidence that HAVE and BE should be treated as two realizations of fundamentally the same element, as argued by the Freeze/Kayne tradition.

    b.   Nevertheless, there are distinctions between HAVE and BE constructions, and within the class of BE constructions, which point to real underlying differences in argument structure.

    c.   The meaning of possession sentences does not come from HAVE and BE verbs themselves, but from other elements in the sentence.

These conclusions place constraints on what plausible solutions to the too-many-(surface)-structures puzzle and the too-many-meanings puzzle can look like.

(161)   *Constraints on Solutions to the Puzzles*

    a.   Solving the too-many-(surface)-structures puzzle involves developing a theory of the syntax-semantics interface that explains how syntactically different argument structures can yield the same semantic result.

    b.   Solving the too-many-meanings puzzle requires abandoning the idea that possession sentences pick out a semantically natural class of elements, which could be stated as the "meaning" of HAVE.

In the rest of this book, I develop an approach that holds to (161), one that takes the position that the solutions to these puzzles are intimately related. If this is correct, then it follows that work on either one of these two puzzles must go on in tandem with work on the other–something which has not always been the case, as this review of the literature has made clear.

3 The Micro-Comparative Syntax of Possession in Quechua

3.1 Outline of the Chapter

The theory of argument structure described in Chapter 1 makes certain predictions about what the typology of possession should look like. Amongst them are the following.

(1)   *Predictions of the Present Approach*

    a.   Possession constructions can vary in the place in the structure where the possessor is introduced.

    b.   The different ways of building possession sentences permitted by (a.) could have somewhat different (albeit potentially overlapping) meanings, depending on the semantic contributions of the pieces that make them up.

These predictions are clearly distinct from the ones made by the strongest interpretation of the Freeze/Kayne tradition: if all possession sentences share the same underlying argument structure from which all the surface typological variation is derived by movement, then (1a) is false by definition, and therefore (1b) cannot be true either. Evaluating the predictions in (1) is thus an obvious way to compare the two theories.

The main aim of this chapter is to provide existence proofs that the predictions in (1) are in fact correct. This is done by presenting analyses of data collected through fieldwork on two Quechua dialects that come from the same sub-group in the family (Quechua IIC in the classification system of Torero 1964). The dialects examined are the Bolivian dialect of Cochabamba and the Argentine dialect of Santiago del Estero, both of which turn out to have more than one predicative possession construction. The secondary aim of this chapter is to offer some speculations as to why Santiago del Estero has HAVE, whereas Cochabamba Quechua does not. Since the two varieties are rather closely related, the comparison has the potential to shed micro-comparative light on the question of what syntactic properties correlate with having HAVE, and why.

The chapter is structured as follows. Section 3.2 gives some necessary background on Quechua and discusses how the data presented here were gathered. Section 3.3 presents an analysis of two existential BE-based possession constructions in Cochabamba Quechua, which I call the BE construction and the BE-APPL construction. These two constructions turn out to be thematically identical in terms of the sorts of possession relation they can and cannot express. However, I will argue that certain morphosyntactic differences between them force the conclusion that they

involve introducing the possessor in different parts of the structure. This constitutes an existence proof for (1a). Section 3.4 provides an existence proof for (1b)
by comparing the Cochabamba Quechua BE-APPL construction to a superficially
near-identical construction in Santiago del Estero Quechua. Despite the superficial
similarities, the two constructions turn out to have very different syntactic and
semantic properties. I show that these differences are partly explicable in terms
of differences in the way in which the copula systems of these two Quechua languages are organized. The superficial similarities between the constructions are
misleading–BE-APPL in Cochabamba is an existential construction, whereas BE-
APPL in Santiago del Estero Quechua is a predicate locative construction. These
syntactic differences in the way BE-APPL is assembled in the two languages explain
why they have different (albeit partially overlapping) meanings, confirming (1b). In
Section 3.5, I show that Santiago del Estero Quechua is a HAVE language, whereas
Cochabamba Quechua is a BE language that lacks HAVE altogether. While I will
not offer definitive answers to the question of why the varieties differ in this way, I
will point out the negative implications that the micro-comparison between these
dialects has for some earlier proposals on parametric variation in predicative possession. I will also propose that variation in a certain subtype of psych constructions
correlates with having HAVE or lacking it in the Quechua family. Section 3.6 summarizes the major conclusions of the chapter.

3.2   Background on Quechua and a Word on the Data

Quechua is an indigenous Amerindian family of languages spoken in Peru, Ecuador,
Bolivia, parts of northern Chile, parts of northern Argentina, and Colombia. Proto-
Quechua is thought to have existed up until some time in the first half of the first
millennium of the Common Era (Torero 1984, 382-383, cited in Adelaar 2004, 181),
and was probably originally spoken in the area around the central Peruvian coast.
Quechua achieved much of its current wide distribution during the expansionary
period of the Inca Empire, of which it was the main language of communication.
However, some groups of speakers, perhaps including those found in Argentina, were
transplanted to their present locations en masse by the Spanish during the early
colonial period. The total number of Quechua speakers is hard to calculate precisely.
Coronel-Molina and Rodríguez-Mondoñedo (2012) estimate the total number of
speakers to be between ten and thirteen million. Adelaar (2004, 168) cites a range
of estimates between eight million and ten million. On the other hand, Sánchez
(2010), based on data from censuses in Peru, Bolivia, and Ecuador since 2007,

cites the much lower figure of approximately five million. There is considerable variation within the family in all areas of grammar and lexis, such that, in the words of Adelaar, "Speakers of different Quechua dialects often have a difficult time understanding each other. If the dialects are not closely related, there may be no mutual comprehension at all" (2004, 168). Nonetheless, all languages in the family share a number of properties, including having SOV as the neutral word order, being Nominative-Accusative in alignment, having heavily agglutinating and exclusively suffixal morphology, and being pro-drop.

As for genetic affiliation, Quechua is not securely linked to any other language family, although there is a long tradition of (controversial) claims that it shares a common ancestor with its close neighbor Aymara. This position, known as the Quechumara hypothesis, is discussed at length in Cerrón-Palomino (2008). See Adelaar (2004, 34-36) for a summary of this debate and further references, as well as discussion of other, even more controversial proposals concerning Quechua's genetic affiliation.

Major subgroupings within the family were proposed by Torero (1964) as follows:

(2)   *The Quechua Family: Major Subgroups*

    a.   Quechua I (central Peruvian dialects–thought to be the oldest sub-branch of the family)

    b.   Quechua II (spread across eastern and northern Peru, through Ecuador, Colombia, Bolivia, and parts of Chile and Argentina).

Quechua II is further subdivided into groups IIA (containing the northern Peruvian variety of Cajamarca and a handful of other varieties), IIB (consisting of the dialects of Ecuador, Colombia, and the Peruvian Amazon) and IIC (which includes the dialects of Bolivia, Chile, Argentina, and southern Peru). Both Cochabamba Quechua and Santiago del Estero Quechua are in the IIC subgroup. Their common ancestor probably existed at least as recently as the fifteenth century, which is when Quechua speakers from the Cuzco area first entered Bolivia and Argentina (Kusters 2003, 249).

Descriptive work on Quechua goes back to the sixteenth century, which saw the first attempts by early Spanish colonists to adequately describe Quechua in order to use it effectively for evangelical and administrative purposes (see especially Domingo de Santo Tomás 1560, a remarkably sophisticated and detailed descriptive grammar of a coastal Peruvian variety). There is also a great deal of descriptive and theoretical work on many Quechua varieties in the structuralist and generative traditions from the early part of the twentieth century on (see Adelaar 2004, 191-194 for review). Descriptive and pedagogical grammars exist for both Cochabamba

Quechua (Lastra 1968; Bills et al. 1969) and Santiago del Estero Quechua (Albarracín 2011; Alderetes 2001; Bravo 1956; Nardi 2002; Prezioso and Torres 2006). While extremely valuable in general, these works record only surface details of the morphosyntax of the different possession constructions, and give very little information on the subtypes of possession relation that the different constructions are compatible with. Since such details were essential for this investigation, fieldwork was undertaken.

The Cochabamba Quechua data presented in this chapter were gathered from three main consultants living in Cochabamba, Bolivia. The Santiago del Estero Quechua data were gathered mainly from two consultants living in the city of Santiago del Estero, and certain judgments that are key to the argument in section 3.4 were rechecked with five additional speakers in Salavina, a small community approximately six hours outside of Santiago del Estero with a high concentration of Quechua speakers (the speakers with whom I worked in the city are originally from near Salavina, and I did not detect any dialect differences between these speakers and the ones currently living in Salavina). All of the consultants were native speakers of Quechua fluent in Spanish.

Some of the judgments gathered were connected with matters of constituency and other morphosyntactic issues, and these judgments were elicited by presenting constructed sentences in the familiar way. The precise nature of the test sentences and my purpose in eliciting them will become clear as the analysis develops, and I will thus not go into them here. For the semantic judgments elicited, however, it is worth taking more time to describe the sort of data that was elicited, why, and how.

The main goal of the semantic part of the fieldwork was to determine, for each possession construction in a given dialect, which of the different cross-linguistically attested subtypes of possession relation that construction is able to express. The taxonomy of possession relations for which I elicited data was a slightly expanded version of a list provided by Heine (1997, 34-35). This list is given below, along with examples from English (or Spanish if relevant English cases are not available).

(3)   John has a cup (with him).   (Physical Possession)

(4)   John has my keys.   (Temporary Possession)

(5)   John has a car.   (Ownership)

(6)   John has black hair.   (Body Parts)

(7)   John has a sister.   (Kinship)

(8)   A weaver has a spindle.   (Canonical Tool)

(9)   This house has a window.   (Part-Whole)

(10)   Juan tiene frío.   (Physical Sensation)
        Juan has   cold
        'John is cold.' (i.e., he's feeling the cold.)

(11)   Juan tiene miedo.   (Psychological State)
        Juan has   fear
        'John is afraid.'

(12)   John has (a great deal of) kindness.   (Abstract Property)

(13)   John has the flu.   (Disease)

(14)   John has a cockroach on his head.   (Locative HAVE)
        That tree has many nests in it.

Semantic judgments of this sort were elicited by presenting instances of each construction in a given contextual scenario. To give the reader a sense for how this was done, take the question of whether the copular BE-based *-yoq* construction in Cochabamba Quechua is compatible with a reading involving temporary possession of a definite DP (the answer turns out to be no; see Chapter 6). One way in which this was tested was by describing to the consultant the following scenario, and subsequently asking him or her whether a constructed Quechua sentence (here reproduced below it) was usable in that context. The contexts themselves were usually described to the consultants in Spanish, in which all were bilingual. For arguments in favor of this methodology for semantic fieldwork, including a defense of the (potentially controversial) idea of describing contexts in an auxiliary language in this way, see Matthewson (2004); Bochnak and Matthewson (2015); Davis, Gillon, and Matthewson (2014).

(15)   *You are staying at a hotel with your friend. Your friend is wondering where the key to the room has gone. You say:*

        Noqa llavi-yoq ka-ni.
        I   key-YOQ be-1SUBJ
        'I have the key.'

Analogous tests were constructed for the other subtypes of predicative possession construction in each of the varieties.

With this background in mind, we turn in the next section to an existence proof for (1a), from Cochabamba Quechua.

3.3   Possession Sentences, Movement, and UTAH

This section provides an existence proof that thematically identical possession constructions cannot always be related by movement. This existence proof will come from a close examination of the following two constructions.[1]

(16)   Noqa-qta auto-s-ni-y   tiya-n.   (BE)
        I-GEN   car-PL-EUPH-1POSS be$_{exist}$-3SUBJ
        'I have cars.' lit. 'There are cars of mine.'

(17)   Noqa-qta auto-s tiya-pu-wa-n.   (BE-APPL)
        I-GEN   car-PL be$_{exist}$-APPL-1OBJ-3SUBJ
        'I have cars.' lit. 'There are cars for me.'

These constructions differ in at least three important ways (the reader will probably be able to infer them already by looking closely at the examples), but for now we will focus on their commonalities, which are striking. In both, the possessor appears in the genitive case, and the possessee appears in the (unmarked) nominative case. Both are existential constructions, as opposed to predicative copular ones (like the -*yoq* construction discussed in Chapter 6). This is shown by three facts. First, the verb root is *tiya-*, which is the form that the existential verb generally takes in the present tense (in contrast, the morphologically distinct predicative copula has the root *ka-* in all tenses).[2]

---

1. The morpheme -*ni*, glossed EUPH in (16), is a *euphonic* suffix inserted whenever the concatenation of nominal morphemes leads to an unacceptable syllable structure (such as a complex coda).

2. The root *tiya-* is also the root of the verb meaning 'to sit', and 'to reside'. In the 'to sit' meaning, it requires the presence of the reflexive marker -*ku*, so that 'to sit, to be seated' is *tiya-ku-y*.
The paradigms of the predicative copula and the existential copula overlap outside the present tense, and are neutralized in favor of *ka-*. Existentials and predicative copular constructions both take the root *ka-* in the past tense, for example. It should also be noted that *ka-* becomes an option even in present tense existentials when certain verbal affixes are present, including applicative -*pu*. In other words, (i) is also a possible rendering of (17). There do not appear to be any syntactic or semantic consequences of the choice of *ka-* or *tiya-* as the spell out of the root of the existential verb in such circumstances.

(i)   Noqa-qta auto-s ka-pu-wa-n.
       I-GEN   car-PL be-APPL-1OBJ-3SUBJ
       'I have cars.' lit. 'There are cars for me.'

We can still be sure that a case like (i) is an existential construction, however, because of the fact that there is obligatory default 3rd singular agreement on the verb (predicative copular constructions would have agreement between the nominative argument and the verb).

(18) Bolivia-pi llama-s tiya-n.
      Bolivia-in llama-PL be$_{exist}$-3SUBJ
      'There are llamas in Bolivia.'

Secondly, existential constructions in Quechua languages have invariant 3rd person singular agreement on the verb, whereas predicative copular constructions display full agreement with the subject of predication (see Hastings 2004). It turns out that this is true of both the BE construction and the BE-APPL construction: the verb must show 3rd singular agreement as in (16) and (17), and attempting to make *tiya-* agree with either the 1st singular possessor or the 3rd plural possessee yields ungrammaticality as shown in (19) and (20).

(19) Noqa-qta iskay pana-s-ni-y   tiya{-n/-*ni/*-n-ku}.
      I-GEN   two   sister-PL-EUPH-1POSS be$_{exist}${-3/-1/-3SUBJ-PL}
      'I have two sisters.'

(20) Noqa-qta iskay pana-s   tiya-pu-wa{-n/-*ni/*-n-ku}.
      I-GEN   two   sister-PL be$_{exist}$-APPL-1OBJ{-3/-1/-3SUBJ-PL}
      'I have two sisters.'

A third diagnostic showing that both the BE and the BE-APPL constructions are existential is the fact that the 3rd singular form of the verb is overt–this is characteristic of existential constructions (as shown by (18)), but it is banned in present tense predicative copular constructions, where the 3rd singular form of the verb must be covert. An illustration for the case of a copular construction with a PP predicate is provided in (21).

(21) a. Noqa Inglaterra-manta ka-ni.
          I   England-from   be-1SUBJ
          'I am from England.'
      b. Pay Inglaterra-manta (*ka-n).
          S/he England-from   be-3SUBJ
          'S/he is from England.'

In addition to these morphosyntactic similarities (the case of the arguments and the use of the existential verb), the two constructions are remarkably similar semantically. In fact, the BE construction and the BE-APPL construction are thematically identical for at least some speakers,[3] in that they pattern the same way with respect

---

3. The only mismatch I found was for one speaker only, who finds abstract property possession somewhat degraded with BE-APPL. The constructions patterned together perfectly for other relations even for this speaker, however.

to the subtypes of possession relation they can and cannot express. This is summarized in the following table.

(22)   *BE and BE-APPL in Cochabamba Quechua*

	BE	**BE-APPL**
Kinship	OK	OK
Body Parts	restricted	restricted
Part-Whole	restricted	restricted
Permanent Possession	OK	OK
Abstract Property	OK	OK (%)
Temporary Possession	*	*
Psychological State	*	*
Physical Sensation	*	*
Disease	restricted	restricted

In the following paragraphs, I present data substantiating (22). Turning first to various types of inalienable possession (including kinship, body parts and part-whole relations), the two constructions are both able to convey these notions. In the case of body parts and part-whole readings, they do so with a degree of awkwardness in the context of adjectival modification. Body parts combined with numerals are fine, on the other hand.

(23)   *Kinship:* BE

    a.   Juan-pata pana-n   tiya-n.
          Juan-GEN sister-3POSS be$_{exist}$-3SUBJ
          'Juan has a sister.'

    b.   Noqa-qta pana-y   tiya-n.
          I-GEN   sister-1POSS be$_{exist}$-3SUBJ
          'I have a sister.'

(24)   *Kinship:* BE-APPL

    a.   Juan-pata pana tiya-pu-n.
          Juan-GEN sister be$_{exist}$-APPL-3SUBJ
          'Juan has a sister.'

    b.   Noqa-qta pana tiya-pu-wa-n.
          I-GEN   sister be$_{exist}$-APPL-1OBJ-3SUBJ
          'I have a sister.'

(25)   *Body Parts:* BE

    (?)? Noqa-qta yana chujcha-y tiya-n.
        I-GEN   black hair-1POSS be$_{exist}$-3SUBJ
    'I have black hair.'

(26)   *Body Parts:* BE-APPL

    (?)? Noqa-qta yana chujcha tiya-pu-wa-n.
        I-GEN   black hair   be$_{exist}$-APPL-1OBJ-3SUBJ
    'I have black hair.'

(27)   *Body Parts:* BE

    Noqa-qta uj ñawi-y   tiya-n.
    I-GEN   one eye-1POSS be$_{exist}$-3SUBJ
    'I have one eye.'

(28)   *Body Parts:* BE-APPL

    Noqa-qta uj ñawi tiya-pu-wa-n.
    I-GEN   one eye be$_{exist}$-APPL-1OBJ-3SUBJ
    'I have one eye.'

(29)   *Part-Whole:* BE

    a.   Kay wasi-qta   uj ventana-n   tiya-n.
           this house-GEN one window-3POSS be$_{exist}$-3SUBJ
           'This house has one window.'

    b.   ? Kay challwa-qta ancha tullu-n   tiya-n.
           This fish-GEN   much bone-3POSS be$_{exist}$-3SUBJ
           'This fish has a lot of bone(s).'

(30)   *Part-Whole:* BE-APPL

    a.   Kay wasi-qta   uj ventana tiya-pu-n.
           this house-GEN one window be$_{exist}$-APPL-3SUBJ
           'This house has one window.'

    b.   ? Kay challwa-qta ancha tullu tiya-pu-n
           This fish-GEN   much bone be$_{exist}$-APPL-3SUBJ
           'This fish has a lot of bone(s).'

Abstract properties and personal attributes like 'strength', which Heine (1997, 10) lists as counting as inalienably possessed in some languages that mark (in)alienability morphosyntactically, seem to be expressible with both constructions. For two of my speakers, both constructions are fine in such contexts. Another speaker found the BE-APPL construction appreciably worse in this environment (this was the only case, except the obligation construction discussed later in this section, where the two constructions did not pattern together–all that my thesis requires is that there are speakers who don't have this difference).

(31)   *Attribute:* BE

Juan-pata ancha kallpa-n   tiya-n.
Juan-GEN much strength-3POSS be$_{exist}$-3SUBJ
'Juan has a lot of strength.'

(32)   *Attribute:* BE-APPL

(??) Juan-pata ancha kallpa   tiya-pu-n.
      Juan-GEN much strength be$_{exist}$-APPL-3SUBJ
'Juan has a lot of strength.'

Ownership of indefinites can be readily expressed by both constructions (including expressing relationships between members of a profession and their canonical tools).

(33)   *Ownership (Indefinites):* BE

a.   Noqa-qta phishqa boliviano-s-ni-y   tiya-n.
      I-GEN   five   boliviano-PL-EUPH-1POSS be$_{exist}$-3SUBJ
      'I have five bolivianos.'

b.   Awa-q-kuna-qpata phushka-n-ku   tiya-n.
      Weave-er-PL-GEN spindle-3POSS-PL be$_{exist}$-3SUBJ
      'Weavers have spindles'

(34)   *Ownership (Indefinites):* BE-APPL

a.   Noqa-qta phishqa boliviano-s tiya-pu-wa-n.
      I-GEN   five   boliviano-PL be$_{exist}$-APPL-1OBJ-3SUBJ
      'I have five bolivianos.'

b.   Awa-q-kuna-qpata phushka tiya-pu-n
      Weave-er-PL-GEN spindle be$_{exist}$-APPL-3SUBJ
      'Weavers have spindles'

Both constructions are equally bad if used to assert ownership of a definite, as might be expected given the existential nature of these constructions (Hastings 2004 shows that the familiar definiteness effect holds in Quechua existentials). The following examples are judged in a context where I point to a particular glass, and assert that it belongs to Juan.

(35)   *Ownership (Definites):* BE

    * Juan-pata chay qeru-n   tiya-n.
    Juan-GEN that glass-3POSS be$_{exist}$-3SUBJ
    'Juan owns that glass.'

(36)   *Ownership (Definites):* BE-APPL

    * Juan-pata chay qeru tiya-pu-n.
    Juan-GEN that glass be$_{exist}$-APPL-3SUBJ
    'Juan owns that glass'

Both constructions appear to be restricted to canonically more permanent forms of possession. Neither of them can express temporary or merely physical possession readings regardless of whether the possessee is definite or indefinite. For example, the following are ungrammatical in a context where my friend and I are staying in a hotel room, and my friend asks what happened to the key.

(37)   *Temporary Possession (Definites):* BE

    * Noqa-qta llavi-y   tiya-n.
    I-GEN   key-1POSS be$_{exist}$-3SUBJ
    'I have the key.'

(38)   *Temporary Possession (Definites):* BE-APPL

    * Noqa-qta llavi tiya-pu-wa-n.
    I-GEN   key be$_{exist}$-APPL-1OBJ-3SUBJ
    'I have the key.'

Similarly, if Juan has a book in his hand that he does not own, these constructions cannot felicitously be used.

(39)   *Temporary Possession (Indefinites):* BE

    * Juan-pata uj libru-n   tiya-n.
    Juan-GEN one book-3POSS be$_{exist}$-3SUBJ
    'Juan has a book.' (bad, unless he owns it)

(40)   *Temporary Possession (Indefinites):* BE-APPL

     * Juan-pata uj libru tiya-pu-n

     Juan-GEN a book be$_{exist}$-APPL-3SUBJ

     'Juan has a book.' (bad, unless he owns it)

Neither construction can be used to express psychological states, physical sensations (like thirst), or most diseases/illnesses.

(41)   *Psychological State:* BE

     * Juan-pata mancha-y-ni-n   tiya-n.

     Juan-GEN fear-INF-EUPH-3POSS be$_{exist}$-3subj

     'Juan is afraid.'

(42)   *Psychological State:* BE-APPL

     * Juan-pata mancha-y tiya-pu-n

     Juan-GEN fear-INF   be$_{exist}$-APPL-3SUBJ

     'Juan is afraid.'

(43)   *Physical Sensation:* BE

     * Noqa-qta ch'aki-y-ni-y   tiya-n.

     I-GEN   thirst-INF-EUPH-1POSS be$_{exist}$-3SUBJ

     'I am thirsty.'

(44)   *Physical Sensation:* BE-APPL

     * Noqa-qta ch'aki-y   tiya-pu-wa-n.

     I-GEN   thirst-INF be$_{exist}$-APPL-1OBJ-3SUBJ

     'I am thirsty.'

(45)   *Diseases:* BE

   a. * Noqa-qta soroqchi-y   tiya-n.

       I-GEN   altitude.sickness-1POSS be$_{exist}$-3SUBJ

       'I have altitude sickness.'

   b. * Noqa-qta ch'uju-y   tiya-n.

       I-GEN   cough-1POSS be$_{exist}$-3SUBJ

       'I have a cough.'

(46)   *Diseases:* BE-APPL

    a. * Noqa-qta soroqchi   tiya-pu-wa-n.
        I-GEN   altitude.sickness be$_{exist}$-APPL-1OBJ-3SUBJ

        'I have altitude sickness.'

    b. * Noqa-qta ch'uju tiya-pu-wa-n
        I-GEN   cough   be$_{exist}$-APPL-1OBJ-3SUBJ

        'I have a cough.'

For the subtypes of possession relation that are bad for both constructions, some are clearly ungrammatical for reasons connected to the existential nature of the construction. It is easy to see why this would be in the case of relations involving definite possessees. The reasons for the ungrammaticality of the other cases could be diverse, and need further probing. Concerning the awkwardness of both constructions with body-part nouns modified by adjectives, it is interesting to note that the existential-based possession constructions of both Hungarian and Russian categorically reject body parts (Dániel Szeredi and Inna Livitz respectively, pers. comm.).[4] I must leave the task of addressing these issues in full for the future.

I conclude that the BE and BE-APPL constructions are indeed thematically identical for some speakers. I must stress that I am not claiming that there are no semantic differences of any sort between the two constructions–although I note that every speaker I have asked for metalinguistic commentary on the two constructions has told me that, for any given subtype of possessee with which the constructions are compatible, they mean the same thing. It is possible that more subtle differences, perhaps with respect to discourse uses, will emerge with further probing. All that I am claiming here, and all that the arguments to come rest on, is that the two constructions are identical with respect to the sorts of possession relation they can and cannot express.

Despite the semantic and morphosyntactic commonalities between these constructions, I will argue that the BE construction and the BE-APPL construction in Cochabamba Quechua differ syntactically in terms of where the possessor is first externally merged: inside the possessed DP in the case of the BE construction, and in spec-ApplP in the case of the BE-APPL. Specifically, I argue for the structures

---

4. The ideal situation would be to be able to reduce all of these ungrammatical cases to the fact that the structures are existential in nature, for then nothing more would need to be said about why the -*yoq* construction, discussed in Chapter 6, is more liberal than either of the constructions discussed in this section–it would follow from the fact that the -*yoq* construction is a predicative copular construction rather than an existential one.

displayed on the next page in (47) and (48). Recall that I adopt the analysis of existentials found in Tremblay (1991), Williams (1994), and Hazout (2004), according to which existentials involve a small clause structure of which the locative element (*there* in English) is the subject. I also follow Hastings (2004) in assuming that Quechua has a null *it*-like expletive in existentials, which raises to spec-TP. As well as explaining the subject agreement facts, this hypothesis has the advantage of accounting for the fact that neither the possessor nor the possessee counts as a subject with respect to the switch-reference system in adverbial clauses (see Hastings 2004, 158-161 for discussion).

Not depicted in (47) is the fact that the possessor subsequently moves out of the possessee DP in the BE construction, just as Szabolcsi (1981) argued for the very similar Hungarian construction. The evidence for this is that clausal material can intervene between the possessor and the possessee in the construction, as shown in (49).[5]

(47)   *BE Construction*

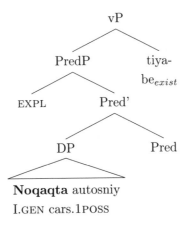

5. This evidence is also compatible with an analysis along the lines of Den Dikken (1999), who argues for Hungarian that the full DP possessor binds a resumptive pronoun inside the possessed DP, rather than (necessarily) raising from that position. The general point of this section, that the BE construction and the BE-APPL construction involve introducing the possessor in different positions, would not be affected if a version of Den Dikken's analysis proved to be correct for the Cochabamba Quechua BE construction. See below for more thorough discussion of Den Dikken's approach as applied to Quechua.

(48) *BE-APPL Construction*

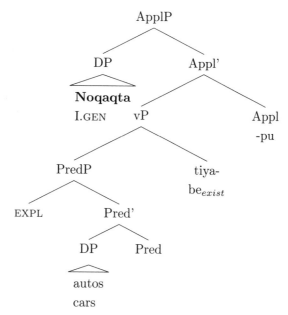

(49) *BE Construction: possessor and possessee are separable*

Juan-pata **sina**   tata-*(n)   tiya-n
Juan-GEN perhaps father-3POSS be$_{exist}$-3SUBJ

'Perhaps Juan is the one who has a father.'

The possibility of such possessor extraction is not surprising, since it is a general feature of Quechua languages that subparts of DP can be extracted (see Hastings 2004; LeFebvre and Muysken 1988). An example is provided in (50).

(50) Juan-pata sina   uj-ni-n   ka-q   masi-n-ta
Juan-GEN maybe one-EUPH-3POSS be-REL fellow-3POSS-ACC
riku-rqa-ni.
see-PAST-1SUBJ

'I saw one of (maybe) Juan's friends.'

This idea that the possessor moves out of the possessed DP in the BE construction will become important later, when the prospects for relating BE and BE-APPL by movement are dicussed (and dismissed).

To summarize, my claim is that the argument structures of these two possession constructions differ in terms of where the possessor is introduced, as follows:

(51)   *BE vs. BE-APPL: Where does the Possessor Come in?*

    a. The possessor in the BE construction is introduced *inside the possessee DP* (see Szabolcsi 1981, 1983, 1994 on Hungarian).

    b. The possessor in the BE-APPL construction is introduced *outside the possessee DP, in spec-ApplP.*

Insofar as (51) is true, it constitutes an existence proof for (1a). In the next subsection, I motivate (51) by showing how it immediately derives the major morphosyntactic differences between the two constructions in terms of other facts about Cochabamba Quechua grammar. Then, I argue explicitly against relating the two constructions by movement, completing the existence proof. Finally, I give full semantic derivations illustrating how the theory of argument structure discussed in Chapter 1 accounts for how these constructions have the same semantics despite their morphosyntactic differences.

3.3.1   Three Arguments for (51)

There are three major morphosyntactic differences between the BE and BE-APPL constructions, all of which are immediately accounted for by the hypothesis in (51) (as represented by the trees in (47) and (48)) once independent facts of Cochabamba Quechua grammar are taken into account.

3.3.1.1   Difference # 1: Applicative *-pu*

The most obvious difference between the BE construction and the BE-APPL construction is the eponymous one: the BE-APPL construction contains a morpheme *-pu*, which is clearly an applicative morpheme elsewhere in the language. In particular, it is a high applicative in Pylkkänen's (2008) sense, as shown by its ability to combine with predicates of any valency, and by its semantics (which are usually described as 'benefactive' in the Quechua literature, though see below).

(52)   Mama-y   (noqa-paq) wayk'u-pu-wa-n
       Mother-1POSS I-BEN   cook-APPL-1OBJ-3SUBJ
       'My mother cooks for my benefit.'

(53)   Tata-y   (noqa-paq) llaqta-man ri-pu-wa-rqa-∅.
       father-1POSS I-BEN   town-DAT   go-APPL-1OBJ-PAST-3SUBJ
       'My father went to town so that I wouldn't have to.'

                                           (Based on van der Kerke 1996, 33)

(54)   Wawqe-y   (noqa-paq) wasi-ta   picha-pu-wa-n.
       Brother-1POSS I-BEN   house-ACC sweep-APPL-1OBJ-3SUBJ
       'My brother sweeps the house for my benefit.'

(55)   Maria (*noqa-paq) wawqe-y-man   misk'i-ta
       Maria I-BEN   brother-1POSS-DAT sweet-ACC
       qo-pu-wa-rqa-∅.
       give-APPL-1OBJ-PAST-3SUBJ
       'Maria gave my brother a sweet so that I wouldn't have to.'

As the above examples show, it is possible in most cases to have the applied
argument realized as a strong pronoun (as well as having it clitic doubled on the
verb).[6] When this happens, though, the case marking on the applied argument is
benefactive. It is thus initially disturbing from the perspective of my account that
the case marking on the possessor in the BE-APPL construction is genitive, not benefactive. I will argue below, however, that the behavior of applicative constructions
within and across Quechua varieties indicates that it is incorrect to think of Appl
as "assigning" benefactive or genitive in the sense of structural or inherent case
assignment. Rather, the meaning of applicative constructions in Quechua appears
to be negotiated between the kind of predicate to which Appl attaches and the
case marking on the applied argument (assuming it is permitted to be overt). In
other words, case marking of applied arguments clearly makes a contribution to
interpretation. I will show in section 3.3.3 that, once this fact is properly taken into
account, the difference in case assignment between benefactive applicatives and the
BE-APPL construction no longer constitutes a threat to my approach.

3.3.1.2   Difference #2: Object Clitic Doubling

The second way in which these two constructions differ morphosyntactially concerns whether an object clitic doubling the possessor appears on the verb. Such
clitic doubling is impossible in the BE construction, but obligatory in the BE-APPL
construction.

---

6. I do not know why it is impossible for the strong pronoun to be overt when the applicative
combines with a ditransitive predicate, as shown in (55).

(56)   *BE Construction: Clitic Doubling of the Possessor Impossible*

Noqa-qta auto-y   tiya-(***wa**)-n.
I-GEN   car-1POSS be$_{exist}$-1OBJ-3SUBJ
'I have a car.'

(57)   *BE-APPL Construction: Clitic Doubling of the Possessor Obligatory*

    a.   Noqa-qta auto-(y)   tiya-pu-**wa**-n.
             car-1POSS be$_{exist}$-APPL-1OBJ-3SUBJ
           'I have a car.'

    b. *Noqa-qta auto-(y)   tiya-pu-n.
             car-1POSS be$_{exist}$-APPL-3SUBJ
           'I have a car.'

The fact that clitic-doubling is obligatory in the BE-APPL case follows from my claim that the possessor is introduced in the specifier of ApplP in that construction, given the following general fact about Cochabamba Quechua: clitic-doubling of a non-nominative argument in the clause is apparently compulsory when possible (van de Kerke 1996, 125-132).[7] This is shown in (58).

(58)   *Clitic Doubling of (Applied and Other) Objects is Obligatory When Possible*

    a.   Juan noqa-ta riku-**wa**-n.
            Juan I-ACC   see-1OBJ-3SUBJ
           'Juan sees me.'

    b. *Juan noqa-ta riku-n.
            Juan I-ACC   see-3SUBJ
           'Juan sees me.'

    c.   Wawqe-y   noqa-paq wasi-ta   picha-pu-**wa**-n.
            Brother-1POSS I-BEN   house-ACC sweep-APPL-1OBJ-3SUBJ
           'My brother sweeps the house for my benefit.'

    d. *Wawqe-y   noqa-paq wasi-ta   picha-pu-n.
            Brother-1POSS I-BEN   house-ACC sweep-APPL-3SUBJ
           'My brother sweeps the house for my benefit.'

---

7. I should note that van de Kerke (1996) takes these markers to be object agreement markers rather than object clitics, but see Myler (forthcoming) for extensive arguments that the clitic analysis is correct.

Since the possessor is a clausal argument in (48), the obligatoriness of clitic doubling in the BE-APPL construction is expected.

The impossibility of clitic-doubling in the BE construction also follows: the possessor is not a clausal argument given the structure in (47). Rather, it is the possessor of a DP. The possessors of possessed DPs cannot be clitic doubled in Cochabamba Quechua, as shown in (59). One way of accounting for this within the so-called big-DP approach to clitic doubling (Torrego 1992; Uriagereka 1995), in which clitics are generated in constituency with their full-DP doubles before moving away, would be to say that the big-DP structures required to allow clitic doubling are not possible for arguments first-merged in DP-internal specifier positions.

(59)   *Possessors of Possessed DPs cannot be Clitic Doubled*

Juan [noqa-qta tata-y-ta]   riku-(***wa**)-rqa-∅.
Juan I-GEN   father-1POSS-ACC see-1OBJ-PAST-3SUBJ

'Juan saw my father.'

3.3.1.3   Difference #3: DP-Internal Possessor Agreement

The final difference that argues in favor of the conclusion that these two constructions differ in terms of the first-merge position of the possessor is the fact that DP-internal possessor agreement is obligatory in the BE construction, but merely optional in the BE-APPL construction.

(60)   *BE Construction: Possessor Agreement Obligatory*

a.   Noqa-qta auto-**y**   tiya-n.
     I-GEN   car-1POSS be$_{exist}$-3SUBJ

     'I have a car.'

b.   * Noqa-qta auto tiya-n.
     I-GEN   car   be$_{exist}$-3SUBJ

     'I have a car.'

(61)   *BE-APPL Construction: Possessor Agreement Optional*

Noqa-qta auto-(**y**) tiya-pu-wa-n.
I-GEN   car-1POSS be$_{exist}$-APPL-1OBJ-3SUBJ

'I have a car.'

The fact in (60) is automatically explained if the BE construction involves the possessor first-merging inside the possessee DP, since such agreement is obligatory in ordinary possessive DPs in the language, as shown in (62).[8]

(62) *Possessor Agreement is Obligatory in Attributive Possession*

    a.   Noqa [Juan-pata tata-**n**-ta]   riku-rqa-ni.

            I   Juan-GEN father-3POSS-ACC see-PAST-1SUBJ

            'I saw Juan's father.'

    b.   *Noqa [Juan-pata tata-ta]   riku-rqa-ni.

            I   Juan-GEN father-ACC see-PAST-1SUBJ

            'I saw Juan's father.'

It is not necessary for possessor agreement to appear in the BE-APPL construction, and this is as expected if the possessor is first-merged outside of the possessee DP in this construction. However, an optional PRO possessor may be merged inside the possessed DP and bound by the "true" possessor in spec-ApplP, yielding a BE-APPL construction with DP-internal possessor agreement.[9] Crucially, when the agreement does appear in (61), there is no change of interpretation. Example (61) with the agreement does not have the flavor of *I have my sister* in English, which has a "have at one's disposal" reading rather than being a statement about a kinship relation. Rather, (61) with the agreement still means what English *I have a sister* means. The analysis in section 3.3.3 explains these facts.

3.3.2 BE vs. BE-APPL: Against a Movement Approach

In the previous subsection, I introduced three morphosyntactic differences between the BE construction and the BE-APPL construction, and showed how they are all captured immediately by the assumption that the possessor is first-merged inside

---

8. I have recently found evidence that this requirement may be becoming weaker among some (Spanish-dominant) bilingual speakers; however, the judgments in the text hold for main informants in this study (and presumably for all monolingual Quechua speakers).

9. Cuzco Quechua, a Peruvian variety closely related to Cochabamba Quechua, requires agreement in the BE-APPL construction across the board (Liliana Sánchez, pers. comm.). This is easily captured micro-parametrically in my system: Poss and n always carry the {D} feature in Cuzco Quechua, but need not do so in Cochabamba Quechua. The result will be that BE-APPL constructions will require PRO in the lower thematic position in Cuzco Quechua. At an even more micro-level, Gladys Camacho Rios differs from my other Cochabamba Quechua consultants in requiring agreement in the BE-APPL construction with some, but not all, possessees. Kinship relations and abstract properties, for instance, require agreement in the BE-APPL construction for her. This can be captured in my system as a requirement on the roots in question, which forces them to merge with $n_{\{D\}}$.

the possessed DP in the former construction, but in the specifier of an Appl head in the latter. In this subsection, I argue that the very same three differences make it impossible to claim that these constructions share a single underlying structure, and are related by movement.

3.3.2.1 Questions Raised by a Movement Approach

Any movement approach to the relationship between the BE and BE-APPL constructions would presumably have to begin from the assumption that the possessor in both constructions starts out inside the possessee DP. It would then postulate that the BE-APPL construction involves movement of the possessor out of the possessee DP, perhaps into the specifier of the ApplP headed by *-pu* (which would thus be a Raising Applicative in the sense of Georgala et al. 2008; Paul and Whitman 2010; see also Georgala 2012). The BE construction would then presumably correspond to a derivation in which no such movement takes place. These derivations are illustrated in (63) and (64).

(63)   *The BE Construction on a Movement Approach* (to be rejected)

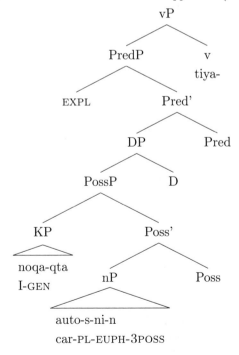

(64)   *BE-APPL on a Movement Approach* (to be rejected)

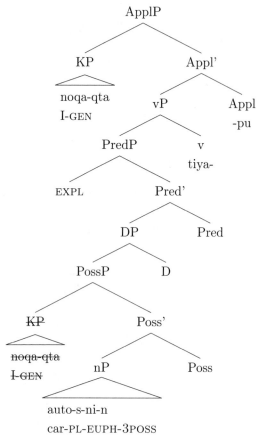

While such an account would have the virtue of potentially unifying the distribution of genitive-marked DPs in the language (whereas my account is forced to postulate two different external merge-sites for genitive–inside DP and in spec-ApplP), there are serious difficulties in implementing it in such a way as to account for the differences between the two constructions.

The first question that arises is what would motivate the putative movement to spec-ApplP in the case of the BE-APPL construction, given that a possessor can clearly be licensed in situ. One must also account for how this movement step makes clitic doubling obligatory (whereas in the BE construction it is impossible), and how it leads DP-internal possessor agreement, which is otherwise obligatory when a possessor is merged inside a DP, to become optional in the BE-APPL construction.

One way of trying to make such an account work might be to follow Deal (2013), and attempt to argue for Quechua DP-internal agreement what she argues for genitive case in Nez Perce: that it only surfaces if the DP associated with it stays in-situ. On this account, a rule would optionally delete the possessor agreement morphology if the possessor has moved away. Such a theory could then claim that the agreement difference follows from the movement difference. As for the clitic doubling facts, one could propose that a "big DP" can be generated even on a possessor inside a DP, but that this clitic is obligatorily deleted if its associated possessor is still inside the DP at Spell Out. Not even these gambits will work, however. The reason for this is that there is evidence that the possessor DP moves out of the possessee DP even in the BE construction. This evidence comes from the fact that it is possible for certain types of clausal material to intervene between the possessor and the possessee, as anticipated above in (49) and discussed in more detail below.

The element *sina* appears to be an evidential particle, with a meaning like "It seems to be the case that...," "I believe that...," or "Perhaps." Like evidentials in many Quechua languages, it is restricted to occurring on major constituents of a finite clause (see Muysken 1995 for this generalization).[10] That is to say, *sina* can occur on whole DP arguments of the verb, but not on DP-internal material, including demonstratives, adjectives, and possessors. Since evidential markers in Quechua languages interact with focus by surfacing to the right of the focussed phrase, there is no reason to expect DP-internal placement of this sort to yield a semantically anomalous interpretation. The ungrammatical cases in (65) and (66) could easily have turned out to have an interpretive effect similar to that of contrastive stress in English. That they do not must therefore reflect a morphosyntactic constraint on the distribution of these particles.

(65)   Chay (*sina) jatun (*sina) runa-ta   (sina)   riku-rqa-ni.
       That perhaps big   perhaps man-ACC perhaps see-PAST-1SUBJ
       'Maybe/it seems it was that big man I saw.'
       '*maybe it was THAT big man I saw (not this one).'
       '*maybe it was that BIG man I saw (not the small one).'

10. Curiously, almost all of the other evidentials found in other Quechua languages appear to be absent from the Cochabamba Quechua of my consultants.

(66)   Juan-pata (*sina) tata-n-ta   (sina)   riku-rqa-ni.
       Juan-GEN perhaps dad-3POSS-ACC perhaps see-PAST-1SUBJ
       'Maybe/it seems it was Juan's dad that I saw.'
       '*Maybe it was JUAN's dad that I saw.'

If we now turn to the BE possessive construction, we find that *sina* can follow
the possessor; this is shown in (67), repeated from (49). This indicates that the
possessor, while it started inside the possessed DP (as indicated by the obligatory
DP-internal possessor agreement), can move out of it.

(67)   *BE Construction: Possessor and Possessee are Separable*

       Juan-pata **sina**   tata-*(n)   tiya-n
       Juan-GEN perhaps father-3POSS be$_{exist}$-3SUBJ
       'Perhaps Juan is the one who has a father.'

The same is true of the Hungarian predicative possessive construction extensively
studied in Szabolcsi (1981, 1994; though cf. Den Dikken 1999). In Hungarian, this
is made more obvious in simple sentences by the word order.

(68)   Nekem van könyvem.   (Hungarian)
       I.DAT is   book.1POSS.NOM
       'I have a book.' (lit: 'there is a book of mine')

As example (68) shows, DP-internal possessor agreement is obligatory in the
Hungarian construction too. So, it seems we have two very similar constructions
in historically unrelated languages which share the mysterious property that the
possessor "runs away from home." Presumably this is not an accident. The motivation for this movement is not easy to discern, nevertheless. In neither language can
it be explained in terms of traditional "licensing" considerations–the possessor can
clearly get a Theta-role, undergo phi-agreement and receive case marking without
leaving its first-merge position. Szabolcsi (1994, 46-47) links the movement to the
need to vitiate the definiteness effect, which would otherwise rule out existential
sentences containing a possessed DP, such as these. She suggests that the extraction
allows the possessed DP to be interpreted as if it were smaller in terms of functional
structure, i.e., as a nonspecific indefinite (although she leaves open how this is to
be implemented). While I will have to leave the development of a full analysis of
the motivation for this possessor extraction for future work, I submit that the fact
that it takes place in the BE construction makes it very difficult to pin down the
morphosyntactic differences between that construction and BE-APPL in terms of
a difference in possessor movement alone. In other words, since movement of the

possessor can in fact take place in the BE construction, one cannot appeal to such movement as the factor that gives the BE-APPL construction its agreement and cliticization properties. I conclude that the morphosyntactic differences between the constructions are to be reduced to a difference in the first-merge position of the possessor. This completes the argument for the structures in (47)-(48), and thus the existence proof for the correctness of prediction (1a).

A version of the same point will go through even if a variant of Den Dikken's alternative (1999) analysis of Hungarian proves to be correct for the Cochabamba Quechua BE construction. On this analysis, the genitive-marked possessor would not be first-merged inside the possessed DP, but would instead be introduced somewhere outside the possessed DP, binding a pronoun inside it. The exact position of the overt possessor would need to be clarified; for the sake of argument, I depict it as adjoined to vP.

(69)   *Den Dikkenian Analysis of the BE Construction*

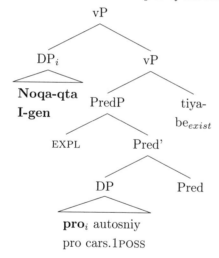

In any case, the place in which the overt possessor is introduced in (69) will have to be of a rather different nature than the position involved in the BE-APPL construction, for otherwise the asymmetry in clitic doubling will go unexplained.[11] The general point–that possessors can be introduced in different first-merge positions– will still go through. While nothing hinges on the choice between a Szabolcsian

11. I note in passing an interesting fact about the scope of quantified possessors with respect to quantified vP modifiers, which might initially seem to point in favor of (69). It turns out that a possessor must scope high over such an adverbial, both in the BE construction and in the BE-APPL construction.

analysis and the one depicted in (69), I will continue to assume the Szabolcsian one for convenience.

In the remainder of this section, I show that the theory of argument structure embraced in this work can explain how the BE and BE-APPL constructions come out with the same meaning despite the difference in their syntactic structure. Crucial to my account will be a certain hypothesis about the meaning of the applicative morpheme -*pu*. The core idea is that -*pu* makes *no contribution of its own to the interpretation*. I will argue that the meanings of all applicative constructions in Quechua languages, including the BE-APPL construction, are computed purely from the denotation of Appl's complement and the denotation of its specifier, and that Quechua case markers make a substantive contribution to the interpretation of applied arguments.[12] The next subsection is concerned with motivating this analysis.

3.3.3   Applicative -*pu* Is Semantically Null

The arguments for this position are of three kinds. First, in all Quechua languages where -*pu* is a productive suffix, it has a number of seemingly unconnected meanings beyond benefactive, so that there is a kind of too-many-meanings puzzle associated with the suffix, analogous to the one found in the domain of predicative possession. Secondly, Quechua languages vary in the set of meanings that -*pu* can have.

(i)   Uj runa-qta sapa llaqta-pi auto-n   tiya-n.
         A man-GEN each town-in car-3POSS be$_{exist}$-3SUBJ

         'A man has a car in each town.' (direct scope only)

(ii)   Uj runa-qta sapa llaqta-pi auto-(n)   tiya-pu-n.
         A man-GEN each town-in car-3POSS be$_{exist}$-APPL-3SUBJ

         'A man has a car in each town.' (direct scope only)

A question that arises for the Szabolcsian analysis of the BE construction, but not for the Den Dikkenian one, is why there is no apparent possibility of reconstruction for the possessor into its putative DP-internal first-merge position. If this were possible, we would predict (i) to allow inverse scope also, contrary to fact. See the appendix of this book for an adaptation of Francez's (2007, 2009) approach to the semantics of existentials which can explain these scope facts even on a Szabolscian analysis of the syntax. Even disregarding this appendix, however, it would be hasty to conclude that this is a decisive point in favor of the approach in (69). Recall that the extraction of the possessor on Szabolcsi's account takes place to alleviate the definiteness effect, the intuition being that such extraction allows the possessee to behave as if it were a non-specific indefinite. However this intuition is ultimately cashed out, it contains within it the seed of an account for the data in (i): presumably reconstruction is impossible because it would "undo" possessor extraction, thereby triggering the definiteness effect anew.

12. I would like to thank David Embick (pers. comm.) for suggesting this approach to the semantics of Quechua applicative constructions.

Given the diversity of the meanings in question, it seems unproductive to attempt to account for this fact by seeding -*pu* with different lexical semantics in different dialects. On the other hand, if we assume that the content of Appl's specifier plays a direct role in determining the sort of applicative meaning generated, this dialectal variation can be accounted for in micro-parametric terms as variation in the sub-categories of phrase that applicative -*pu* allows in its specifier. Thirdly, in at least one dialect (Santiago del Estero Quechua) it is possible to point to case alternations in applicative constructions in which a change of case marking goes along with a change of interpretation.

The first point can be established very easily within Cochabamba Quechua. Aside from the benefactive and possessive uses discussed above, -*pu* has a range of other meanings, some of which seem to be available only with certain types of predicate. For instance, motion verbs such as *riy* 'to go' allow at least two interpretations for the applicative morpheme. Alongside the familiar benefactive meaning shown in (70) (repeated from (53)), -*pu* also allows a reading comparable to English 'away' in combination with such verbs.

(70)   Tata-y   (noqa-paq) llaqta-man ri-pu-wa-rqa-∅.
       father-1POSS I-BEN   town-DAT   go-APPL-1OBJ-PAST-3SUBJ
       'My father went to town so that I wouldn't have to.'
                                        (Based on van der Kerke 1996, 33)

(71)   *'Away' Readings of Applicatives in Cochabamba Quechua*
     a.   Noqa ri-rqa-ni.
          I   go-PAST-1SUBJ
          'I went.'

     b.   Noqa ri-pu-rqa-ni.
          I   go-APPL-PAST-1SUBJ
          'I went away/I left.'
          'I went for him/her.'

A plausible suggestion is that (71b) on its first reading involves -*pu* hosting a silent counterpart of English *away*. Consonant with this, note that examples with an overt object clitic, like (70), are unambiguously benefactive, and do not have the "away" reading. This will follow on the suggested analysis, since silent AWAY would be competing for the same specifier position as the applied argument represented by the clitic. Examples like (71b), however, are ambiguous between an "away" reading and a benefactive reading with a 3rd person beneficiary argument. This is explained by the fact that there is no overt object clitic corresponding to

3rd person in Quechua–(71b)'s ambiguity can then be understood as a structural ambiguity (depending on whether AWAY or a silent 3rd person argument is merged as spec-ApplP). The structures for each reading of (71b) are given in (77) and (78). I assume that the "away" part of the meaning comes from a silent PP, which raises into spec-ApplP to be licensed; its denotation is shown in (72). The benefactive reading comes from merging a benefactive KP in the same specifier position. I assume that the beneficiary thematic role is associated with the K-head *-paq* itself (as shown by the denotation in (73)), and that *-paq* is silent when it combines with silent *pro* (just as all case-markers are in Quechua languages).

(72) $[\![\text{AWAY}]\!] = \lambda e_s.\text{away-from-here}(e)$

(73) $[\![\text{-paq}]\!] = \lambda x_e.\lambda e_s.\text{Beneficiary}(e,x)$

Other interpretations for *-pu* mentioned by van de Kerke (1996, 32-33;169-171), but which I have not explored with my own consultants, are "the result of an action [...] is considered to prevail for at least a relatively long period," and a sort of restitutive reading analogous to 'back' (available with ditransitive verbs and certain motion verbs). Here I will sketch an analysis of each of these two readings based on what I believe their semantic properties to be based on van de Kerke's description.

The restitutive reading of *-pu* is illustrated by the following contrast, based on an example from van der Kerke (1996, 192; his (42)).

(74)   Noqa kay libru-ta   Ana-man haywa-rqa-ni.
         I   this book-ACC Ana-DAT hand-PAST-1SUBJ
         'I handed the book to Ana.'

(75)   Noqa kay libru-ta   Ana-man haywa-**pu**-rqa-ni.
         I   this book-ACC Ana-DAT hand-**APPL**-PAST-1SUBJ
         'I handed the book **back** to Ana.'

I take it that the restitutive meaning here comes from a silent predicate BACK, which syntactically modifies a pP (this explains why this reading is associated only with ditransitives and motion verbs), and subsequently raises into spec-ApplP. I take the denotation of BACK to be as shown in (76). This denotation passes the meaning of its complement up the tree, but adds the presupposition that an eventuality of the same sort has held before at some point in the past. The syntactic and semantic derivation of the example in (75) is given in (79). Note that, for space reasons, not every node in the tree is annotated.

(76) $[\![\text{BACK}]\!] = \lambda P_{\langle s,t \rangle}.\lambda e_s.[P(e) : \exists t.\exists e'_s.\text{PAST}(t) \wedge P(e') \wedge \text{rt}(e') \subset t]$

(77)   *'AWAY' reading of (71b)*

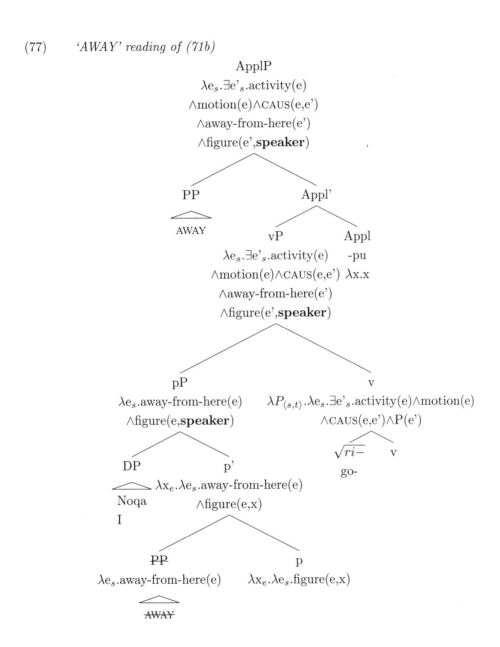

(78)   *Benefactive Reading of (71b)*

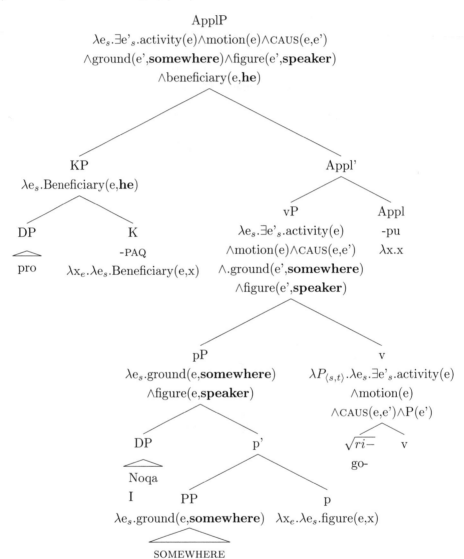

(79) *Restitutive Meaning of -pu*

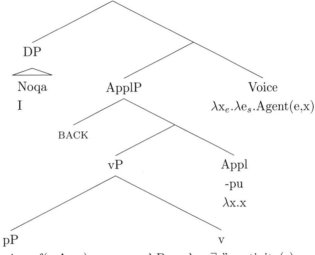

VoiceP
$\lambda e_s.\exists e"_s.$activity(e)$\wedge$hand(e)$\wedge$Agent(e,**speaker**)
$\wedge$CAUS(e,e")$\wedge$in-possession-of(e",**Ana**)$\wedge$figure(e",**this-book**)
$:\exists t.\exists e'_s.$PAST(t)$\wedge$in-possession-of(e',**Ana**)
$\wedge$figure(e',**this-book**)$\wedge$rt(e')$\subset$t

DP

Noqa
I

BACK

ApplP

vP

Voice
$\lambda x_e.\lambda e_s.$Agent(e,x)

Appl
-pu
$\lambda x.x$

pP
$\lambda e_s.$in-possession-of(e,**Ana**)
$\wedge$figure(e,**this-book**)$:\exists t.\exists e'_s.$PAST(t)
$\wedge$in-possession-of(e',**Ana**)
$\wedge$figure(e',**this-book**)$\wedge$rt(e')$\subset$t

v
$\lambda P_{\langle s,t\rangle}.\lambda e_s.\exists e"_s.$activity(e)
$\wedge$hand(e)$\wedge$CAUS(e,e")$\wedge$P(e")

$\sqrt{haywa-}$ v

~~BACK~~
$\lambda P_{\langle s,t\rangle}.\lambda e_s.$P(e):
$\exists t.\exists e'_s.$PAST(t)
$\wedge$P(e')$\wedge$rt(e')$\subset$t

pP
$\lambda e_s.$in-possession-of(e,**Ana**)
$\wedge$figure(e,**this-book**)

kay libru-ta Ana-man
this book-ACC Ana-DAT

What we might call the "enduring end-state" reading is illustrated by the following examples (adapted from van de Kerke 1996, 171, his (86) and (88)).

(80)   Wijch'u-pu-n.
         throw.away-APPL-3SUBJ
         'He throws something away for good.'

(81)   Apa-yka-pu-n.
         carry-inside-APPL-3SUBJ
         'He carries it inside and the object stays there.'

Based on van de Kerke's characterization of the meaning of this construction, I will assume that it comes from a silent predicate FOR-GOOD that modifies the end state of the main predicate and moves into spec-ApplP. I take the denotation of FOR-GOOD to be as follows.

(82) $[\![\text{FOR-GOOD}]\!] = \lambda P_{\langle s,t \rangle}.\lambda e_s.P(e) \wedge \text{enduring}(e)$

The tree in (84) is a structure for (81). I take *-yka* 'inside' to be analogous to a Germanic-style adpositional particle, which cliticizes onto the verb later in the derivation.

The second fact pointing towards *-pu* itself being a simple syntactic scaffold is the fact that Quechua languages vary in the possible meanings for applicative constructions. This can be illustrated by comparing Cochabamba Quechua to its very near relative, Santiago del Estero Quechua. The latter dialect turns out to systematically lack the "away" reading for applicatives combined with motion verbs, although it retains the benefactive reading, as shown in (83).

(83)   Noqa ri-po-ra-ni.
         I   go-APPL-PAST-1SUBJ
         NOT:'*I went away/I left.'
         ONLY: 'I went for him/her'

One could attempt to come up with distinct (yet overlapping) lexical semantics for Appl in these two Quechua varieties, and attempt to account for the difference in that fashion. We saw in Chapter 2 that this approach has been attempted for the too-many-meanings puzzle in the HAVE/BE domain, with unsatisfying results.

(84)

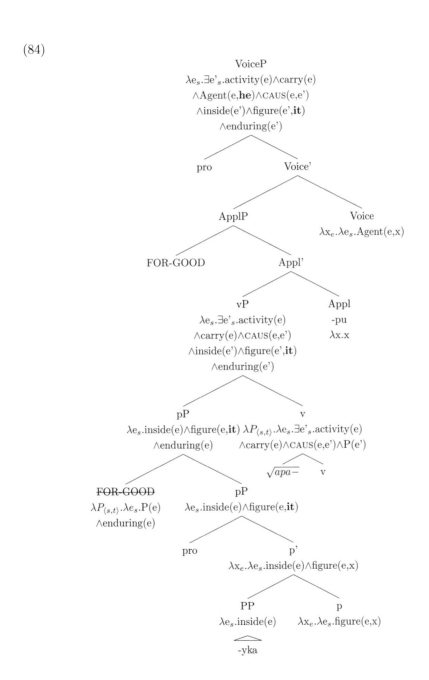

This strategy is likely to fail for the applicative *-pu* for the same reasons–the possible meanings of *-pu* are so varied as to defy the search for a lexical semantic core, and postulating one will not avoid the need for more than one lexical entry for *-pu*. Instead, it seems more plausible to adopt the same strategy here as for the HAVE/BE question, and argue that *-pu* itself is meaningless.

The third argument gives key support to the idea that the case marking of applied arguments makes a contribution of its own. In Santiago del Estero Quechua, unlike in Cochabamba Quechua, it is possible for applied arguments to surface in the accusative case.[13] Santiago del Estero also allows benefactive case, which is also possible in Cochabamba Quechua, as we have seen. There is, however, an interpretive difference between these two possibilities in Santiago del Estero Quechua. Benefactive marking yields a benefactive interpretation along the lines of "X did Y so that Z wouldn't have to", whereas accusative yields either a malefactive or an intended-transfer-of-possession reading.[14]

(85)   *Acc/Ben Alternation in Santiago del Estero Applicatives*

   a.   Noqa pay-paq   challwa-s-ta wachi-pu-ni.
        I   s/he-BEN fish-PL-ACC scale-APPL-1SUBJ

        'I scale fishes so that s/he doesn't have to.'
        (Albarracín and Alderetes 2013, 7)

   b.   Noqa pay-ta   challwa-s-ta wachi-pu-ni.
        I   s/he-ACC fish-PL-ACC scale-APPL-1SUBJ

        'I scale fishes on him/for him to have.'
        (Lelia Albarracín, pers. comm.)

Let us see how this works in detail. The syntax and semantics of (85a) will be exactly analogous to the parallel case in Cochabamba Quechua illustrated in (78). The example in (85b) is ambiguous between an *intended possession* reading and a *malefactive reading*, and I will take this to be a structural ambiguity determined,

---

13. The following example shows that this alternation is not available in Cochabamba Quechua.

   (i)   Wawqe-y   noqa{-paq/*-ta} wasi-ta   picha-pu-wa-n.
         Brother-1POSS I-BEN/*-ACC   house-ACC sweep-APPL-1OBJ-3SUBJ
         'My brother sweeps the house for my benefit.'

14. Given this latter reading, it is tempting to conclude that *-pu* is actually the spell-out of a low applicative head (in Pylkkänen's 2008 sense) when it assigns accusative in Santiago del Estero Quechua. This temptation should be resisted, however: as Albarracín and Alderetes (2013, 9-10) show, *-pu* is not obligatory in any ditransitive verbs of the *give/send* sort, and when added to such verbs it always has a benefactive interpretation.

once again, by the material in spec-ApplP. The malefactive reading I will take to
be supplied by a silent oblique marker, ON, with the following denotation.

(86) $[\![ON]\!]=\lambda x_e.\lambda e_s.\text{maleficiary}(e,x)$

The structure of (85b) on its malefactive reading will then be as illustrated in (89).
I assume that the appearance of the accusative case marker *-ta* on the malefactive
argument is due to the applicative head itself: in Santiago del Estero Quechua, Appl
may assign accusative to its specifier if no other overt case marker is available. Appl
in Cochabamba Quechua does not have this ability.

Partly following Wood and Marantz (2015, 25; to appear) on possessor raising,
I will assume that the intended possession reading of (85b) involves delayed gratification of a possessive thematic role from inside of the direct object DP. The
structure involved is depicted below in (90). I also follow Partee (1999) and Wood
and Marantz in taking it that determiners can, in such derivations, existentially
close the possessee argument. The v head in this derivation takes its causative
allosome, because the DP complement denotes an eventuality. The denotations of
the DP object and the verbal complex compose together via function composition
(which allows the verbal complex to take the DP object as its complement). Once
again, the appearance of accusative case on the applied argument comes from Appl
itself.

I noted above that Cochabamba Quechua differs from Santiago del Estero
Quechua in not allowing accusative case on its applied arguments. This will explain
why Cochabamba Quechua does not permit overt malefactive applied arguments:
such arguments would receive no case marking.[15]

(87)   *Malefactives in Cochabamba Quechua: Silent Only*

    a.   Juan wawa-y-ta   ch'eqni-pu-wa-n.
           Juan child-1POSS-ACC hate-APPL-1OBJ-3SUBJ

           'Juan hates my child on me'

    b.   * Juan noqa{-ta/-paq/-qta} wawa-y-ta   ch'eqni-pu-wa-n.
           Juan I-ACC/-BEN/-GEN   child-1POSS-ACC hate-APPL-1OBJ-3SUBJ

           'Juan hates my child on me'

---

15. Somewhat mysteriously, the malefactive reading of *-pu* is much more restricted in terms of
the predicates it is available with in Cochabamba Quechua than in Santiago del Estero Quechua.
In particular, I have only been able to find acceptable cases involving stative verbs. I have no
explanation for this difference.

(88)   *Structure for* (85a)

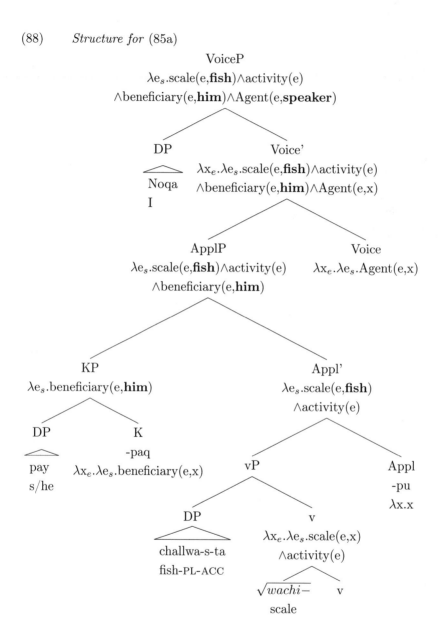

(89)   *Structure for the Malefactive Reading of* (85b)

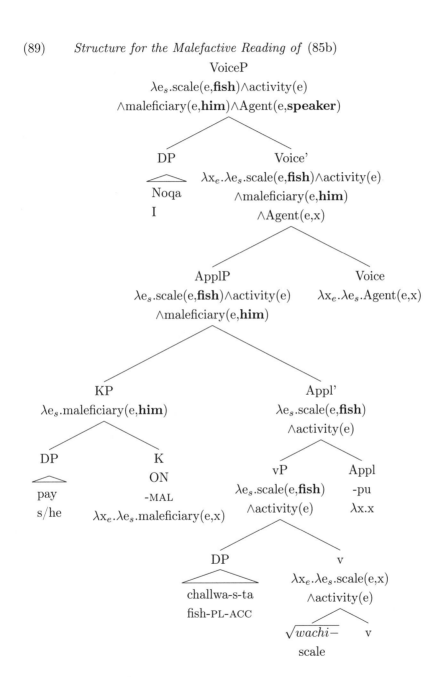

(90)   *Structure for the Intended Possession Reading of* (85b)

VoiceP
$\lambda e_s.\exists e'_s.\text{scale}(e)\wedge\text{activity}(e)\wedge\text{CAUS}(e,e')$
$\wedge\exists z_e.\text{fish}(z)\wedge\text{Poss}(\mathbf{him},z,e')\wedge\text{Agent}(e,\mathbf{speaker})$

DP

Noqa
I

ApplP

Voice
$\lambda x_e.\lambda e_s.\text{Agent}(e,x)$

DP

pay-ta
s/he-ACC

vP
$\lambda v_e.\lambda e_s.\exists e'_s.\text{scale}(e)$
$\wedge\text{activity}(e)\wedge\text{CAUS}(e,e')$
$\wedge\exists z_e.\text{fish}(z)\wedge\text{Poss}(v,z,e')$

Appl
-pu
$\lambda x.x$

DP
$\lambda v_e.\lambda e_s.\exists z_e.\text{fish}(z)$
$\wedge\text{Poss}(v,z,e)$

v
$\lambda P_{\langle s,t\rangle}.\lambda e_s.\exists e'_s.\text{scale}(e)$
$\wedge\text{activity}(e)$
$\wedge\text{CAUS}(e,e')\wedge P(e')$

PossP
$\lambda v_e.\lambda w_e.\lambda e_s.\text{fish}(w)$
$\wedge\text{Poss}(v,w,e)$

D
$\lambda R_{\langle e\langle e\langle s,t\rangle\rangle\rangle}.$
$\lambda v_e.\lambda e_s\exists z_e.$
$P(v)(z)(e)$

$\sqrt{wachi-}$
scale

v

nP
$\lambda x.\text{fish}(x)$

Poss
$\lambda P_{\langle e,t\rangle}.\lambda v_e.$
$\lambda w_e.\lambda e_s.P(w)$
$\wedge\text{Poss}(v,w,e)$

challwa-s-ta
fish-PL-ACC

Putting all of the foregoing evidence together, we can see that there is ample motivation for taking the contribution of High Appl in Quechua to be vacuous. Appl's role is as a sort of syntactic scaffold–it makes the construction of a certain semantic edifice possible, but is not itself part of the finished edifice. That edifice consists entirely of the independent semantic contributions of the vP and of whatever comes to occupy spec-ApplP.

Before moving on to the impact of this conclusion on the analysis of the alternation between the BE construction and the BE-APPL construction in Cochabamba Quechua, let us first consider its implications for the analysis of High Applicatives more generally. An obvious question to ask is the following: should this analysis be extended to all cases of High Appl cross-linguistically, or should it be restricted to Quechua -*pu*?

I would like to suggest that the analysis should be generalized to all cases of High Appl (it will always be possible, of course, to retreat to the more conservative position if necessary). This is because I believe that the account solves a number of problems in the standard analysis of High Appl (that of Pylkkänen 2008), without introducing any new problems.

A worry (or complaint) about the standard analysis of High Appl that I have often met with is encapsulated by the following footnote from Kim (2010, 503; fn 45): "The proposed analysis raises the issue of what high applicatives are. As an anonymous reviewer points out, high applicatives have become prevalent in the literature, introducing various semantic types of arguments since Pylkkänen's work (2002/2008), and it is not clear what the exact nature of high applicatives is."

Now, it ought to be noted that the fact that many thematic roles can be associated with High Appl is a real empirical challenge, which has been acknowledged for a long time on the basis of data from languages with overt applicative morphemes (see Baker 1988b on the various interpretations of High Applicatives in Bantu languages; also Jeong 2007). The problem is therefore by no means an artifact of Pylkkänen's account. Nevertheless, the theoretical challenge raised by Kim's reviewer is clearly an important one: how can one head be associated with so many meanings? Of course, this problem is immediately solved on my approach: we are not dealing with a single head with multiple meanings, but rather syntactically different types of phrase in the specifier of ApplP (with unsurprisingly different meanings).[16]

---

16. Although variation in oblique case marking is not visible in the Bantu languages, this is presumably reducible to the fact that Bantu languages do not have overt case markers generally. I would therefore propose that the same sort of analysis applies to Bantu, but that the different oblique markers are silent in those languages.

Secondly, the position argued for here is supported by some recent analyses of rather different languages. Kalin (2014, 173-174) has shown that an approach related to this one can account for the complementary distribution of indirect objects with Differentially Marked objects in Hindi. Kalin proposes that Differentially Marked objects are licensed by raising into spec-ApplP, thereby precluding the introduction of an indirect object in this position. This account presupposes that the Appl head itself does not necessarily assign a thematic role, as asserted here. Moreover, work on Amharic (including Baker and Kramer 2014; Demeke 2003) has noted that the case markings on applied arguments in that language vary with the interpretation. Baker and Kramer (2014) propose a syntax very like my own, in which spec-ApplP can be occupied by KPs, although they do not draw out the semantic consequences of this idea as I have done here.

Thirdly, the analysis helps to solve a long-standing puzzle in the syntax and semantics of High Applicative heads; namely, the way in which they interact with causatives in affix order. In particular, in many languages in which the order of causative and applicative may only come in that order, it is often possible for the applied argument to nonetheless scope under the causative, in apparent violation of the Mirror Principle (Baker 1985). Many cases of this sort from Bantu are discussed in Hyman (2003). An example from Quechua is given below (van de Kerke 1996, 192; his (42)), in which the restitutive meaning of *-pu* clearly "belongs" to the predicate embedded under the causative *-chi*, despite the fact that *-pu* follows *-chi*:[17]

(91)   Juan kay libru-ta   Ana-man haywa-chi-**pu**-wa-n-qa.
        Juan this book-ACC Ana-DAT hand-CAUS-APPL-1OBJ-3SUBJ-FUT
        'Juan will make me hand this book back to Ana.'

My approach to High Appl can explain this pattern: since specifiers of High Appl can get there by being first-merged there OR by raising there, in principle applied arguments are expected to be able to scope under the causative even though the applicative morpheme itself follows the causative morpheme. This is illustrated by the following structure for (91):

---

17. The reverse order is impossible in Quechua, as is the equivalent in many Bantu languages. Example (i) shows this for Cochabamba Quechua:

(i)   * Juan kay libru-ta   Ana-man haywa-pu-chi-wa-n-qa.
         Juan this book-ACC Ana-DAT hand-APPL-CAUS-1OBJ-3SUBJ-FUT
         'Juan will make me hand this book back to Ana.'

I have no explanation for this fact, nor for why much Bantu and Quechua differ in this respect from languages like Hiaki, which allows both Caus-Appl and Appl-Caus order (Harley 2013).

(92)

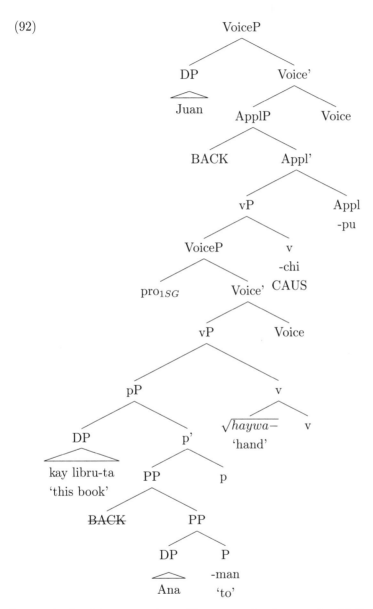

Interestingly, this approach predicts not only that we should find Mirror Principle violations involving applicative morphemes, but also *what kind* of Mirror Principle violations we should see. Since movement is always up the tree and never downward, we predict that although cases of Appl seeming to scope too low given its position should be attested, there should be no cases in which it seems to scope too high. In other words, we should never find cases of suffixes ordered Appl-Caus in which the applicative meaning takes the causative argument as its complement. As far as I know, this prediction is correct. While Hyman (2003) contains some surface counterexamples from Bantu, Hyman shows that their morphophonology indicates an underlying Root-Caus-Appl order consistent with their semantics (see also Myler In Press).

Having established that the Appl head is a meaningless syntactic scaffold, we are now in a position to understand how the BE construction and the BE-APPL construction have the same meaning, despite the difference in structure I have been arguing for, repeated below from (47) and (48).

The BE construction turns out to be an instance of instant gratification, since it involves introducing the possessor in the specifier of the DP-internal head that introduces the semantics of the relevant possession relation. The BE-APPL construction involves delayed gratification, with Appl pushing the semantics of the same possession relation up the tree. The next subsection illustrates this in detail, via sample derivations.

(93)   *BE Construction*

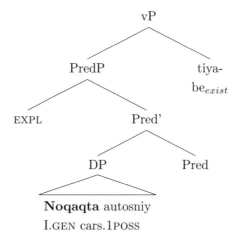

(94) *BE-APPL Construction*

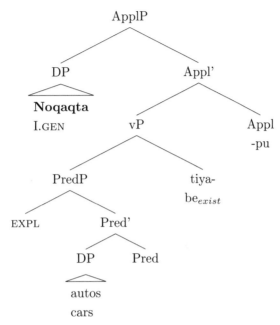

3.3.4 How Two Syntaxes Can Have the Same Semantic Result

I will provide sample derivations for alienable possession relations, which are introduced by the Poss head as we saw in Chapter 1 (following Barker 1995). All of the lexical items in the following derivations are familiar except for the denotation of the genitive suffix. For this, I follow Partee and Borschev's (2001/2004, 296) suggestion that genitives take an individual as their first argument and a relation as their second argument, but I adjust it by adding an eventuality variable, and giving it a second alloseme allowing it to also take relations whose second argument has been existentially closed (i.e., predicative types).[18] The choice between these allosemes is technically free, but the "wrong" choice will lead to a type-mismatch.

18. For an antecedent to this dual allosemy approach to a possession-related morpheme, see Francez and Koontz-Garboden (2015a, 2015b); Koontz-Garboden and Francez (2010).

(95)   *Denotation of the Genitive Suffix*

$[\![\text{-qta}_{GEN}]\!] = \lambda x_e.\lambda R_{\langle e\langle e\langle s,t\rangle\rangle\rangle}.\lambda y_e.\lambda e_s.R(x)(y)(e)$

$[\![\text{-qta}_{GEN}]\!] = \lambda x_e.\lambda R_{\langle e\langle s,t\rangle\rangle}.\lambda e_s.R(x)(e)$

The denotations of all of the pieces involved in the ensuing derivations are listed in (96), for reference. With respect to (96g) and (96h), recall from Chapter 1 that I am assuming that the difference between predicative and existential copulas is a matter of conditioned allomorphy. The existential interpretation of an existential sentence does not come from the copula itself, but from the "expletive" in spec-PredP (so that "expletive" becomes a misnomer). For Cochabamba Quechua, this means that predicative copula *ka-* and existential copula *tiya-* are suppletive allomorphs of the same meaningless v head, conditioned as seen in (97).

(96)   *Semantics: The Pieces*

    a. $[\![\text{Noqa}]\!] = \textbf{speaker}_e$

    b. $[\![\text{auto}]\!] = \lambda x_e.\text{car}(x)$

    c. $[\![\text{Poss}]\!] = \lambda P_{<e,t>}.\lambda v_e.\lambda w_e.\lambda e_s.P(w)\wedge\text{Poss}(v,w,e)$

    d. $[\![\text{Pred}]\!] = \lambda x.x$

    e. $[\![\text{-qta}_{GEN}]\!] = \lambda x_e.\lambda R_{\langle e\langle e\langle s,t\rangle\rangle\rangle}.\lambda y_e.\lambda e_s.R(x)(y)(e)$

        $[\![\text{-qta}_{GEN}]\!] = \lambda x_e.\lambda R_{\langle e\langle s,t\rangle\rangle}.\lambda e_s.R(x)(e)$

    f. $[\![\text{-pu}_{APPL}]\!] = \lambda x.x$

    g. $[\![\text{tiya-}]\!] = \lambda x.x$

    h. $[\![\text{EXPL}]\!] = \lambda f_{<e,<s,t>>}.\lambda e_s.\exists x_e.f(x)(e)$

(97)   *Copula Allomorphy in Cochabamba Quechua*

    a. v $\Leftrightarrow$ tiya- / [PredP ~~EXPL~~ [Pred' ...]] ___

    b. v $\Leftrightarrow$ ka- / elsewhere

The motivation for this approach was that existential and predicative copulas, even in languages where they are morphologically distinct, often undergo morphological neutralization in marked environments–a situation analyzable in terms of Impoverishment. Such neutralization occurs in non-present tenses in Cochabamba Quechua, as we have seen in footnote 2. On my approach, this can be analyzed in terms of an Impoverishment rule that obliterates the copy of the moved EXPL from the representation in marked tenses, so that the conditioning environment for (97a) is not met.

On, then, to the sample derivations. We begin with the derivation of a BE construction seen in (98). First, the nP denotation goes in for the first argument of

Poss. The genitive KP takes the resulting denotation as its argument, and yields a function from a set of individual-eventuality pairs to propositions that are true so long as the individual is a car and is owned by the speaker in that eventuality. The existential semantics supplied by EXPL then takes this function as its argument, resulting in the existential closure of the entity variable corresponding to the car. Since the copula v is semantically vacuous, the meaning of the verb phrase is the set of eventualities in which there is a car owned by the speaker, as desired. Syntactically, since the genitive KP is first-merged inside the possessee DP, it triggers possessor agreement (here represented as being hosted on D).

The same result is achieved in a somewhat different way in the BE-APPL construction, as shown in (99). The derivation involves the version of Poss which *doesn't* take a specifier. This means that the possessed DP ends up denoting what Poss' denoted in the previous sample derivation. Once again, EXPL existentially closes over the individual variable corresponding to the car (although this time it composes with Pred' via Function Composition, rather than Functional Application), and v passes this denotation up, so that the vP denotes the set of individual-eventuality pairs such that there is a car owned by that individual in that eventuality. Applicative *-pu*, being meaningless, simply passes up that denotation so that it can compose with the denotation of the KP in its specifier. In the present case, this is a genitive KP, which takes the denotation of Appl' as its argument semantically.

The resulting denotation is the set of eventualities in which there is a car owned by the speaker–the same result as in the BE construction. Syntactically, no agreement is triggered inside the DP, because there is no syntactic representation of the possessor there.[19] However, since the possessor is an applied argument, it triggers clitic doubling, as applied arguments in Cochabamba Quechua always do.

---

19. Recall that agreement is optionally possible in the BE-APPL construction–this would be represented by first-merging PRO in spec-PossP, and having PRO be controlled by the "real" possessor in spec-ApplP. Agreement would then be triggered DP-internally, but the compositional semantics will be identical to the derivation above.

(98)   Noqa-qta auto-y   tiya-n.   (BE Construction)
         I-GEN   car-1POSS be$_{exist}$-3SUBJ
         'I have a car.'

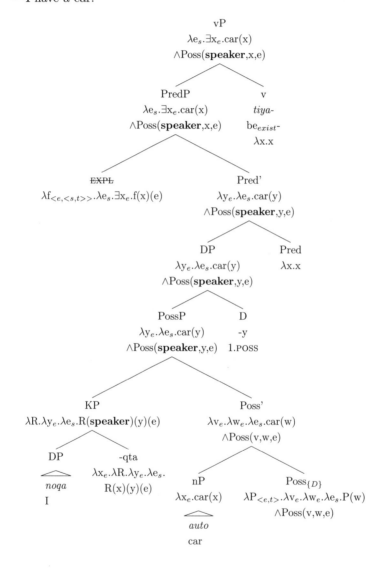

(99)   Noqa-qta auto tiya-pu-wa-n.   (BE-APPL Construction)
         I-GEN   car   be$_{exist}$-APPL-1OBJ-3SUBJ
         'I have a car.'

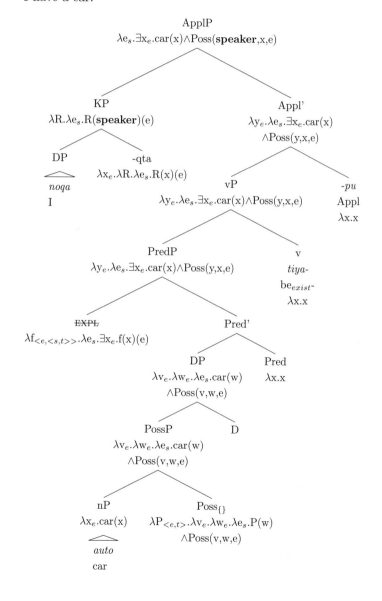

3.3.4.1   An Excursus on the Obligation Construction

Before closing, I note an interesting asymmetry between the BE construction and the BE-APPL construction concerning the expression of obligation.

There is an obligation construction in Cochabamba Quechua that has interpretations similar to that of English *have* in *John has to leave*. This construction involves a nominalized form of the embedded verb (which employs the same nominalizer as appears in subjunctives and irrealis relative clauses)[20] in an existential construction. It turns out that only the plain existential verb is allowed in this construction–an existential verb marked by applicative *-pu* cannot be used. Another way of putting this is that the BE construction can be used to express obligation, but the BE-APPL construction cannot.

(100)   Llank'a-na-y   tiya-n.
         Work-SUBJUNCTIVE-1POSS be$_{exist}$-3SUBJ

         'I have to work.'

(101)   * Llank'a-na-(y)   tiya-pu-wa-n.
         Work-SUBJUNCTIVE-1POSS be$_{exist}$-APPL-1OBJ-3SUBJ

         'I have to work.' (good on an irrelevant derived nominal reading- 'I have a thing for working with; a piece of work')

(102)   Ri-pu-na-y   tiya-n.
         go-APPL-SUBJUNCTIVE-1POSS be$_{exist}$-3SUBJ

         'I have to go away.'

(103)   * Ri-pu-na-(y)   tiya-pu-wa-n.
         go-APPL-SUBJUNCTIVE-1POSS be$_{exist}$-APPL-1OBJ-3SUBJ

         'I have to go away.'

Given that my account has it that these two constructions are thematically indistinguishable, how is this contrast to be accounted for? The answer comes from the structure of the nominalized clause, in particular, the amount of verbal structure that is embedded in it. If the arguments of this embedded clause are spelled out overtly, the subject turns out to be nominative and the object turns out to be accusative. This, combined with the fact that genitive or any other case marking on these arguments is impossible, indicates that there is enough verbal structure in

---

20. This nominalizer, *-na*, also has a derived nominal use on which it means *thing or place for verb*ing.

the nominalized clause for the introduction and licensing of the verbal arguments
to proceed just as it does in finite clauses.

(104)   Noqa wasi-ta   picha-na-y   tiya-n.
        I   house-ACC sweep-SUBJUNCTIVE-1POSS be$_{exist}$-3SUBJ
        'I have to sweep the house.'

(105)   * Noqa-qta wasi-(ta)   picha-na-y   tiya-n
          I-GEN   house-ACC sweep-SUBJUNCTIVE-1POSS be$_{exist}$-3SUBJ
        'I have to sweep the house.'

While I am not in a position to give a full analysis of the obligation construction's
syntax and semantics, it is clear that the structure includes a subjunctive nominalized clause embedded in an existential construction, and that the nominalized
clause contains at least TP, as shown in the structure for example (104) on the next
page.

Note that it is almost certainly the case that more structure is present in this
construction than is represented in (106),[21] but the structure already present in
(106) is enough to explain why there is no BE-APPL equivalent of the obligation
construction. This is because there is no way to relate the applied argument to
the embedded subject position: none of delayed gratification, control/pronominal
binding, or raising results in a convergent derivation. Let us see why this is, taking
each subtype of derivation in turn.

A delayed gratification structure for a BE-APPL obligation construction would
look as shown in (107). This derivation crashes, because a syntactically required
argument is left out–namely, the external argument of the embedded VoiceP (which
is required by the {D} feature on Voice). Recall that, in order for a delayed gratification derivation to take place, it has to be syntactically permissible to leave
an argument-introducing head without an argument in the sentence. Quite generally, this is not possible in the case of a core argument of a verb, since these are
syntactically obligatory. This means that it will never be possible to arrive at a
BE-APPL version of the obligation construction via delayed gratification: to do so

---

21. Thinking of Cattaneo (2009, Chapter 5), one might even propose that this construction
involves a silent nominal NEED head of which a subjunctive clause is the complement, so that
(104) is close in syntax and interpretation to *there is a need for me to sweep the house.* In that
case, there will be a relative clause boundary between the thematic domain of the prejacent clause
and the thematic domain of the existential verb, in which case there will also be locality reasons why the BE-APPL construction cannot convey obligation, in addition to the considerations
discussed in the main text.

would require leaving out the embedded verb's subject, and this will always lead to a crash.

(106)   *The Obligation Construction*

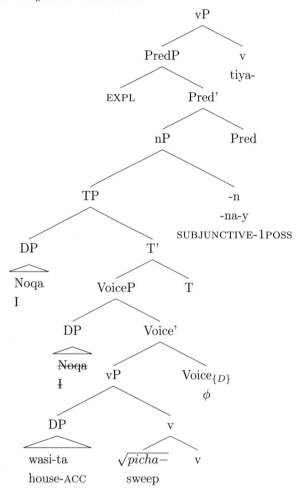

(107)   *Delayed Gratification: BE-APPL Obligation Construction*

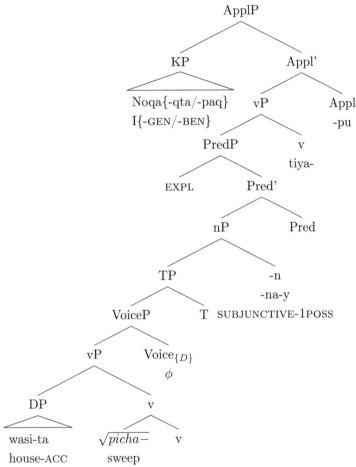

What of a derivation involving a controlled PRO, or a bound little *pro*? Such a structure is displayed in (108). This structure evades the problem of the delayed gratification derivation, since spec-VoiceP is filled by a DP, as required. The relationship between the applied argument and the subject of the prejacent clause is mediated by co-indexation with *pro*, or control of PRO. I propose that it is precisely this crucial coindexation relationship that makes the derivation invalid. The subordinate clause in this construction is a subjunctive, and subjunctives are inherently obviative. This makes the binding/control relationship in (108) impossible, thereby ruling out reaching a BE-APPL version of the obligation construction by this route.

(108)   *Control/Binding: BE-APPL Obligation Construction*

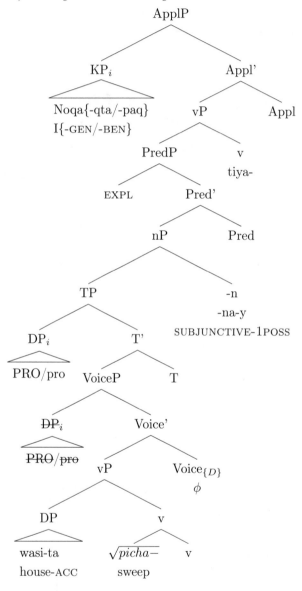

(109)   *Raising: BE-APPL Obligation Construction*

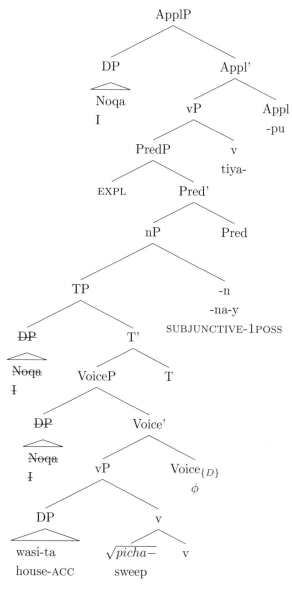

The final possibility to consider is a raising derivation, as shown above in (109). This derivation is ruled out on two grounds. First, it involves *hyper-raising*–raising of an already-licensed argument from the subject position of a finite clause into a higher argument position (see Carstens and Diercks 2010, and references cited there). While permitted in some languages, I know of no evidence that such hyper-raising is permitted in Quechua languages. A second problem for the raising structure in (109) is that it involves illegally moving a nominative argument into spec-ApplP. Recall that in Cochabamba Quechua this position is able to accommodate only (a subset of) oblique arguments.

Since this exhausts the possible sorts of derivation, I conclude that the incombatibility of the BE-APPL construction with the obligation construction is explained.

3.3.5   Conclusions

This section was concerned with demonstrating that (1a) (repeated below) is correct, by showing that the alternation between BE and BE-APPL constructions in Cochabamba Quechua is best accounted for in terms of a difference in where the possessor is first-merged.

(110)   *Predictions of the Present Approach*

    a.   Possession constructions can vary in the place in the structure where the possessor is introduced.

    b.   The different ways of building possession sentences permitted by (a.) could have somewhat different (albeit potentially overlapping) meanings, depending on the semantic contributions of the pieces that make them up.

The next section aims to provide an existence proof for (110b), by comparing the BE-APPL construction of Cochabamba Quechua with a superficially identical construction in Santiago del Estero Quechua.

3.4 BE-APPL in Cochabamba vs. Santiago del Estero Quechua

The striking similarity between the BE-APPL constructions of Cochabamba Quechua and of Santiago del Estero Quechua is illustrated in (111) and (112).[22]

(111) *BE-APPL in Cochabamba Quechua*

Juan-pata kallpa   tiya-pu-∅-n.
Juan-GEN strength be$_{exist}$-APPL-3OBJ-3SUBJ
'Juan has strength.'

(112) *BE-APPL in Santiago del Estero Quechua*

Juan-ta   kallpa   tiya-pu-∅-n.
Juan-ACC strength be-APPL-3OBJ-3SUBJ
'Juan has strength.'

Aside from the case on the possessor, the two constructions look identical. However, they turn out to be extremely different in terms of the possession relations they can express. In fact, (111) and (112) constitute an example of the only kind of possession relation on which the constructions converge (abstract properties). This is summarized in the table in (115).

There is a further fundamental difference. It turns out that BE-APPL in Santiago del Estero, unlike its Cochabamba counterpart, is not an existential construction, since it allows possessees bearing strong quantifiers and demonstratives. In contrast, we saw in the last section that the Cochabamba Quechua BE-APPL construction exhibits a strong definiteness effect.

(113) *Santiago del Estero: Possessee can Have a Strong Quantifier*

Qam-ta   kutis tukuy mosca-s tiya-∅-su-n-ku.
You-ACC again all   fly-PL   be-APPL-2OBJ-3SUBJ-PL
'You have all the flies on you again.'

---

22. Santiago del Estero Quechua appears to be losing its equivalent of the BE construction. Lelia Albarracín tells me (pers. comm.) that it used to be productive in the language, but none of my consultants allowed a possessive reading for sentences like (i).

(i)   # Juan-pa   pana-n   tiya-n.
     Juan-GEN sister-3POSS be-3SUBJ

     *'Juan has a sister.'
     OK: 'Juan's sister is here.'

As indicated, (i) is fine on a predicate locative reading in which *Juan's sister* is construed as the subject–a fact to which we return.

(114) *Santiago del Estero: Possessee can Have a Demonstrative*

Qam-ta kutis cha mosca tiya-∅-su-n.
You-ACC again that fly   be-APPL-2OBJ-3SUBJ
'You have that fly on you again.'

(115) *BE-APPL in Cochabamba vs. Santiago del Estero: Semantics*

	Cochabamba	Santiago del Estero
Kinship	OK	*
Body Parts	restricted	OK
Part-Whole	restricted	OK
Permanent Possession	OK	*
Abstract Property	OK	OK
Temporary Possession	*	%
Psychological State	*	OK
Physical Sensation	*	OK
Disease	restricted	OK

Note that (114) was judged in a context where one particular fly keeps coming back to bother the addressee, so that there is no possibility that it involves a kind reading.[23]

The reason for this difference starts to become clear when one compares the structure of the copula systems in the two dialects. Although the same morphemes (*ka-* and *tiya-*) are involved, their distribution turns out to be dramatically different. In particular, *tiya-* is used not only for existentials in Santiago del Estero Quechua, but also for (roughly) stage-level predicative copula sentences. In turn, *ka-* is limited to (roughly) individual-level copular predication. This *ka-/tiya-* distinction in Santiago del Estero mirrors rather closely the *ser/estar* distinction in Spanish, by which it is no doubt influenced.[24] This distribution is summarized in the table below.

23. Notice that the applicative morpheme itself is silent in both of these examples. It turns out that *-pu* disappears in combination with a 1st or 2nd person object clitic in Santiago del Estero Quechua, but only in the BE-APPL construction and with certain physical sensation verbs. With other predicates, *-pu* surfaces as normal when combined with overt object clitics, as shown below in (123). I have no principled account of this conditioned silence of Appl, but it is certainly interesting that it treats a possession construction and physical sensation predicates as a natural class (thinking of Isačenko 1974; Noonan 1993; Harley 2002).

24. The fact that Santiago del Estero has a transitive verb HAVE, discussed in Section 3.5, may also be because of Spanish influence.

(116)   *Structure of the Copula System: Cochabamba vs. Santiago del Estero*

	Cochabamba	**Santiago del Estero**
ka-	predicative only (present tense)	predicative (individual-level)
tiya-	existential only	existential and predicative (stage-level)

I have been arguing throughout this work that, at the level of the syntax, there is only one meaningless copular v element, and that both HAVE and BE are suppletive realizations of this same v. It follows that languages that are described as having more than one BE verb, or more than one HAVE verb, will have to be treated as involving conditioned allomorphy of the same v head (see also Roy 2013; Welch 2012). Below I illustrate how such an analysis would work for each of the distributions in (116) (see Chapter 4 for an analysis of a language with more than one HAVE verb). The system for Cochabamba Quechua is repeated from (97). Notice that the system for Santiago del Estero Quechua includes the additional form *api-*, which is inserted only when v combines with a transitive Voice head;[25] this is the HAVE verb discussed in section 3.5.

(117)   *Allomorphy of Copular v: Cochabamba*

    a.   v ⇔ tiya- / [PredP ~~EXPL~~ [Pred' ...]] ___

    b.   v ⇔ ka- / elsewhere

(118)   *Allomorphy of Copular v: Santiago del Estero*

    a.   v ⇔ tiya- / [$Pred_{stage-level}$P]___$Voice_{\{\}}$

                   / [PredP ~~EXPL~~ [Pred' ...]]___$Voice_{\{\}}$

    b.   v ⇔ ka- / elsewhere

    c.   v ⇔ api- / ___$Voice_{\{D\},\phi}$

Aside from the presence of the *api-* allomorph in Santiago del Estero Quechua, the main important difference between the two dialects concerns the conditioning environment for the insertion of *tiya-*. In Cochabamba Quechua, this allomorph is inserted only when v takes as its complement a PredP introducing EXPL; this is what

---

25. Recall that the term "transitive" in the present system means a Voice head that both introduces an external argument and bears phi-features with which it licenses some DP.

restricts *tiya-* to existential contexts in that variety. Santiago del Estero Quechua, on the other hand, uses the *tiya-* allomorph whenever v takes a stage-level PredP OR one introducing EXPL in the environment of an intransitive Voice head.[26] In both dialects, *ka-* is the elsewhere allomorph, so that it "mops up" whatever contexts remain (recall that this also accounts for why it is *ka-* that replaces *tiya-* in certain morphosyntactically marked environments in Cochabamba Quechua, rather than the other way around).

Data illustrating the distribution of allomorphs in Santiago del Estero Quechua are shown below. Note that titles and professions must employ the copula *ka-*, as in (119). The version with *tiya-* in (120) must instead be interpreted as a predicative copula sentence with a hidden locative predicate (with *presidenta* 'president' interpreted as an appositive). I note in passing that Santiago del Estero is unlike Cochabamba Quechua in allowing (and, for most speakers I have consulted, preferring) the 3rd person singular present tense form of *ka-* to be overt (compare (119) with (21b)).

(119) *Santiago del Estero: Copula ka- is Individual Level*

Kirchner presidenta ka-n.
Kirchner president be-3SUBJ
'Kirchner is the president.'

(120) *Santiago del Estero: Copula tiya- is Stage Level/Locative*

a. # Kirchner presidenta tiya-n.
    Kirchner president be-3SUBJ
    'Kirchner, the president, is here.' NOT: 'Kirchner is the president.'

b. Mesa na   chura-sqa   tiya-n.
    Table already put-PARTICIPLE be-3SUBJ
    'The table is aready set.'

The example in (121) shows that *tiya-* is also the form of the existential copula in Santiago del Estero Quechua.

---

26. These two contexts could potentially be reduced to one if it were assumed that EXPL itself is always introduced by stage-level PredP. It would then be possible to state that *tiya-* is inserted in Santiago del Estero Quechua in the environment of stage-level PredP and an intransitive Voice head. I have not attempted to implement this alternative in this chapter, since it would complicate the exposition of the semantics considerably (in particular, it would require a new semantics for stage-level Pred, different from the one I have assumed following Adger and Ramchand 2003; Balusu 2014; and Markman 2008).

(121) *Santiago del Estero: Existential tiya-*

Kay-pi yaku tiya-n.
this-in water be$_{exist}$-3SUBJ
'There is water here.'

The lack of definiteness effects in the BE-APPL construction in Santiago del Estero can then be explained if this construction involves predicative *tiya-*, rather than existential *tiya-*.[27] The question then becomes what kind of predicate the BE-APPL construction of Santiago del Estero Quechua involves. There is good semantic evidence that the predicate is a locative of some kind. To see this, consider speakers' metalinguistic commentary on why the following is bad on an ownership reading:

(122) *Santiago del Estero BE-APPL Means 'Y Has X on/in Y'*

\# Juan-ta wasi tiya-pu-∅-n.
Juan-ACC house be-APPL-3OBJ-3SUBJ

Speaker comment: "Would mean the house is on top of Juan, or growing out of his body."

I propose therefore that the BE-APPL construction in Santiago del Estero is a locative predicative copula construction with the meaning 'Y has X on/in Y'. Meanings like abstract properties, mental states, and diseases are to be compared to archaic English *strength was in him, fear was upon him, a terrible cold was upon him*, etc; also Irish English *he's got fear in him*.[28]

We must now ask ourselves where this locative meaning comes from. It seems unlikely that it comes from Appl itself, for reasons discussed in detail in the previous section: *-pu* is compatible with a range of meanings (benefactive, malefactive, and others) in Santiago del Estero Quechua, in a manner that interacts in an interesting way with (a) the sort of predicate it combines with and (b) the case that the applied argument bears. The following example shows that *-pu* allows benefactive meanings, for instance.

27. One might wonder whether the BE-APPL construction in Santiago del Estero Quechua could not be structurally ambiguous. That is, Santiago del Estero Quechua could, in principle, build BE-APPL constructions using either an existential structure or a stage-level predicative copula structure. However, if Santiago del Estero Quechua really could build a BE-APPL construction using an existential structure, the semantic differences between the constructions (seen in (115)) would become inexplicable. We must therefore conclude that existential structures are not compatible with *-pu* in Santiago del Estero Quechua, even though they are in Cochabamba Quechua, and ask why this is. At present I do not see a clear answer to this question, but it is probably related to the fact that for many speakers (including all of my own consultants) there is no equivalent of the BE possession construction in Santiago del Estero Quechua either (see footnote 22).

28. Thanks to Jim Wood (pers. comm.) for the Irish English data.

(123)   Wawqe-y   noqa-paq wasi-ta   picha-p-a-n.
         Brother-1POSS I-BEN   house-ACC sweep-APPL-1OBJ-3SUBJ
         'My brother sweeps the house for me.'

There are many possible explanations for where the locative part of the meaning of this construction comes from, and it is not necessary to choose between
them in order to establish the main point, which is that the structure and interpretation of this construction are rather different than in the case of Cochabamba
Quechua. However, a promising possibility is displayed in (125). In this structure,
the possessee is the subject of a silent locative small clause. The complement of the
preposition in this structure is a pronoun bound by the possessor in spec-ApplP.
Amongst the virtues of this structure are that it predicts that the possessee in
this construction is the true subject of predication, rather than the possessor. This
prediction is correct, as shown by certain control facts.

In Santiago del Estero Quechua, as in many languages, the PRO subject of an
infinitive embedded under a verb like *want* can be controlled by the matrix subject.
If the embedded clause has a subject different from the matrix, the subjunctive must
be used instead. This is shown in (124).

(124)   a.   Noqa amu-y-ta   muna-ni.
              I   come-INF-ACC want-1SUBJ
              'I want to come.'

        b.   *Noqa qam-(ta) amu-y-ta   muna-ni.
              I   you-ACC come-INF-ACC want-1SUBJ
              'I want you to come.'

        c.   Noqa qam amu-na-yki-ta   muna-ni.
              I   you come-SUBJUNCTIVE-2POSS-ACC want-1SUBJ
              'I want you to come.'

(125) *Suggested Structure for BE-APPL in Santiago del Estero*

Juan-ta   cha chuspi tiya-pu-n.
Juan-ACC that fly   be-APPL-3SUBJ

'Juan has that fly on him.'

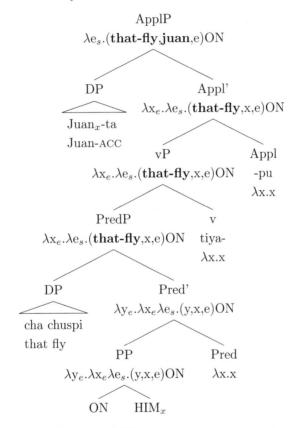

If we now turn to the Santiago del Estero BE-APPL construction, we find that the possessee position can be controlled into, but that the possessor position cannot (compare (126) and (127)). In order for the matrix subject to be understood as coreferent with the possessor, the subjunctive must be used, as shown in (128).

(126) *Santiago del Estero: Control into Possessee Position*

Cha chuspi [qam-ta PRO tiya-∅-su-y-ta]   muna-n.
That fly   you-ACC PRO be-APPL-2OBJ-INF-ACC   want-3SUBJ

'That fly wants to be on you.' (Lit: that fly wants you to have it on you.)

(127)   *Santiago del Estero: No Control into Possessor Position*

     * Qam [PRO cha chuspi tiya-∅-su-y-ta]   muna-nki.
       You PRO that fly   be-APPL-2OBJ-INF-ACC want-2SUBJ
       'You want to have that fly on you.'

(128)   *Santiago del Estero: Subjunctive must be Used to Mean (127).*

     Qam [cha chuspi tiya-∅-su-na-n-ta]   muna-nki.
     You that fly   be-APPL-2OBJ-SUBJUNCTIVE-3POSS-ACC want-2SUBJ
     'You want to have that fly on you.'

To conclude this section, although they have an overlapping meaning (both can convey possession of abstract attributes) and look superficially very similar, the BE-APPL construction found in Santiago del Estero is very different in nature from its Cochabamba counterpart. This is because the two constructions differ markedly in the type of copular construction employed (predicative copula vs. existential) and in the type of structure the possessee itself is embedded in (it is the subject of a locative PP in Santiago del Estero, but not in Cochabamba). This can be seen by comparing the structures of the superficially identical sentences with which we started this discussion ((111) and (112)), shown below in (129) and (130):

(129)   *BE-APPL in Cochabamba Quechua*

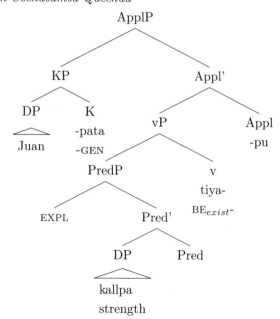

(130)   *BE-APPL in Santiago del Estero Quechua*

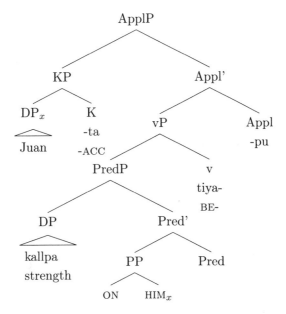

We thus have our existence proof for (1b), which states that the meanings of possession constructions might vary cross-linguistically because of differences in the pieces used to build them.

This completes our discussion of micro-variation in the BE constructions of Cochabamba Quechua and Santiago del Estero Quechua. The next section looks instead at micro-variation in the domain of HAVE.

3.5   To HAVE and to HOLD Across the Quechua Family

This section begins in 3.5.1 by establishing that, of the two dialects, only Santiago del Estero has a true HAVE verb. Section 3.5.2 discusses what light this micro-comparison can shed on the question of what goes along with having HAVE or lacking it. Although I will point out some negative implications that the micro-comparison of these dialects has for some earlier proposals on parametric variation in predicative possession, I also propose that variation in a certain subtype of psych constructions correlates with having HAVE in the Quechua family.

3.5.1   Santiago del Estero Has HAVE

The HAVE verb in Santiago del Estero Quechua has the infinitive form *apiy*. We will see that this is a true transitive HAVE verb that allows inalienable uses. Cochabamba Quechua has a cognate of this verb in the form of *jap'iy*. The two overlap in some of their uses, for instance, in expressing temporary possession of definite, portable objects. Interestingly, (131) does not require the speaker to have the key in their hands–it only requires that the speaker be in control of the key.

(131)   Noqa llavi-ta jap'i-(sha)-ni.   (Cochabamba)
       I   key-ACC hold-DUR-1SUBJ
       'I have the key.'

(132)   Noqa llavi-ta api-ni.   (Santiago del Estero)
       I   key-ACC have-1SUBJ
       'I have the key.'

The transitive verb *jap'iy* has two entries in Laime Ajacopa's (2007) dictionary of Bolivian Quechua. One is "to grab, to seize forcefully, to grasp;" and the other is "to possess, to have in one's power."[29] While descriptive grammars I had consulted had led me to believe that Cochabamba Quechua (which is a Bolivian variety) is not a HAVE language, those grammars do not contain any conclusive demonstration that *jap'iy* lacks inalienable possession readings or ownership readings. My fieldwork data indicate that *jap'iy* does not have any such uses. While the definitions that Laime Ajacopa gives are right to suggest that *jap'iy* is less specific in meaning than its usual English glosses ('grab' and 'hold') indicate, *jap'iy* remains an ordinary lexical transitive verb in Cochabamba Quechua, and is thus to be represented as in (133). Santiago del Estero Quechua's *apiy*, on the other hand, has inalienable readings and ownership readings. Santiago del Estero Quechua thus constitutes a HAVE language, whereas Cochabamba Quechua does not.

---

29. The original Spanish is respectively "Agarrar. Asir fuertemente, coger" and "Poseer. Tener uno algo en su poder."

(133) *Structure of jap'iy in Cochabamba Quechua*

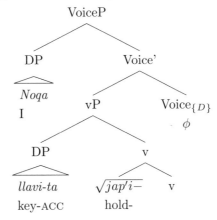

To review the evidence, it is striking that no inalienable possession uses are available for *jap'iy*, whereas these are fine with its Santiago del Estero cognate *apiy*.

(134)   *Kinship*: *jap'iy* (Cochabamba)

    * Noqa pana-ta   jap'i-(sha)-ni.
      I   sister-ACC hold-DUR-1SUBJ

    'I have a sister.'

(135)   *Kinship*: *apiy* (Santiago del Estero)

    Noqa pana-ta   api-ni.
    I   sister-ACC have-1SUBJ

    'I have a sister.'

(136)   *Body Parts*: *jap'iy* (Cochabamba)

    * Noqa yana chujcha-ta jap'i-(sha)-ni.
      I   black hair-ACC hold-DUR-1SUBJ

    'I have black hair.'

(137)   *Body Parts*: *apiy* (Santiago del Estero)

    Noqa yana chujcha-ta api-ni.
    I   black hair-ACC have-1SUBJ

    'I have black hair.'

(138)   *Part-Whole*: *jap'iy* (Cochabamba)

    a.   *Kay wasi uj ventana-ta jap'i-(sha)-n.
        This house one window-ACC hold-DUR-3SUBJ
        'This house has one window.'

    b.   *Kay challwa ashka tullu-ta jap'i-(sha)-n.
        This fish   much bone-ACC hold-DUR-3SUBJ
        'This fish has a lot of bone(s).'

(139)   *Part-Whole*: *apiy* (Santiago del Estero)

    a.   Ka wasi suj ventana-ta api-n.
        This house one window-ACC have-3SUBJ
        'This house has one window.'

    b.   Ka challwa ashka tullu-s-ta api-n.
        This fish   much bone-PL-ACC have-3SUBJ
        'This fish has a lot of bones.'

Additionally, *jap'iy* is unable to express abstract properties, personal attributes like 'strength', psychological states, diseases, or physical sensations, whereas *apiy* is able to convey such relations in at least some cases, although it seems to lack physical sensation readings.

(140)   *Attribute*: *jap'iy* (Cochabamba)

    *Juan ancha kallpa-ta jap'i-(sha)-n.
    Juan much strength-ACC hold-DUR-3SUBJ
    'Juan has a lot of strength.'

(141)   *Attribute*: *apiy* (Santiago del Estero)

    Juan ancha kallpa-ta api-n.
    Juan much strength-ACC have-3SUBJ
    'Juan has a lot of strength.'

(142)   *Psychological State*: *jap'iy* (Cochabamba)

    *Juan mancha-y-ta jap'i-(sha)-n.
    Juan fear-INF-ACC hold-DUR-3SUBJ
    'Juan is afraid.'

(143)   *Psychological State*: *apiy* (Santiago del Estero)

        Juan penqa-y-ta   api-n.

        Juan shame-INF-ACC have-3SUBJ

        'Juan is ashamed.'

(144)   *Diseases*: *jap'iy* (Cochabamba)

    a.   * Noqa soroqchi-ta   jap'i-(sha)-ni.

           I   altitude.sickness-ACC hold-DUR-1SUBJ

           'I have altitude sickness.'

    b.   * Noqa ch'uju-ta jap'i-(sha)-ni.

           I   cough-ACC hold-DUR-1SUBJ

           'I have a cough.'

(145)   *Diseases*: *apiy* (Santiago del Estero)

    a.   Noqa uma nana-q-ta   api-ni.

           I   head hurt-rel-ACC have-1SUBJ

           'I have a sore head.'

    b.   Noqa uju-ta   api-ni.

           I   cough-ACC have-1SUBJ

           'I have a cough.'

(146)   *Physical Sensations*: *jap'iy* (Cochabamba)

        * Noqa ch'aki-y-ta   jap'i-(sha)-ni.

        I   thirst-INF-ACC hold-DUR-1SUBJ

        'I am thirsty.'

(147)   *Physical Sensations*: *apiy* (Santiago del Estero)

        * Noqa chaki-y-ta   api-ni.

        I   thirst-INF-ACC have-1SUBJ

        'I am thirsty.'

To conclude, *jap'iy* is less specific than the gloss 'hold' suggests, since it does not require that the possessor actually have the possessee in his/her hands. Nevertheless, it lacks inalienable possession and ownership readings, from which we can infer that it lacks the ability to pass such relations up the tree to the argument in spec-Voice; in other words, *jap'iy* is not a HAVE verb. The fact that *apiy*, its cognate in Santiago del Estero Quechua, is a HAVE verb in this sense sets up an interesting challenge from the point of view of comparative syntax. Namely, why is a structure of the sort displayed in (148), in which transitive Voice combines with meaningless copula v, possible in Santiago del Estero Quechua, but not in Cochabamba Quechua?

(148)   Noqa pana-ta   api-ni.
           I   sister-ACC have-1SUBJ

           'I have a sister.'

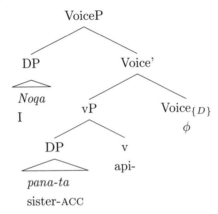

3.5.2   HAVE, BE and Parametric Variation: the View from Quechua

As discussed in Chapter 2, a great deal of work has investigated what else is required in order for a language to have HAVE; that is, what properties having HAVE depends upon. Micro-comparative work on closely related dialects that differ with respect to having HAVE has a potential advantage with respect to this question, since the number of other differences between the languages being compared is more manageable than would be the case in a more "macro" comparison (see Kayne 1996 for discussion).

It remains my hope that continued comparative work on Cochabamba Quechua and Santiago del Estero Quechua (and other dialects, of course) will ultimately lead to interesting new answers to this question. Unfortunately, the descriptive and analytical challenges inherent in studying the possession constructions of each dialect independently have prevented me from arriving at definitive new answers during the preparation of this book. Therefore, the ensuing discussion will mostly have only a negative bearing on this question, serving only to rule out certain hypotheses that have been proposed. On the other hand, at least some positive (but still speculative) light can also be shed, since there seems to be a one-way

correlation between having HAVE and exhibiting a certain psych verb alternation in
the Quechua family.

3.5.2.1   Negative Implications of the Micro-Comparison

The comparison of Cochabamba Quechua and Santiago del Estero Quechua makes it
seem unlikely that having HAVE can be linked to head directionality in the manner
suggested by Mahajan (1994). Amongst Mahajan's proposals was the idea that
head-finality is incompatible with having HAVE (see Chapter 2 for more thorough
discussion of the proposal). As earlier examples in this chapter attest, however,
Santiago del Estero Quechua is a HAVE language despite having a number of head-
final properties, including OV order and having postpositions/suffixal case markers.
In addition, auxiliaries in compound tenses follow the main verb, as shown in the
following progressive example.

(149)   *V-Aux Order in Santiago del Estero Quechua*

    a.   Juan qaa-su-s   tiya-n.
          Juan look.at-2OBJ-GERUND be-3SUBJ

          'Juan is looking at you.'

    b.   * Juan tiya-n   qaa-su-s.
          Juan be-3SUBJ look.at-2OBJ-GERUND

          'Juan is looking at you.'

It is possible, however, that Santiago del Estero Quechua will be compatible with
a somewhat weaker proposal in the spirit of Mahajan's, suggested to me by Richard
Kayne (pers. comm.). Kayne suggests that the right generalization is as follows:

(150)   *Conjecture (due to Richard Kayne)*

    In order for a language to have HAVE, it must have at least one preposi-
    tion.

While Santiago del Estero Quechua is predominantly postpositional, Nardi (2002,
61) mentions that it has borrowed the Spanish preposition *hasta* 'up to, until', and
sometimes uses it along with the equivalent native postposition *-kama*. If having
a single preposition is all that is required, as per (150), then Santiago del Estero
Quechua arguably falls under the generalization.

(151)   (Hasta) wasi-y-kama
       up.to   house-1POSS-up.to

       'up to my house'

I will leave the validity of (150) as an open question here–investigating it is difficult for practical reasons, since available typological databases tend to classify languages in terms of being "predominantly postpositional" or "predominantly prepositional," rather than in terms of whether a given sort of adposition exists in the language at all. If (150) proves correct, it would potentially be necessary to re-evaluate my claim (made most explicitly in Chapters 2 and 5, but at least implicit throughout this book) that preposition incorporation has no role to play in the derivation of HAVE sentences. This is because my approach predicts no interaction between the head-directionality of PPs (or, indeed, any other properties of PPs) and the HAVE/BE question.

3.5.2.2   (Un)accusative Psych Verbs and Having HAVE

Many Quechua languages have a class of psychological and physical sensation predicates that assign accusative case to their experiencer argument. These predicates have been especially well-studied in Ecuadorian dialects, most prominently Imbabura Quechua (Cole 1982; Hermon 1985, 2001; Jake 1985; Muysken 1977; Willgohs and Farrell 2009). As well as a list of predicates which lexically select for such an accusative experiencer, there is also a productive suffix (often termed *desiderative*, although see Cathcart 2011 for arguments that *impulsative* is a more appropriate term) that can be added to a verb to introduce an accusative experiencer. A non-exhaustive list of lexical experiencer predicates in Imbabura Quechua is given in (152). Example sentences containing such verbs are given in (153), and examples of the impulsative suffix are provided in (154).

(152)   *Some Lexical Experiencer Verbs in Imbabura Quechua*
          (Hermon 2001:151, her (7))

          nanana 'to hurt'

          rupana 'to be hot'

          chirina 'to be cold'

          yarjana 'to be hungry'

(153)   *Lexical Experiencers*
          (Hermon 1985, 151 and 62; her (8) and (40))

      a.   Ñuka-ta chiri-wa-rka-∅-mi.
            I-ACC   cold-1OBJ-PAST-3SUBJ-EVID

            'I was cold.'

      b.   Ñuka-ta uma-ta   nana-wa-∅-n-mi.
            I-ACC   head-ACC hurt-1OBJ-PRES-3SUBJ-EVID

            '(My) head hurts me.'

(154)   *Impulsative Experiencers*
          (Hermon 2001, 152, her (13) and (14))

      a.   Ñuka-ta-ka puñu-naya-rka-∅.
            I-ACC-TOP sleep-IMPULS-PAST-3SUBJ

            'I feel like sleeping.'

      b.   Ñuka-ta-ka aycha-ta   miku-naya-rka-∅.
            I-ACC-TOP meat-ACC eat-IMPULS-PAST-3SUBJ

            'I feel like eating meat.'

Such accusative experiencers are present in both Cochabamba Quechua and Santiago del Estero Quechua also. Below are the translations of (153a) in each dialect.

(155)   *Cochabamba Quechua*

       (Noqa-ta) chiri-wa-rqa-∅.
       I-ACC   cold-1OBJ-PAST-3SUBJ

       'I was cold.'

(156)   *Santiago del Estero Quechua*

       (Noqa-ta) chiri-a-ra-∅.
       I-ACC   cold-1OBJ-PAST-3SUBJ

       'I was cold.'

While the existence of these verbs cuts across the HAVE/BE difference within the Quechua family, there is a generalization concerning them that does appear to interact with the HAVE/BE difference:

(157)   If a Quechua language has HAVE, then at least some lexical experiencer predicates or the impulsative suffix can take a nominative experiencer.

Imbabura Quechua is a HAVE language, and has extremely productive alternations between the accusative experiencer pattern and another pattern in which the experiencer is marked nominative, and triggers subject agreement on the verb.

(158)   *HAVE in Imbabura Quechua* (Cole 1982, 94; his (373))

Juzi iskay kaballu-ta chari-n.
Jose two   horse-ACC have-3SUBJ
'Jose has (i.e., owns) two horses.'

(159)   *Accusatives Made Nominative* (Hermon 2001, 157)

    a.   Ñuka-ta-ka chiri-wa-rka-∅-mi.
           I-ACC-TOP   cold-1OBJ-PAST-3SUBJ-EVID
           'I was cold.'

    b.   Ñuka-ka chiri-chi-rka-ni.
           I-TOP   cold-CHI-PAST-1SUBJ
           'I was cold.'

(160)   *Impulsative Accusatives Made Nominative* (Hermon 2001, 157)

    a.   Ñuka-ta-ka puñu-naya-rka-∅.
           I-ACC-TOP sleep-IMPULS-PAST-3SUBJ-EVID
           'I felt like sleeping.'

    b.   Ñuka-ka puñu-naya-chi-ni.
           I-TOP   sleep-IMPULS-CHI-1SUBJ
           'I feel like sleeping.'

The nominative versions of (159) and (160) are accompanied by an additional suffix on the verb, *-chi*, which is obligatory for some (but not all) Imbabura Quechua speakers in order to make the experiencer argument nominative. This morpheme is identical in form to the causative suffix, but there is no causative interpretation in (159b) or (160b). This alternation is completely unavailable in the BE language Cochabamba Quechua. Hence, while (161a) is grammatical, (161b) is not, and (161c) can only have a causative interpretation.

(161)   *No Acc-Nom Alternation in Cochabamba Quechua*

    a.   Juan-ta   puñu-naya-n.
           Juan-ACC sleep-IMPULS-3SUBJ
           'Juan feels like sleeping.'

    b.   * Juan puñu-naya-n.
           Juan sleep-IMPULS-3SUBJ
           'Juan feels like sleeping.'

c.   # Juan puñu-naya-chi-n.
   Juan sleep-IMPULS-CAUS-3SUBJ
   'Juan makes someone feel like sleeping.'

If we now turn to Santiago del Estero Quechua, we find that, though it lacks productive alternations of the Imbabura Quechua sort, its impulsative morpheme obligatorily introduces a nominative experiencer. This is seen in (162).

(162)   *The Impulsative in Santiago del Estero Quechua*

a.   * Juan-ta   puñu-naa-n.
   Juan-ACC sleep-IMPULS-3SUBJ
   'Juan feels like sleeping.'

b.   Juan puñu-naa-n.
   Juan sleep-IMPULS-3SUBJ
   'Juan feels like sleeping.'

If (157) proves to be valid more generally,[30] then it would dovetail in an interesting way with my hypothesis that having HAVE involves being able to delay gratification of a thematic role until spec-VoiceP–one can think of the nominative versions of these experiencer predicates as involving the same mechanism, with the experiencer thematic role (associated with a low position for these predicates) being satiated higher up in the thematic domain. To illustrate what is meant here, I provide sample derivations for the Imbabura Quechua alternation seen in (160a). Following Cathcart (2011, 14), I assume that *-naya* is a v head which assigns accusative case to any DP in its specifier, and that it has the following denotation, where 'IMPULSE(w,e,x)' means the set of things that x wants to do in e in w:

(163) $[\![\text{-naya}]\!] = \lambda P_{\langle e\langle s,t\rangle\rangle}.\lambda x_e.\lambda e_s.\lambda w.\forall w'.[w'\text{-is-compatible-with-}$
   $\text{IMPULSE(w,e,x)}] \rightarrow \exists e'$ in w' s.t. $P(x)(e')$

The structure of (160a) will then be as shown in (164), following Cathcart (2011, 11). This derivation involves instant gratification of the thematic role introduced by *-naya*. I propose that the nominative experiencer construction in (160b) involves delayed gratification, such that the experiencer argument is introduced by the matrix Voice head, which is spelled out as *-chi* and interpreted with its expletive alloseme. The resulting structure is shown in (165). It is intuitively plausible

30. I note that this generalization has to be a one-way implication, since Cajamarca Quechua (Quechua IIA, northern Peru) has nominative experiencers in the impulsative construction (Coombs-Lynch et al. 2003, 192), despite being a BE language (Coombs-Lynch et al. 2003, 53-54).

that allowing delayed gratification in such experiencer constructions might go along with allowing it in order to derive HAVE sentences.

(164)

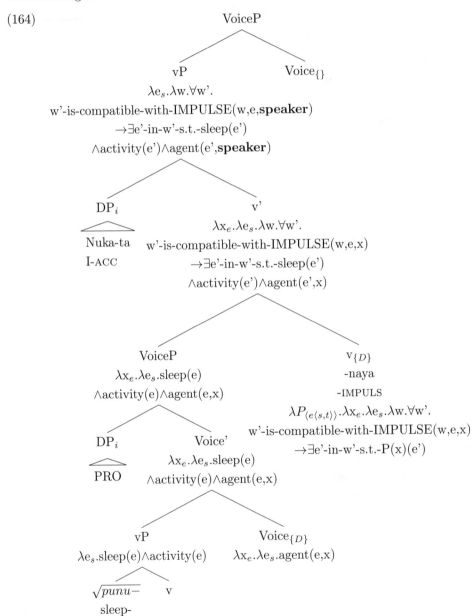

(165)

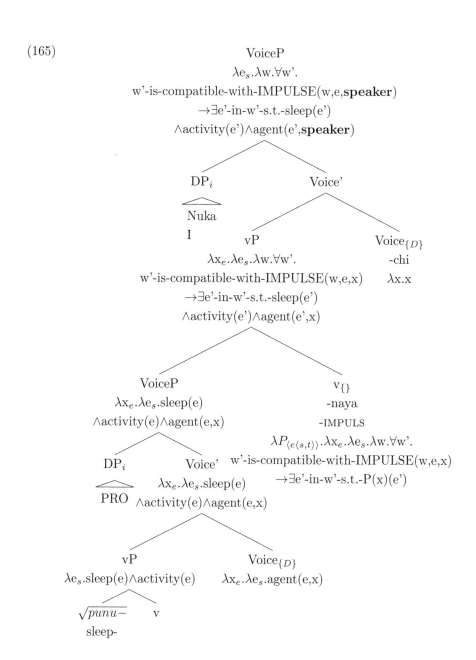

3.6   Conclusions

In this chapter, I used a number of case studies from two closely related Quechua
languages to show that possession constructions can differ in terms of the first-
merge position of the possessor, and that possession constructions can have different
interpretations depending on the contributions of the pieces that make them up.
Both of these facts are expected if there is a certain amount of independence between
the notions "syntactic argument of head X" and "semantic argument of head X," as
claimed by the theory of argument structure adopted in this book. In addition, the
case studies serve as useful demonstrations that the present approach is capable of
addressing the too-many-(surface)-structures puzzle.

Where this chapter has focussed on motivating my approach within the domain
of BE, the next two turn to the domain of HAVE, showing that the approach yields
improvements on previous analyses of this well-studied type of possession construction.

Building and Interpreting HAVE Sentences

In Chapter 1, I argued that BE-based possession constructions can arise from a variety of structures (this conclusion is backed up with evidence from Quechua in Chapter 3, from Quechua, Hungarian, and West Germanic languages in Chapter 6, and from Icelandic and Bantu in Chapter 7; see also Boneh and Sichel 2010 on Palestinian Arabic; Levinson 2011 on Icelandic). In all of them, BE is a light-verb that takes a complement, and the structure is either unaccusative or unergative. The variation we see in BE-based possession constructions both within and across languages comes from the fact that the internal structure of BE's complement can vary. This is shown schematically in (1) and (2).

(1)   *Unaccusative Configuration for Predicative Possession: Leads to BE*

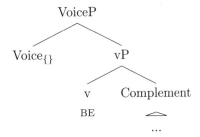

(2)   *Unergative Configuration for Predicative Possession: Leads to BE*

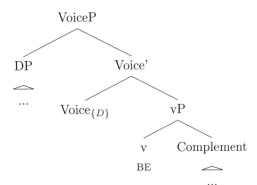

Throughout, I have been following a long tradition in assuming that the thematic roles involved in the possession relation itself are mediated entirely internally to the complement of BE, so that BE itself is thematically inert.

This view on BE does not entail that BE is totally meaningless–only that it neither adds to nor subtracts from the set of Theta-roles available. Nonetheless, for simplicity, I will continue to take BE to be meaningless in this chapter, and I will continue to implement that idea as follows:

(3)   BE is morphosyntactically a light-verb (little-v) that has the semantics of a type-neutral identity function.

My proposal for HAVE-based possession constructions is that they contain the structure in (1), but introduce the higher of the two arguments of that structure (i.e. the possessor) in the specifier of a Voice head bearing phi-features (which, following Schäfer 2008, Wood 2015, and Alexiadou et al. 2014 may assign a Theta-role or be semantically vacuous). This will lead to a transitive structure in which the Theta-role corresponding to the possessor is assigned to spec-VoiceP under what I have been calling *delayed gratification*. HAVE is therefore the spell-out of BE when Voice introduces an external argument and bears phi-features–it is the transitive form of BE (Hoekstra 1994; Isačenko 1976, 60; Jung 2011). The cross-linguistic question about HAVE vs. BE can then be attacked as a question about when and why certain arguments can be projected externally in this way. The schema for main-verb HAVE sentences is given in (4).

(4)   *HAVE as BE+Voice$_{\{D\},\phi}$*

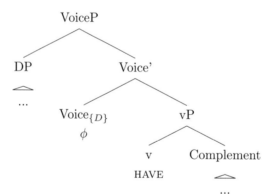

To summarize, the relationship between HAVE and BE can be encapsulated by the following schematic rules of Vocabulary Insertion:

(5)   a.   v ⇔ HAVE / ___Voice$_{\{D\},\phi}$

      b.   v ⇔ BE / elsewhere

This chapter focusses on *have* in English, with occasional forays into certain other languages when the comparison illuminates the discussion of English. The central claim will be that the approach to HAVE sentences schematized in (4), plus the usual options for how to interpret Voice, is enough to predict the many different interpretations that English *have* can have. Recall from Chapter 1 the rules of allosemy that govern the interpretation of Voice (we will have cause to add one more rule to this list by the end of this chapter).

(6)   *Rules for the Interpretation of Voice (Adapted from Wood 2015, 30)*

    a.   [[Voice]] $\Leftrightarrow \lambda x_e.\lambda e_s.\text{Agent}(x,e)$ / ___(agentive, dynamic event)

    b.   [[Voice]] $\Leftrightarrow \lambda x_e.\lambda e_s.\text{Holder}(x,e)$ / ___(stative eventuality)

    c.   [[Voice]] $\Leftrightarrow \lambda x.x$ / ___(elsewhere)

It is clear that Kratzer (1996) intends for the holder role to cover experiencers as well as other sorts of state-holders, since she assumes that this is the role assigned to the subject of a stative experiencer verb like *love* in a sentence such as *John loves Mary*. It also must include causer as a subcase, given the existence of stative sentences such as *This situation worries me*. Combining these rules of allosemy with the approach to HAVE in (4), we expect the following sorts of interpretation for *have* sentences:

(7)   *Interpretations of Have Constructions*

    a.   Cases where the meaning of a *have* sentence = that of *have*'s complement (if Voice = Expl)

    b.   Cases where the meaning of a *have* sentence = that of *have*'s complement+that of Voice (if Voice $\neq$ Expl)

I will show that each of the cases in (7) are attested in some use of *have*. It will also be demonstrated that together (7a) and (7b) cover much of the *have* paradigm as discussed in Beavers, Ponvert, and Wechsler (2009), Brugman (1988), Belvin (1996), Harley (1997, 1998), Partee (1999), Partee and Borschev (2001/2004), and Ritter and Rosen (1997). The resulting analysis of *have* will be very similar in spirit to those found in Ritter and Rosen (1997), Sæbø (2009) and Iatridou (1995), but it will have an advantage over the latter two proposals in not requiring that HAVE's complement be a small clause in all cases (I will show that this allows my account to avoid awkward English-internal and typological questions about when and why the predicate of this small clause has to be overt and when it can be covert). I will also raise numerous new observations that require friendly amendments to Ritter and Rosen's (1997) account. Let me note additionally that the analysis owes much to the work of Belvin (1996), whose insight that many of *have*'s properties follow if these properties are thought of as being inherited from *have*'s complement was a key inspiration for the present approach.

The remainder of this chapter is structured as follows. In the first section, I will go through the two cases in (7) one after the other, showing which interpretations

of *have* instantiate them and how the structures that my account assigns to *have*
sentences predict those interpretations. Section 4.2 briefly examines modal *have* in
English, showing how a recent analysis by Bjorkman and Cowper (2013) can be
readily assimilated to the assumptions of the present work. Section 4.3 explains
how the present approach deals with languages with more than one HAVE verb,
focussing on a case-study from Icelandic (the discussion here will be based on joint
work with Einar Freyr Sigurðsson and Jim Wood). Section 4.4 is the conclusion.

4.1   The Syntax and Semantics of *Have*

4.1.1   Cases Where the Meaning of a *Have* Sentence = That of *Have*'s Complement (If Voice = Expl)

There appear to be three cases of this sort in English. These are what I will call
relational *have* (which for me covers traditional inalienable possession and the *have*
of ownership), locative *have*, and experiencer *have*.

4.1.1.1   Relational *Have*

Relational *have* covers kinship relations, part-whole relations, body part relations
(these three traditionally being classified as inalienable possession), and ownership
(traditionally classified as a type of alienable possession).

(8)   *Relational have*

    a.   I have a sister.   (Kinship)

    b.   This tree has many branches.   (Part Whole)

    c.   John has black hair.   (Body Part)

    d.   I have a Playstation 3.   (Ownership)

Of course, by uniting these, I do not mean to imply that they are syntactically
indistinguishable. There is ample evidence from the morphosyntax of possessive
DPs in many languages that the inalienable relations are distinct from ownership,
as we saw in Chapter 1. This is even detectable to some extent in English. Barker
(1995) suggested the ability of the possessor to surface inside an *of* PP as a test
that sets inalienable possession off from alienable possession (some speakers further
restrict *of* PPs to part-whole relations with inanimate possessees).

(9)   *Inalienable Possession Allows of PP Possessors*

    a.   % The sister of John (is a best-selling author).   (Kinship)

    b.   The branches of this tree (are large).   (Part Whole)

    c.   % The blue eyes of his father (were glistening with pride). (Body Part)

    d.   * The Playstation 3 of John (broke down). (Ownership)

The three inalienable possession relations are also almost certainly distinguishable from each other in their syntactic behavior, even for speakers who treat them as equivalent with respect to the *of* PP diagnostic. Evidence that kinship is syntactically distinguishable from the other two comes from the existential-based BE possession constructions in Cochabamba Quechua discussed in Chapter 3, which are perfect with kinship relations but have some degree of deviance with some part whole and inalienable body part meanings. In Icelandic, which we will see has two HAVE verbs, kinship relations involve one verb (*eiga*) but other inalienable relations are expressed with other constructions. Subtler evidence that part whole is also to be distinguished from the other two comes from English. Compare the ability of such relations to be bound by a topic (with no overt possessive determiner) in the following contexts.[1]

(10)   *Kinship versus Part-Whole*

    a.   * The thing about Bart is that the dad is an idiot.

    b.   The thing about the Simpson family is that the dad is an idiot.

(11)   *Body Parts versus Part-Whole*

    a.   * The thing about John is that the eyes are shifty.

    b.   The thing about John's face is that the eyes are shifty.

The important issue is that the differences between these subtypes of relation have to do with their status in DP-syntax; plausibly, given the foregoing, all of the possessors involved in these different relations are introduced into the DP in different positions, or perhaps by different relation-denoting heads, as argued by Adger (2013). But this has no bearing on their status with regard to the verb *have* itself. My justification in uniting them under the banner of relational *have* is therefore that, whatever these positions are, leaving them without a possessor argument will give rise to the same result: a DP that denotes a relation that *have*

---

1. I first noticed this effect as it applies to kinship relations. I would like to thank Alec Marantz for pointing out to me that it extends to body part relations too, and providing the examples in (11).

can then pass up the tree to Voice, to be satiated under delayed gratification.[2] Let us consider how these different cases would be derived under the present approach. Recall that, for simplicity, I am treating the inalienable possession relations as on a par with each other syntactically, and I assume that the possessors in such relations are introduced as complements of little-n. Semantically, I will assume that these relations are inherent to the roots themselves (although it would not matter for my purposes if these relations were instead introduced by a suite of different relational functional heads, in the style of Adger 2013). The ownership relation, on the other hand, will be introduced by a Poss head, which takes nP as its complement (Poss is taken in slightly adapted form from Barker 1995, 54). This difference is enough to explain the asymmetry between the inalienable relations and ownership with regard to Barker's *of* test. The denotations of the pieces that play a role in the derivations of the sentences in (8) are listed in (12).

(12)   *Relational Have: the Pieces*

    a. $[\![\sqrt{sister}]\!] = \lambda y_e.\lambda x_e.\lambda e_s.\text{female}(x) \wedge \text{sibling-of}(y,x,e)$

    b. $[\![\sqrt{branch}]\!] = \lambda y_e.\lambda x_e.\lambda e_s.\text{branch}(x) \wedge \text{part-of}(y,x,e)$

    c. $[\![\sqrt{hair}]\!] = \lambda y_e.\lambda x_e.\lambda e_s.\text{hair}(x) \wedge \text{body-part-of}(y,x,e)$

    d. $[\![\sqrt{Playstation3}]\!] = \lambda x_e.\text{Playstation3}(x)$

    e. $[\![n]\!] = \lambda x.x$

    f. $[\![\text{Poss}]\!] = \lambda P_{<e,t>}.\lambda y_e.\lambda x_e.\lambda e_s.P(x) \wedge \text{Poss}(y,x,e)$

Of course, roots that denote body parts and the parts of inanimate wholes can appear outside of *have* sentences, with no apparent possessor. The question arises of how to account for this if these relations are inherent to the roots themselves.

(13)   I like beards.

(14)   I picked up a branch.

---

2. Thinking ahead to the discussion in Chapter 5, having ownership relations be introduced inside the DP leads to the expectation that ownership *have* sentences should give rise to definiteness effects. This is indeed the case, as Iatridou (1995, 197) showed. If placed in a context where the ownership of the possessee has to be construed as part of the assertion, *have* is not compatible with a definite direct object ((i) and (ii) are Iatridou's examples in her (36); (iii) is added by me).

    (i)   Do you see all the antiques in this room? I own/*have them.

    (ii)   That's a nice car you're driving. Do you own/*have it?

    (iii)   Now look here, I own/*have that china, so don't you go smashing it like that!

One possibility is suggested by a phenomenon found in certain languages that exhibit special morphosyntax for inalienably possessed nouns. In some such languages, including many Kampan languages (Michael 2012), inalienably possessed nouns ordinarily *must* have an overt possessor when used in a sentence. However, it is also possible to combine such nouns with what Michael (2012, 154) calls an *alienator* suffix. An example from Matsigenka is given in (15) and (16).

(15)   *(No)-gito   (Matsigenka)
        1POSS-head
        'my head'

(16)   gito-tsi
        head-ALIENATOR
        'a head'

Plausibly, the semantic function of the alienator is to existentially (or, perhaps in some contexts, generically) close the possessor variable in the possession relation. Sentences of the sort in (13) and (14) can then be explained if a silent version of the alienator exists in English.[3]

I will illustrate a full derivation only for the ownership relation, since the derivations of the other cases are exactly analogous save for where the possessor role is introduced and the relation which is associated with it. As we can see in (17), Poss takes the common noun denotation of *Playstation 3* as its argument and yields the set of individual-individual-eventuality triples such that the second individual is a Playstation 3 and is alienably possessed by the first individual in that eventuality. Since Poss is left specifierless in this derivation, this becomes the denotation of the whole DP. Given that *have* is a type-neutral identity function, this same denotation is passed up to Expletive Voice, with the result that the DP in spec-VoiceP goes in for the possessor argument in that relation. Assuming that the entity variable corresponding to the direct object undergoes existential closure at the VoiceP level (Diesing 1992), the denotation of the VoiceP will be the set of states in which there

---

3. A different question arises for part-whole relations. Quite probably, more or less anything can be construed as part of some larger whole given the right context, and then used in a part-whole *have* sentence. Given this, it cannot be the case that all part-whole relations are stored as such as the meanings of specific roots–there must be a way of introducing such relations on the fly. Two possibilities suggest themselves. One is that there is a separate functional head capable of introducing the part-whole relation. (See Adger 2013 for the view that this is the right analysis for *all* inalienable relations.) I do not know if any language displays overt evidence for such a head, but it does not strike me as an outlandish possibility. If no such evidence is forthcoming, another possibility is that it is possible to coerce a predicate of individuals into a part-whole relation in the semantic component. I will leave this matter open here.

is a Playstation 3 owned by John–a desirable result. Note that all of the semantic action in composing the meaning of the possession relation itself is already complete inside the possessee DP. It is in this sense that relational *have* is a case where the meaning of the *have* sentence = the meaning of *have*'s complement.

(17)   John has a Playstation 3.

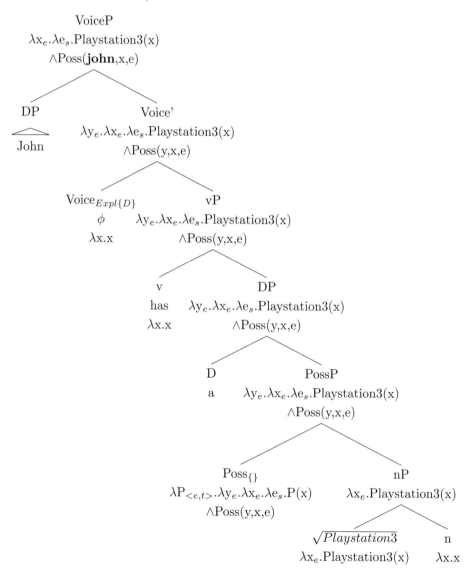

An alternative way of ensuring that the variable corresponding to the possessee is existentially closed would be to assign a denotation of the following sort to the determiner in this derivation, following Partee (1999) and the discussion of possessor raising in Wood and Marantz (2015/to appear) (cf. also the discussion of the "intended possession" reading of *-pu* in Santiago del Estero Quechua in Chapter 3 of this book):

(18) $[\![a]\!] = \lambda R_{\langle e, \langle e, \langle s, t \rangle \rangle \rangle}.\lambda y_e.\lambda e_s.\exists x_e.R(y)(x)(e)$

This denotation would compose with PossP to yield the following as the meaning of the whole DP, and this meaning can be passed up the tree by HAVE much as in the derivation illustrated above.

(19) $[\![a \text{ Playstation } 3]\!] = \lambda y_e.\lambda e_s.\exists x_e.\text{Playstation3}(x) \wedge \text{Poss}(y,x,e)$

I will leave this matter open here.

An alternative to the delayed gratification analysis of relational *have* presented above is given by Ritter and Rosen (1997, 313), who suggest that the subject of *have* binds a pronoun inside the possessed DP, as in (20) (this tree represents an updating of Ritter and Rosen's own structure to reflect my assumptions about the structure of Verb Phrases). There is a predictive difference between (20) and the delayed gratification analysis. This difference arises from the fact that in (20) there is a syntactic representation of the possessor inside the possessee DP. There is no such syntactic reflex of the possessor inside the possessee DP according to the delayed gratification analysis. Here is a way of testing these predictions: suppose we find a language that exhibits transitive HAVE, and also requires Hungarian-style agreement between the head noun and its possessor in possessed DPs. The approach in (20) predicts that HAVE sentences in such a language should require DP-internal possessor agreement, triggered by the presence of the silent pronoun. The delayed gratification approach makes no such prediction. We have, in fact, already encountered a relevant language in Chapter 3: Santiago del Estero Quechua. It turns out that, despite the fact that the dialect has obligatory DP-internal possessor agreement, it does not exhibit such agreement in relational HAVE sentences.

(20)

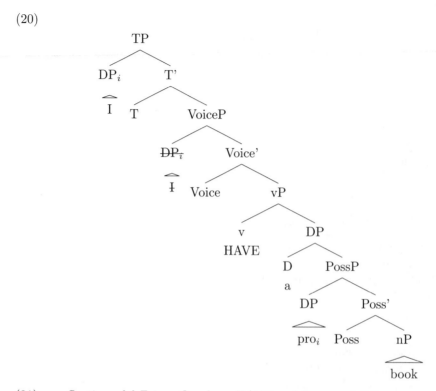

(21)   *Santiago del Estero Quechua: HAVE and Possessed DPs*

  a. Juan-pa pana-*(n)
   Juan-GEN sister-3POSS
   'Juan's sister'

  b. Juan-pa auto-*(n)
   Juan-GEN car-3POSS
   'Juan's car'

  c. Juan pana-ta api-n.
   Juan sister-ACC have-3SUBJ
   'Juan has a sister.'

  d. Juan auto-ta api-n.
   Juan car-ACC have-3SUBJ
   'Juan has a car.'

These facts from Santiago del Estero thus support the delayed gratification analysis presented here over the alternative in (20).

4.1.1.2   Locative *Have*

Another case of a *have* sentence involving expletive Voice, I will now argue, is so-called locative *have*, illustrated in (22).[4]

(22)   *Locative Have*

  a.   This tree has nests in it.

  b.   I have a cockroach on my head.

  c.   The stadium has two pubs flanking it.

A well-known constraint on this construction is that it requires a locative small clause (which is usually a PP but may also be headed by a verb, as shown in (22c)) containing a pronoun anaphoric to the subject of *have*. Absent such a pronoun, the result is either ungrammaticality or a non-locative interpretation for the sentence. The argument structure of this obligatory small clause exhausts the thematic content of a locative *have* sentence, meaning that this construction is another case where the meaning of the *have* sentence = the meaning of *have*'s complement.

(23)   *Non-Locative Have*

  a.   * This tree has nests.

  b.   * This tree has nests on me.

  c.   I have a cockroach. (= as a pet, not on my body somewhere)

  d.   I have a cockroach on John's head. (=I balanced it there/that's where I keep my cockroach)

  e.   The stadium has two pubs. (=the pubs are a built-in part of the stadium.)

Why should there have to be an overt small clause for a locative interpretation, and why must it contain such a pronoun? My proposal is that the pronoun we see in such small clauses is interpreted as a variable. This variable is lambda-abstracted-over once the PredP is completed. Hence, the PredP *nests in it* in (22a) has an interpretation along the lines of (24).

(24) $\lambda x_e.\lambda e_s.\exists y_e[\text{nests}(y)\wedge\text{in}(y,x,e)]$

---

4. Harley (1997, 77, fn 1) anticipates this idea, when she proposes the relationship between the subject of *have* and this bound pronoun is analogous to the relationship between the subject of *have* and the possessor role in an inalienably possessed NP.

Such a denotation can be passed up the tree by *have*. If Voice is interpreted expletively, then this gives rise to a locative interpretation.[5]

(25)   This tree has nests *(in it).

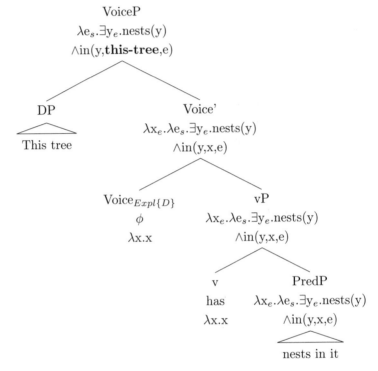

Now consider what would happen if the PP were absent. In that case, the structure assigned to this example would involve a simple DP *nests* as the complement of *have*. The only way to interpret such a sentence would be to assume that *nests* has the denotation of an inalienable or alienable possession relation, but none of these are pragmatically plausible in the case of a tree and some nests, and this is why (23a) is rejected as anomalous by native speakers ((23c) and (23e) respectively have a plausible ownership reading or a part-whole reading, and so they are grammatical without such a PP on those readings, but not on the locative reading). If the PP

---

5. The role played by this pronoun is inspired by Kratzer's (2009) approach to bound variable readings of pronouns, although the mechanisms involved cannot be quite identical, since variable binding by quantifiers does not obey the same locality constraints– a matter which I must leave aside now.

is present but contains a pronoun not coreferent with the subject of *have*, then the pronoun cannot be interpreted as a variable and the PP will be saturated. Thus, the denotation that *have* passes up the tree will be that of a simple predicate of eventualities. Given the rules of allosemy for Voice, this gives rise to the expectation that the subject of *have* will be interpreted as an external argument of that event semantically. We will see in section 4.1.2 that this situation usually allows for a causer or temporary possession *have* reading (indeed, the causer reading is a possible reading of (23d)), but since neither of these is pragmatically plausible in the case of a tree, (23b) is ruled out. Thus, the fact that the locative reading is dependent on the presence of a small clause containing such a pronoun is accounted for. Relational *have* sentences do not require a small clause, because there the relation being passed up the tree by *have* is supplied from within the possessee DP itself.[6]

4.1.1.3   Experiencer *Have*

Another subtype of *have* sentence has been called experiencer *have* (Belvin 1996; Belvin and Den Dikken 1997; Harley 1997, 1998, 2002). We shall see that experiencer *have* sentences can be either stative or eventive. It turns out that only the eventive subcase of experiencer *have* involves expletive Voice, so I will discuss the eventive subcase first here. These are constructions in which the subject of *have* is understood to have been affected in some way by the event or state in *have*'s complement. As shown in the examples in (26), the complement of *have* in experiencer *have* constructions can be headed by a bare infinitive, a participle, a preposition,

---

6. This is not to say that such a small clause is banned, and some languages may in fact require an existential PredP to be there even in a relational HAVE sentence. Some regional varieties of Italian require the presence of the "locative" clitic *ci* in all HAVE sentences, including relational ones. For relational HAVE sentences, it is plausible that this *ci* is the same *ci* as appears in existential sentences (see Kayne 2008). (Thanks to Guglielmo Cinque (pers. comm.) for the judgement on (i), and to both him and Richard Kayne for discussion).

    (i)   Gianni *(**c**)' ha una sorella.
               Gianni there has a   sister

           'Gianni has a sister.'

    (ii)   **C'**   è molto tè.
              There is much tea

           'There is a lot of tea.'

In the context of my approach, the structure of (i) will involve v embedding a PredP with *ci* (=my EXPL) in its specifier. I do not know why such a PredP complement is required by HAVE in some Italian, but not in other languages.

or even an adjective.[7] The case of (26c) is notable in that it shows that experiencer *have* sentences need not be malefactive. (Examples (26d)-(26g) are based on ones from Harley 1998.)

(26) *Experiencer Have*

    a.   I had John's dog die (on me) at 2pm.

    b.   We had a thousand people turn up all at once (on us). It was too much to handle.

    c.   John had something wonderful happen (to him) today.

    d.   We've had little Johnny crying all night (on us).

    e.   We've had half the neighborhood reduced to ashes (on us).

    f.   We've had everyone on the verge of quitting (on us).

    g.   We've had little Johnny crazy ??(on us) all day.

Contra Harley (1998), experiencer *have* readings are compatible with bare infinitival eventive complements, as we can see in (26a) and (26b), which include modifiers which are only compatible with eventive interpretations (like *at 2pm* and *all at once*).[8]

Before introducing an analysis of experiencer *have*, we must first address an observation that Belvin (1996) and Harley (1997, 1998) discuss at length concerning the role that pronouns anaphoric to the subject of *have* play in such sentences. Why is it that the presence of a PP containing a pronoun anaphoric to the external argument of *have* favors an experiencer reading over a causer one? I agree with Belvin and Den Dikken (1997)–*pace* Belvin (1996) and Harley (1998)–that this *linking requirement* (as Belvin and Den Dikken 1997, 166 call it) is semantic/pragmatic in nature (and cancellable given the right context) rather than syntactic.[9] The pronoun makes it

---

7. Although in the case of an adjective the presence of an *on* PP is virtually obligatory, and some speakers find adjective cases like (26g) awkward even with the PP (Jim Wood (pers. comm.)).

8. Ritter and Rosen (1997, 306) also err, therefore, when they claim that experiencer *have* sentences are always stative (in earlier work, Ritter and Rosen 1993 correctly stated that experiencer *have* constructions could be either stative or eventive).

9. One feature of Belvin and Den Dikken's (1997) account that I have not included here concerns extraction facts. Belvin and Den Dikken (1997, 161) note that A-bar extraction of the embedded subject in an eventive experiencer *have* sentence sometimes leads to deviance. The data includes sentences of the following sort (their footnote 11), which is claimed to be grammatical only on a causative reading.

    (i)   (*?) Who did you have ask you for money?

In fact, as the authors note themselves, the judgments on these extraction cases are contested (I accept (i) quite readily on an experiencer reading, although in other cases extraction is somewhat

easier to construe the embedded eventuality as something that "happens to" *have*'s subject, and therefore makes an experiencer reading easier to find, but it is not necessary. Nor does the presence of a pronoun actually force an experiencer reading. Hence, while (27) may favor the experiencer reading out of the blue, it can get a causer reading if, for example, John is my butler and I have ordered him to pour custard over my head repeatedly owing to a belief that it is good for one's hair. Similarly, while (28) leans in the direction of a causer reading out of context, it can be understood as an experiencer *have* sentence if I have been trying to keep Bill clean for a family photo, but his naughty brother John keeps frustrating my efforts.

(27)   I've had John pouring custard over my head all day.

(28)   I've had John pouring custard over Bill's head all day.

However, if the pronoun is contained in an *on* PP, it seems that an experiencer reading is forced, and moreover that a malefactive experiencer reading is forced.

(29)   We had little Johnny run off on us.

(30)   We had little Johnny running off on us (every five minutes).

To explain these effects, I will partly follow Kim (2012, 86) in postulating that the complement of *have* contains a functional head that introduces an experiencer thematic role, and which merges above the embedded VoiceP. I will depart from Kim, however, in refraining from calling that projection ApplP (since this would be at variance with my conclusions about Appl from the previous chapter). Instead I will call it FreeP, since this head, as I shall argue, introduces free datives in languages other than English. My assumptions regarding where the experiencer argument itself is introduced will also be different. Kim (2012, 93) assumes that the experiencer argument is introduced in the specifier of ApplP (my FreeP) below *have*. I will instead claim that this argument is introduced in the specifier of the VoiceP above *have*. My proposal has the advantage that it does not lead to the prediction that *have* is an unaccusative verb (see Chapter 5). My account will also allow for an attractive explanation of the structural role of *on* PPs, as well permitting a parametric approach to the relationship between experiencer HAVE sentences and

---

more difficult), and even for speakers that have them, are quite easily ameliorated by the inclusion of adverbs like *today*. Given this, I do not think that the correct reaction to (i) is to assign eventive experiencer *have* a radically different argument structure from other variants of *have*.

free datives cross-linguistically,[10] neither of which is provided by Kim's approach.[11] In the ensuing discussion, I will focus on eventive experiencer *have* sentences, and in particular on those where the complement of *have* is headed by a bare infinitive. I will temporarily leave stative experiencer *have* sentences to one side, since there is some comparative syntactic evidence that the presence of a Free head may not be necessary to introduce an experiencer role in stative cases. I will suggest later on that this is because Voice introduces a holder role in stative contexts (Kratzer 1996), and one way to be the holder of a state is to be an experiencer of it. Because Voice is able to introduce an experiencer in stative contexts, the presence of the Free head turns out not to be a necessary condition for the derivation of an experiencer reading with statives. In eventive contexts, on the other hand, the presence of Free *is* necessary to derive such a reading.

Let us begin with the case of an experiencer *have* sentence where no *on* PP is present. For these, I propose the structure in (31). Note that the Appl head above the embedded VoiceP introduces an experiencer role, but that this role is not saturated until the matrix VoiceP level, where the subject of *have* is introduced. The embedded VoiceP denotes the set of running-off events that took place this morning and of which Johnny is the agent. Free, which takes this VoiceP as its complement, introduces an experiencer argument semantically. These two denotations combine via Krazter's (1996) rule of Event Identification. However, since this FreeP is unable to introduce a specifier in English (as I will argue below, when I contrast English with other languages), the experiencer role introduced by FreeP is not saturated straight away, and is instead passed up the tree by v=HAVE, where it is saturated by the argument introduced in the matrix spec-VoiceP.

---

10. I would like to thank Alec Marantz for suggesting this connection and encouraging me to pursue it.

11. I will also note that Kim's account has an empirical consequence that is presented as advantageous (Kim 2012, 85), but that actually fatally undermines it–namely, the (false) generalization that the subjects of VoicePs embedded under experiencer *have* are invariably agentive. See (26a) and (26c) for disconfirming evidence.

(31)   We had little Johnny run off this morning.

VoiceP
λe_s.run-off(e)$\wedge$this-morning(e)
$\wedge$Agent(e,**johnny**)
$\wedge$Experiencer(e,**speaker+**)

DP   Voice'

we $\lambda x_e.\lambda e_s$.run-off(e)$\wedge$this-morning(e)
$\wedge$Agent(e,**johnny**)$\wedge$Experiencer(e,x)

Voice$_{\{D\}}$ vP
ϕ $\lambda x_e.\lambda e_s$.run-off(e)
$\lambda x.x$ $\wedge$this-morning(e)
$\wedge$Agent(e,**johnny**)
$\wedge$Experiencer(e,x)

v   FreeP
had $\lambda x_e.\lambda e_s$.run-off(e)
$\lambda x.x$ $\wedge$this-morning(e)
$\wedge$Agent(e,**johnny**)
$\wedge$Experiencer(e,x)

Free$_{\{\}}$ VoiceP
$\lambda x_e.\lambda e_s$.Experiencer(e,x) λe_s.run-off(e)
$\wedge$this-morning(e)
$\wedge$Agent(e,**johnny**)

little Johnny run
off this morning

Let us now consider sentences including *on* PPs. The intuition I would like to argue for here, following Wood (2013, 283), is that *on* PPs are to the Free head in (31) what *by*-phrases are to passive VoicePs (on an analysis of *by*-phrases along the lines of Bruening 2013). That is to say, the *on* PP adjoins to FreeP and has the effect of transmitting the thematic role introduced by Free to the DP in its complement. To ensure this, I give malefactive *on* the following denotation, based on Bruening's (2013, 25) denotation for the *by* of English passives, in (32a). The denotation of an *on* PP like *on us* will then be as in (32b).

(32)   *The Interpretation of on PPs*

    a. $\llbracket \text{on} \rrbracket = \lambda x_e.\lambda f_{<e,<s,t>>}.\lambda e_s.f(x)(e) \wedge \text{adversely-affect}(e,x)$

    b. $\llbracket \text{on us} \rrbracket = \lambda f_{<e,<s,t>>}.\lambda e_s.f(\textbf{speaker+})(e)$
        $\wedge \text{adversely-affect}(e,\textbf{speaker+})$

Unlike English *by* in passives, however, *on* does not merely transmit this role in a neutral way–it also imposes a malefactive meaning, encoded in (32a) by an 'adversely-affect' relation between an eventuality and an individual. Since the argument introduced by *on* is able to saturate the role introduced by Free, sentences with Free and an *on* PP can still compose semantically even if they are not embedded under *have*. We thus correctly predict that sentences like the one diagrammed in (33) on the next page are grammatical.

What of experiencer *have* sentences that contain an *on* PP, such as *we had little Johnny run off on us*? Recall that, in the analysis of locative *have* sentences, we invoked Kratzer's (2009) idea that pronouns can be interpreted simply as variables that are lambda-abstracted-over at a certain point in the derivation. I propose that the same sort of pronoun is at issue in the case of such experiencer *have* sentences. That is, the *us* in *on us* can be interpreted as such a variable and lambda-abstracted-over at the level of FreeP. The derivation of such a sentence will then proceed in a familiar fashion, as shown in (34) two pages below.

(33)   Little Johnny ran off on us.

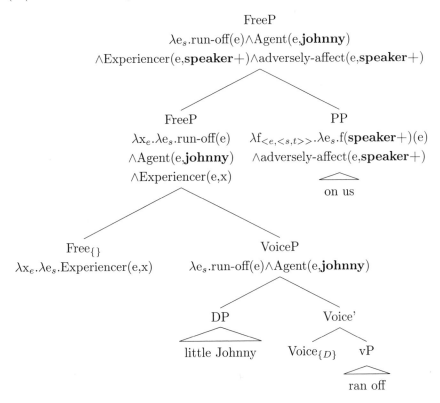

The general picture of experiencer *have* sentences in English that I am advocating is this: they involve a Free head that is able to introduce a thematic role at semantics but is not able to project a specifier. This idea raises the expectation that there will be languages out there in which the relevant Free head *can* project a specifier. Also, if a language happened to *require* this Free to take a specifier in derivations where it appears, we would expect it to lack experiencer HAVE entirely–there would never be any need or opportunity to introduce Free's argument in a higher specifier position. As I will now show, these expectations are correct. The evidence comes from the presence of Free datives and the absence of eventive Experiencer HAVE in Romance (cf. the situation in English, which is the reverse).

(34)   We had little Johnny run off on us.

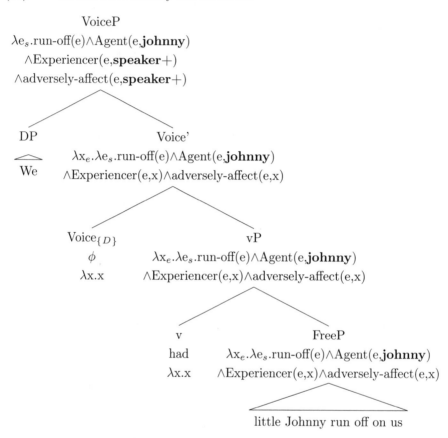

The table in (35) displays the expected space of parametric variation, and the languages that instantiate it. I do not yet know of any languages that radically lack the relevant Free head altogether, and perhaps Universal Grammar forbids such radical absence of a functional head (Cinque 1999; Kayne 2000, 2005, 2010b), but for completeness I include this possibility in the table.

(35)   *Parametric Variation in FreeP*

Available Free heads	Phenomena	Instantiating Languages
Free$_{\{\}}$	Eventive Experiencer HAVE, No free datives	English
Free$_{\{D\}}$	No Eventive Experiencer HAVE, Yes free datives	Spanish
Free$_{\{\}}$ & Free$_{\{D\}}$	Both Eventive Experiencer HAVE and free datives	None Known
None	Neither Eventive Experiencer HAVE nor free datives	None Known

This table is incomplete in that it does not include *on* PPs and their cross-linguistic equivalents. The existence of these makes it logically possible for a language to have the Free$_{\{\}}$ head in its grammar but still lack eventive experiencer HAVE and free datives if independent factors rule these out (although I do not know what independent factors would lead to such a situation). Such a language would simply be forced to use its counterpart of the *on* PP in every derivation in which the relevant Free head was included. Note also that there is a predicted language type in which free datives alternate with experiencer HAVE. I have not found a convincing case of such a language yet.

As pointed out by Belvin (1996, 202-213), Spanish completely lacks correspondents of eventive experiencer *have* in English. Examples like the following are completely out (example (36a) is from Belvin's discussion).[12]

(36)   *Spanish Lacks Eventive Experiencer HAVE*

a.   * Juan tuvo una abeja picar=lo en la   nariz.
     Juan had a   bee sting-him on the nose
     'Juan had a bee sting him on the nose.'

b.   * Tuve el   perro de Juan morir=se.
     I.had the dog   of Juan die-refl
     'I had John's dog die (on me).'

---

12. Given facts about Spanish word order in small clauses, it is worth pointing out that these examples remain bad if the infinitive precedes the embedded subject: **Juan tuvo picarlo una abeja en la nariz*. Thanks to Pablo González Martínez for judgments on the Spanish sentences reported here.

My proposal is that the badness of (36) is linked to the fact that Spanish conveys these sorts of meaning using a simple finite clause containing a dative clitic, as seen in (37).

(37)   *Spanish Has Free Datives*

    a.   (A Juan) una abeja le   picó en la   nariz.
           To Juan a   bee   him.DAT stung on the nose

           'Juan had a bee sting him on the nose.'

    b.   Se   me   murió el   perro de Juan.
           REFL me.DAT died   the dog   of Juan

           'I had John's dog die (on me).'

I claim that this dative clitic is introduced in the specifier of the same Free head that is involved in deriving eventive experiencer *have* sentences (following the spirit of Cuervo 2003, but departing from her assumption that the clitic instantiates Free [her Appl] itself).[13] In English, this head cannot take a specifier–hence, in order to use the head at all, English must avail itself of an *on* PP and/or embed the FreeP in a vP, which then allows it to introduce the experiencer argument in spec-VoiceP (yielding an experiencer *have* sentence). In Spanish, I propose that this Free head not only can take a specifier, but *must* do so. This requirement is met by the dative clitic in examples like (37). However, this same requirement means that it is impossible to build an eventive *have* sentence by leaving Free specifierless and introducing the experiencer argument higher up–and this is why (36) is bad in Spanish, whereas its equivalent is good in English.

Before moving on from experiencer *have*, I must make a brief comment on stative experiencer *have* constructions (recall that we have been focussing on eventive variants until now). Some examples of these are gathered below (some are repeated from (26)).

(38)   *Stative Experiencer Have Sentences*

    a.   Juan had bees stinging him all over his body (at 2pm).

    b.   We've had little Johnny crying all night (on us).

    c.   We've had half the neighborhood reduced to ashes (on us).

    d.   We have everyone on the verge of quitting (on us).

    e.   We've had little Johnny crazy ??(on us) all day.

---

13. Recall that Quechua languages have an overt Appl morpheme *-pu* which coexists with overt object clitics, which might be taken to undermine Cuervo's proposal for Spanish.

That these uses of *have* are stative is shown by the interpretation of temporal modifiers–*at 2pm* in (38a) does not mean that any particular change in the situation occurred at 2pm, but rather that a particular state of affairs still held (when the speaker checked) at 2pm. In addition, examples in the simple present tense are compatible with a non-generic reading ((38d) can describe a state of affairs that is true right now–it does not require a habitual reading like an eventive sentence would). I will show how the stativity of these constructions follows from the current approach in more detail in the next section. For now, I wish to note that, unlike eventive experiencer HAVE sentences, such stative experiencer HAVE sentences do not appear to rely on the properties of Free in the same way. This is shown by the fact that stative experiencer HAVE is attested in Romance languages that have free datives, such as Spanish, as discussed by Belvin (1996, 202) (see also Tremblay 1991 on French).

(39)   *Spanish Allows Stative Experiencer HAVE*

Juan tiene abejas picando=le   por todo el   cuerpo.
Juan has   bees   stinging-him.DAT for all   the body
'Juan has bees stinging him all over his body.'

It seems, therefore, that stative experiencer HAVE is in some sense 'easier' to have than the eventive subcase is. Moreover, and relatedly, the distribution of stative experiencer HAVE does not appear to interact with the existence of free datives in the same way that eventive experiencer HAVE does. What is the source of this asymmetry?

I propose that these facts are a natural consequence of ideas about the Voice head that have been standardly assumed since at least Kratzer (1996). Kratzer proposed the following two variants of the Voice head. The choice between them depends upon the nature of Voice's complement–in particular, whether it is stative or eventive (recall that I am following Wood 2015 in assuming that these are in fact two conditioned allosemes of the same syntactic Voice head).

(40)   *Allosemes of Voice*

  a.   [[Voice]] $= \lambda x_e.\lambda e_s.$ Agent(x,e) / ___(agentive, dynamic event)

  b.   [[Voice]] $= \lambda x_e.\lambda e_s.$ Holder(x,e) / ___(stative eventuality)

Since holder ranges over the causer and experiencer role, there is nothing to stop Voice introducing an experiencer argument in a stative HAVE sentence ((40a) already explains why it can't do this in eventive HAVE sentences, of course). This, I propose, is how Spanish is able to build stative experiencer HAVE sentences despite the fact that its Free head requires a specifier (which prevents it from being able to build eventive experiencer HAVE sentences): it can build them without using Free and instead simply using the Voice head. This is illustrated schematically for English in the tree in (41) (I assume that the *-ing* morpheme is responsible for stativizing the event denoted by *sting*, and that this denotation is passed up the tree by *have*, making the whole construction stative). To avoid any potential confusion, let me stress that I am not claiming that Free is barred from stative contexts. What I am claiming is that, thanks to the independently needed holder alloseme of Voice, Free is not the only way to introduce an experiencer role in a stative sentence (whereas Free *is* the only way to introduce an experiencer role in an eventive sentence).

(41)   Juan had bees stinging him.

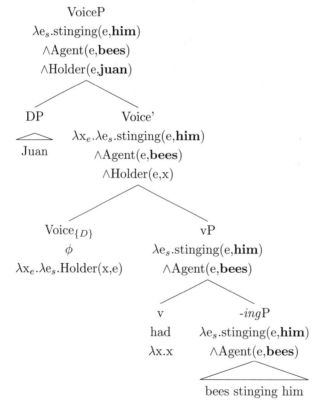

This concludes the discussion of *have*/HAVE sentences in which Voice assigns no thematic role (I will later claim that modal *have*/HAVE in sentences like *John has to leave* is another such case, but I postpone discussion of this construction for the time being). Because *have*/HAVE itself is semantically vacuous, all of the thematic content of such sentences comes from *have*/HAVE's complement. In the next subsection, we consider cases in which Voice does assign a Theta-role, so that the meaning of the *have*/HAVE sentence is a combination of the meanings of *have*/HAVE's complement and the meaning of Voice. In (41) we have already seen a brief illustration of one such case; I will now show that there are many more.

4.1.2   Cases Where the Meaning of a *Have* Sentence = That of *have*'s Complement+That of Voice (If Voice ≠ Expl)

4.1.2.1   Light-Verb *Have*

Perhaps the simplest case of this kind is what we might call light-verb *have*. In these cases, the DP that *have* takes as its complement denotes an event or state. When this denotation is passed up the tree by *have*, Voice will relate the argument in its specifier to it in the standard way. This derivation, spelled out in (43), is essentially a translation into Kratzerian terms of Ritter and Rosen's (1997, 302-305) analysis of light-verb *have*.

(42)   *Light-Verb Have*

    a.   We had a conversation.

    b.   John had an accident.

    c.   We had an argument.

    d.   I had a bath.

    e.   We're having fun.

    f.   You'll have trouble getting that to work.

Before moving on, I will note an interesting puzzle (first brought to my attention by Anna Szabolcsi) raised by the analysis of light-verb *have* constructions in (43).[14] It seems that, unlike simplex event nominals like those in (42), complex event nominals (in the sense of Grimshaw 1990) are ungrammatical under light-verb *have*. That is, complex event nominals systematically resist delayed gratification of the sort that I have argued takes place in relational *have* sentences. This is true regardless of whether the agent or the theme argument of the derived nominal ends up as the subject of *have*. The examples in (44)-(46) show this.

---

14. It turns out, however, that no previous theory of HAVE has a ready account of Szabolcsi's observation, either.

(43)   We had a conversation.

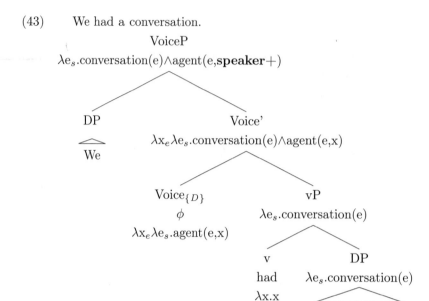

(44) a.   The Romans' destruction of the city (was merciless).

      b.   * The Romans' had {a/the} destruction of the city.

      c.   * The city had {a/the} destruction.

(45) a.   John's completion of his homework (was a turn-up for the books).

      b.   * John had {a/the} completion of his homework.

      c.   * His homework had {a/the} completion.

(46) a.   John's payment of his bills (was prompt).

      b.   * John had {a/the} payment of his bills.

      c.   * His bills had {a/the} payment.

A priori, given that my account allows DP-internal relations like kinship and ownership to give rise to *have* sentences via delayed gratification, the facts in (44)-(46) are not automatically expected. It seems that the situation has to be characterized as follows: complex event nominals make more demands on their syntactic argument structure than do relation-denoting roots like *sister*, or relationalized DPs like *Playstation 3* in *John has a Playstation 3*. That is to say, unlike the case of the latter kinds of nominal, Poss and n always have a {D} requirement in complex event nominalization contexts. This would then force instant gratification in complex event nominal structures, explaining (44)-(46). From what might this follow?

A plausible answer, thinking of Alexiadou and Grimshaw (2008), stems from the idea that complex event nominals contain more verbal substructure than simplex event nominals or relational(ized) nouns, which arguably contain no verbal substructure at all.

(47)   a. $[\; [\sqrt{destruct}-\emptyset_v \;]_{vP}$ -ion$_n \;]_{nP}$

     b. $[\sqrt{argue}$ -ment$_n \;]_{nP}$

     c. $[\sqrt{sister}$ -$\emptyset_n \;]_{nP}$

The idea would be that it is the presence of the v head in (47a) that forces instant gratification in complex event nominals in *have* sentences. While Wurmbrand's (2001) approach to restructuring allows delayed gratification from verbal argument positions, it is permitted only under restructuring verbs–presumably main verb *have* is not a restructuring predicate in this sense when it selects a DP. Consonant with this, as Alec Marantz points out to me (pers. comm.), the following example is grammatical on a reading where the Romans are the agent of the destruction event. This is expected on Wurmbrand's approach combined with what I have said here, since *finish* is a restructuring verb.

(48)   The Romans finished the destruction of the city.

The absence of the v head in simplex event nominals (47b) and relational nouns (47c) would then account for their compatibility with delayed gratification, and therefore with *have*.

This account is compatible with what is known about languages that make strikingly extensive use of light-verb constructions. Choi and Wechsler (2002) argue (mostly for Korean, but with some reference to Japanese) that light-verb constructions never involve transfer of core arguments from the derived nominal to the light-verb, *contra* Grimshaw and Mester's (1988) description and analysis of Japanese light-verb constructions. In particular, they argue for cases like (49) that the agent argument (*John* in this case) is always assigned a Theta-role chosen by the light verb itself, and that the theme argument (*English* in (49)) is always introduced inside the nominal (indicated by brackets).[15]

---

15. Oblique arguments may apparently be introduced either inside or outside the nominal in these Korean light-verb constructions, but these cases need not be analyzed in terms of delayed gratification. Indeed, they cannot be so analyzed, since the oblique case markings involved are the same regardless. The behavior of obliques in this construction is presumably a matter of ambiguity of attachment (which in these cases would be semantically vacuous or close to it, since the light verb itself adds very little to the lexical semantics of the predicate).

(49)   John-i   [yenge-lul   kongpu-lul] ha-yess-ta.   (Korean)
         John-NOM English-ACC study-ACC do-PAST-DEC
         'John studied English.'

Choi and Wechsler adduce numerous arguments in favor of this conclusion and
against that of Grimshaw and Mester (1988), who argued that light verbs could
inherit and project the arguments of complex event nominals in Japanese. One of
them is the fact that the complement of *ha* must be eventive and cannot be stative,
and the external argument must therefore be an agent and not the holder of a state.
This indicates that the external argument is introduced by the Voice head above the
light verb, and its agentive semantics are not percolating up from the nominal itself.
Secondly, the fact that the theme argument is internal to the nominal projection
(headed by *study* in (49)) is shown by numerous constituency tests.

It therefore seems plausible that the core arguments of a complex event nominal are never transferred under delayed gratification cross-linguistically in light-
verb constructions (although they can be under certain restructuring predicates–see
(48)).[16] The fact that *have* does not allow this either is therefore scarcely anomalous.

4.1.2.2   ECM *Have*: Causers, Engineers, and Experiencers

Sentences of the kind discussed in this subsection are often called causative and
experiencer *have* (Belvin 1996; Harley 1997, 1998, 2002). My terminology will be
slightly different. For reasons that will become clear presently, I splinter causative
have into engineer *have* and causer *have*.[17] The need for such splintering of causative
have has been recognized by Copley and Harley (2009), who use the term *director*

---

16. An anonymous reviewer asks whether this generalization is true even in languages that have
very few actual verbs, and make extensive use of light-verb constructions involving a root and one
of a handful of 'true' light verbs, like Jingulu (Pensalfini 1997). Jingulu, at least, does not appear
to be relevant to testing this generalization: it could only be so if eventive derived nominals were
able to act as the root in such a structure. Pensalfini (1997, 138) himself argues that the root in
such Jingulu structures is acategorial (he shows that the roots themselves are not always usable
as nouns, and so certainly cannot be derived nominals).

17. My analysis of such sentences differs in its essentials from that of Ritter and Rosen (1997)
only in that it distinguishes engineer and causer *have* (which they do not), and in that it does
not require that experiencer *have* sentences be stative (something which Ritter and Rosen 1997
do require–erroneously, as we have seen).

reading for a subset of the cases I am calling the engineer reading.[18] Examples of each one are provided in (50)-(52).[19]

(50)   I had John bathe his dog.   (Engineer)

(51)   We have everyone on the verge of quitting (on us).
        (Experiencer)

(52)   a.   The article had me angry at the government/weeping in fury.
              (Causer)

        b.   Superman has the bad guy pinned to the floor/begging for mercy.

In these cases, the subject of *have* does not seem to correspond to an argument of the embedded predicate (except when (51) appears with *on us*, for reasons covered in the previous section). I will argue however that these subjects are not receiving a Theta-role from *have*, which is a type-neutral identity function in (50)-(52) just as it always is. Instead, these Theta-roles are being assigned by allosemes of Voice that are needed outside of HAVE constructions. That Voice can introduce causer and experiencer roles (as subcases of the holder role) is not controversial; the engineer role, as I call it, is less familiar (although its properties are well discussed by Belvin 1996; Harley 1997, 1998; and Copley and Harley 2009), and so it is worth discussing its nature a little more. The engineer reading requires a sentient subject, and in that sense is not merely a causer:

(53)   * The up-coming dog show had John bathe his dog.

Yet, the engineer role goes beyond agentivity in requiring that the argument to which it is assigned not be a direct causer of an event, but rather a sort of backstairs orchestrator of it. In this it differs from the agent in a *make* causative or an ordinary transitive sentence, for instance. Hence, (54a) and (54b) can be felicitous descriptions of a situation in which I stick my leg out in front of John and thereby cause him to fall, but (54c) cannot be (although it can describe a situation in which I arrange for John to fall over with his complicity, perhaps in order to fool a soccer referee into giving a free kick).[20]

18. The approach to engineer *have* in this work unfortunately does not make hay of the very interesting parallelism that Copley and Harley point out between futurate uses of the present tense (like *we leave tomorrow*) and the semantics of engineer *have*. This may prove to be a disadvantage in the long run.

19. Example (52a) is based on one in Pesetsky (1995, 61, his (172a)).

20. Example (54c) and others like it disprove Kim's (2012, 75) claim that unaccusatives are not permitted in *have* causatives. Kim's evidence for this claim consists of two examples. One of these

(54)   a.   I made John fall over.

       b.   I tripped John.

       c.   I had John fall over.

A sharp contrast between causer *have* and engineer *have* can be brought out
by employing a verb like *cough*, which is usually ambiguous between meaning an
involuntary reflex caused by some respiratory irritation or a deliberate act.

(55)   a.   Robin had me coughing. (Causer *have*)

       b.   Robin had me cough. (Engineer *have*)

Example (55a) has a reading that (55b) lacks: namely, one in which my coughing
was an involuntary reaction to something about Robin or something that Robin
was doing (e.g., perhaps her perfume was too strong, she was blowing smoke at me,
etc.). In contrast, (55b) requires that I coughed on purpose at Robin's instigation
(e.g., if Robin is a doctor and asks me to cough as part of a test she is running).

   Why is the engineer role so restricted in its distribution, and why does it differ so
much from the causer of *make* causatives, as shown by (54), and from the causers of
causer *have* sentences, as shown by (55)? I conjecture that this reading emerges only
when Voice is trying to semantically relate an argument directly to an eventuality
that already contains a saturated VoiceP, which is not something that happens in
make causatives (since *make* presumably introduces a causing event of its own) or
ordinary transitive contexts (in which Voice is relating the argument in its specifier
to vP). A rule of allosemy encapsulating this distribution is given below:

(56) $[\![\text{Voice}]\!]= \lambda x_e.\lambda e_s.\text{Engineer}(e,x)$ / ___v_{BE} Eventive-VoiceP$_{\langle s,t \rangle}$

   There is perhaps one other situation in English, beyond the engineer *have* construction, in which the engineer role emerges. I suggest that it is also at work in
the so-called *secondary agentivity* phenomenon in *get* passives, whereby the subject

---

is poorly chosen, since it employs *die*, which, although unaccusative in many languages, actually
has some unergative properties in English (such as allowing cognate objects in cases like *he died
a gruesome death*). Her other example is *(*)John had Mary arrive*, which is straightforwardly
ameliorated (cf. *John had Mary arrive early to help set up*). What is actually crucial for engineer
have, as we will see, is not that the complement of *have* have a true external argument. Rather,
the crucial thing is that the embedded event be something that some other agent is capable of
bringing about voluntarily (this is why *John had Mary die* improves to perfection if John is a film
director and Mary is an actress playing a character who dies, as Copley and Harley 2009 note).
This fact in turn is hard to reconcile with Kim's claim that *have* causees are non-agentive (2012,
85). Her evidence for this claim is the generalization that adverbs like *deliberately* are not allowed
underneath engineer *have*, but this is also false (cf. *The coach had the player deliberately fall to
the floor to win a penalty*).

argument (which apparently correponds to the direct object of the main verb) is also interpretable as having engineered the situation denoted by that verb.[21]

(57)   Blackadder deliberately got shot by the Germans (to get sent home).

There are two main advantages of the view that all three of engineer *have*, eventive experiencer *have*, and causer *have* are cases in which *have*'s meaning is nothing more than that of Voice plus that of *have*'s complement. First, it explains why the interpretation of the external argument of *have* is determined by the nature of its complement (we will turn to the evidence for this presently): the alloseme of Voice is chosen by the denotation of this complement, which *have* simply pushes up the tree. Secondly, it explains why the aspectual properties of engineer/experiencer/causer *have* sentences (i.e. whether they are stative or eventive) are also determined by *have*'s complement (as Belvin 1996 showed and Harley 1998 pursued). These two advantages are intertwined, as we will now see: if the complement of *have* is an eventive bare infinitive, then only the engineer or experiencer reading are allowed. If the complement of *have* is a stative small clause, then causer or experiencer readings are allowed depending on other factors. Both advantages follow if *have* simply passes the interpretation of its complement up to Voice.

Let us now review the evidence for these generalizations. Engineer *have* takes a bare infinitive in active contexts. This infinitive, as proposed in (56), must be an eventive VoiceP. The whole construction itself becomes eventive as a result, as can be seen by the fact that *have* is allowed in the progressive[22] and by the fact that it can only be interpreted habitually if put into the simple present tense (i.e., (58b) cannot mean "my butler is shaving the cow right now, and I engineered this").

---

21. If this conjecture were true it would entail, given the allosemy rule in (56), that *get* contains v_{BE} in some way. This idea, of course, is commonplace in lexical decomposition analyses (Harley 1995; Richards 2001; many others).

22. This fact, along with similar ones involving event-denoting complements of *have* like *we're having a party*, shows that *have* itself cannot be inherently stative, as many suppose. Instead, as predicted by the current account, *have* is stative or eventive depending on its complement. Richard Kayne asks in this connection why not all languages allow the equivalent of *we're having a party*. The answer to this question will be a complex one, since it is closely related to the question of how a language with many light-verbs "chooses" which one to use in particular contexts. This is something that can differ quite markedly between dialects of the same language, and it is seldom clear why at this point. For instance, I reject *I'm taking a piss* and accept *I'm having a piss*, but the judgments are reversed for an American consultant I asked. I must leave this important question, which might fruitfully be pursued via micro-comparative work on English dialects, for future research.

(58)   *Engineer Have Is Eventive*

    a.   I'm having my butler shave the cow.

    b.   I have my butler shave the cow.

Crucially, the progressive aspect in (58a) modifies the embedded shaving event.[23] My approach will explain this fact, because it predicts that *have* introduces no causing event of its own, and simply passes the eventuality denotation of its complement up the tree, whereupon the latter will end up getting linked to the matrix Tense and Aspect heads.

If the complement of *have* is stative (which will be the case if it is a small clause headed by an AP, PP, adjectival passive, or gerund) then a causer reading is available (see (59) and (60)). With animates, an experiencer reading is also available, and this is the only reading that survives if an *on* PP is included (for reasons discussed earlier).

(59)   We've had little Johnny crying all night (on us).

(60)   We've had half the neighborhood reduced to ashes (on us).

(61)   We've had everyone on the verge of quitting (on us).

(62)   We've had little Johnny crazy ??(on us) all day.

Because such small clauses are stative, the whole construction is stative. It is thus incompatible with the progressive, and the simple present tense form can have a non-habitual reading.

(63)   *Causer Have Is Stative*

    a.   * We're having little Johnny crying.

    b.   We have little Johnny crying.

One apparent wrinkle in the generalization that engineer readings emerge in eventive contexts and causer readings emerge in stative small clause contexts comes from the fact that small clauses headed by a passive participle seem to allow all three of engineer, causer and experiencer readings.

---

23. Of course, (58a) can mean that the cow-shaving will take place in the future. But this is no threat to the generalization in the text, since the same is true of simple progressive cases quite generally:

    (i)   My butler is shaving the cow tomorrow.

(64)   The general had the bridge blown to smithereens.   (Engineer)

(65)   The wind had our belongings strewn across the field.   (Causer)

(66)   We've had half the neighborhood reduced to ashes (on us). (Experiencer)

However, this actually reduces to the well-known structural ambiguity between eventive passive participles and adjectival (=stative) ones, as Harley (1998) shows. The progressive test confirms that this is what is at issue.

(67)   The general is having the bridge blown to smithereens.
          (Engineer)

(68)   * The wind is having our belongings strewn across the field.
          (Causer)

(69)   We're having half the neighborhood reduced to ashes (on us).
          (Experiencer)

Example (68) is ungrammatical because causer *have* sentences involve a stative complement. The presence of the progressive is incompatible with this. In contrast, (67) and (69) are fine, because engineer *have* and eventive experiencer *have* embed eventive complements. Interpreting the passive participle as eventive will not help with (68), because this will give rise to an engineer reading, which is incompatible with an inanimate subject like *the wind*.

Let us now examine the derivations of some individual cases, to see how the relevant allosemes of Voice are selected in each case (omitting experiencer cases, which were discussed in the previous subsection). The structure in (70) depicts the derivation of an engineer *have* sentence.

(70)   I had John bathe his dog.   (Engineer *have*)

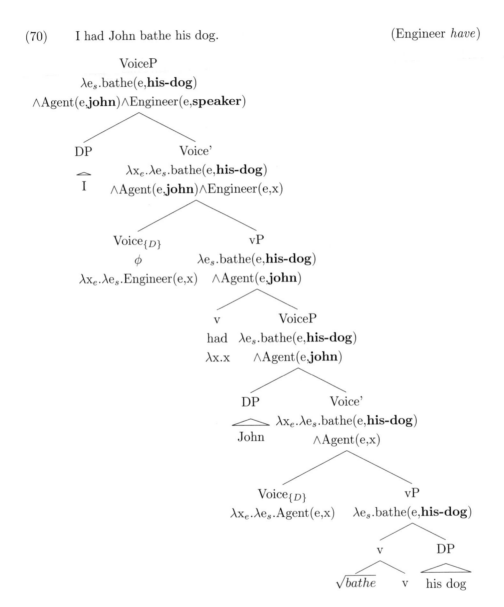

The embedded VoiceP is composed in the familiar way, and comes to denote the set of bathing events of which John is the agent and his dog is the theme. This denotation is simply passed up the tree by *have*, and Voice finds itself having to relate the argument in its specifier to this same eventuality. Since this eventuality is a full, saturated VoiceP, the engineer alloseme of Voice is chosen, and this is the reading we get. The fact that no independent causing event is introduced by *have* is crucial here: it is because of this that the engineer alloseme of Voice is chosen rather than agentive Voice. There is independent evidence that there is indeed no independent causing event in *have* sentences of this sort. As observed by Brugman (1988, 132), it is impossible to use modifiers that would modify the causing event in engineer *have* and causer *have* sentences, whereas *make* causatives do allow this. This is, of course, readily explained if *make* introduces its own event variable but *have*, being a type-neutral identity function, simply pushes the eventuality in its complement up the tree.[24]

(71)   I made Bill eat his soup by threatening him with a ladle.

(72)   * I had Bill eat(ing) his soup by threatening him with a ladle.

(73)   I made Bill eat his soup by sucking it through a straw.

(74)   I had Bill eat(ing) his soup by sucking it through a straw.

Next, consider the derivation of a causer *have* sentence, exemplified in (75). In this case, the complement of *have* is an adjectival small clause denoting the set of states in which the speaker is angry at the government. Voice is then fed this denotation by *have* in the by-now familiar way. Faced with relating an external argument to this state, Voice does so via its causer alloseme (a special case of holder).

---

24. It is for this reason that I have been assuming all along that relational DPs contribute the eventuality variable in predicative possession sentences–this variable must come from somewhere, and given the behavior of engineer and causer *have*, we cannot assume that this variable is contributed by *have* in those sentences and maintain a unified analysis of HAVE itself. See Chapter 1 for empirical evidence for the assumption that possession relations include their own eventuality variable.

(75)   The article had me angry at the government.   (Causer *have*)

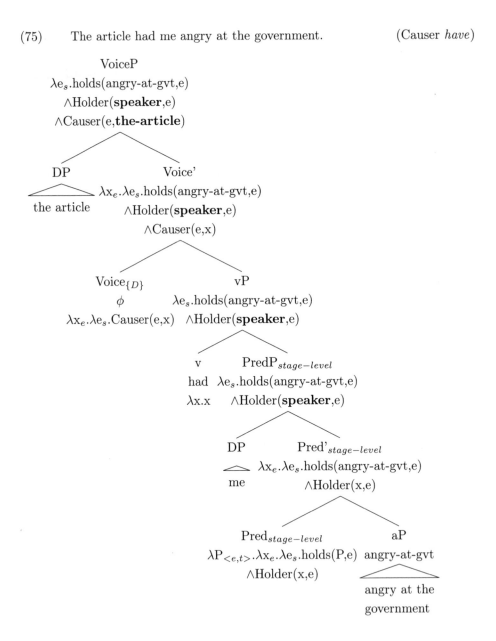

Before moving on I must address comparative questions analogous to the ones that arose in the discussion of experiencer *have* in the previous subsection. It turns out that engineer HAVE is more or less unique to English (Kayne 1993, fn16; Den Dikken 1997), although causer HAVE is found elsewhere. Belvin (1996, 202-213) gives a number of examples from Spanish, including this one (causer HAVE sentences are also available in French, as shown by Tremblay 1991).

(76)   *Spanish Allows Causer HAVE*

      El   hielo tuvo patinando al   carro.

      The ice   had sliding   to.the car

      'The ice had the car sliding around.'

Belvin (1996, 202-213) also shows that what I am calling engineer HAVE is impossible in Spanish.[25]

(77)   *Spanish Does Not Allow Engineer HAVE*

      * Juan tuvo a   Miguel bailar.

      Juan had ACC Miguel dance

      'Juan had Miguel dance.'

This distinction between engineer and causer HAVE cuts in an identical fashion to the distinction we saw earlier between eventive experiencer HAVE and stative experiencer HAVE. In both, the event/state distinction is crucial (with the eventive one missing outside of English). Also in both, infinitives behave differently than other sorts of complement cross-linguistically. This raises the possibility, explored by Richard Kayne in recent work, that the availability of what I am calling eventive experiencer HAVE and engineer HAVE in English is contingent on rather unique (amongst closely related languages) properties of English infinitives–Kayne suggests the existence of a complementizer *for* as the crucial feature (which he in turn relates to the lack of infinitive morphology in English). One issue with Kayne's suggestion is that engineer readings in English are also available with eventive passive participles (e.g. *They had the defendant savagely beaten by the court bailiffs*), showing that the reading in question does not require the presence of an infinitive complement per se. At any rate, Kayne's line of explanation is not open to me, since I have argued that the eventive experiencer HAVE facts are related to the distribution of free datives cross-linguistically, and it seems highly unlikely that the free dative facts would be similarly implicated in engineer HAVE.

---

25. Just like in the eventive experiencer HAVE cases discussed in the previous section, this example cannot be rescued by inverting the infinitive and the causee.

Out of a desire to retain the account of eventive experiencer HAVE given in the previous section, I am forced to pursue a non-unified approach to the availability of engineer HAVE vis-a-vis eventive experiencer HAVE. As Richard Kayne points out to me, this leads to the expectation that it should be possible for a language to have one without the other. While I know of no such language as of yet, I have the impression that ECM HAVE sentences are much less well studied typologically than predicative possession uses of HAVE are, and so the apparent absence of such a language may prove to be an artifact of this gap in the literature. Nevertheless, this expectation should be noted as a strong predictive difference between the present approach and a unified account along the lines of Kayne's, and one that ought to be tested in future work.

Here is the approach that I suggest to the absence of engineer HAVE in languages closely related to English. Perhaps these languages can in fact build structures equivalent to engineer HAVE sentences, but for one reason or another they realize those structures with a different light verb from English. The light-verb in question could be LET in much of Germanic, as Jim Wood points out to me. In Romance, the verb MAKE looks like a likely candidate:

(78)   *(Some) Romance Causatives as Hidden Engineer Sentences?*

Juan me   hizo abrir=le   la puerta.
Juan me.DAT made open=him.dat the door.
'Juan had me open the door for him.'

Note that I am not claiming that Romance MAKE causatives are always engineer HAVE sentences in disguise. Rather, on this account Romance MAKE causatives would be structurally ambiguous between a structure like an English *make* causative and a structure like an English engineer *have* sentence (and likewise *mutatis mutandis* for Germanic LET causatives).

Similar considerations potentially apply to other readings of English *have* that are not available in other HAVE languages. The general expectation is that all languages ought to be able to build such structures, so long as independent morphosyntactic facts do not intervene. And where they do intervene, it could be that the language has an alternative way of generating the same reading in a HAVE sentence. For example, a reviewer of this book points out to me that German does not allow the direct equivalent of *John has bees stinging him all over his body*, but it can arrive at the same sort of stative experiencer reading for its HAVE verb *haben*, by using a (reduced) relative clause as follows (example provided by the reviewer):

(79)   Hans hat überall   auf seinem körper {ihn stechende Bienen/Bienen
       Hans has everywhere on his   body {him stinging   bees/bees
       die ihn stechen}.
       that him sting}
       'Hans has bees (which are) stinging him all over his body.'

It could be that, as a matter of (micro)parametric variation, v_{BE} (and thus HAVE) is unable to select present participles in German in the same way that it can in English, and that German is therefore left with the options we see in the above example to arrive at the same reading. These options are, as we would expect, also available in English:

(80)   John has bees all over his body, which are stinging him.

This concludes the discussion of clear cases of ECM *have* in English.[26] In the next subsection, I address another use of *have* that is less obviously of the ECM type, but which I will argue (following a long tradition) nonetheless is one.

4.1.2.3   (Hidden) ECM *Have*: Temporary Possession

The sentences I have in mind in this subsection are of the following sort:

(81)   I have your money.

(82)   John has the keys.

The idea that these sorts of sentence contain a hidden small clause predicate of which the possessee is the subject, entailing that these examples are also of the ECM type, is nothing new. It also appears in Belvin (1996), Levinson (2011), Ritter and Rosen (1997), Sæbø (2009), Iatridou (1995), and many other places. The notion

---

26. One very interesting fact concerning this domain is noted by Harley (1997) (citing a personal communication from Andrew Carnie). The presence of a logophoric reflexive pronoun co-indexed with the subject of *have* disambiguates between the engineer and eventive experiencer *have*. Namely, the experiencer reading is eliminated by the presence of such a pronoun.

(i)   John had water splashed all over him. ([OK]Engineer, [OK]Experiencer)

(ii)   John had water splashed all over himself. ([OK]Engineer, [*]Experiencer)

Harley's account of this generalization involves two premises: first, that the experiencer *have* reading requires the complement of *have* to contain an open variable; and second, that a logophor, unlike an ordinary pronoun, cannot introduce such an open variable. On my approach, the same facts might be captured if the projection of FreeP interferes with the licensing of logophors in some way. I will leave the matter open.

that they might contain such a predicate is made more plausible by the fact that it is possible to have an overt version of one.[27]

(83)   I have your money here.

(84)   John has the keys with him.

As for the interpretation of temporary possession sentences, it has often been noted (see Levinson 2011 for a recent case) that they imply that the possessor has "control" over the possessee. I claim that this interpretation comes about because Voice is assigning a causer role in these constructions. The structure of a case like *John has the keys* will then be as in (85).

I assume that the silent PP involved in such structures can have a variety of meanings that need not be synonymous with *with him*, which I use in (85) only for the sake of the example. In fact, there is direct evidence that this silent PP need not contain a silent counterpart of *with* (cf. *John has the keys–but not with him, they're on his desk back in his office*, which does not have the flavor of a contradiction).

The VoiceP in (85) denotes a set of states in which the keys are with John, and John is the causer of this state of affairs. I think that this is a reasonable paraphrase of the temporary possession meaning.[28]

This concludes the discussion of cases where *have*'s meaning actually comes about from the way Voice interacts with the denotation of *have*'s complement and assigns a Theta-role to *have*'s subject.

---

27. This gives rise to the awkward question of why, internal to English, the small clause is allowed to be silent in temporary possession sentences but not in locative *have* sentences like *this tree has nests *(in it)*. I will not attempt to solve this problem here.

28. Levinson (2011) assumes the control reading actually originates with the PP *with* itself, and that it is the incorporation of silent *with* that yields *have* in English. As I show in Chapter 7, the assumption that P Incorporation is involved in such sentences, while not logically incompatible with the present approach, does not buy us anything that the rest of the present account does not derive by other means, and for this reason I do not adopt it here. Furthermore, as discussed extensively in Chapters 2 and 5, there are a number of problems raised by P Incorporation accounts of the HAVE/BE relation in general. Note also that Levinson's paper concentrates on temporary possession, whereas the present work aims to account for the entire main-verb *have* paradigm.

(85)   John has the keys.

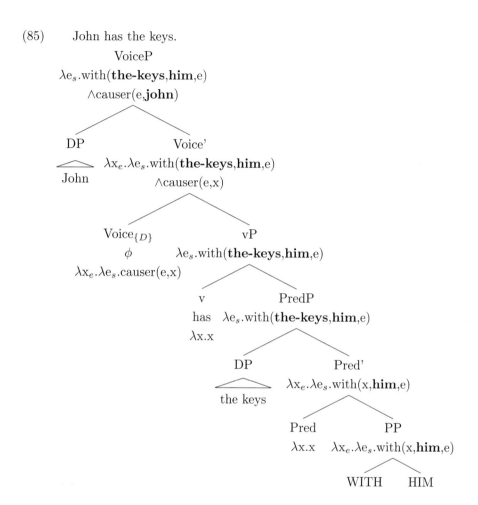

4.2   A Loose End: Modal *Have*

This chapter aims to provide a comprehensive account of the different uses of main verb *have* in English. A conspicuous absentee from most of the discussion so far has been modal *have*. The very fact that modal *have* is a raising verb initially seems to undermine my hypothesis that HAVE is the result of combining BE with external-argument-introducing transitive Voice. How can this be, if there are raising *have* sentences (examples from Brillman 2012, 50, her (79))?

(86)   *Modal HAVE is a Raising Construction*

    a.   The cat has to be let out of the bag if we want to win this election.

    b.   There has to be someone in the garden.

    c.   It has to rain today.

The answer can only be that something other than a DP occupies spec-VoiceP in modal *have* sentences, something which, because it is not a DP, cannot interfere with the raising to spec-TP that is clearly taking place in (86). The plausibility of this idea is raised by the fact that, unlike any of the other types of *have* sentence that we have been considering so far, modal *have* sentences do not relate individuals to eventualities. Instead, they relate sets of worlds, and it is thus unsurprising that the nature of the external argument in a modal *have* sentence is somewhat different syntactically from the nature of the external argument in other types of *have* sentence, as Bjorkman and Cowper (2013, 14) rightly note. These authors also note (2013, 4) that, while modal uses of possession constructions are common cross-linguistically, it is by no means the case that all languages can employ their possession constructions in this way. Hence, it seems prudent to build into the theory enough wiggle room to accommodate languages where this parallelism does not hold. Bjorkman and Cowper (2013) provide such a theory, and since it is compatible with the broad theory of HAVE sentences I am advocating, I will adopt it in what follows.[29]

The core of Bjorkman and Cowper's idea is that Modal *have*/HAVE sentences are fundamentally about an inclusion relation between sets of worlds. Specifically, if we take the sentence *John has to eat an apple*, what is being asserted is that the set of words denoted by the TP [*<John> to <John> eat an apple*] properly contains the set of worlds denoted by the (in this case, deontic) modal base (a notion they borrow from Kratzer 1981, 1991). In other words, modal *have* is like a part-whole *have* sentence such as *this table has four sturdy legs*, except that the relation involves sets of worlds rather than individuals. The TP [*<John> to <John> eat an apple*] is the whole in our example sentence, and it possesses the modal base as its subpart. The following is a tree schematizing Bjorkman and Cowper's analysis, translated into my assumptions about the structure of verb phrases.

---

29. A revision of this analysis, not compatible with the approach I have taken here, is given in Bjorkman and Cowper (2014).

(87)

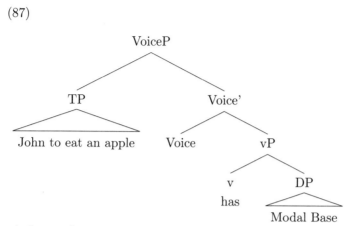

A flurry of questions immediately arise, of course–not the least of which is how the correct word order is derived in English (and how extraction from inside the TP in spec VoiceP is possible). But this approach has a syntacticosemantic virtue not shared by alternative approaches to modal HAVE sentences cross-linguistically (such as Bhatt 1997; Cattaneo 2009). Namely, it automatically predicts the (to my knowledge true) generalization that modal HAVE sentences invariably involve universal, rather than existential, quantification over worlds (Bjorkman and Cowper 2013, 14). Another way of putting this is that there are no modal HAVE constructions in any language where *John has to leave* means *John has permission to leave*. This fact does not follow on an analysis like Bhatt (1997) or Cattaneo (2009), which postulate a silent modal element meaning OBLIGATION or NEED, which is existentially quantified over in these constructions. These analyses raise the question of why the silent element involved could never be something like PERMISSION. On Bjorkman and Cowper's approach, according to which modal HAVE involves expressing a containment relation between sets of worlds, this typological fact about the interpretation of modal HAVE sentences is captured straightforwardly.

4.3   A Language with Two HAVEs: Icelandic

Alongside the *vera með* construction discussed in Chapter 7, Icelandic has (at least) two other predicative possession constructions. Interestingly, both of them involve a transitive verb, with the usual nominative-accusative case frame this entails. In other words, Icelandic has two HAVE verbs, as illustrated in (88a) and (88b) (see Irie 1997; Myler, E.F. Sigurðsson, and Wood 2014).

(88)   *Two Icelandic HAVEs*

    a. Þeir   **hafa** augu.
       they.NOM have$_1$ eyes.ACC
       'They have eyes.'

    b. Þeir   **eiga** stóra bók.
       they.NOM have$_2$ big   book.ACC
       'They have a big book.'

How can the present approach deal with such a case? The account developed so far forces a certain analytical strategy on us. According to this approach, all transitive configurations (and therefore, all HAVE constructions) involve an external argument-introducing Voice head bearing phi-features. Furthermore, all HAVE/BE verbs are analyzed as conditioned allomorphs of the same meaningless v head. This requires me to assume that *hafa* and *eiga* are both HAVE verbs in the sense of being a spell-out of copula v in the environment of transitive Voice.[30] The VIs *hafa* and *eiga* are suppletive allomorphs of this head, and the choice between them must be dictated by some aspect of this v's complement. Furthermore, whatever it is about v's complement that determines the choice between *hafa* and *eiga* at PF must also account for the semantic differences between *hafa* and *eiga* at LF. That is, if PF and LF really are both being read off from the syntactic structure, as the present approach claims, then getting the allomorphy analysis right should ensure that the semantic analysis follows, and vice versa.

Myler, E.F. Sigurðsson, and Wood (2014) have recently proposed an account of the data in (88) which has these properties. Specifically, they argue that the following rules of Vocabulary Insertion determine the distribution of *hafa* and *eiga*.

(89)   a. v$_{BE}$ ⇔ *hafa* / Voice$_{\{D\},\phi}$___Pred

     b. v$_{BE}$ ⇔ *eiga* / Voice$_{\{D\},\phi}$___

In prose: v in a transitive context is spelled out as *hafa* when it takes a small-clause complement (a PredP), and as *eiga* otherwise. Notice that the rule inserting *hafa* in (89a) is sensitive to context on both sides of v. This plugs a gap in the typology of copula allomorphy predicted by the present approach. So far, we have seen upwardly-sensitive allomorphy (which induces the spell out of HAVE rather than BE), and downwardly-sensitive allomorphy (which accounts for languages with

---

30. Recall that *transitive* has a technical meaning in the present framework: it refers to a configuration in which Voice introduces an external argument and bears phi-features with which it can license a direct object.

multiple copulas depending on the nature of BE's complement). We therefore expect the possibility of suppletion conditioned from both directions at once, and this is precisely what happens in (89a).

Myler, E.F. Sigurðsson, and Wood (2014) defend the rules in (89) by pointing out that they derive the following novel generalizations concerning the manner in which *hafa* and *eiga* carve up the domain of possession in Icelandic.

(90)   a.   **Generalization 1**: Clausal possession can be expressed with *eiga* only if DP-internal possession <u>cannot</u> be expressed with a PP.

       b.   **Generalization 2**: Clausal possession can be expressed with *hafa* only if DP-internal possession <u>can</u> be expressed with a PP.

To see the validity of (90), consider first the following data, which shows the subtypes of possession relation with which each of these verbs is compatible.

(91)   a.   *Concrete*

            Þeir   { *hafa / **eiga** } stóra bók.
            they.NOM { *have$_1$ / have$_2$ } big   bookACC

            'They have (i.e. own) a big book.' [31]

       b.   *Kinship*

            Þeir   { *hafa / **eiga** } systur.
            they.NOM { *have$_1$ / have$_2$ } sister.ACC

            'They have a sister.'

       c.   *Body part*

            Þeir   { **hafa** / *eiga } augu.
            they.NOM { have$_1$ / *have$_2$ } eyes.ACC

            'They have eyes.'

       d.   *Abstract*

            Þeir   { **hafa** / *eiga } ekki hugmynd.
            they.NOM { have$_1$ / *have$_2$ } not idea.ACC

            'They have no idea.'

---

31. Note that (91a) is grammatical with *hafa* for a number of speakers, but only with a reading where the subject has the book at its disposal, as opposed to owning it. This fact is predicted given the idea that temporary possession HAVE sentences always involve a silent small clause. Those speakers who reject (91a) with *hafa* presumably lack this silent predicate in their grammar.

Turning to attributive possession, we find that Icelandic has two main ways of introducing a possessor DP-internally. Some possession relations involve a possessive adjective/genitive DP.[32] Other possession relations are instead conveyed by introducing the possessor inside a PP. The following table, adapted from Myler, E.F. Sigurðsson, and Wood (2014, 5, their (13)), summarizes this distribution.

(92)   *Attributive Possession in Icelandic*

	A: NP - POSS.PRON	**B**: NP-DEF poss.pron	**C**: NP-DEF - PREP - PRON
Concrete 'my book'	# bók mín book my	bók-in mín book-def my	* bók-in hjá mér book-def at me
Kinship 'my sister'	systir mín sister my	* systir-in mín sister-def my	* systir-in hjá mér sister-def at me
Body part 'my eyes'	# augu mín eyes my	% augu-n mín eyes-def my	augu-n í mér eyes-def in me
Abstract 'my idea'	hugmynd mín idea my	* hugmynd-in mín idea-def my	hugmynd-in hjá mér idea-def at me

Of most relevance to our current concerns is Column C. Notice that the relations that permit a PP possessor in DP-internal possession are the very same ones that take *hafa* in clausal possession: body parts and abstract possession.

Myler, E.F. Sigurðsson, and Wood (2014) propose that these two DP-internal possession configurations have the following structures (the surface word order is derived via movement of $_x$nP to spec-DP):

(93)   *Option A*

augu-n í mér
eyes-def in me

'my eyes'

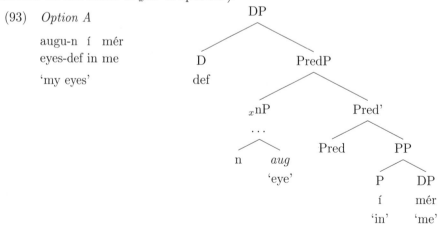

---

(94) *Option B*

bók-in   mín
book-def my

'my book'

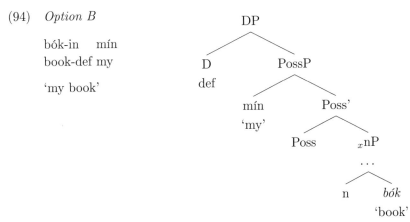

In keeping with Szabolcsi (1981), Kayne (1993), and the assumptions of the present work, Myler, E.F. Sigurðsson, and Wood (2014) assume that possession sentences are constructed by embedding an attributive possession substructure underneath a meaningless v. The resulting structures differ depending on whether the relation in question is expressed via Option A or Option B, as follows:

(95)   'They have eyes.'

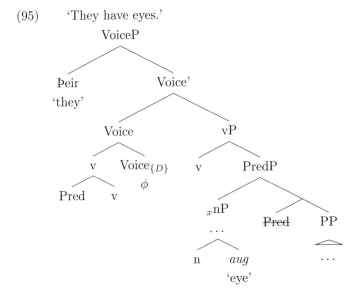

(96)   'They have a big book.'

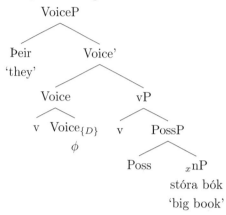

Given these assumptions, the spell-out rules in (89) correctly ensure that *hafa* is inserted as the realization of v in (95), whereas *eiga* will be selected in (96). The broader distribution of *hafa* and *eiga* is also captured, including the fact that *hafa* is compatible with a range of small-clause complements that have nothing to do with the domain of possession per se.

(97)   *Non-Possessive Hafa+Small Clause*

  a.   Haf-ðu   hljóð!
       have₁-you quiet
       'Be quiet!'

  b.   Hann   hafði orð   á   því.
       he.NOM had₁ word on it
       'He spoke about it.'

  c.   Sindri hefur Það fínt.
       Sindir has₁ it fine
       'Sindri has it fine.' (i.e., Sindri is well)–Stolz et al (2008, 170)

  d.   Hann   hafði Það upp úr   henni.
       he.NOM had₁ it up out.of her
       'He got it out of her.'

While the account sketched here only scratches the surface of the complexity in the domain of possession in Icelandic, it is sufficient to illustrate that the present framework is in principle equipped to analyze languages with more than one HAVE verb, using much the same strategy as is employed to analyze languages with more than one BE verb.

4.4   Conclusions

The table in (100) summarizes how the different uses of *have* (and HAVE generally)
are derived in this system. As well as the readings discussed earlier in the chapter,
table (100) contains a reading that has not been discussed so far (in parentheses),
and a number of starred readings, which are ruled out by the system. It is worthwhile
to see how the starred cells in this table are ruled out, and that the reading in
parentheses is not incorrectly ruled in, in order to show that the analysis does not
overgenerate. In every case, the account depends crucially on the rules of allosemy
for Voice, which are repeated in full here for convenience (now including the engineer
alloseme, which was first introduced in this chapter).

(98)   *Rules for the interpretation of Voice*

    a.   [[Voice]] $\Leftrightarrow \lambda x_e.\lambda e_s.$Agent$(x,e)$ / ___(agentive, dynamic event)

    b.   [[Voice]] $\Leftrightarrow \lambda x_e.\lambda e_s.$Holder$(x,e)$ / ___(stative eventuality)

    c.   [[Voice]] $\Leftrightarrow \lambda x_e.\lambda e_s.$Engineer$(e,x)$ / ___v_{BE} Eventive-VoiceP$_{\langle s,t \rangle}$

    d.   [[Voice]] $\Leftrightarrow \lambda x.x$ / ___(elsewhere)

First, let us take the parenthesized reading in (100), which arises when *have*
takes a FreeP complement, and Voice simultaneously introduces a holder role. Such
a derivation should lead to the subject of *have* bearing both thematic roles. Con-
cretely, the prediction is that the subject of (99) could simultaneously receive an
experiencer role (from Free) and a holder role (from Voice).

(99)   I had John washing cars.

The fact that this prediction does follow from the theory can be seen from the
structure in (101), which represents the example in (99) (recall that I take *-ing*
to be a stativizer, so that the complement of *have* is stative despite containing
an eventive predicate). Since the approach to argument structure here does not
forbid arguments to receive more than one thematic role (indeed, the account of the
temporary possession reading presented above crucially invokes it), the derivation in
(101) is valid. However, I suggest that the reading derived here is vacuously different
from one in which expletive Voice is chosen. This is because an experiencer of a
state is a subcase of a holder of a state, so that the holder role adds no additional
information to the semantic component in (101). Therefore, the existence of this
additional reading predicted by the system does neither good nor harm.

(100)   *Building and Interpreting HAVE Sentences*

have's complement / Voice alloseme	DP	Saturated eventive VoiceP	FreeP	Stative small clause
Voice$_{agent}$	light-verb *have*	*	*	*
Voice$_{holder}$	light-verb *have*	*	(holder + experiencer subj.)	stative experiencer or causer *have* (includes temporary possession)
Voice$_{expl}$	relational *have*	*	eventive experiencer *have*	eventive locative *have*
Voice$_{engineer}$	*	engineer *have*	*	*

(101)

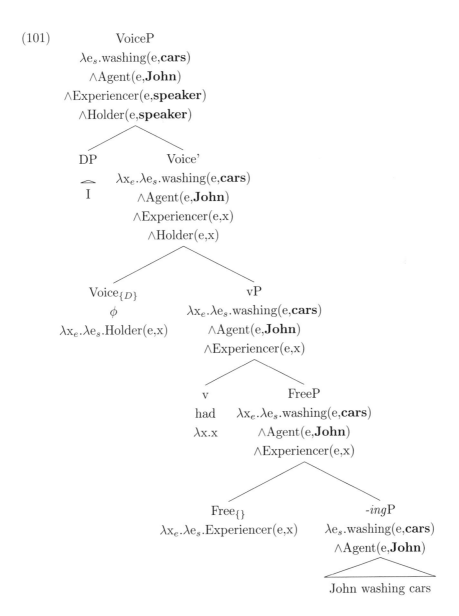

Turning to the starred readings, let us begin with the bottom row of the table in (100), corresponding to the engineer alloseme of Voice. Given the allosemy rule in (98c), this interpretation can only arise when *have* takes a saturated eventive VoiceP as its complement. The other categories of complement do not meet this conditioning environment, and this explains the stars on this row.

Further, the fact that the engineer reading is highly specified to take a saturated eventive VoiceP means that it will beat out all the other allosemes when *have* takes such a complement. This explains the stars in the third column of (100).

The next star to explain is the one in the top-right-hand corner of (100): why is it that the agentive alloseme of Voice cannot be chosen when the complement of *have* is a stative small clause? The answer is simply that such a small clause will not satisfy the conditioning environment for that alloseme: (98a) requires an eventive complement.

The final starred subcase is one in which Free introduces an experiencer role and Voice introduces an agent role, both of which are assigned to the subject of *have*. To see how this subcase is ruled out, consider the sample structure in (102) on the next page. The final semantic representation of this structure is one in which a single event has two separate and contradictory statements as to its agent. I assume that this makes the structure uninterpretable.

This chapter has shown that a non-trivial proportion of the interpretations of English *have* (and HAVE verbs cross-linguistically) fall out from the simple assumption that it denotes a type-neutral identity function, once the role of the allosemy of Voice and the availability of delayed gratification are taken into account. I believe that this is a significant result that puts an important dent in the too-many-meanings puzzle. We have also seen that the analysis extends readily to languages with more than one HAVE verb. Now that the present approach to HAVE verbs has been set out in full, we are in a position to compare it directly with the standard approach: the Freeze/Kayne tradition. Such a comparison is the goal of the next chapter.

(102)   I had the flies exterminated by the caretakers.

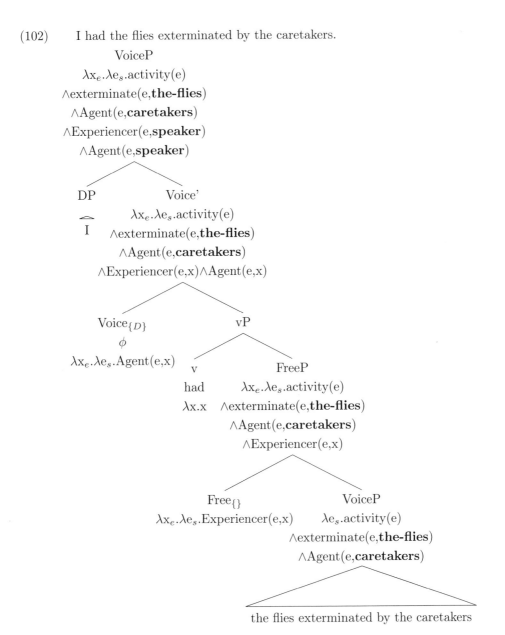

5

Consequences and Comparisons

The previous chapter showed in detail how the present approach handles HAVE languages, focusing on data from English in comparison with a number of other languages. The present chapter compares this approach with the influential Freeze/Kayne tradition, which can be regarded as the standard approach to predicative possession within generative grammar. After a brief reminder of the basic properties of the two approaches in section 5.1, I point out some conceptual and empirical problems for the Freeze/Kayne approach on its own terms in section 5.2. In section 5.3 I identify some crucial predictive differences between the two approaches with respect to the nature of HAVE sentences. These have to do with definiteness effects in HAVE sentences, and with the argument structures that HAVE sentences are predicted to exhibit. The Freeze/Kayne tradition predicts that definiteness effects in HAVE sentences should be identical to those found in existential sentences. It also predicts that HAVE sentences should be underlyingly unaccusative. My approach makes rather different predictions. I show that, in both cases, the present account makes the better predictions. Section 5.4 is a conclusion.

5.1   Comparing the Approaches

According to my approach, HAVE constructions have a different argument structure than BE constructions do. HAVE constructions involve a transitive configuration, whereas BE constructions can be found in every available intransitive configuration. The Freeze/Kayne tradition is rather different. This approach reduces HAVE to the same underlying structure as BE. On its strongest interpretation, the Freeze/Kayne tradition involves saying that all possession sentences share a single underlying argument structure.

The details of this approach differ somewhat between Freeze (1992) and Kayne (1993), so I will begin with a brief reminder of the basics of each of these papers (see Chapter 2 for a more detailed introduction).

5.1.1   Freeze (1992)

Freeze proposes that predicate locatives, existentials, and HAVE sentences are "all derived from a single and maximally simple abstract syntactic structure" (1992, 553). This structure is shown in (1) (Freeze 1992, 558, his (7)).

(1)   *The D-Structure of Predicate Locatives, Existentials and Possession Sentences (Freeze 1992)*

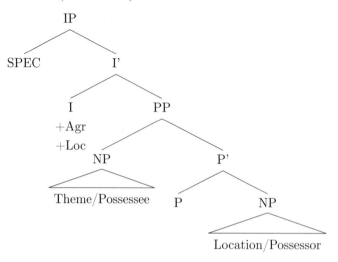

The surface differences between predicate locatives, existentials, and HAVE sentences all result from movement differences. If the theme argument raises to spec-IP, the result is a predicate locative. Note that it is I itself that spells out as the copula BE.

(2)   *Predicate Locative: Theme Moves to Spec-IP*

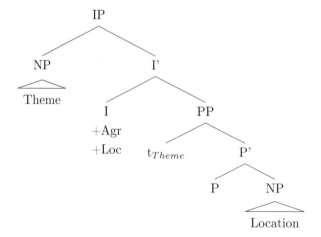

Thus, (2) would be the structure of a sentence like *A book is on the table*. An existential sentence is derived by instead raising P' into spec-IP, as in (3):[1] This is also the structure of possession sentences in BE-languages like Russian for Freeze.

(3)   *Existential: P' Containing Location Moves to Spec-IP*

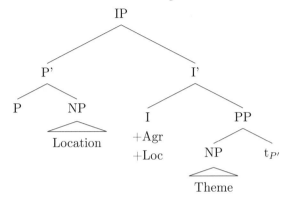

In HAVE languages, possession sentences involve incorporation of P into I (which then spells out as HAVE instead of BE). The possessor (equivalent to the location argument in existential and predicate locatives) then moves into spec-IP, as shown in (4):

(4)   *HAVE: Possessor Moves to Spec-IP; P Incorporates into I*

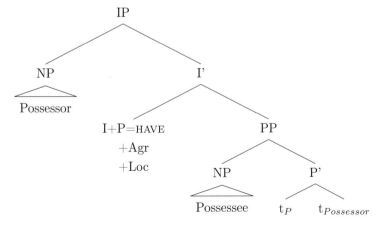

---

1. In languages like English, which Freeze (1992, 556) treats as exceptional, spec-IP is instead filled by a locative proform (*there* in English).

Which of these three different derivations ensues from the D-Structure in (1) depends on certain features of the arguments involved. If the theme is definite, then it raises to spec-IP. If the theme is indefinite, then the P' containing the location moves to spec-IP, yielding an existential sentence. Finally, if the theme is indefinite and the location is human, then a HAVE derivation ensues (in languages that allow this).

5.1.2   Kayne (1993)

Like Freeze, Kayne proposes that HAVE sentences share a D-structure with existential BE sentences. He differs from Freeze on the nature of this D-structure. For Kayne, HAVE sentences involve embedding a possessed DP underneath an existential BE verb; this D-Structure is inspired by Szabolcsi's account of possession in Hungarian (Szabolcsi 1981, 1983).[2]

(5)   *D-Structure for Possession Sentences, Kayne (1993/2000)*

...BE [$_{DP}$ Spec D/P [$_{AgrP}$ DP$_{poss}$ [$_{Agr'}$ Agr QP/NP]]]

Following Szabolcsi (1981, 1983), BE-based possession constructions result from the extraction of the possessor from the possessee DP, via an escape hatch. This escape hatch is the specifier of a category D/P, a prepositional determiner (analogous to a prepositional complementizer), as shown in (6).

(6)   *Schematic S-Structure for Possession, Kayne (1993/2000)*

...DP$_{poss}$ BE [$_{DP}$ t$_{poss}$ D/P [$_{AgrP}$ t$_{poss}$ [$_{Agr'}$ Agr QP/NP]]]

In Hungarian and languages like it, D/P assigns case to the possessor, and its specifier is thus clearly an A-position. Kayne proposes that in languages like English, D/P is not a case-assigner, and thus its specifier is an A-bar position. This means that the movement in (6) should be ruled out as a case of improper movement. To rescue the derivation, D/P incorporates into BE, voiding the latter's A-bar status via the Government Transparency Corollary. The result of incorporating D/P into BE is spelled out as HAVE.

Most of Kayne's paper is devoted to analyzing alternations between HAVE and BE in auxiliary systems (especially Romance auxiliary systems). Kayne argues that compound tenses in these systems involve a similar D/P structure embedded under

---

2. We shall see below that Freeze (1992) also allows a structure like (5) as the D-structure for a subset of BE constructions.

BE. What differs is the complement of D/P: in the case of compound tenses, this complement is a VP substructure as shown in (7), rather than a nominal one.

(7)   *Schematic D-Structure for the Perfect, Kayne (1993/2000)*

        ...BE $[_{DP}$ SPEC D/P ... $[_{VP}$ DP$_{Subj}$ [V DP$_{Obj}$]]]

The nature of this VP substructure can vary across dialects, accounting for the various subtypes of auxiliary alternation found in Romance languages (including those based on the person of the subject, those based on the argument structure of the main predicate, and those based on whether clitic climbing has applied or not).

   With this summary of Freeze (1992) and Kayne (1993) in hand, we now examine some problems internal to these approaches.

5.2   Problems for the Freeze/Kayne Approach

5.2.1   Problems for Freeze (1992)

Perhaps the most problematic aspect of Freeze's paper from the point of view of solving the too-many-(surface)-structures puzzle is that it fails to do what it sets out to do; namely, it does not deliver on its promise to solve this puzzle by reducing the surface variation in HAVE-BE constructions to a single underlying syntactic structure. This is because Freeze (1992, 590-591) assigns a different underlying structure to what we have been calling Adnominal Possessives (such as the Cochabamba Quechua BE construction, and the very similar Hungarian construction discussed by Szabolcsi 1981).[3] This structure is shown in (8). This is not to say that I disagree with Freeze's decision to assign these constructions distinct underlying syntaxes. On the contrary, I argue elsewhere in this book that this is precisely the correct approach. But one must note that this part of Freeze's analysis effectively concedes the point that the similarities between existentials, locatives and possession sentences cannot all be explained in terms of their being distortions of the same

---

3. This failure is sometimes forgotten in discussions of Freeze's work in later generative literature, much of which omits all mention of the different D-structure that Freeze assigns to the Adnominal Possessive. To give two examples, take Jung's statement that "Freeze (1992) proposes a unified structure of the existential, possessive and locative constructions involving *be* or *have*" (2011, 46); and Harves' comment that "Freeze (1992) argues that locative, existential and possessive sentences are all syntactically derived from a single underlying structure" (2002, 171). Note that this omission is found even in generative literature that is ultimately critical of Freeze's approach, as Harves' is.

underlying structure. Instead, the similarities result from the fact that these structures involve many of the same pieces, but certain differences among them indicate
that they vary in the way that these pieces are put together.

(8)   *The D-Structure of Adnominal Possessives* (Freeze 1992)

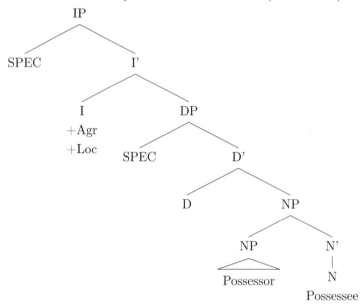

The foregoing is only reinforced by the observation that Predicativization, which
clearly involves predicative copula BE rather than existential BE in languages where
these can be distinguished, is not dealt with in Freeze's paper. Moreover, even the
parts of Freeze's unification upheld in the paper itself turn out to unravel upon
closer scrutiny. In the ensuing paragraphs, I will show this with respect to (i) the
proposed unification of predicate locatives and existentials, (ii) the analysis of HAVE
sentences as arising from an existential structure involving incorporation of P into
I, and (iii) the analysis of WITH-Possessives as involving reanalysis of I and P into
a single rebracketed complex head.

    In claiming that predicate locatives and existentials involve the same D-structure
and are differentiated only by which argument moves to spec-IP, Freeze (1992, 557)
maintains that the two structures are in complementary distribution, determined
by whether the theme is definite or indefinite. The idea is that a predicate locative results if the theme is [+Definite], and an Existential results if the theme is
[−Definite]. However, as anticipated already in Clark (1970, 1978) and explicitly
pointed out by Heine (1997, 220), this complementarity is at best tendential, and is

not absolute in the way that Freeze would require it to be in order for it to explain how the grammar chooses one of these movement options over the other. Freeze (1992, 557) himself notes that the complementarity breaks down in one direction due to the existence of indefinite subjects in locative sentences in many languages (Freeze cites Russian as one example). Although Freeze claims that the other side of the complementarity does go through ("Probably no language allows the existential to have a definite theme," 557), this also turns out to be systematically false in some languages (Catalan according to McNally 1998; also Irish according to McCloskey 2014, if the pivot moves to the higher of Irish's two subject positions), and is false in some special subcases even in languages where it generally holds, like English.[4]

Even if the problem of the trigger of movement is solved, however, Freeze's (1992) attempted unification predicts that existentials and predicate locatives will be syntactically identical up to this movement difference. But this prediction is false. First, the status of the PP involved is clearly very different–in predicate locatives, it serves as the predicate, whereas in existentials it has adjunct-like behavior (see Francez 2007, who cites evidence from Keenan 1987 that the PP in question is adjoined to VP). Hartmann and Milićević (2008, 1, their (1) and (2)) make this point forcefully using Serbian data. As they show, the PP in existentials is clearly optional (9a), compatible with it being an adjunct, whereas in predicate locatives it is obligatory (9b). Similar contrasts can be replicated in many other languages.[5]

(9)   *Serbian: Status of the PP Differs between Existentials and Predicate Locatives*

   a.   Ima nekih studenata   (ovde) koji hoće samo diplomu.
        Has some students.GEN here   who want just   certificate

        'There are some students (here) who just want the certificate.'

   b.   Neki studenata   su *(ovde) koji hoće samo diplomu.
        Some students.NOM are here   who want just   certificate

        'Some students are *(here) who just want the certificate.'

In addition, there is an important agreement asymmetry between predicate locatives and existential sentences, which is not satisfactorily dealt with on Freeze's

---

4. One case is the famous list reading (Rando and Napoli 1978):

   A: What shall we have for dinner?

   B: Well, there's the chicken, or there's the beef.

5. See also Francez (2009, 30-46) for a range of arguments against codas as predicates.

approach–namely, the fact that agreement of the copula with the theme is obligatory in predicate locatives, but subject to much cross-linguistic variation in existentials. Recall, for instance, that the existential verb in Cochabamba Quechua does not agree with the pivot, but the predicative copula does agree with the subject of its predicate.

(10)   *Cochabamba Quechua: Agreement in Existentials vs. Predicate Locatives*

a.   Kay-pi llama-s   tiya-n-(*ku).
      This-in llama-PL be$_{exist}$-3SUBJ-PL
      'There are llamas here.'

b.   Llama-s   kay-pi ka-n-*(ku).
      Llama-PL this-in be-3SUBJ-PL
      'Llamas are here.'

Freeze claims that the variability in existential agreement patterns is a reflection of the fact that "Whether or not agreement is morphological is highly idiosyncratic cross-linguistically" (1992, 562), and proposes that there is syntactic agreement with the theme in existentials even when it is not apparent. But if so, the question becomes why the predicate locative is not subject to similar morphological idiosyncrasies across languages.

Finally, as noted by Harves (2002, 174), technical problems arise (within Government and Binding Theory, the theory that Freeze adopts) for Freeze's assumption that the Existential involves movement of P' to a specifier position. Movement of P', which is rendered necessary in Freeze's approach to void the barrierhood of PP, was ruled out in the theory of the time as a violation of the structure preservation constraint on movement of Chomsky (1986, 4), based on earlier work by Emonds (1976).

A central pillar of Freeze's approach–the reduction of predicate locatives and existentials to a single D-structure–thus turns out to be fundamentally misguided. As I will now argue, the same turns out to be true of his analysis of HAVE sentences as involving an existential BE structure along with incorporation of the adposition.

I begin by noting some severe problems for Freeze's account of Case-assignment in transitive HAVE constructions. Freeze entertains two possibilities here. The first idea is that the I+P complex assigns Case to the possessor, with the possessee receiving a default Case (Freeze notes that default Case "is often accusative"). The problem here is that default Case is not always accusative, but the direct object of a transitive HAVE verb in a nominative-accusative language always is–thus, we falsely predict that a language with a nominative default (like Icelandic) should assign nominative to the direct object of its HAVE verb(s). The second possibility raised by Freeze is that the possessor is Case-licensed by P before movement, and the I+P complex assigns Case to the theme. The latter possibility fails to explain why the possessor subject of a HAVE sentence surfaces in nominative Case rather than some oblique Case. This exhausts the possibilities named by Freeze, and it is thus unclear how the Case-marking patterns associated with transitive HAVE verbs can be reconciled with his approach. It is also unclear why agreement would be invariably with the possessor subject on Freeze's account–in particular, his second suggested analysis would predict that subject agreement with the possessee should sometimes be possible, contrary to fact.

A second problem concerns Freeze's notion that possession sentences are distinguished from existentials only by the fact that they involve a [+human] location. While Freeze notes the existence of *have* sentences in English that have non-human subjects, and even has a fairly detailed descriptive discussion of the semantic and syntactic constraints on such constructions (e.g., that locative *have* sentences require a PP complement containing a pronoun coindexed with *have*'s subject (Freeze 1992, 583)), he does not provide any insight into how the derivation that yields *have* is triggered in sentences where the possessor has the feature [−human]. Moreover, as noted by Belvin (1996, 222), Freeze's approach will not extend to ECM-like uses of *have*, such as *John had Bill clean the dishes*, which appear to have no equivalent in the domain of existentials.

These arguments force us to the conclusion that Freeze's assimilation of transitive HAVE to his Locative Paradigm fails. His attempt to assimilate WITH-Possessives to this paradigm is also problematic. Fatal flaws for this analysis as it would apply to the Icelandic WITH construction have been identified by Levinson (2011). Here, I will concentrate on the problems that arise for Freeze's analysis as it applies to Portuguese, a language that Freeze himself discusses (the Icelandic construction is not discussed in Freeze 1992).

Recall from Chapter 2 that Freeze argues that WITH-Possessive constructions like the following have fundamentally the same syntax as existentials, but with reanalysis of the preposition so that it is rebracketed with the copula. This, according to Freeze, creates the appearance that the preposition is taking the theme as its complement, whereas in reality it originates with the location/possessor. This alleged constituency is depicted by the bracketing in (11).

(11)   *Portuguese WITH-Possessive*

        O   menino [está com] fome.
        The child   is   with hunger
        'The child is hungry.'

Recall also that Freeze presents apparent evidence for this constituency (and against the idea that *com* takes *fome* as its complement) in the form of the fact that wh-movement of the PP *com X* is ungrammatical.

(12)   * Com que   está o   menino?
          With what is   the child
        'With what is the child?' = 'What does the child have?'

While the badness of (12) seems to be a real fact and is certainly interesting, Freeze was mistaken to conclude that it shows *com fome* to be non-constituent. First, note that if constituency were the only issue with (12), it ought to be possible for interrogative *que* to move on its own, stranding *com* to the right of the copula. Such a string would involve movement of a constituent and would not violate the predictions of Freeze's reanalysis account. The fact that it is nonetheless ungrammatical means that there must be some independent factor ruling out (12).[6]

(13)   * Que   está com o   menino?
          What is   with the child
        'With what is the child?' = 'What does the child have?'

Positive evidence against the reanalysis of *com* with *está* comes from the fact that it is possible to place adverbs between the two.

(14)   *Portuguese With-Possessive: Adverbs may Intervene*

        O   menino está sempre com fome.
        The child   is   always with hunger
        'The child is always hungry.'

There is also positive evidence from pseudo-clefting that *com fome* is a constituent after all.

(15)   *Portuguese With-Possessive: Pseudo-Clefting*

        O   que   ele está é [com fome].
        The which he is   is with hunger
        'What he is is hungry.'

---

6. For judgments on the next three sentences in European Portuguese, and for volunteering the pseudo-clefting example, I thank Salvador Mascarenhas. Thanks also to Ananda Lima for providing judgments from Brazilian Portuguese. The two varieties coincide with respect to the phenomena discussed here.

Hence, there can be no assimilation of the WITH-Possessive to the Locative Paradigm along the lines envisaged by Freeze. This means that we have yet another possession construction whose syntax cannot be assigned the same underlying D-structure as the others, reinforcing the point that the solution to the too-many-(surface)-structures puzzle should not be sought by trying to identify such a unified D-structure.

Before closing, I wish to discuss two further aspects of Freeze's paper that are of great interest from the present perspective. Both of these are connected to the [+Loc] feature that Freeze postulates on the copular verb in the Locative Paradigm. The first of them involves the appearance of locative clitics in existentials in certain languages. The second involves the question of copula suppletion.

Freeze (1992, 566-571) goes into some depth regarding the status of a class of "locative"[7] proforms found in existentials. An example of such a proform is found in (16), in the form of the French locative clitic *y* (Freeze 1992:567, his (21a)).

(16)   *The French Locative Proform y*

         Il **y**   a   deux enfants dans l'   auto.
         it there has two   children in   the car
         'There are two children in the car.'

As Freeze discusses, such proforms are found in many Romance languages, as well as further afield (Freeze 1992, 569 names Palestinian Arabic, Palauan, and Tongan). Elsewhere in this book, I make the claim (following and adapting Tremblay 1991) that such proforms in Existentials are the subject of a PredP of which the pivot is the complement. Since Freeze's analysis of these elements is rather different, it behooves me to compare the two approaches systematically.

For Freeze, these locative proforms are nothing other than morphological realizations of the [+Loc] feature on I. One question that this idea must face is the status of other instances of such clitics which clearly have non-locative meanings, as documented extensively by Kayne (2008). As an example of such cases, consider these examples from Kayne (2008, 177-178, his (7) and (8); glosses adapted).

(17)   *(Non)-Locative Clitics in French and Italian*

    a.   Jean **y**   pense. (French)
          Jean there thinks
          'Jean thinks of it.'

---

7. See Kayne (2008) for recent discussion of the status of these proforms, which points out numerous problems with using the term "locative" to describe them.

    b.   Gianni **ci**   pensa. (Italian)
           Gianni there thinks
           'Gianni thinks of it.'

A further question is why Predicate Locatives do not obligatorily involve the realization of such a pronoun, given the fact that Predicate Locatives involve the same [+Loc] I head in Freeze's approach. Even laying these problems aside, Freeze's hypothesis that locative proforms spell out a [+Loc] feature on I makes a prediction that turns out to be unfortunate. The prediction is that it should be impossible to separate the clitic from the existential copula, since both are realizations of the same I head. As evidence that this is correct, Freeze (1992, 567) points out that the clitic y in French cannot undergo raising when embedded under the verb *sembler* 'seem' (the example is Freeze's (22b)).

(18)   * Il **y**   semble avoir   du   soleil. (French)
          It there seems have.INF some sun
          'There seems to be some sun.'

However, to fully test this prediction, one wants to test a Romance language that allows clitic climbing in the general case (i.e. not modern French), and one wants to use an embedding predicate known to allow clitic climbing straightforwardly in Romance (i.e., not 'seem', which is known to vary in its restructuring behavior across the family–see Cinque 2006, 52n27). When one does this, one finds that the locative clitic is, in fact, capable of moving away from the copula. This is shown for Italian in (19). I conclude that this key prediction of Freeze's account of such clitics is incorrect.

(19)   *Clitic Climbing of Locative ci in Italian Existentials*

    a.   Può esser=**ci** amore senza   attrazione.
          can be=there love   without attraction
          'There can be love without attraction.'

    b.   **Ci**   può essere amore senza   attrazione.
          There can be   love   without attraction
          'There can be love without attraction.'

Nevertheless, Freeze's discussion of such proforms contains an observation that is of potential interest. I am unable to offer an account of this observation here, and Freeze's own account is itself unsatisfying. Despite this, I will note it here in the spirit of reminding the field of its existence, in the hope that others will be able to investigate it more deeply. The observation is that SOV languages with head-final IPs seem to systematically lack such proforms (Freeze 1992, 572). Freeze accounts for this generalization by stipulating a surface filter that requires the locative proform to precede the Location PP–an SOV language is guaranteed to violate this filter if it has a head-final IP, on Freeze's assumption that these proforms are the realization of a feature on the I-head.[8]

Interestingly, so-called locative proforms are not the only phenomenon that Freeze attempts to explain as a realization of the [+Loc] feature on I. Another possible realization of this feature is copula suppletion (Freeze 1992, 570). This aspect of Freeze's approach is attractive, since it offers a way to understand the allomorphy of the copula in languages which observe a split between a locative/existential copula (which would have the [+Loc] feature) and another predicative copula (which would presumably be [−Loc]); recall that Clark (1970, 1978) discusses many such languages.

While Freeze is to be commended for at least recognizing that such suppletion is an issue, his approach is not immediately generalizable to other suppletion patterns. In particular, it has difficulty with languages where Existentials have a separate copula, but Predicate Locatives are marked with the copula used for other categories of predicate. Freeze does in fact bring up such languages; one of them is Tagalog (Freeze 1992, 556, his (5)).

(20)   *Copula Allomorphy in Tagalog*

    a.   **Na** sa baaba?i aŋ saŋgol.
          BE at woman NP baby
          'The baby is with the woman.'

    b.   **May**   gera sa ewropa.
          BE_{exist} war in Europe
          'There is war in Europe.'

Freeze describes the pattern as follows: "In Tagalog the copula has a distinct morphological form in the (locative-subject) existential" (1992, 570). More precisely, *may* spells out the [+Loc] copula only when IP has P' in its specifier. The conditioning environment in this formulation does not respect any of the standard notions of locality for conditioned allomorphy, and for this reason it is unsatisfactory, but Freeze's discussion constitutes an important first step in addressing the problem of copula suppletion.

---

8. As Richard Kayne points out to me, one would need to find an SOV language that has locative proforms of the *y* sort outside of existential and predicate locative structures in the first place, in order to properly test Freeze's generalization.

To summarize this section, we have seen that Freeze (1992) contains many important observations but ultimately fails in its mission to unify locatives, existentials and possession sentences under a single underlying syntactic analysis.

5.2.2 Problems for Kayne (1993)

While the focus of my discussion here will be on issues for Kayne's approach to variation in possession sentences, I will first make brief mention of criticisms that have been made of the theory as it applies to auxiliary selection, as well as pointing out a previously unnoticed issue. Some problems that have arisen are empirical in nature. Ledgeway (2000, 194-195), for example, points out that Kayne's account of why clitic climbing forces the selection of HAVE is too strong. As stated, the account predicts that clitic climbing should always force HAVE in such dialects, but this is false (Kayne 1993/2000, 128, note 37, acknowledges this issue; Ledgeway provides examples from peripheral Neapolitan dialects). Ultimately, Ledgeway (2000, Ch 6) makes minor adjustments to Kayne's approach, preserving the central mechanisms.

An additional issue is pointed out by Iatridou (1995, 186), who notes that any decompositional approach of the sort advocated by Kayne is supported in so far as HAVE and BE share complementation patterns in a language–for example, in both being compatible with a participial complement. It is therefore potentially worrying that Greek lacks a periphrastic passive in which BE takes a participle as its complement, despite the fact that it *does* have a periphrastic perfect in which HAVE takes a participle as its complement.[9] Apart from these issues, some work on auxiliary selection in languages where unaccusativity is the conditioning factor have pointed out a number of semantic subtleties to the conditioning–Bentley (2006) and Sorace (2004) are prominent examples. Such subtleties are often probabilistic in nature and based on a number of lexical semantic and other factors, leading these authors to doubt whether a preposition incorporation account can capture them.

---

9. The worry is only a potential one, however, since participial passives might fail to be grammatical in a HAVE language for independent reasons.
Of course, since my own approach to the HAVE/BE question is itself a decompositional account, one might legitimately wonder whether Iatridou's qualm applies equally to it. The full answer to this question must await a more thorough-going extension of the present approach to the domain of aspectual auxiliaries than I am able to provide in this book. However, recall that my approach casts HAVE as the realization of a certain v head in the environment of transitive Voice. This leaves room for optimism that Iatridou's puzzle will be solved once a fully worked-out account of aspectual auxiliaries is placed alongside a developed theory of the middle/passive morphology of Greek (itself presumably a manifestation of non-transitive Voice). For recent accounts of the middle/passive morphology of Greek in a framework compatible with the present work, see Alexiadou and Doron (2012); Alexiadou, Anagnostopoulou, and Schäfer (2014).

As well as these issues noted by earlier scholars, I would point out an inconsistency in the consequences that Kayne attributes to incorporation with respect to the A/A-bar distinction.[10] Recall that D/P incorporation into BE is meant to void the A-bar status of spec-D/P. The directionality of the inheritance here is the same as in more canonical cases of Baker's (1988) Government Transparency Corollary (GTC), whose spirit Kayne invokes: D/P, by incorporating into BE, inherits the A-related status of BE. However, if we now turn to Kayne's account of person-sensitive auxiliary selection, we find that the incorporation of AgrS from below into D/P is similarly able to undo the A-bar status of spec-D/P. But here the normal directionality of the GTC is reversed: to be consistent, it should be AgrSP that inherits properties from D/P as a result of this incorporation, not the other way around. But this would mean that spec-AgrSP would become an A-bar position, rather than D/P becoming an A-position, and we will be left with the incorrect result that the subject of the participial clause should be unable to raise to the matrix subject position. It is not clear whether there is a way to resolve this inconsistency in a manner that preserves the intuition behind the approach.

Nevertheless, Kayne's account of auxiliary selection remains influential, and many recent generative contributions to the topic are friendly amendments to Kayne's basic idea that preposition incorporation into auxiliary BE yields HAVE unless some other factor prevents the incorporation (Coon and Preminger 2012; Steddy and van Urk 2013; see also Bjorkman 2011 for an analysis that eschews preposition incorporation but still makes reference to an adpositional feature on an aspectual functional head). None of these have attempted to match the intended empirical scope of Kayne's original proposal, however, instead restricting themselves to certain subtypes of auxiliary alternation to the exclusion of others.

More pertinent to us are the issues with Kayne's account of predicative possession. An issue of particular importance in the present context is the nature of the relationship between BE and HAVE themselves, and how this relationship in turn affects the argument structure of possession sentences, as well as their differing case and agreement properties. It turns out that there are a number of technical problems with Kayne's proposal even with respect to syntactic theory as it stood when the proposal was first set out, and these problems do not look any less formidable in the context of more recent syntactic theory.

All of these issues revolve around the key role that the incorporation of D/P into BE plays in the account. Recall that this incorporation is responsible both for the

10. As I will show below with respect to possession sentences, Kayne's invocation of incorporation here also faces implementation problems when considered in a wider theoretical context.

appearance of HAVE itself (since HAVE is the realization of BE+D/P) and for the differing argument structural properties of HAVE sentences and BE sentences, since the incorporation is what allows the possessor embedded inside the possessed DP to raise to the matrix subject position, triggering agreement and receiving nominative Case. The incorporation has this effect, according to Kayne, because it transfers the A-position nature of BE to the specifier position of D/P, which would otherwise be an A-bar position. This transfer of A-status is held to be "in the spirit of Baker's (1988) Government Transparency Corollary." A serious issue arises here. As Den Dikken puts it: "it is essential here that Kayne appeals to the *spirit* of Baker's GTC; the letter of the GTC would guarantee nothing of the sort that Kayne needs" (1997, 139, fn 9).

To see why this is so, we need to consider what the GTC as originally presented by Baker is a corollary of, and how it was defined. The definition from Baker (1988, 64, his (65)) is as shown in (21).

(21)   *Baker's Government Transparency Corollary (GTC)*

A lexical category which has an item incorporated into it governs everything which the incorporated item governed in its original position.

The GTC follows in the theory assumed by Baker because incorporation creates complex heads with the familiar adjunction structure, illustrated in (22) (adapted from Baker 1988, 64, his (63b)).

(22)   *Head Adjunction*

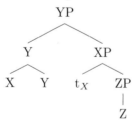

Hence, once two heads X and Y are part of the same complex head, they no longer count as *distinct* in the sense defined in (23) (Baker 1988:64, his (65)).

(23)   *Distinctness*

X is *distinct* from Y only if no part of Y is a member of a (movement) chain containing X.

Since X and Y in (22) are not distinct by the definition in (23), the movement depicted in (22) has made it impossible to distinguish XP and YP for the purposes of calculating which phrases are barriers to government in the sense of Chomsky (1986). The GTC follows: Y is able to govern ZP in (22) by virtue of the incorporation step that has taken place; without this movement, it would be impossible for Y to govern ZP, since XP would act as a barrier.

Now, since incorporation merely alters possible government configurations, it follows that the only impact it can have is on grammatical relations that rely on government. In the Government and Binding theory presupposed by both Baker (1988) and Kayne (1993/2000), the grammatical relations predicated on government included Case assignment, Theta-role assignment, and some types of agreement, but crucially did not include the A or A-bar status of heads. It is for this reason that the letter of the GTC will not suffice to derive the result Kayne needs.

One might in principle salvage this situation by altering the definition of the A/A-bar distinction so that it is parasitic on government–for example, one might define an A-position as any position governed by a head which participates in Theta-role assignment and/or Case assignment, and let A-bar position denote heads that lack this property. But for reasons mentioned by Kayne (1993/2000, 125, endnote 13) and emphasized by Den Dikken (1997, 139 fn 9), it would have been undesirable to do this, since other instances of incorporation of an A-related head into an A-bar related head do not seem to void the A-bar status of the latter (Kayne and Den Dikken both mention that I-to-C movement does not seem to circumvent Improper Movement violations). Hence, a central pillar of Kayne's approach was not technically implementable within the version of syntactic theory it presupposed, and plausible alterations to the theory that would have made it implementable were undesirable for other reasons. These are non-trivial deficits.

Further problems become apparent when one considers the case and agreement properties of possession sentences cross-linguistically. Restricting consideration to nominative-accusative languages, existential constructions vary cross-linguistically in terms of their subject agreement patterns–in some languages, one finds default 3rd singular agreement; in others, subject agreement is with the pivot. In an existential BE-based possession construction, the pivot will be the possessee, so that subject agreement will be with the possessee if it is not default. Similarly, the case of the possessee will be as appropriate for pivots in the language in question; often, this is nominative. Both the case and agreement facts of transitive HAVE constructions are radically different, since the possessor invariably takes nominative and determines subject agreement, and the possessee is assigned accusative. Kayne is not explicit about how any of these differences would follow on his approach. Somehow, the incorporation of D/P into BE must endow BE with the ability to appear in structures that will license accusative as well as nominative (i.e., both AgrS and

AgrO must be present), an ability which, in many languages, it does not normally have. It is by no means clear how to implement this incorporation-induced change of case and agreement properties. Furthermore, even if a way of implementing it could be found, it would require changes to Baker's theory of incorporation. This is because incorporation merely extends government domains, and it is not capable of increasing the Case-assigning abilities of a verb beyond what that verb started with. This is formalized in Baker's Case Frame Preservation Principle (1988, 122, his (99)).

(24)   *Baker's Case Frame Preservation Principle (CFPP)*

   A complex X^0 of category A in a given language can have at most the maximal Case assigning properties allowed to a morphologically simple item of category A in that language.

Amongst the consequences of the CFPP is that P Incorporation cannot, for example, endow an unaccusative verb with the ability to assign Accusative Case. Baker explicitly assumes that unaccusative verbs count as a category for the purposes of the CFPP–this plays a key role in Baker's explanation of the fact that applicative constructions, which Baker treats as involving P Incorporation, in many languages are not compatible with unaccusatives. This, then, is another case where the details of Kayne's proposal are not readily implementable within the theory that is being invoked. Nor has any development in more recent syntactic theory had the effect of allowing head-movement to change case-assignment in the required way (see Levinson 2011, 378 for related points).

   Finally with respect to the theoretical problems for Kayne's proposal, I note that the existence of the Improper Movement constraint has recently been called into question by the apparent existence of constructions that require the postulation of an A-bar movement step feeding an A-movement step. Cases of this in recent literature include Hartman's (2009, 2012) analysis of *tough*-movement; Brillman's (2014) extension of (aspects of) this analysis to Gapped Degree Phrases like *Mary is *(too) shy to talk to*; and Wood's (2014b) analysis of the movement of certain accusative arguments of infinitives into matrix subject position in Icelandic. If these analyses are correct and there is nothing improper about A-bar movement feeding A-movement, then at the very least the rationale for D/P-incorporation in the context of Kayne's analysis would have to be rethought.

   On the empirical side, an important problem concerns Kayne's treatment of definiteness effects in certain subtypes of HAVE sentence, and the absence of such effects in some others, such as temporary possession sentences.

(25) a.   John has a/*the sister.

      b.   John has your article (with him).

Since Kayne treats HAVE sentences as having the same D-structure as existential sentences, he effectively unifies (25a) with the wider class of definiteness effects in existentials (Milsark 1977). We will see later that this is incorrect. More damaging still are the consequences of Kayne's proposed solution to the apparent problem posed by examples like (25b), where no definiteness effect is in evidence. Kayne suggests that "such examples might be analyzed as containing a substructure with a prepositional small clause (cf. in part Freeze (1992)) in place of QP/NP, but with D still indefinite" (1993/2000:125, endnote 14). This structure is depicted in (26) (Kayne's (ii)).

(26)   ... SPEC D [DP$_{Poss}$ Agr [DP [P DP]]] ...

The problem with this idea is that there is no apparent reason why an existential BE-based Adnominal Possessive construction of the Hungarian sort could not embed a similar substructure; in fact, given the general unificatory nature of the approach, the expectation is that this should be possible. Importantly, however, such Adnominal Possessive constructions are crucially unlike HAVE constructions in that they systematically forbid possession of definites cross-linguistically. Kayne's approach fails to predict this–a serious typological shortcoming.[11]

Finally, just as with Freeze's (1992) approach, it is not clear that Kayne's (1993/2000) account can be extended to the complete typology of possession sentences, unless more underlying D-structures are available. Kayne's paper itself is restricted to Adnominal Possessives of the Hungarian type and HAVE constructions of the English type, and these are held to share the same D-structure. There is

---

11. Richard Kayne points out to me the following example from Koopman (2012), which looks like a potential counter example. The case hinges on the status of the determiner *le*, which is in some cases translated as definite. However, the same determiner is translated as being ambiguous between definite and indefinite interpretations in various non-existential examples in Koopman's paper, so that it is hard to evaluate whether *le* is relevant to a discussion of definiteness effects. K.C. Lin informs me (pers. comm.) that Austronesian determiners operate on a specific/non-specific distinction rather than a definite/indefinite one, so that *le* in (i) may be signalling a specific indefinite.

(i)   e   iai   le   ta'avale a   ioane. (Samoan)
       PRES exist DET.SG car   POSS John

       'John has a car.'

some doubt concerning whether the approach can be extended to cases like Predicativization, Icelandic-style WITH-Possessives,[12] or Locational Possessives of the
sort found in Russian. Focussing on the latter, Harves (2002, 178) presents a number of problems that this construction poses for Kayne's approach (the example is
Harves' (32)).

(27)   *The Locational Possessive in Russian*

       U menja   est' kniga.
       at me.GEN is   book.NOM
       'I have a book.'

As Harves points out, the most straightforward mapping of Kayne's analysis onto
these Russian data would be as follows (adapted from Harves 2002, 178, her (33)).

(28)   *Russian D-structure on Kayne's Approach*

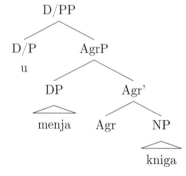

Harves notes that this structure makes an incorrect claim about constituency,
since it predicts that *u menja* 'at me' is not a constituent. One way to fix this
problem is via a remnant-movement derivation of the following sort (adapted from
Harves 2002, 180, her (35)).

---

12. Levinson (2011, 356) frames her analysis of the Icelandic *vera með* 'be with' possession construction as offering broad support for Kayne's (1993/2000) approach, but it is important to
note that Levinson's analysis entails that not all types of possession sentence involve the same
underlying syntax.

(29)   *Kaynian Approach to Russian Possession Sentences,*
       with Remnant Movement

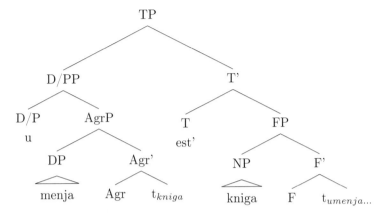

In this derivation, the NP *kniga* has first moved out of the possessed DP into the
specifier of a functional projection FP. Then, the remnant DP containing *u menja*
t_{kniga} moves into the subject position, spec-TP. Even if a motivation for these two
movements can be found,[13] however, Harves highlights an enduring problem: *menja*
in the structure in (29) is not the complement of the preposition *u*, and it should
therefore be possible to extract *menja* without running the risk of violating Russian's ban on preposition stranding. Such extraction turns out to be impossible,
and it is not clear why this would be, given that Russian generally permits extraction from left branches. As Harves concludes, this undermines the structure in (29)
(Harves 2002, 180, adapted from her (36)).

(30)   *Russian: u-Stranding Is Impossible*

   a.   * Menja   est' u t_{menja} kniga.
        me.GEN is   at $t_{me.GEN}$ book

   b.   * [U t_{menja} kniga] est' menja $t_{u...kniga}$
        [at $t_{me.GEN}$ book] is   me.GEN $t_{at...book}$

---

13. Harves (2002, 179-180) offers further arguments against this remnant-movement analysis
partly based on the lack of apparent motivation for the movements, and partly based on the
fact that the derivation violates the Minimal Link Condition. Jung (2011) proposes a version of
the account that circumvents these problems. Her idea is that Harves' FP is a focus projection,
and that the second remnant movement step is in fact a form of topicalization. Since each movement step is motivated, and takes place for different featural reasons (topic vs. focus), Harves'
objections do not apply to Jung's version of this analysis. The problem of preposition stranding
mentioned in the text remains, however.

To conclude, there is reason for serious doubt about the generality of the approach in Kayne (1993/2000) when it is confronted with the wider typology of possession sentences.

5.2.3   Conclusions

The Freeze/Kayne tradition is widely associated with the idea that all types of possession sentence are to be derived from a single underlying syntactic structure. We have seen that this leads to a range of empirical and implementational problems.

Both papers take the position that HAVE constructions and BE constructions differ from each other only in terms of two movement differences: the movement of the possessor DP into subject position in HAVE sentences, and the movement of an adpositional element into BE, yielding HAVE itself. Since the assumed D-structure is unaccusative, the apparent transitivity of HAVE sentences (both in terms of agreement and case-assignment) must somehow come about as a result of these movement differences. However, neither Freeze (1992) nor Kayne (1993/2000) alight upon satisfying ways of implementing this idea. Additionally, the implementational problems are not merely an artifact of changes that have taken place in the armamentarium of syntactic theory—I have shown that no good way of implementing these ideas existed in syntactic theory even at the time these proposals were made.

While it is always possible that future changes in the theory of morphosyntax will eliminate these implementational issues, two particular predictive differences between my own approach and the Freeze/Kayne tradition will remain regardless. These are the topic of the next section.

5.3   Crucial Predictive Differences

Any implementation of the Freeze/Kayne tradition will have the properties in (31):

(31) a.   HAVE sentences are existential sentences.

  b.   HAVE sentences are only *apparently* transitive; they are underlyingly unaccusative (in that their subject raises from below the verb, rather than originating in spec-VoiceP).

From these properties, the following predictions follow:

(32) a.   Definiteness effects in HAVE sentences should be the same as those in existential sentences.

  b.   HAVE sentences should show signs that their subject has raised from below, and they should pass tests for unaccusativity.

My own approach does not force an identical syntax on HAVE sentences and existentials, and so it makes no general prediction that definiteness effects in HAVE sentences should match up with those found in existential sentences. I show below that my approach yields a somewhat different approach to definiteness effects in HAVE sentences. In addition, HAVE is genuinely transitive on my approach, and so it predicts the negation of (32b). Let us now test each of these predictions in turn, starting with (32a).

5.3.1   The Nature of Definiteness Effects in HAVE Sentences

In the previous chapter, I defended an approach to *have* sentences in English (and HAVE sentences generally) that does not give them the same underlying syntax as existentials (*contra* Freeze 1992 and a long tradition of related proposals). For some subtypes of *have*, my position is easy to argue for on the basis of the fact that the definiteness effect is absent. This is true of locative *have* and temporary possession *have*. (Interrogatives are employed to militate against the possibility of the list reading for the existential cases).

(33)   a.   Does that tree have my hat in it?

        b.   * Is there my hat in that tree?

(34)   a.   Does John have the keys?

        b.   * Are there the keys with John?

As is well-known, however, some subtypes of *have* sentence do show a type of definiteness effect (Partee 1999; Keenan 1987). These include kinship *have*, body part *have*, and the *have* of ownership.

(35)   *Definiteness Effects: Kinship*

        a.   John has a son.

        b.   * John has the son. (Good only on a non-relational reading)

(36)   *Definiteness Effects: Body Parts*

        a.   John has blue eyes.

        b.   * John has the blue eyes. (Good only on an attribute reading, a post-transplant reading, or a gruesome temporary possession reading)

(37)   *Definiteness Effects: Ownership*

    a.   Do you see all the antiques in this room? I own/*have them.

    b.   That's a nice car you're driving. Do you own/*have it?

(Iatridou 1995, 197, her (36))

One might be tempted to take this as evidence that at least these sorts of *have*/HAVE sentences do have the same underlying syntax as existentials. I think that this is a mistake, and that the definiteness effects that we see in a subset of HAVE sentences should be accounted for separately from those we see in existentials. That the two types of definiteness effect are indeed separate from each other is suggested by the fact that the effects found in relational HAVE sentences do not match up with what happens in existentials in all languages. This will also pose a problem for any attempt to explain definiteness effects in possessive HAVE sentences that reduces them to the same mechanism that explains definiteness effects in existential sentences, even if that approach does not assign possessive HAVE sentences the same underlying syntax as existential BE sentences.[14]

Romance languages provide some key evidence. Firstly, as far as I know all Romance has the definite article cropping up in inalienable possession sentences involving body parts, irrespective of whether they allow such definite DPs in existentials (Catalan does, as shown in (39), standard Castillian Spanish does not, as seen in (38)). Unlike in English, which does not allow definite articles in body part sentences like (36) except with very specific readings, the body part sentences in Romance languages have a small clause structure of some kind, in which the body part is the subject of the small clause that HAVE embeds.[15]

(38)   a.   * Había   (la) Juana en la fiesta

              there.was the Juana in the party

              'There was Juana at the party'

---

14. Tham (2004) is an example of such an approach, although Tham notes a number of interesting interactions between information structure, definiteness effects, and animacy restrictions on *have* sentences, which it will not be possible to assimilate in full here—see Chapter 2 for discussion of these observations.

15. As proof that these cases have a small clause structure, witness the fact that the body part DP can be cliticized to the exclusion of the adjective, in the following Spanish example.

    (i)   Me   dicen   que tengo los ojos azules, pero los_i tengo t_i marrones.

           me.DAT they.say that I.have the eyes blue,   but them.ACC I.have t_{them} brown

           'They tell me I have blue eyes, but I have brown ones.' (lit.: I have them brown.)

b. Tengo los ojos azules.
I.have the eyes blue
'I have blue eyes.'

(Spanish)

(39) a. Hi   havia la Joana a la festa
there was   the Joana in the party
'There was Joana at the party'

(Catalan; McNally 1998, 367, her (23a))

b. Tinc els ulls blaus
I.have the eyes blue
'I have blue eyes.'

(Catalan; Txuss Martin, pers. comm.)

A second type of mismatch in Romance comes from the following striking fact. Despite allowing definite articles in existentials and inalienable possession sentences with body parts, Catalan patterns like English with regard to kinship HAVE and ownership HAVE: these reject definites.

(40) a. Tinc el nen.
I.have the child
'I have the child (with me).' '*I am the father of the child.'

b. *Tinc el fill.
I.have the son
'I have the son.' (Bad out of context because *fill* is an obligatorily relational noun)

c. Veus   aquesta pintura? Es meva/ *Jo la tinc.
You.see this   painting is mine/ I   it have
'You see this painting? It's mine/*I have it.'

(Catalan; Txuss Martin, pers. comm.)

I will leave aside the question of what permits the definite article in body part sentences in Romance languages,[16] which is surely related to their small clause structure.

A further sort of mismatch concerns certain uses of *that* in English *have* sentences, as against existential sentences. Note that the following example permits a sort of

---

16. This feature manifests itself outside of predicative possession sentences too, in so-called external possession structures with datives–see Gueron (1985, 1986); Hoekstra (1994).

ownership reading of *that book*, with an indefinite interpretation along the lines of *a copy of that book*. That this is not a case of the list reading is shown by the grammaticality of the interrogative case in (41b).

(41)   a.   I have that book.

       b.   Do you have that book?

Analogous uses of *that* are not possible in existential sentences, however.

(42)   a.   There is that book. (list reading only)

       b.   * Is there that book?

Let us now consider why these definiteness effects fail to match up across relational HAVE sentences and existential sentences. it seems to me that the added robustness of the definiteness effect in the relevant HAVE sentences is expected on the present approach from the normal semantic effects of definite determiners, which all map common noun denotations either to individual denotations (in the case of definite articles and demonstratives) or to generalized quantifier denotations (which subsequently undergo QR and leave an individual-denoting trace, following Heim and Kratzer 1998). That these determiners have this effect on ordinary noun denotations is already standardly assumed. That they have the same effect on relational nouns is indicated by the following observation: when triggers of the definiteness effect, including definite articles and strong quantifiers like *every*, are used with such nouns, both argument variables in the relation end up getting bound in some way.

(43)   The son is a complete idiot.
       (felicitous if there is a unique contextually salient male individual AND a unique contextually salient family unit of which that individual is a part.)

(44)   Every son is precious.
       =either 'every person's sons are precious to him or her' OR 'every son of mine is precious to me'(where one of the variables is contextually bound by the speaker somehow)

Because individual denotations of this sort are not relations, they will never trigger a relational HAVE reading–this is the true origin of the definiteness effects we see in such HAVE sentences. The best that they are predicted to get on my approach is a temporary possession reading, in which case they will have the somewhat different structure shown below for the case of the definite determiner (corresponding to temporary possession HAVE).

It seems that these sentences do indeed have the predicted reading: *John has the son* can mean, for instance, that John has kidnapped the son of the wealthy family we've just been discussing. Similarly, I think that HAVE sentences with strong quantifiers can have such readings, although these are harder to get. Here is a context that allows such a reading for some speakers, including the present author. A large kidnapping ring of which John is a member has just abducted the members of several wealthy families. To make the plot more difficult for the police to foil, the abductees have been split up into various groups and sent to different places, where they are held captive by different members of the gang. It happens that John has been assigned all of the young males from all of the abducted families, a situation we can describe as follows:

(45)   John has every son.

A sample derivation, showing how this reading arises in the case of *John has the son*, is given in (47).

The fact that there is no definiteness effect in locative *have* sentences follows from the syntax I have already given to such cases: they have a small clause structure, and the relation denotation they have comes from the presence of the lambda-abstracted variable-denoting pronoun in the predicate of the small clause.

(46)   Does that tree have [[my hat] [in it]] ?

Any definite determiner/possessor like *my* thus does not take the relevant relation as its argument semantically, and so will not close it off, as shown in the derivation of the verb phrase of (46) presented in (48).[17]

---

17. Not all morphosyntactically definite DPs trigger definiteness effects in relational HAVE sentences, however, and it is not yet clear to me what alleviates the effects in these cases. One subcase, pointed out to me independently by Richard Kayne and by Jim Wood, involves relative clauses, shown in (i). The post-transplant reading of (ii), pointed out to me by David Pesetsky, is also problematic, since the DP *the heart of an 18-year-old* really does pick out a specific individual semantically on the reading where John has just undergone a heart transplant (namely, the heart that used to belong to the 18-year-old). (For reasons unknown to me, not all speakers accept this post-transplant reading.) Yet a third kind of case, again pointed out to me independently by Jim Wood and by Richard Kayne, concerns the definiteness effects in ownership sentences discussed by Iatridou (1995). These effects are (bafflingly) mitigated by the simple expedient of putting the sentence in the present perfect, or by using certain kinds of adverbial like *why*, as shown in (iii) and (iv).

   (i)   John has the sister he always wanted.
   (ii)   John has the heart of an 18-year-old.
   (iii)   Do you like my car? I've had it for a while now.
   (iv)   This computer is useless; I don't even know why I have it in the first place.

(47)   John has the son.

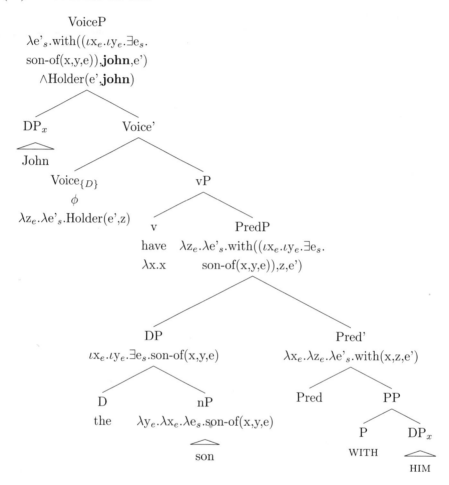

---

(48)   That tree has my hat in it.

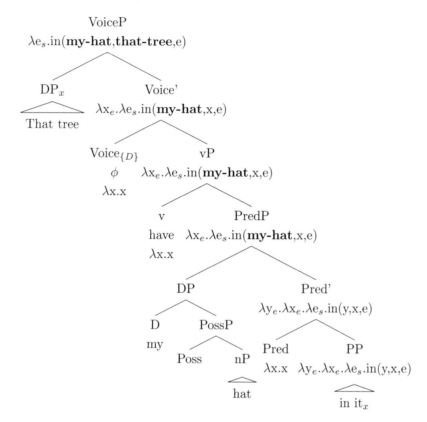

I would also point out that the absence of definiteness effects in locative *have*
sentences is very striking given that, of all the *have* sentences, these are the ones
that arguably bear the greatest surface resemblance to existentials (see Emonds
1976 for a proposal that derives one from the other, and which surely cannot be
defended in the light of the evidence just reviewed).

To conclude this discussion, definiteness effects in existentials should be treated
in a partially separate way from definiteness effects in HAVE sentences, because the
two do not match in behavior within and across languages. On the present approach,
definiteness effects in relational HAVE sentences are composition problems, whereas
there seems to be a consensus evolving in the semantics/pragmatics literature (see
especially McNally 1992, 1998; Francez 2007; Abbott 1997; McCloskey 2014) that
the definiteness effect in existentials as it applies to definite articles, demonstratives, and proper names arises from information-structural issues rather than a

composition problem. I thus predict that, *modulo* body-part contexts with definite articles in Romance (which is a problem that goes far beyond HAVE structures *per se*), the definiteness effect should always be robust in relational HAVE contexts even in languages where it is not robust in ordinary existentials. So far, this seems to be true (McNally 1998; McCloskey 2014). On the other hand, definiteness effects involving strong quantifiers like *every* seem to be robust in all languages in a way that cuts across existentials and relational HAVE sentences. This is as expected given McNally's (1998) analysis of existentials, in which definiteness effects triggered by strong quantifiers are compositional rather than information-structural in nature. All of the foregoing leaves us with an important argument against the prediction of the Freeze/Kayne tradition that HAVE sentences have the same underlying syntax as existentials, and in favor of my alternative, which seems to make the right distinctions.

5.3.2   HAVE Is Transitive, Not Unaccusative

The analysis of HAVE in this chapter explicitly endorses the view that HAVE is a transitive verb syntactically, in agreement with Beavers, Ponvert, and Wechsler (2009), Brugman (1988), Belvin (1996), Hoekstra (1994), Jung (2011), Partee (1999), Partee and Borschev (2001/2004), and Ritter and Rosen (1997), along with many others. Translated into present assumptions, this means it is a verb with an external argument in the specifier of a Voice head bearing phi-features. This position has a lot of *prima facie* plausibility, since it immediately derives the Nom-Acc case pattern that distinguishes HAVE constructions from BE constructions in nonergative languages. We have also seen in Chapter 4 that such a theory is capable of delivering a unified account of the many meanings of HAVE. Nevertheless, the Freeze/Kayne tradition claims that HAVE's apparent transitivity is a red herring, and that HAVE is in fact underlyingly unaccusative (see Belvin and Den Dikken 1997; Den Dikken 1997; Freeze 1992; Gueron 1986; Kayne 1993; many others). My approach constitutes a sharp departure from this tradition on the syntactic side (although I share with this tradition the assumption that possession-related thematic roles originate below HAVE).

In this section, I defend this departure by examining and dismissing a couple of arguments that have been mustered in favor of the unaccusative analysis of HAVE. I will also add a novel empirical argument from *-able* affixation, and one involving the genitive of negation in Polish, pointed out to me by Stephanie Harves. Both of these come down in favor of the transitive analysis of HAVE.

5.3.2.1   HAVE Doesn't Passivize(?)

HAVE verbs in English and other languages generally disallow passivization (at least in their core possessive uses–see below). This fact has occasionally been taken to support the idea that HAVE is underlyingly unaccusative, on the assumption that a true transitive verb ought to passivize straightforwardly (cf. the 1-Advancement Exclusiveness Law of Perlmutter and Postal 1984). The same restriction holds of ECM *have*, however. This makes *have* strikingly different from *make*, which allows passivization so long as *to* is included. While I will not be able to offer an explanation for the badness of passivization in ECM *have* contexts here, I will note that on many analyses such sentences would indubitably involve *have* taking a true external argument.[18] Straight away, therefore, (49b) should make one wonder whether some factor independent of transitivity might be responsible for the judgement in (49a).

(49)   a.   * {a sister/a Playstation 3/red hair} was had by John.

     b.   * John was had (to) leave early by the teacher.

     c.   John was made *(to) leave early by the teacher.

For relational *have* sentences, I would suggest that the reason for the ungrammaticality of (49a) is semantic: the passive morpheme combines with VoicePs that denote a function from a set of individuals to a function from a set of eventualities to truth values (see Bruening 2013). However, in a relational *have* sentence, this is not the denotation that VoiceP will have: instead, it will denote a function from a set of individuals to a function from a second set of individuals to a function from eventualities to truth values. The resulting type mismatch will cause sentences like (49a) to be uninterpretable at semantics.

---

18. I also note that (49b) may be a contingent fact about English, since ECM uses of one of Icelandic's two HAVE verbs (*hafa*) do permit passivization in certain cases (Einar Freyr Sigurðsson and Jim Wood (pers. comm.)).

    (i)   Þeir höfðu orð   á því.
        they had   words on that
        'They spoke about that.'

    (ii)   Það var haft orð   á því.
        there were had words on that
        'That was spoken about.'

    (iii)   Hundurinn var hafð í bandi.
        Dog.DEF   was had on leash
        'They had the dog on a leash.' (literally 'the dog was had on a leash.')

In support of this account, I will now introduce some novel evidence that the constraints on the passivization of HAVE have been overstated, at least for English *have*. It turns out that the possibility of passive with English *have* is much more widely attested than many suppose. Moreover, the cases where passivization is allowed have a systematicity to them that should lead us to question the idea that they are mere idioms. In particular, passivization is often acceptable so long as the complement of *have* is an event-denoting DP (for some reason, the cases are often a lot better if a modal is present or if infinitival relativization is used):

(50)   *Light-Verb Have can be Passivized*

   a.   A terrible fight was had at that street corner.

   b.   A thorough discussion needs to be had before we proceed.

   c.   A debate was had to resolve the issue.

   d.   He's unlikely to leave while there's still fun to be had.

Now, recall that my analysis of *have* treats light-verb constructions like *have a fight* as involving *have* passing up the eventive denotation of its complement to Voice, which in transitive clauses will then relate the individual in its specifier to that event (as an Agent, for instance). This means that the Voice' node in such sentences has a denotation exactly like the denotation of Voice' in a normal transitive sentence. As a result, the semantic problem that rules out (49a) will not arise in light-verb *have* cases, so that the ability to passivize is expected–correctly, as (50) shows. On the other hand, the unaccusative analysis of HAVE is in no position to explain (50).

5.3.2.2   HAVE as Similar to a Raising Verb(?)

In many of its guises, the unaccusative analysis of HAVE amounts to the claim that HAVE will be similar in interesting respects to a raising verb like *seem* (this is most clearly true of Kayne's 1993 analysis). This claim initially appears to be vindicated by the behavior of modal *have* in English, which does have raising properties (including allowing expletive and idiom chunk subjects)–these examples are drawn from Brillman (2012, 50; her (79)).

(51)   *Modal HAVE is a Raising Construction*

   a.   The cat has to be let out of the bag if we want to win this election.

   b.   There has to be someone in the garden.

   c.   It has to rain today.

How might this prediction be tested in the case of possessive HAVE? One way is to seek out DP-sized idioms containing a possessor that is part of the idiom, constructing a related *have* sentence of which the possessor is the subject, and then seeing if idiomaticity is maintained. It is very hard to find DPs of the relevant sort in English, and those that do exist tend to be (i) very similar in meaning, and (ii) predicate-denoting rather than individual-denoting in their ordinary uses, making them very different from standard possessed DPs. This makes it difficult to conclude a great deal from the following facts, but it is still of some interest that these idioms do not survive into the corresponding *have* sentences for most speakers.[19] Note that example (54) is from colloquial English as spoken in the United Kingdom.

(52) a.   the cat's pyjamas = 'the feline's sleepwear'/'something outstanding'

      b.   the pyjamas that the cat has = 'the feline's sleepwear'/'*something outstanding'

      c.   The cat has pyjamas. = 'the feline has sleepwear'/'*this is outstanding'

(53) a.   the bee's knees = 'the bit of *Apis mellifera*'s body corresponding to our *articulatio genus*'/'something outstanding'

      b.   the knees that the bee has. = 'the bit of *Apis mellifera*'s body corresponding to our *articulatio genus*'/'*something outstanding'

      c.   The bee has knees. = *Apis mellifera*'s body has parts corresponding to our *articulatio genus*'/'*this is outstanding'

(54) a.   the dog's bollocks = 'the canine's testicles'/'something outstanding'

      b.   the bollocks that the dog has = 'the canine's testicles'/'*something outstanding'

      c.   The dog has bollocks. = 'the canine has testicles'/'*this is outstanding'

19. Richard Kayne tells me he can still detect the idiomatic reading for *the devil has an advocate*, however. Somewhat surprisingly, Anna Szabolcsi informs me that the same case loses its idiomatic reading in Hungarian, despite Hungarian looking like a language where the possessor really does raise out of the possessee DP. This result is perhaps a feather in the cap of Den Dikken's (1999) counter-analysis of that construction, according to which such sentences in Hungarian crucially involve a resumptive pronoun inside the DP, if we assume that the resumptive pronoun is incompatible with the idiomatic interpretation (not, itself, being part of the idiom). As Richard Kayne reminds me, however, Italian Clitic Left Dislocation is possible with some idioms and an overt clitic connected to the idiom chunk, meaning that even more might need to be said even from a Den Dikken-like perspective.

(55)   a.   the devil's advocate = 'Satan's lawyer/'the person deliberately argu-
             ing a contrary position'

       b.   the advocate that the devil has = 'Satan's lawyer'/'*the person delib-
             erately arguing a contrary position'

       c.   The devil has an advocate. =
             'Satan has a lawyer'/'??there is a person deliberately arguing a con-
             trary position'

If there are never any robust DP/HAVE sentence idiom doublets of the relevant
sort, then this should, at the very least, cast a shadow of suspicion on any raising
approach to main verb HAVE, of which the unaccusative analysis is one.[20]

There are comparative syntactic arguments to be made here too. The first concerns auxiliary selection. Within the four Romance and Germanic languages with
argument-structure-based auxiliary alternations that I was able to check, the SEEM
verb patterns either with the transitives (French, German, Dutch) or the unaccusatives (Italian) as regards auxiliary selection. The main verb HAVE, on the other
hand, takes the transitive auxiliary (HAVE) in all four or them. If HAVE is never
like SEEM and never takes BE as its auxiliary in languages with the relevant sort
of auxiliary alternation, then this is another argument against analyzing main verb
HAVE as a raising verb.

Finally, there is an argument from Imbabura Quechua. Like all Quechua languages, this variety has nominalized clauses which receive accusative case when
they occur as the complement of a transitive verb. The verb meaning SEEM does
not assign accusative case to its complement in this way.

(56)   *Imbabura Quechua: Transitive Clause-Taking Verb*
       (Jake 1985, 158, her (63a))

       Maria-ka   cri-n   [Francisco kaypi ka-j]-ta.
       Maria-TOP believe-3SUBJ Francisco here be-NMLZ-ACC

       'Maria believes that Francisco is here.'

---

20. An important question is whether my own approach avoids making the same prediction.
Insofar as the DP-idiom would not be structurally whole at any point in the derivation on my
approach, standard assumptions about idioms lead to the conclusion that it does not make the
same prediction. However, given the way that HAVE passes denotations up the tree in my account,
one can imagine other approaches to the semantics of idioms on which my account would predict
idiom preservation to be possible. In that case, the argument in the text will not decide between
my approach and the Freeze/Kayne tradition. I would like to thank John Beavers for raising this
issue.

(57)   *Imbabura Quechua: SEEM Does Not Assign Acc*
         (Hermon 2001, 160, her (38))

         kan$_i$-ka   [t$_i$ puñu-naya-y]   yari-ø-ngi.
         you-TOP   t$_{you}$ sleep-IMPULS-INF   seem-PRES-2SUBJ
         'You seem to want to sleep.'

The other interesting property of Imbabura Quechua that is crucial in this context is that it is a HAVE language. Crucially, its HAVE verb patterns against its SEEM verb, in that the former *does* assign accusative case.

(58)   *Imbabura Quechua: HAVE Does Assign Acc*
         (Cole 1982, 94, his (373))

         Juzi iskay kaballu-ta chari-ø-n.
         Jose two   horse-ACC have-PRES-3SUBJ
         'Jose has two horses.'

This is disconfirming evidence for the raising analysis of HAVE, which predicts morphosyntactic parity between HAVE and SEEM. The fact that we find a difference in case assignment in a language where we can detect case on embedded clauses is thus a severe problem for the unaccusative analysis of HAVE.

5.3.2.3   The Unaccusative Analysis Predicts that *haveable* Should Be Unhaveable

It has been pointed out (Oltra-Massuet 2010; Wood and Sigurðsson 2014) that the affix *-able* and its correspondents in other languages can be productively used only with transitive verbs, and not unaccusative ones.[21] If correct, then the fact that

---

21. Richard Kayne points out to me a few apparent exceptions to this generalization. Interestingly, however, these exceptions all implicate unaccusative configurations that are independently pseudo-passivizable.

   (i)   That kind of mat isn't fallable on/This mat has been fallen on by many stuntmen.

   (ii)   That kind of solution isn't arrivable at using these kinds of methods/This solution was arrived at only after much discussion.

If the configuration is not pseudo-passivizable, it will not submit to *-able* affixation either. Note that non-motion uses of *arrive at* are different from motion uses in this respect.

   (iii) * The station isn't arrivable at by bus/*The station was arrived at by the passengers.

   (iv)   * The pub isn't comable to without friends/*This pub is come to by many undergraduates.

   (v)   * This bridge isn't goable over without a guide/*The bridge was gone over by many cars.

examples of the following sort[22] are attested on the internet (and acceptable to me and other speakers) is a knock-down argument against the unaccusative analysis of HAVE.

(59)   ...the thesis can be defended that the addiction to the **haveable**, which characterizes the affluence variety of externalization, is reinforced not only by...

I pause to note that this discovery has interesting implications for the semantics of *-able* as compared with the passive morpheme–since (59) appears to involve a possessive use of *have*, we have to conclude that *-able* is more flexible than the passive morpheme in that the former can combine with relational denotations (which, by hypothesis given the contrast between (49a) and (50), the passive morpheme is not able to do). The affix *-able* must also be assumed to be more permissive in this respect than other derivational morphology in English. As Richard Kayne points out to me, *have* cannot be combined with *-ion*, *-er*, or any other nominalizing derivational morphemes (in this, Kayne also points out, *have* contrasts sharply with true lexical verbs that pick out a subset of possession related meanings, cf. *ownership*, *possession*, vs. **havership*, **haveion*).

5.3.2.4   Genitive of Negation in Polish

As Stephanie Harves points out to me, the genitive of negation is a diagnostic for transitivity in Polish. Unlike in some other Slavic languages (for instance, Russian, where the genitive of negation can be assigned to underlying direct objects, including the subjects of unaccusatives–Harves 2002; Pesetsky 1982), in Polish the genitive of negation can only be assigned to the direct object of a transitive verb. By this diagnostic, the Polish HAVE verb is clearly transitive rather than unaccusative ((60a) is drawn from Błaszczak 2007, 325, her (4.23)).

(60)   *Polish Genitive of Negation*

a.   Samochód ma silnik.
         car.NOM   has engine.ACC
         'The car has an engine.'

Whatever exceptional property licenses pseudo-passives in configurations that allow it, I presume that it will explain the exceptions to Oltra-Massuet and to Wood and Sigurðsson's claims also.

22. Found at http://tinyurl.com/lzlgp5a on December 14, 2013.

   b.   Samochód nie   ma silnik-*(a).
         car.NOM   NEG has engine-GEN
         'The car doesn't have an engine.'

   c.   *Samochódu nie   ma silnik-(a).
         car.GEN   NEG has engine.GEN
         'The car doesn't have an engine.'

5.3.2.5   Conclusion: HAVE Is Not Secretly Unaccusative

This section has defended my analysis' departure from the assumption, long held
in many parts of the possession literature, that HAVE is really an unaccusative
verb. The defense took the form of a series of counter-arguments to this assumption, pointing out numerous cases from English and other languages in which the
expectations of this unaccusative analysis are not met. These same cases all fall out
straightforwardly if we accept that HAVE is, in fact, transitive after all.

5.4   Conclusion

This chapter has identified a number of problems for the Freeze/Kayne tradition
that do not arise on my own approach. Regardless of the validity of the details
of the approach defended in this book, I think that these problems tell us something about what the correct solution to the too-many-(surface)-structures puzzle
must look like: it will not involve reducing all of the surface variation in possession
sentences to a single underlying argument structure. It is for this reason that my
own proposal departs from the Freeze/Kayne tradition in seeking another approach
to capturing the syntactico-semantic core of predicative possession. Nevertheless,
my own proposal also carries over certain subparts of the Freeze/Kayne tradition
that I believe must play a role in any satisfying solution to this puzzle. One of
these is the idea that predicative possession builds on top of attributive possession,
in the sense that the semantic relations associated with possession originate from
DP-internal functional heads–this core idea originates with Szabolcsi (1981, 1994)
and is extended by Kayne (1993/2000). Another idea from the Freeze/Kayne tradition that I adopt is that HAVE and BE are manifestations of the same syntactic
elements. While my implementation of this proposal is different from Freeze's or
Kayne's (and closer in spirit to those of Hoekstra 1994 and Jung 2011), the core
idea is abundantly vindicated by the cross-linguistic morphological profile of HAVE
and BE.

In this chapter, I briefly alluded to the fact that the Freeze/Kayne tradition does not readily generalize to certain subparts of the typology of possession. These include so-called Predicativization and the WITH-Possessive. My own approach does extend to these sorts of construction, as the next two chapters show.

Stassen (2009, 157-185) points out what looks like a set of possession constructions in which the possessee appears as the predicate in a copular construction. In these constructions, the possessee appears to be marked by a derivational morpheme, which can be a nominalizer or an adjectivalizer.[1] Some examples are given below. Arguably, the English *-ed* of *John is blue-eyed* falls into the same class–this morpheme is clearly adjectival, as shown by the ability of *blue-eyed* to pass the *seem* test in (3b) (cf. (3c)).

(1)   *Andoke (Witotoan–Colombia)*

      Puke-koá   b-aya.
      canoe-NMLZ FOC-3SG.M
      'He has a canoe.'

                                      (Stassen 2009, 162)

(2)   *Mundari (Austro-Asiatic–Munda)*

      Ne   hodo odaq-an   menaq-i-a.
      This man house-ADJ be-3SG.OBJ.-PRED
      'This man has a house.'

                                        (Stassen 2009, 163)

(3)   *Clear Adjectival Case from English*

      a.   John is blue-eyed.

      b.   John seems blue-eyed (in this light).

      c.   John seems {*president/presidential}.

If Stassen is correct, there are derivational morphemes that can convert a possessee into a nominal or adjectival predicate, which can then serve as the predicate of a copular construction in order to derive a possession sentence. This would be surprising on a strong interpretation of the Freeze/Kayne tradition, since it would be an instance of a type of possession structure that cannot be related to other HAVE and BE constructions via movement. Stassen's discussion still leaves some room for skepticism, however. Firstly, many of the languages from which Stassen exemplifies Predicativization are understudied–this is the case for Andoke in (1) and Mundari in (2), for example. This makes it possible that (1) and (2) will turn out on closer inspection to be assimilable to more familiar subtypes of possession construction.

---

1. Stassen also discusses subcases of Predicativization in which the relevant morpheme is verbal (what he calls the flexional variant). I set such cases aside in this chapter, since it is hard to distinguish them from cases of Noun Incorporation into a HAVE verb.

For the English case in (3), where the descriptive issues are not nearly so extreme, there is a plausible analysis by Pesetsky (1995, 311, endnote 123) that attempts to assimilate it to the HAVE-Possessive structure. Pesetsky proposes that a silent counterpart of *have* takes the possessee as its complement, with adjectival passive *-ed* then selecting that.[2]

The aim of this chapter, then, is to use detailed fieldwork data to give an existence proof that Predicativization is permitted by Universal Grammar, and to give a generative account of its properties. The result not only vindicates Stassen's discussion, but goes beyond it by embedding the hypothesis in a particular theory of argument structure in which different possession relations are associated with functional heads at different heights in the extended projection of the noun. This yields added value in the form of predictive power–we predict that the meanings that a Predicativization structure can express should correlate with the size of the DP substructure that the predicativizing derivational morpheme embeds. I will argue that this prediction is correct via a comparison of the Quechua *-yoq* construction with the English *-ed* construction in (3). I will also offer a preliminary typology of Predicativization cross-linguistically, building on joint work with Andrew Nevins.

The rest of the chapter is structured as follows. In 6.1, I introduce the *-yoq* construction of Quechua and give a sketch of the analysis to come. In 6.2, I use distributional tests to show that phrases marked by *-yoq* have the external syntax of nouns for at least some speakers. Then, I argue that this nominal nature comes about because *-yoq* is a derivational little-n in section 6.3, dismissing certain plausible counter-analyses that would assimilate *-yoq* to the HAVE-possessive or WITH-possessive type. Section 6.4 offers a detailed account of the semantics of the *-yoq* construction (and hence of Predicativization in general). The basic idea will be that *-yoq* takes a relational(ized) DP "missing" its possessor, and converts it into the type of a predicate, which can then be predicated of the possessor in a predicative copular construction. The *-yoq* construction thus turns out to involve another case of delayed gratification of a possessive thematic role, but one of a rather different sort than the BE-APPL construction analyzed in Chapter 3 and the HAVE constructions analyzed in Chapter 4, which cannot possibly be derivationally

---

2. As Nevins and Myler (2014, 2) point out, however, this analysis runs into a problem with the fact that HAVE verbs do not passivize on their possessive uses.

(i)   * Brown eyes are had by Sarah.

related to it. In Section 6.5, we turn to the comparative syntax of Predicativization, outlining the parameters of variation that are expected to affect it. Section 6.6 concludes.

6.1   Introducing -*yoq*

The -*yoq* construction is illustrated in (4). This example is from Cochabamba Quechua, as are all the examples in this section unless otherwise noted.

(4)   Noqa [ashkha puka auto-s]-ni-yoq   ka-ni.
      I   many   red   car-PL-EUPH-YOQ be-1SUBJ
      'I have a lot of red cars.'

Unlike the BE and BE-APPL constructions of Cochabamba Quechua, (4) is a predicative copular construction rather than an existential one. This is diagnosed by the fact that the copular verb in (4) is *ka-* rather than *tiya-* even in the present tense; recall the Vocabulary Insertion rules for copular v we established for Cochabamba Quechua in Chapter 3:

(5)   *Allomorphy of Copular v: Cochabamba*
   a.   v ⇔ tiya- / [PredP ~~EXPL~~ [Pred' ...]] __
   b.   v ⇔ ka- / elsewhere

The fact that the copula shows phi-feature agreement with the subject in the -*yoq* construction is another piece of evidence that the structure is predicative (existential sentences have invariant 3rd person singular agreement in Quechua languages–see Chapter 3, as well as Hastings 2004). This subject is the possessor in the possession relation. The predicate of the construction is made up of the possessee (bracketed in (4)) and the eponymous -*yoq* suffix, whose status will be the main focus of the discussion to come.

While this section will focus exclusively on the -*yoq* construction as it occurs in Cochabamba Quechua, it is important to note that it is extremely widespread in the Quechua family. In fact, I know of no Quechua dialects lacking the -*yoq* construction. Nor does Pieter Muysken (pers. comm.); and Cole explicitly states that "this construction is found in all Quechua languages" (1982, 94).

My claims concerning this construction are as follows.

(6)   *Main Claims about the -yoq Construction*

  a. **Morphosyntax I:** The *-yoq*-marked phrase is nominal in nature, hence (4) is a copular construction with a nominal predicate.

  b. **Morphosyntax II:** *-yoq* itself is a phrasal derivational little-*n*. That is, it merges with a DP and starts a new nominal extended projection.

  c. **Semantics:** *-yoq* takes as its first argument a possessed DP "missing" its possessor, and outputs something of the type of a common noun. This common noun can then go on to serve as the predicate in a copular construction, be used as an attributive modifier, or be embedded in a larger DP substructure and used in argument position.

Note that claims (6a) and (6b) are in fact (Distributed Morphology/Minimalist Program translations of) the standard analysis of the *-yoq* construction in the descriptive Quechua literature (Cole 1982, 172-173; Hoggarth 2004, 103; Quesada 1976, 104; Weber 1989, 42), including in work by linguistically-trained native speakers of Quechua (Soto-Ruiz 2006, 230; Cerrón-Palomino 1987, 271). The analysis thus has a long pedigree in Quechua studies. However, with the exception of Hoggarth (2004), this literature does not provide explicit argumentation in favor of these claims, and none of it provides evidence against plausible alternatives. One of my contributions will be to provide such evidence.

The claims in (6) add up to the tree in (7). Note that I depict the structure as unergative, which, in the present approach, means that it involves Voice introducing an external argument but not bearing any phi-features.[3] Although I have no particular Quechua-internal evidence that the structure is unergative, I do this for consistency with the literature on copular predication in other languages, which has found predicate nominal structures to be reliably unergative (Cinque 1990a; Harves 2002; Irwin 2012). In any case, no aspect of the analysis to come hinges on the question of unergativity. In the following sections, I motivate the various facets of (7), beginning with the idea that *-yoq* marked phrases are nominal.

---

3. Recall that a Voice head that introduces an external argument *and* bears phi-features gives rise to a transitive structure, which would yield HAVE rather than BE.

(7)   Noqa pana-yoq   ka-ni.
      I   sister-YOQ be-1SUBJ
      'I have a sister.'

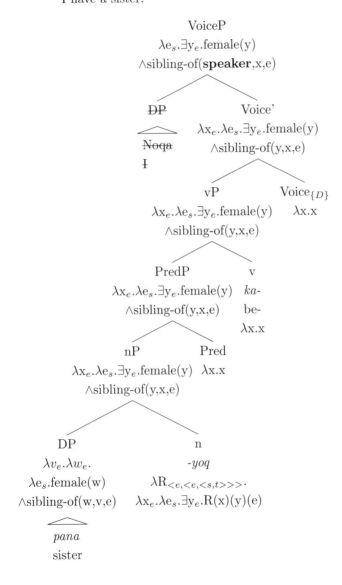

6.2   *-yoq*-Marked Phrases Are Nominal (for at Least Some Speakers)

The examples in (9)-(11) show that the copula *ka-*, which appears in the *-yoq* construction, is the same predicative copula as appears with nominal, adjectival, and adpositional predicates.

(8)   Noqa pana-yoq   ka-ni.
      I   sister-YOQ be-1SUBJ
      'I have a sister.'

(9)   Noqa linguista ka-ni.   (Nominal Predicate)
      I   linguist be-1SUBJ
      'I am a linguist.'

(10) Noqa jatun ka-ni.   (Adjectival Predicate)
      I   big   be-1SUBJ
      'I am big.'

(11) Noqa Inglaterra-manta ka-ni.   (Adpositional Predicate)
      I   England-from   be-1SUBJ
      'I am from England.'

In principle, then, *-yoq*-marked phrases might be any one of these categories. An initially attractive option is to propose that *-yoq* is adpositional,[4] since this would allow the construction to be assimilated to Icelandic-style WITH-Possessives.

(12) Jón   er með blá augu.
      John is with blue eye.ACC
      'John has blue eyes.'   (Icelandic; Levinson 2011, 360)

(13) Juan anqas ñawi-s-ni-yoq   (*ka-n).
      Juan blue   eye-PL-EUPH-YOQ be-3SUBJ
      'John has blue eyes.'

However, there are strong distributional arguments that indicate for all speakers I have consulted that *-yoq* is not adpositional, but must be either nominal or adjectival. Additionally, for some speakers there is evidence that *-yoq* cannot be adjectival and must be nominal, although one of my speakers differs from the others in ways that may suggest that she treats *-yoq* as adjectival. For the purposes of the typological conclusions I am arguing for, however, this difference is unimportant.

---

4. Sánchez (1996, 21) appears to adopt this analysis. She glosses *-yoq* simply as POSS, but labels the phrase dominating it as a postpositional phrase.

6.2.1   Distributional Argument #1: Nominals but Not PPs Can Stand Alone in Argument Position.

An important restriction on PPs is that they may not stand alone in certain core argument positions, whether as a subject (14) or a direct object (15). Of course, this restriction does not hold of nominals, which readily occur in such positions. It is not clear why the (c) examples are somewhat deviant compared with the (a) examples; for some reason, Quechua is much more restricted than English when it comes to PP modifiers inside DPs, and it does not treat all types of PP equally in this respect. The important point here is the contrast between the (a) and (c) examples on the one hand, and the (b) and (d) examples on the other.

(14)   *PPs not Allowed Alone as Subject*

     a.   Inglaterra-manta runa pisi-lla-ta   qheshwa-ta   yacha-n.
           England-from   man little-only-ACC Quechua-ACC know-3SUBJ
           'The man from England knows only a little Quechua.'

     b.   * Inglaterra-manta pisi-lla-ta   qheshwa-ta   yacha-n.
           England-from   little-only-ACC Quechua-ACC know-3SUBJ
           'The *(one) from England knows only a little Quechua.'

     c.   ?? Kay wawa-s-wan   runa reqsi-wa-n.
           This child-PL-with man know-1OBJ-3SUBJ
           'This man with (i.e. in the company of) the children knows me.'

     d.   * Kay wawa-s-wan   reqsi-wa-n.
           This child-PL-with know-1OBJ-3SUBJ
           'This one who is with the children knows me.'

(15)   *PPs not Allowed Alone as Object*

     a.   Noqa Inglaterra-manta runa-ta   reqsi-ni.
           I   England-from   man-ACC know-1SUBJ
           'I know the man from England.'

     b.   * Noqa Inglaterra-manta-ta reqsi-ni.
           I   England-from-ACC   know-1SUBJ
           'I know the one (who is) from England.'

     c.   ?? Noqa kay wawa-s-wan   runa-ta   reqsi-ni.
           I   this child-PL-with man-ACC know-1SUBJ
           'I know this man with (i.e. in the company of) children.'

d. * Noqa kay wawa-s-wan-ta   reqsi-ni.
    I   this child-PL-with-ACC know-1SUBJ
    'I know this one (who is) with children.'

If we now turn to *-yoq*-marked phrases, we find unequivocal evidence that they
are not adpositional, since they are allowed in both sorts of argument position.

(16)   *-yoq-Marked Phrases Allowed Alone as Subject*

    a.   Kay wawa-s-ni-yoq   runa reqsi-wa-n.
          This child-PL-EUPH-YOQ man know-1OBJ-3SUBJ
          'This man who has children knows me.'

    b.   Kay wawa-s-ni-yoq   reqsi-wa-n.
          This child-PL-EUPH-YOQ know-1OBJ-3SUBJ
          'This one who has children knows me.'

(17)   *-yoq-Marked Phrases Allowed Alone as Object*

    a.   Noqa kay wawa-s-ni-yoq   runa-ta   reqsi-ni.
          I   this child-PL-EUPH-YOQ man-ACC know-1SUBJ
          'I know this man who has children.'

    b.   Noqa kay wawa-s-ni-yoq-ta   reqsi-ni.
          I   this child-PL-EUPH-YOQ-ACC know-1SUBJ
          'I know this one who has children.'

The contrast between (14d)/(15d) on the one hand and (16)/(17) on the other
hand is especially striking, since it shows that *-yoq* is very different from *-wan*,
which is the true correspondent of English *with* (having as it does instrumental and
comitative uses, which are not found with *-yoq*).

As mentioned above, there is evidence that shows that *-yoq* is nominal as opposed
to adjectival for some speakers. It is rather difficult to tell adjectives and nouns apart
in Quechua, since they share most of their morphophonological and distributional
properties. It is possible for a noun to attributively modify another noun within a
DP in a compound-like structure, for instance.

(18)   Kay qhuya runa ri-pu-n-qa.
        This mine man go-APPL-3SUBJ-FUT
        'This miner (lit. 'mine man') will go away.'

This difficulty has led some researchers to deny that there is a noun-adjective
distinction in the grammar of Quechua (e.g. Weber 1989). However, Adelaar (1994,
2004) discovered one apparently robust difference between the two.

(19)   *Adelaar's Generalization*

Adjectives may not appear in subject position by themselves–they must be modifying an overt nominal or appear along with a relativized form of the verb BE.

Two out of the three main speakers I worked with treat nouns and adjectives differently in accordance with Adelaar's generalization, although the other did not. For the first pair, the contrast between (16) and (20) confirms that *-yoq* is not adjectival.

(20)   *Adjectives not Allowed Alone as Subject (Some Speakers)*

    a.   Jatun runa jamu-sha-n,   huch'uy runa-taq

            Big   man come-DUR-3SUBJ small   man-and

            qhepa-ku-sha-n.

            stay-REFL-DUR-3SUBJ

            'The big man is coming, but the small man is staying.'

    b.   Jatun %(ka-q) jamu-sha-n,   huch'uy %(ka-q)-taq

            Big   be-REL come-DUR-3SUBJ small   be-REL-and

            qhepa-ku-sha-n.

            stay-REFL-DUR-3SUBJ

            'The *(one who is) big is coming, but the *(one who is) small is staying.'

For speakers who treat *-yoq* as adjectival, the structure of the overall construction will be minimally different from that assumed in (7). The only difference will reside in the category of *-yoq* (*a* rather than *n*) and in the category of the phrase headed by it (*aP* rather than *nP*).

6.2.2   Distributional Argument #2: Nominal Plural Morphology

When *-yoq*-marked phrases appear in argument positions, it turns out that the possessee can itself be plural marked, and that *-yoq* itself can go on to take plural morphology (with the interpretation that there is a plurality of possessors).

(21)   *-yoq Takes Nominal Plural Morphology*

    a.   Ashkha wasi-s-ni-yoq   jamu-sha-n.

            Many   house-PL-EUPH-YOQ come-DUR-3SUBJ

            'One who has many houses is coming.'

b.   Ashkha wasi-s-ni-yoq-kuna   jamu-sha-n-ku.
     Many   house-PL-EUPH-YOQ-PL come-DUR-3SUBJ-PL
     'People who have many houses are coming.'
     'Many people who have houses are coming.'

The structural ambiguity in the attachment height of the quantifier *ashkha* 'many' in (21b) fits nicely into the idea that *-yoq* is starting a new nominal extended projection, as entailed by the analysis pursued here.

6.2.3   Reassuring Distributional Facts: Modification by Numerals and Determiners

It is possible for speakers who clearly treat *-yoq* as nominal to have a sequence of a determiner and a numeral, such that the numeral is understood as part of the DP under *-yoq* and the determiner is understood as part of the DP above it.

(22)   [Tukuy [iskay wawa-s-ni]-yoq]   masi-ta   muna-n.
       Every   two   child-PL-EUPH-YOQ friend-ACC want-3SUBJ
       'Everyone who has two children wants a friend.'

It is even possible to have sequences of two differently-attached numerals, but such cases are extremely hard to parse.

(23)   [Uj [iskay wasi-s-ni]-yoq]   jamu-sha-n.
       One two   house-PL-EUPH-YOQ come-DUR-3SUBJ
       'One who has two houses is coming.'

I conclude that the external syntax of *-yoq*-marked phrases indicates that *-yoq* is nominal for at least some speakers, and that *-yoq*-marked phrases involve one nominal extended projection embedded in another (i.e., *-yoq* starts a new nominal extended projection). The account embodied in (6) and (7) above explains this by claiming that *-yoq* is a nominal derivational affix that selects a nominal phrasal category. In the next section, I defend this idea against some plausible alternatives.

6.3   Against Decompositional Approaches to *-yoq*

The three counter-analyses to be entertained here all involve some decomposition of *-yoq* into multiple morphemes. Such a decomposition is rendered plausible by the fact that *-q*, which is the final segment of *-yoq*, occurs as a nominalizing morpheme elsewhere in the language. The first two analyses I will consider involve decomposing

yoq into -*yo*, an affixal transitive HAVE verb, and -*q*, the nominalizer. The third
counter-analysis, suggested to me by Richard Kayne (pers. comm.), decomposes
-*yoq* as -*yo*-∅-*q*, with -*yo* an adposition, a silent BE verb, and -*q* a nominalizer. All
three of these counter-analyses would have the potentially attractive consequence
of assimilating -*yoq* to more familiar types of possession construction (the HAVE-
Possessive type or the WITH-Possessive type). All three will turn out to have fatal
problems, however.

Let us first consider the idea that -*yoq* contains a transitive HAVE verb and the -*q*
nominalizer. This counter-analysis can be cashed out in two ways, which are best
illustrated by first thinking about the examples in (24).

(24)   a.   waka ranti-**q**   asi-ku-sha-n.
            cow   buy-REL laugh-REFL-DUR-3SUBJ
            'The cow-buyer is laughing.'

       b.   waka-ta ranti-**q**   asi-ku-sha-n.
            cow-ACC buy-REL laugh-REFL-DUR-3SUBJ
            'The one who buys/bought a cow is laughing.'

Gladys Camacho Rios (pers. comm) comments that (24a) gives the impression
that the person laughing is someone who buys cows frequently or for a living,
whereas (24b) is more like a description picking out a person who just happens to
be buying (or to have bought) a cow. We might then split this counter-analysis into
two sub-cases (whilst recognizing, along with Collins (2006) and Kayne (2008/2010),
that the two sub-cases may in fact have a great deal in common syntactically).

(25)   *Two Versions of the Decompositional Counteranalysis*

       a.   -*yoq*-marked phrases are synthetic compounds like English
            cow-buyer/house-owner, and are thus like (24a).

       b.   -*yoq*-marked phrases are subject relative clauses like (24b), where
            the possessor corresponds to the head of the relative clause and the
            possessee is the direct object of the verb inside the relative clause.

Counter-analysis (25a) is falsified by the distribution of plural morphology. It
turns out that synthetic compounds in Quechua do not allow plural marking on the
non-head any more than their English counterparts do. Yet we saw in the previous
section that -*yoq* can attach outside plural morphology.

(26)   *Plural Morphology Banned Inside Synthetic Compounds*

    a.   * waka-s ranti-q   asi-ku-sha-n.

             cow-PL buy-REL laugh-REFL-DUR-3SUBJ

             'The cow(*s)-buyer is laughing.'

    b.   Noqa waka-(*s) miku-q ka-ni.

             I   cow-PL   eat-REL be-1SUBJ

             'I am the cow(*s) eater.'

(27)   *Plural Morphology Allowed Inside -yoq*

    Ashkha wasi-s-ni-yoq   jamu-sha-n.

    Many   house-PL-EUPH-YOQ come-DUR-3SUBJ

    'One who has many houses is coming.'

Counter-analysis (25b) is schematized in (30) (See Hastings (2004) for a thorough discussion of the properties of relative clauses in Quechua). This analysis has a number of attractive properties. It provides an appealing way to get a handle on the interpretation of *-yoq* itself: it would presumably mean something like *one who has x*. In addition, the way in which it derives the interpretation has an apparent conceptual advantage: my own semantic analysis of *-yoq* involves stipulating the sort of function *-yoq* is so as to get the denotation of the *-yoq*-marked phrase to be something that can be predicated of the possessor. Counter-analysis (25b) does the same work with nothing more than a familiar operator-gap dependency. Nevertheless, the analysis also has a number of problems that make it untenable. One problem is that it seems to be impossible to question a subpart of a relative clause; some speakers reject this possibility even in an echo question with the wh-word in situ. In contrast, the possessee in a *-yoq* construction can readily be wh-questioned. This is shown in (28).

(28)   *Questioning Sub-Parts of Relative Clauses Is Difficult*

    a. % Ima-(ta)   ranti-q   asi-ku-sha-n?

             What-ACC buy-REL laugh-REFL-DUR-3SUBJ

             'the one who buys/bought *what* is laughing?'

    b.   * Ima-(ta)   yacha-chi-q   kay runa?

             What-ACC know-CAUS-REL this man

             Lit. 'What is this man one who teaches?'

(29)   *Questioning Sub-Parts of -yoq Phrases Is Easy*

Ima-yoq   Juan?
What-YOQ Juan
'What does Juan have?'

(30)   *Schematic Version of (25b) for pana-yoq 'one who has a sister'*

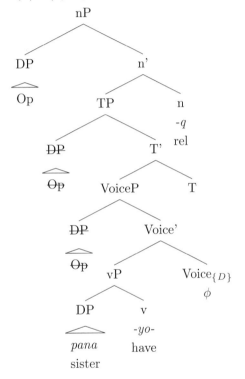

A second problem is that the structure in (30) leads us to expect the possibility of accusative case assignment to the possessee, since the direct objects of subject relatives in Cochabamba Quechua are marked with accusative, as seen in (24b). This prediction is false; assigning accusative case to the possessee under -*yoq* is not possible.

(31)   *Accusative Case Banned under -yoq (cf. (24b))*

* Noqa pana-ta-yoq   ka-ni
I   sister-ACC-YOQ be-1SUBJ
'I have a sister.'

Third, there is a micro-comparative problem with this analysis. If -*yoq* contains a HAVE verb, then why don't Quechua languages vary with respect to whether they have it or not (given that Quechua languages do vary as to whether they have a free-standing transitive HAVE verb)?

Finally, the analysis in (30) runs into a macro-comparative problem. We will see in the next section that the -*yoq* construction is incompatible with definite possessees, even in temporary possession contexts. This would make -*yoq* an extremely unusual HAVE construction, since there is no HAVE language that is unable to express temporary possession of definites using HAVE (Stassen 2009, 63).

A third counter-analysis, which avoids these comparative issues and the problem with accusative case assignment faced by counter-analysis (25b), has been suggested to me by Richard Kayne. Kayne suggests that the -*yo* be taken to be an adposition rather than a HAVE verb. This immediately does away with the accusative case problem of (25b), since adpositions do not assign accusative case in Quechua. The presence of -*q* is explained by postulating a silent BE verb whose subject is relativized. The analysis is summarized in (34) on the next page.

The structure in (34) seems plausible in principle, and I see no reason to exclude it from UG. Its applicability to Quechua is doubtful, however. First, -*yoq* is incompatible with definite DPs. This fact is unexpected on the above approach, since it is not a property of adpositions (in Quechua or in general). Importantly, it is not a general property of true WITH-Possessives of the Icelandic sort, which readily allow temporary possession readings of definite possessees (thanks to Einar Freyr Sigurðsson for the judgment on Icelandic (pers. comm.)).

(32)   * Noqa llavi-yoq ka-ni.
        I   key-YOQ be-1SUBJ

        'I have the key.' (in answer to a friend who has asked 'where's the key (to the hotel room)?')

(33)   Ég er með lyklana.   (Icelandic)
        I   am with keys.DEF.ACC

        'I have the keys.' (in answer to a friend who has asked 'where are the keys (to the hotel room)?')

(34)   *Kayne's Counter-Analysis*

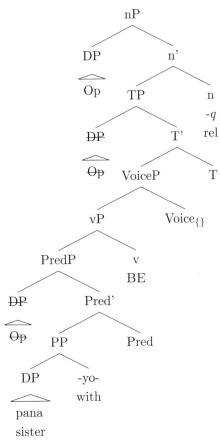

Second, questioning material inside relative clauses is not straightforward in Cochabamba Quechua, whereas questioning material inside -*yoq* phrases is easy, as we have seen. Finally, there is a comparative issue with respect to Ecuadorian Quechua varieties (Cole 1982; Muysken 1977), in which relative clause markers are distributed rather differently than in other Quechua varieties. Outside of Ecuadorian varieties, relative clause markers in most Quechua languages are distributed based partly on grammatical function and partly on tense. Subject relatives are invariably marked -*q*, whereas non-subject relatives are marked -*na* in future/irrealis contexts and -*sqa* in present or past-tense contexts. In Ecuadorian varieties, on the other hand, the distribution of the relative clause markers is not tied to grammatical function. Instead, the choice between nominalizers -*k* (=-*q*), -*na*, and

-shka is entirely tense-based, with *-k* for the present, *-na* occurring for the future tense, and *-shka* for the past. However, these dialects do not have **-yuna* (one who will have x) and **-yushka* (one who had x) to go along with *-yuj* (as *-yoq* is written in those dialects).

I conclude that the *-yoq* construction cannot be assimilated to the HAVE-Possessive type or the WITH-Possessive type, and is best analyzed as a derivational little-n that converts a possessee into a predicate–what Stassen (2009) would call Predicativization.

6.4   *-yoq* and the Semantics of Predicativization

Given the latter conclusion, and the syntactic structure for the *-yoq* construction that it gives rise to, how do we account for the way this construction is interpreted? I propose the following denotation for the *-yoq* suffix.

(35) $[\![\text{-yoq}]\!] \Leftrightarrow \lambda R_{<e,<e,<s,t>>>}.\lambda x_e.\lambda e_s.\exists y_e.R(x)(y)(e)$

The derivation of a *-yoq* sentence will look as in (37) on the next page. Note that the nP *pana* 'sister' is relational and so requires a possessor semantically. However, in this derivation nP is not given a specifier, so that the DP as a whole comes to denote a relation. It is this denotation that *-yoq* takes as its first argument. The derivation is mostly self-explanatory, but since the composition of *-yoq* with its complement involves several iterations of lambda conversion, I unpack it here to aid the reader. Derivations with an alienable possessee will proceed in much the same fashion, except that the possession relation will be introduced by specifierless Poss, rather than the noun root itself.

(36) $[\![\text{pana-yoq}]\!] = [\![\text{-yoq}]\!]([\![\text{pana}]\!])$

$= \lambda R_{<e<e<s,t>>>}.\lambda x_e.\lambda e_s.\exists y_e.[R(x)(y)(e)]([\![\text{pana}]\!])$

$= \lambda x_e.\lambda e_s.\exists y_e.[[\![\text{pana}]\!](x)(y)(e)]$

$= \lambda x_e.\lambda e_s.\exists y_e.[\lambda v_e.\lambda w_e.\lambda e_s.[\text{female}(w) \wedge \text{sibling-of}(v,w,e)](x)(y)(e)]$

$= \lambda x_e.\lambda e_s.\exists y_e.[\lambda w_e.\lambda e_s.[\text{female}(w) \wedge \text{sibling-of}(x,w,e)](y)(e)]$

$= \lambda x_e.\lambda e_s.\exists y_e.[\lambda e_s.[\text{female}(y) \wedge \text{sibling-of}(x,y,e)](e)]$

$= \lambda x_e.\lambda e_s.\exists y_e.[\text{female}(y) \wedge \text{sibling-of}(x,y,e)]$

(37) Noqa pana-yoq ka-ni.
I sister-YOQ be-1SUBJ
'I have a sister.'

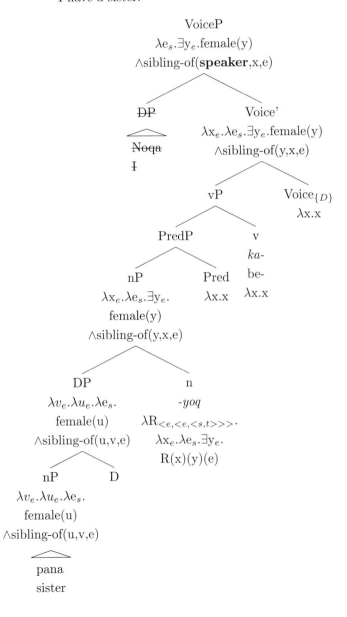

At this point, a reader might wonder what the motivation for such a delayed gratification analysis of *-yoq* is. Why not just have the possessed DP denote an individual and have *-yoq* do all the semantic work of introducing the possession relation? There are in fact a number of arguments against this alternative.

First, there is positive evidence that *-yoq* cannot combine with individual denoting expressions–in particular, it is not usable to convey permanent or temporary possession of a definite.

(38)   *Ownership (Definites)*

     * Juan chay qeru-yoq.

     Juan that glass-YOQ

     'Juan owns that glass.'

(39)   *Temporary Possession (Definites)*

     * Noqa llavi-yoq ka-ni.

     I   key-YOQ be-1SUBJ

     'I have the key.' (in answer to a friend who has asked 'where's the key (to the hotel room)?')

All apparent exceptions to the ban on definite possessees in the *-yoq* construction demonstrably involve kind readings–for instance, (38) is grammatical on a reading like 'John has that (kind of) glass at home too'.[5] There is good reason to believe that kind readings might be syntactically distinct from true definite DPs in Cochabamba Quechua, so that they are neither morphosyntactically nor semantically definite. Take the morphosyntactic and semantic facts about this example:

(40)   a.   Wawa [tata-n-pa   senqa]-yoq.

         child father-3POSS-GEN nose-YOQ

         'The child has his father's nose.'

     b.   * Wawa [tata-n-pa   senqa-n-ni]-yoq.

         child father-3POSS-GEN nose-3POSS-EUPH-YOQ

         'The child has his father's nose.'

First, note that this sentence must have a kind reading in Cochabamba Quechua: it is not compatible with either of (i) a temporary possession reading in which the

---

5. In Myler (2010), I gave an example similar to this one from Cuzco Quechua, but I was insufficiently sensitive to the possibility that it had a kind reading, and thus gave a misleading translation of it.

child has grabbed his father's nose; nor (ii) a post-transplant body-part reading, where the baby literally has as its nose the nose that used to be its father's (Gladys Camacho Rios, pers. comm.). Second, note that the possessee *senqa* 'nose' does not display possessor agreement, and cannot. This is unusual, since normally DP-internal possessors in the language *obligatorily* trigger such agreement, as we saw in Chapter 3. An additional example showing this is provided below.

(41)   Tata-n-pata   senqa-*(n) jatun.
        father-3POSS-GEN nose-3POSS big

        'His father's nose is big.'

I would therefore suggest that examples like (40a) are to be represented as follows: [[[*tata-n-pa KIND*] *senqa*] *-yoq*], with a silent noun KIND agreeing (silently) with the possessor. This idea is supported by the fact that the genitive marker in (40a) appears in its short form *-pa*, and cannot appear in its long form *-pata*. The short form appears to be required in at least some NP-ellipsis contexts, too, suggesting that this form is conditioned by the presence of a silent element adjacent to it in DP.[6]

(42)   Gladys-pata wasi-n-man   ri-saq,   chay-manta
        Gadys-GEN   house-3POSS-DAT go-1FUT that-from
        Gillan-pa(*ta)-man ri-saq.
        Gillian-GEN-DAT   go-1FUT

        'I will go to Gladys' house, then I will go to Gillian's.'

---

6. Pieter Muysken points out to me (pers. comm.) that for many speakers, including those described by Bills et al. (1969) and Lastra (1968), what I have described as the long form of the genitive only arises when possessed DPs in object position are split up. For such speakers, the *-ta* part of the long forms is in fact the accusative case morpheme, which is obligatorily spelled out on both the possessor and the head noun in split-DP contexts. The distribution of this long form is rather different for the urban speakers consulted for this work, and apparently for those consulted by Grondin (1980, 42-43), who gives the following example in which the long form appears DP-internally:

(i)   Pedro-qpata tata-n   jamu-n.
        Pedro-GEN   father-3POSS come-3SUBJ

        'Pedro's father comes.'

Clearly there is some micro-variation in play here, but I must leave a description and analysis of its nature for the future.

The same analysis might apply *mutatis mutandis* to cases like (38) on its kind reading.[7]

Hence, there are no genuine exceptions to the generalization that *-yoq* is incompatible with definites. This is unexpected if *-yoq* takes an individual as its first argument and introduces its own possession relation, but it is derived immediately if *-yoq* demands a relational(ized) DP as its first argument.

The second argument for not having *-yoq* introduce its own possession relation, and instead passing one up the tree, is the by-now familiar argument from the too-many-meanings puzzle. It turns out that *-yoq* (just like possession constructions in other languages) can convey a non-coherent set of alienable and inalienable relations, depending on its complement.[8] In fact, *-yoq* is more liberal in the possession relations it can convey than either of the two existential BE-based possession constructions in Cochabamba Quechua, as can be seen in the following comparative table.[9]

(43)

	-yoq	**BE**	**BE-APPL**
Kinship	OK	OK	OK
Body Parts	OK	restricted	restricted
Part-Whole	OK	restricted	restricted
Permanent Possession	OK	OK	OK
Abstract Property	OK	OK	OK (%)
Temporary Possession	OK	*	*
Psychological State	OK	*	*
Physical Sensation	OK	*	*
Disease	OK	restricted	restricted

7. An anonymous reviewer suggested that an analysis in which KIND is a type-lifting operation absent from the syntax might be able to handle the facts discussed here equally well, but I cannot see how such an analysis would handle the morphosyntactic contrast between (40) and (41).

8. This fact could in principle be handled by having *-yoq* introduce its own underspecified relation in the style of Barker (1995). However, we saw in Chapter 2 that such a vagueness-based approach leads to unsatisfactory solutions in the domain of HAVE, and so I am loath to reintroduce the idea in the domain of Predicativization.

9. In Chapter 3 I conjectured that the added restrictions on the BE and BE-APPL constructions are to be attributed to their existential semantics. Making this follow, and checking its validity against the behavior of other languages with existential BE-based possession constructions, are tasks left for the future.

This situation, which is amply illustrated in the examples below, is best accounted for by simply having *-yoq* pass up the tree whatever possessive relation is handed to it.

(44)   *Kinship*

Noqa wawa-yoq ka-ni.
I   child-YOQ be-1SUBJ
'I have a child.'

(45)   *Body Parts*

Noqa yana chujcha-yoq ka-ni.
I   black hair-YOQ   be-1SUBJ
'I have black hair.'

(46)   *Part-Whole*

a.   Kay wasi uj ventana-yoq (*ka-n).
     This house one window-YOQ be-3SUBJ
     'This house has one window.'

b.   Kay challwa ancha tullu-yoq (*ka-n).
     This fish   much bone-YOQ be-3SUBJ
     'This fish has a lot of bones.'

(47)   *Attribute*[10]

Juan ancha kallpa-yoq   (*ka-n).
Juan much strength-YOQ be-3SUBJ
'Juan has a lot of strength.'

(48)   *Ownership (Indefinites)*

a.   Noqa phishqa boliviano-s-ni-yoq   ka-ni.
     I   five   boliviano-PL-EUPH-YOQ be-1SUBJ
     'I have five bolivianos.' (That's how much money I own)

b.   Awa-q-kuna   phushka-yoq ka-n-ku.
     weave-REL-PL spindle-YOQ be-3SUBJ-PL
     'Weavers have spindles.'

10. This usage of *-yoq* is reminiscent of recent discussions by Itamar Francez and Andrew Koontz-Garboden on the "possessive strategy" of encoding property concept sentences, in which *being red* is encoded as *having redness*, *being strong* is encoded as *having strength*, and so on (see Francez and Koontz-Garboden 2015a, 2015b; Koontz-Garboden and Francez 2010).

(49)   *Temporary Possession (Indefinites)*[11]

    a.   Mama-y   pollera-yoq ka-sha-n,   mana-taq pay-pata-chu.
        Mother-1POSS pollera-YOQ be-DUR-3SUBJ not-and   s/he-GEN-NEG

        'My mother has a *pollera* (traditional skirt), but it's not hers.'

    b.   Maria auto-yoq ka-sha-n,   mana-taq pay-pata-chu.
        Maria car-YOQ be-DUR-3SUBJ not-and   s/he-GEN-NEG

        'Maria has a car, but it's not hers.'

(50)   *Diseases*

    a.   Noqa pisti-yoq ka-(sha)-ni
        I   cold-YOQ be-DUR-1SUBJ

        'I have a cold.' (absence of the durative indicates that the condition is chronic)

    b.   Noqa soroqchi-yoq   ka-(sha)-ni
        I   altitude.sickness-YOQ be-DUR-1SUBJ

        'I have altitude sickness.' (absence of the durative indicates that the condition is chronic)

I conclude that derivational morphemes that convert a possessee into a predicate really do exist, as claimed by Stassen (2009), and that *-yoq* is one of them. In the next section, I compare the syntax and semantics of Quechua *-yoq* with English *-ed*, and similar constructions in Dutch, German, and Hungarian. The similarities and differences between them are easily captured given the approach to predicative possession and the theory of argument structure embraced here. Moreover, the resulting picture makes strong predictions concerning correlations between the semantics of the construction and structural constraints on the height of attachment of the morphemes involved.

6.5   The Comparative Syntax of Predicativization

In the foregoing discussion, I developed an approach to Predicativization on the basis of *-yoq*. This approach suggests at least two ways in which such structures might vary (two more parameters will be added to this in the coming sections).

---

11. A reviewer for *Linguistic Inquiry* points out that this example provides interesting additional evidence that a full DP is embedded under *-yoq*: the possessee noun *pollera* is clearly referential, since it is picked out anaphorically by the ellipsis in the second part of the sentence.

(51)   *Parameters of Variation in Predicativization (to be extended)*

    a.   The category of the derivational morpheme itself
        (e.g. *-yoq* = *n*; English *-ed* = *a*).

    b.   The size of the DP substructure that it embeds
        (e.g. a DP for *-yoq*; an n for *-ed*).

Recall that possession relations are associated with different DP-internal positions, on the present approach. In particular, thematic roles associated with inalienable relations are brought in by relational noun roots themselves, but those associated with alienable relations are introduced by a Poss head, higher up in the functional sequence of the DP. We thus predict a correlation between (51b) and the sorts of possession relation the derivational morphemes in Predicativization structures are compatible with. In particular, alienable possession should be available in a language with Predicativization only if the derivational morpheme embeds a DP substructure big enough to contain PossP. On the other hand, if the derivational morpheme selects a DP substructure too small to accommodate the Poss head, then we expect that the morpheme will be able to express only inalienable relations (i.e., relations inherent to the possessee noun itself). As shown by Nevins and Myler (2014, submitted), comparing English and Quechua reveals some evidence that this is correct.

(52)   a.   * John is blue-carred.

      b.   John is blue-eyed.

      c.   * John is lovely big blue-eyed.

(53)   Noqa [ashkha puka auto-s]-ni-yoq   ka-ni.
       I   many   red   car-PL-EUPH-YOQ be-1S
       'I have a lot of red cars.'

Nevins and Myler (2014, submitted) argue that English *-ed* is a derivational little-a head that can combine with things of maximally compound size, hence the badness of examples like (52c). Since *-ed* is exactly like *-yoq* in requiring a relation semantically, this means that *-ed* is restricted to a subset of relations that often show up as inalienable in languages that mark alienability morphologically (compare (52a) and (52b)).[12] This follows because only these roots denote a relation on their

---

12. These restrictions are noted by Pesetsky (1995, 311, endnote 123); they are also noted by Tsujioka (2002, 165), who provides a similar structural explanation for them, albeit a less explicit one than that of Nevins and Myler (2014).

own, without the need for Poss to introduce it. On the other hand, we have seen that
-yoq can select large phrasal DP structures, presumably large enough to contain
the Poss head, and it can therefore express a variety of alienable and inalienable
relations. Future work should further test this predicted correlation between the
size of the embedded possessee DP and the types of possession relation that can be
expressed on a wider range of languages which have Predicativization.

In the ensuing subsections, I elaborate on Nevins and Myler's (2014, submitted)
approach to the English *-ed* facts, and similar facts in other European languages.[13]

First, I defend the idea that the *-ed* of the *brown-eyed girl* construction is the
realization of a derivational little-a head. That is, despite looking like the passive
participle morpheme, this *-ed* does not always embed a verbal substructure. More

---

13. Hagit Borer points out to me (pers. comm.) that adjectival construct states in Semitic languages share a number of properties with the Predicativization structures analyzed here (thanks
also to Itamar Kastner for discussion). They are limited to a subset of the inalienable possession
relations, the subset in question excludes kinship, and they can serve as predicates or as attributive
modifiers (see Berman 1978; Borer 1996; Hazout 1991, 2000; Siloni 2002). These properties, the
first two of which are illustrated for Hebrew in (i)-(iv), are shared with the English *brown-eyed
girl* construction. The examples come from Siloni (2002, 165-166).

(i)   yalda yefat   'eynayim/se'ar
         girl   beautiful eyes/hair

         'a girl with beautiful eyes/hair'

(ii)   xadarim gvohey tikra
         rooms   high   ceiling

         'high-ceilinged rooms'

(iii) * yalda yefat   'ofana'im/mexonit/bayit
         girl   beautiful bicycle/car/house

         'a girl with a beautiful bicycle/car/house'

(iv)   * yalda yefat   'axot/'em/savta
         girl   beautiful sister/mother/grandmother

         'a girl with a beautiful sister/mother/grandmother'

Despite these similarities, there are some differences between the adjectival construct state and
the English *brown-eyed* construction, which lead Siloni (2002, 166) to reject a unified analysis of
them. One is that adjectival constructs never give rise to idiomatic readings, whereas the English
construction does (e.g. *lily-livered* 'cowardly'). The second is that adjectival constructs allow coordination of the possessee element in a manner that the English construction does not:

(v)   yalda 'arukat yadyim ve-raglayim
         girl   long   arms   and-legs

         'a girl with long arms and legs'

(vi)   * a long armed and legged girl

I agree with Siloni that these two types of construction must have a rather different syntax. I will
leave open what the exact relationship between them is.

specifically, I will claim that cases of body-parts (*a gilled mammal, a brown-eyed girl*) and inanimate part-whole relations (*a walled house*) involve a predicativizing a-head selecting a noun directly. Apparent cases of the *brown-eyed* construction involving clothing being worn, such as *a spectacled gentleman* and *the ragged-trousered philanthropists*, will be argued to be a separate phenomenon: these involve an adjectival passive participle *-ed* embedding a silent verbal head (which can sometimes be spelled out as *be-*, as in *bespectacled, bejewelled*). Comparative evidence in favor of this analysis will be adduced from Dutch and German, which use somewhat different morphology for the two subcases. Then, in Section 6.5.2, I go on to discuss an apparent wrinkle in the prediction that relation-denoting nouns should be acceptable in the *brown-eyed girl* construction; namely, the fact that kinship terms are systematically barred from the construction in English and in other languages. I suggest that this is due to a syntactic constraint on possessed kinship terms, which seem to need to enter into a relationship with the D position (a position that will be absent if the kinship term is embedded under a predicativizing head that selects n rather than DP). In Section 6.5.3, I attempt to account for the fact that, in many languages, such predicativizing structures require the possessed noun to be modified in some way. I argue that these restrictions cannot be accounted for in terms of a pragmatic requirement that these structures be informative (*contra* a long tradition in the literature on this topic; cf. Ackerman and Goldberg 1996; Beard 1976; Hirtle 1970; Hudson 1975; Ljung 1976; Tsujioka 2002), even if that requirement is restricted to a particular syntactic domain (as proposed in Nevins and Myler 2014). Instead, I propose that modification requirements, when they arise, are syntactic and semantic in nature. Thus, there is a distinction between simple Predicativizing heads of the *-yoq* sort, and what I will call *Co-Predicativizing* heads, which take a modifier as a specifier in the syntax, and have a semantics which applies the modifier's denotation to that of the possessee noun. Co-Predicativizing heads also vary within and across languages with regard to how complex the modifier can be, a parameter I formulate in terms of *Complexity Filters*, in the sense of Koopman (2002, 2005) and Koopman and Szabolcsi (2000). A concluding subsection sums up the typology predicted by combining all of the parameters proposed in this chapter.

6.5.1   The Accidental Participle

Nevins and Myler (2014, submitted) argue that a word like *brown-eyed* has a structure along the following lines (this structure is slightly adapted, in part for compatibility with present assumptions about the structure of small clauses):[14]

(54)   Sarah is brown-eyed.

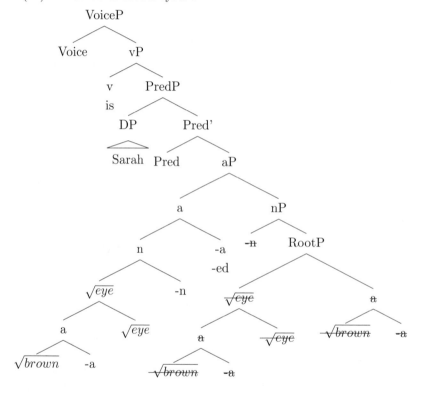

14. More precisely, we argued that *-ed* took a root as its complement rather than a categorized noun. I now think that there is evidence against this approach. In particular, it is possible for a morphologically complex noun to appear in the construction in some cases (example (iii) was found in a Google Books search; it appears in the novel *Sweet Forever*, by Becky Lee Weyrich):

   (i)   a well-intentioned man

   (ii)   a big-bumpered car

   (iii)   silver-lininged musings

Since *-ion*, *-er*, and *-ing* are overt manifestations of little-n, it cannot be the case that predicativizing *-ed* is restricted to taking roots as a complement.

The denotation of this -*ed* is taken to be the same as the one argued for -*yoq* in the previous section. Since -*ed* embeds a nominal substructure too small to contain PossP, it is limited to the expression of inalienable possession (see the next section on why kinship nouns are excluded).

Note that the analysis in (54) contains no verbal substructure below -*ed*, entailing that this instance of -*ed* is not the passive-participle morpheme.[15] One might wonder whether this constitutes a flaw in the analysis–is it an accident that this morpheme is identical to the passive participle morpheme?

In response to this question, Nevins and Myler point out that this homophony is not shared by Dutch and German, and might therefore be a red herring. As shown in (55) and (56), both of these languages have a Predicativization construction which is capable of expressing body-part possession. In both languages, the construction is subject to the same modification requirement as the English case, as indicated in (55b) and (56b) (see Section 6.5.3 for discussion of such modification requirements). Yet the suffix used to mark the possessee is the adjectival derivational morpheme -*ig*, cognate to English -*y*, rather than a participial morpheme.[16]

(55)   *Predicativization in German*

    a.   ein blau-äug-ig-es   Mädchen.

           a   blue-eye-y-NEUT.SG girl

           'a blue-eyed girl.'

    b.   * ein äug-ig-es Mädchen.

           a eye-y-NEUT.SG girl

           '*an eyed girl.'

(56)   *Predicativization in Dutch*

    a.   dik-buik-ig

           fat-belly-y

           'fat-bellied.'

    b. % buik-ig

           belly-y

           '*bellied.'

---

15. This analysis is therefore incompatible with that of Pesetsky (1995, 311, endnote 123), which proposes that the *brown-eyed* construction involves the passive form of a silent counterpart of HAVE. As noted in footnote 2, this analysis is undermined by the fact that HAVE verbs do not passivize on their possessive uses. Additionally, an analysis of this sort will not generalize to the facts discussed below concerning the suffix -*ig* in Dutch and German.

16. German and Dutch have another Predicativization construction that *does* involve participial morphology, to which we return presently.

Nevins and Myler conclude on the basis of this evidence that it is partly an accident of history that the English *brown-eyed girl* construction involves *-ed*, rather than some other adjectival morpheme (albeit a natural accident–participles are themselves morphologically adjectival in many languages, and it is therefore not altogether surprising that *-ed* might be recruited to spell out an *a* head in such a context). The structure in (54) is therefore a plausible one.

However, the Dutch and German evidence also indicates that a subset of the English cases *does* involve some verbal substructure. As well as the construction in *-ig*, Dutch and German display examples of Predicativization with participial morphology. For Dutch, Coppe van Urk points out (pers. comm.) that forms with participial morphology often indicate that the possessee is attached to or covering something else.

(57)   be-haar-d (Dutch)
        be-hair-ed
        'hairy; covered with hair'

It is of some interest that, in both German and Dutch, possession of clothing being worn can only be expressed via this participial form. In such cases, Predicativization in *-ig* is not possible. Note that *ge-*, where it appears, is traditionally described as part of the participial morphology, which is therefore taken to be circumfixal. Somewhat at odds with this traditional description is the fact that *ge-* is in complementary distribution with certain other verbal prefixes, including *be-*. I will take no position on the nature of *ge-* here, but see footnote 17 below.

(58)   *German: Clothing Being Worn*
    a.   ge-stiefel-t
          ge-boot-ed
          'booted'
    b.   * stiefel-ig
          boot
          'booted'

(59)   *Dutch: Clothing Being Worn*

    a.   ge-laars-t

         ge-boot-ed

         'booted'

    b.   be-laars-t

         be-boot-ed

         'booted'

    c.   * laars-ig

         boot-y

         'booted'

Nevins and Myler (submitted) propose, therefore, that the structure of cases involving clothing-being-worn is different from (54) even in English. Instead, these cases involve verbal substructure, and exhibit true participial morphology rather than a Predicativizing morpheme of the sort defined in previous sections of this chapter. Here I will assume, for concreteness, that the verbalizing head involved may be silent, or be spelled out as *be-*.[17] I will take the denotation of this v head to be as shown in (61), where the 'adorn' predicate stands in for van Urk's intuition that the construction refers to a possessee attached to or covering the possessor (which would naturally include clothing). The *-ed* suffix in this construction is thus the true adjectival passive participle morpheme, here labelled Part to distinguish it from the Predicativizing case of *-ed*.

---

17. Alternatively, the verbalizer in question is always silent, and *be-* represents some other category when it appears. This alternative is supported by the fact, pointed out by an anonymous reviewer of Nevins and Myler (submitted), that *be-* participates in Spray-Load alternations of the following sort in Dutch, perhaps suggesting it is a prepositional aspect particle of some sort (cf. the line taken for incorporated particles in Dutch by Koopman and Szabolcsi 2000, 134-136, amongst others).

    (i)   Jan legt vlees op het brood.

         Jan puts meat on the bread.

         'Jan puts meat on the bread.'

    (ii)   Jan be-legt het brood met vlees.

         Jan be-puts the bread with meat

         'Jan decorates the bread with meat.'

This, in turn, might suggest that the so-called participial *ge-* is itself an adpositional particle of some kind, and that it is for this reason that *ge-* is in complementary distribution with *be-* and certain other prefixes. I believe that something like this analysis is correct, but to avoid overcomplicating the exposition, in the main text I will make the (over-)simplifying assumption that *be-* is a verbalizing prefix.

(60)   *Clothing Being Worn in West Germanic*

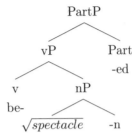

(61) $[\![v_{be-}]\!]=\lambda P_{\langle e,t\rangle}.\lambda x_e.\lambda e_s.\exists y_e.P(y)\wedge adorn(y,x,e)$

The reason that items of clothing are not compatible with *-ig* in German and Dutch would then be that, at least in West Germanic, clothing terms do not count as inherently relational (cf. %*the brother of John is here* vs. **the hat of John is here* in English), and hence cannot be taken as a first argument by a Predicativizing morpheme.

We have seen that the English *brown-eyed girl* construction is to be subdivided into two types: one involving some verbal substructure and a true passive participle morpheme, the other involving a predicativizing morpheme in Stassen's sense. This distinction is more transparent in Dutch and German, where it is marked in the surface morphology. In the next subsection, we return to the predicativizing subcase of *-ed*, and ask why it (and its West Germanic brethren) eschews an important subcase of inalienable possession; namely kinship and other social relations.

6.5.2   Restrictions Against Kinship and Other Social Relations

The fact to be explained in this section is illustrated in (62) and (63). The English *brown-eyed girl* construction and its counterparts in Dutch and German cannot convey kinship (or other social relations). The same is not true, however, of the Quechua *-yoq* construction.

(62)   a.   * a three-sistered boy

         b.   * ein drei-schwestr-ig-er   Junge (German)
                a   three-sister-y-MASC.SG boy
                'a boy with three sisters.'

         c.   * een drie-zuster-ig-e   jongen (Dutch)
                a   three-sister-y-NON.NEUT boy
                'a boy with three sisters.'

(63)   kinsa pana-s-ni-yoq   wayna (Cochabamba Quechua)
        three sister-PL-EUPH-YOQ boy
        'a boy with three sisters.'

In this section, I will argue that the restriction on show in (62), and its absence
from (63), are both explained by the following generalization.

(64)   In order for a kinship term to project a possessor argument, it must enter
        into a syntactic relationship with a D-head.

I will assume that the syntactic relationship referred to in (64) is sometimes Agree
alone, and sometimes Agree plus movement of some kind. The explanation for
the badness of (62) is then that the kinship term has no D head in its extended
projection to enter into a relationship with, since -ed and -ig select nP. In contrast,
(63) is fine because -yoq embeds a whole DP, and the kinship term is thus able to
enter into an Agree relation with D.

Before presenting independent empirical evidence for (64), I will first dismiss an
apparent problem for it from derivational morphology in English (the same issue
no doubt arises in many other languages). The question is whether (64) is falsified
by examples of the following sort:

(65)   a.   brotherly, sisterly, fatherly, motherly...

        b.   brotherhood, sisterhood, fatherhood, motherhood...

The derivational suffixes -ly and -hood can no more take full DP complements
than -ed can (e.g. *our [this brother]-hood, *he is very [my brother]-ly), and yet
the examples in (65) are grammatical. However, this in no way undermines (64),
because the cases in (65) do not involve the projection of a possessor argument.
The meanings of these forms in -ly and -hood only make reference to the possessee
argument in the kinship relation: *brotherly* means 'like/characteristic of a brother',
and *brotherhood* means 'the property or state of being a brother/brothers'. These
forms are thus not subject to (64), because they do not involve the projection of
a possessor argument. In contrast, if *(two)-brothered* were grammatical, it would
mean 'having {two brothers/a brother}'. Since this involves the projection of a
possessor argument, but -ed cannot take a whole DP complement, the structure
violates (64).

While I am not sure why (64) holds, I believe that there is considerable cross-
linguistic evidence that it does.

First, certain possessed kinship terms are known to be able to undergo overt
movement to D in Italian, or combine with a silent determiner (they share these

properties with proper names, as mentioned in Longobardi 1994, 625, fn 19). Other possessed nouns do not allow this. This is illustrated in (66).

(66) a.   (*il) mio fratello (Italian)
            the   my brother

            'my brother'

      b.   fratello mio (Italian)
            brother my

            'my brother'

      c.   *(il) mio libro (Italian)
            the   my book

            'my book'

      d.   * libro mio (Italian)
            book my

            'my book'

Secondly, and relatedly, in Icelandic, possessed kinship terms are unable to combine with the suffixal article, in contrast with alienable possessors and other kinds of possessed inalienable nouns (see Pfaff 2015, Ch 6; Julien 2005, Ch 5, amongst many others). One possible explanation for this is that the suffixal article has a silent allomorph triggered by the hypothesized Agree relation between possessed kinship terms and D.

(67) a.   systir(*-in) mín (Icelandic)
            sister-the   my

            'my sister'

      b.   bók-#(in) mín (Icelandic)
            book-the   my

            'my book'

      c.   augu-*(n) í mér (Icelandic)
            eyes-the   in me

            'my eyes'

    With this explanation of the restriction against kinship and other social relationship terms in hand, we now turn to another apparent restriction: in many languages, Predicativization structures require that the possessee be modified.

6.5.3   Modification Requirements

This requirement is illustrated for English in (68). In English, many nouns must be modified in order to appear in the *brown-eyed* construction (68b), but other nouns do not require this (68c). Similar patterns can be replicated for Dutch and German, as shown in the following examples from Nevins and Myler (submitted, 24-25).

(68)   a.   John is blue-eyed.

       b.   * John is eyed.

       c.   John is bearded.

(69)   *The Modification Requirement: Dutch*

       a.   twee-ben-ig
            two-leg-y
            'two-legged.'

       b.   * ben-ig
            leg-y
            '*legged.'

       c.   baard-ig
            beard-y
            'bearded'

(70)   *The Modification Requirement: German*

       a.   ein blau-äug-ig-es   Mädchen.
            a   blue-eye-y-NEUT.SG girl
            'a blue-eyed girl.'

       b.   * ein äug-ig-es   Mädchen.
            a   eye-y-NEUT.SG girl
            '*an eyed girl.'

       c.   ein bärt-ig-er   Mann.
            a   beard-y-MASC.SG man
            'a bearded man.'

Much work on English -*ed* has analyzed the modifier requirement as pragmatic in nature (Ackerman & Goldberg 1996; Beard 1976; Hirtle 1970; Hudson 1975; Ljung 1976; Tsujioka 2002:140-1). The intuition behind these analyses is that (68b) is ruled out because it is insufficiently informative: people and many other animals have eyes by default, and so (68b) is unlikely to be news. On the other hand, beards are not obligatory body-parts, and so *bearded* can be informative on its own in (68c).

As Nevins and Myler (2014, submitted) point out, however, there are some serious problems for this general idea. In particular, no manipulation of the sentence can render forms like *eyed* acceptable, even if it would make the proposition as a whole informative. This is illustrated for negation in (71), and for a subject that canonically does not have eyes in (72).

(71)   * John isn't eyed.

(72)   * The hills are eyed.

Nevins and Myler (2014, submitted) propose a reformulation of the informativeness approach that attempts to avoid the problem posed by (71), (72), and similar examples. The idea was that the informativeness constraint is evaluated at the level of the aP phase headed by *-ed*. This means that elements outside of this constituent, including the subject and sentential negation, will not be present in the structure when the constraint is evaluated. This, at least in principle, is able to explain why (71) and (72) are still ungrammatical. However, as a reviewer of Nevins and Myler (submitted) points out, it is not entirely clear how to formulate an informativeness constraint over a predicate, as opposed to a whole proposition.

Another problem that affects both formulations of the informativeness idea comes from Hungarian (thanks to Anna Szabolcsi for alerting me to this issue). Hungarian displays two Predicativization constructions, one involving the suffix -U, and another involving the suffix -OS (here I follow the convention of using capital letters to represent morphemes whose surface vowel quality is determined by vowel harmony). Note that neither of these suffixes resembles a participial morpheme in Hungarian. The examples are from Anna Szabolcsi and Daniel Szeredi (pers. comm.).

(73)   *Hungarian -U and -OS*

    a.   fekete szakáll-u.
           black   beard-U
           'black bearded'

    b.   fekete szakáll-as.
           black   beard-OS
           'black bearded'

These suffixes differ with respect to whether or not they generally require a modifier: -U does, even with body parts like *beard* that do not require a modifier in the West

Germanic counterparts of these constructions; -OS, on the other hand, does not require the possessee to be modified (see also Kenesei 1996, 162).

(74)   *The Modification Requirement: Hungarian*

    a.   * szakáll-u.
         beard-U
         'bearded'

    b.   szakáll-as.
         beard-OS
         'bearded'

    c.   * púp-ú.
         hump-U
         'humped, hunchback'

    d.   púp-os.
         hump-OS
         'humped, hunchback'

Clearly, no informativeness-based explanation will generalize to this difference between -U and -OS; nor will such an account be able to explain the contrast between Hungarian (74a) and its West Germanic translations.

I propose that the micro-variation we see between -U and -OS in Hungarian is indicative that a syntactic approach to these modification requirements is needed. In other words, (74) represents evidence for another microparameter in the syntax of predicativizing morphemes. Let us assume that -U bears a requirement for a specifier, whereas -OS exists in two versions: one requiring a specifier, and one not. The feature *mod* here, short for modifier, is a placeholder–I assume it is some feature that adjectives, numerals, and weak quantifiers have in common. It is an element with this feature that -U and morphemes like it require in their specifier.

(75)   *Specifier Requirements in Hungarian Predicativization*

    a. $-U_{\{mod\}}$

    b. $-OS_{1\{\}}$

    c. $-OS_{2\{mod\}}$

The micro-parameter itself can then be stated in prose as follows:

(76)   *The Modifier Requirement Parameter*

    A predicativizing morpheme {does/does not} require a specifier bearing the feature *mod*.

Formulating the modifier requirement in this way allows us to understand why the modifier is obligatory when it is–the apparent modifier is actually a required specifier.[18] This has an initially counter-intuitive consequence: the modifier is not merging directly with the possessee nP in examples like (73), despite the apparent semantic relationship between the two. This is illustrated in the following tree for (73a). Clearly, arriving at the desired semantic interpretation for such structures will require a denotation of -U and morphemes like it slightly different from the one proposed for *-yoq* in the previous section. My proposal for the denotation of -U is given in (78), along with the denotation of *-yoq* for comparison.

(77)

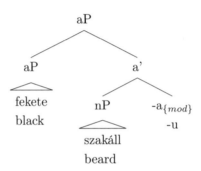

(78)   *Semantics: Predicativization vs. Co-Predicativization*

   a. $[\![\text{-yoq}]\!] \Leftrightarrow \lambda R_{\langle e,\langle e,\langle s,t\rangle\rangle\rangle}.\lambda x_e.\lambda e_s.\exists y_e.R(x)(y)(e)$

   b. $[\![\text{-U}]\!] \Leftrightarrow \lambda R_{\langle e,\langle e,\langle s,t\rangle\rangle\rangle}.\lambda P_{\langle e,t\rangle}.\lambda x_e.\lambda e_s.\exists y_e.R(x)(y)(e)\wedge P(y)$

The denotation in (78b) is minimally different from the one given for *-yoq*; it still takes a relation as its first argument, and the end result is still a predicate that can be applied to the possessor. But (78b) takes an additional argument of type $\langle e,t\rangle$ (namely, the modifier in its specifier), which it predicates of the possessee argument. Quechua *-yoq* and Hungarian -U thus represent two different subtypes of Predicativizing morpheme. Hungarian OS$_1$ and OS$_2$ in (75) provide additional examples of each type: OS$_1$ will have the denotation in (78a), whereas OS$_2$ will have the denotation in (78b).

   Morphemes like -U and -OS$_2$ not only transform the possessee into a predicate, but also simultaneously predicate something of the possessee. For this reason, I propose that morphemes like -U and OS$_2$ be called Co-Predicativizing morphemes.

---

18. It will not be self-evident at this point how such an account can be extended to the modification requirement (and exceptions to it) apparent in West Germanic, but I return to this presently.

This approach can be readily adapted to the modification requirements found in West Germanic. Recall the following contrasts in English, repeated from (68).

(79)   a.   John is blue-eyed.

       b.   * John is eyed.

       c.   John is bearded.

Since modification is required in cases like (79b) but not in cases like (79c), I will take it that -*ed* is like -OS in coming in two versions, one of which has a specifier requirement and is thus Co-Predicativizing.

(80)   *Specifier Requirements in English Predicativization*

       a. $-ed_{1\{\}}$

       b. $-ed_{2\{mod\}}$

Given data like those in (79), it seems that ed_1 is unable to combine with all nouns in English. The question is then what restricts -ed_1 in this way. I have already argued above that informativeness cannot be the issue. It might be, as Anna Szabolcsi suggests to me (pers. comm.), that the modifierless version of the *brown-eyed girl* construction is simply unproductive. In the context of the present analysis, this would mean that -ed_1 is only able to select a very specific set of listed nouns. Alternatively, it could be that -ed_1 is barred from selecting certain nouns (this class might consist of stereotypical human body parts, as suggested by a reviewer) but is otherwise productive. I will leave the question open.

The analysis of Co-Predicativization proposed here, in which these structures involve the predicativizing morpheme introducing the modifier in its specifier, has a further advantage: it allows us to state yet another point of parameteric variaton simply and elegantly. The variation in question can once again be illustrated via a comparison of -U and -OS in Hungarian. It turns out that -U allows the modifier to be a full-fledged AP, which may include comparative morphology, but that -OS allows only single-word modifiers, and bars comparative morphology (Kenesei 1996, 163-164).

(81)   *Hungarian -U Allows a Full AP Modifier*

       a.   A   nagy-obb kalap-u férfi
            the bigg-er   hat-U   man

            'the bigger-hatted man; the man with the bigger hat'

       b.   */?? A   nagy-obb kalap-os férfi
                the bigg-er   hat-OS man

            'the bigger-hatted man; the man with the bigger hat'

c. Háromnál kevesebb lámpáj-ú/ujj-ú
    three.than less   lamps-U/fingers-U
    'with less than three lamps/fingers'

d. * Háromnál kevesebb lámp-ás/ujj-as
    three.than less   lamps-OS/fingers-OS
    'with less than three lamps/fingers'

In a series of works over the past fifteen years, Hilda Koopman has pointed out a number of cases in which certain heads have restrictions on how complex their specifiers can be. She dubs such restrictions *Complexity Filters* (see Koopman 2002, 2005; Koopman and Szabolcsi 2000). I propose that Co-Predicativizing morphemes are parameterized with respect to whether they are subject to such a filter or not, as follows:

(82)   *The Complexity Filter Parameter*

       For a predicativizing head that requires a specifier, that specifier {may/-may not} be phrasal.

In Hungarian, -U has the "may" setting for this parameter, whereas -OS has the "may not" setting. The Co-Predicativizing versions of the West Germanic morphemes *-ed* and *-ig* also have the "may not" setting.

This concludes the discussion of modification requirements in Predicativization.

6.5.4   A Typology of Predicativization

In the preceding four subsections, we have needed to distinguish four parameters of variation for Predicativization structures cross-linguistically. These are gathered together in (83).

(83)   *Parameters of Variation in Predicativization* (Final)

       a. **Category of the Morpheme:** n vs. a

       b. **Category of the Complement:** DP vs. nP

       c. **Modifier Requirement:** Yes vs. No

       d. **Complexity Filter on Modifier:** Yes vs. No vs. Not Applicable

Parameters (83a), (83b), and (83c) are logically independent of each other. In contrast, (83d) is logically dependent on (83c), because the existence/non-existence of a complexity filter on modifiers is only relevant if the construction has a modifier in the first place. Thus, the space of construction types predicted to exist cross-linguistically comes to a total of twelve. These types are exhaustively laid out in the following table. Double horizontal lines mark the dividing line between different grammatical categories of Predicativizing morpheme.

(84)

Category (n/a)	Complement (DP/nP)	Modifier Required (Y/N)	Complexity Filter (Y/N/NA)	Example
n	DP	N	NA	Quechua -*yoq*
n	DP	Y	Y	???
n	DP	Y	N	???
n	nP	N	NA	???
n	nP	Y	Y	???
n	nP	Y	N	???
a	DP	N	NA	???
a	DP	Y	Y	???
a	DP	Y	N	???
a	nP	N	NA	English -ed_1, Hungarian -OS_1
a	nP	Y	Y	English -ed_2, Hungarian -OS_2
a	nP	Y	N	Hungarian -U

There are clearly many subtypes of Predicativization predicted to exist by this typology which are not yet attested. The eight as-yet-unattested types can be subsumed under some simpler generalizations, as follows:

(85) a.   No cases in which a Predicativizing morpheme of category n takes an
           nP complement are attested.

      b.   No cases in which a Predicativizing morpheme of category n requires
           a modifier are attested.

      c.   No cases in which a Predicativizing morpheme of category a takes a
           DP complement are attested.

My approach predicts that each of the gaps in (85) is accidental, i.e., a mere artifact
of the lack of large-scale generative typological work on these constructions so far.
Whether this position proves to be tenable is a question that only such work can
resolve.

6.6   Conclusion

This chapter has used a case study of the *-yoq* construction in Quechua to demonstrate that Predicativization in the sense of Stassen (2009) is a real phenomenon
that cannot be related to more familiar subtypes of possession construction via
movement. Predicativization thus constitutes an additional counter-example to the
strong interpretation of the Freeze/Kayne tradition. The chapter also sketched a
preliminary generative account of the comparative morphosyntax and semantics of
such constructions, building on Nevins and Myler (2014, submitted).

7 Extending the Typology II: The WITH-Possessive

This chapter sketches an analysis of WITH-Possessives. Section 7.1 reintroduces the phenomenon. Section 7.2 examines Levinson's (2011) account of the WITH-Possessive in Icelandic. I argue that Levinson's approach is correct in its essentials, and that it can be broadened to account for other subtypes of possession structure (beyond temporary possession, on which Levinson herself focuses). However, I argue against the specific relationship that Levinson proposes between WITH-Possessives and HAVE-Possessives (that the latter are derived from the former via P Incorporation). In Section 7.3, I compare the Icelandic WITH-Possessive with similar structures in Bantu languages. It turns out that the WITH-Possessives of Bantu languages are able to express a wider selection of "possessive" meanings than the Icelandic WITH-Possessive can. I argue that this is because the WITH preposition of the Icelandic WITH-Possessive retains its comitative semantics, whereas these semantics have been lost in the Bantu equivalent. I analyze this as a case of grammaticalization, understood as a subtype of reanalysis along the lines of Roberts and Rousseau (2003). Section 7.4 is a brief conclusion.

7.1 Re-introducing WITH-Possessives

Recall from Chapter 2 that Stassen (2009, 55) proposes the following definition of the WITH-Possessive.

(1)   *Definition of the WITH-Possessive*

    a.   The construction contains a locative/existential predicate in the form of a verb with the rough meaning of 'to be'.

    b.   The Possessor NP (PR) is constructed as the grammatical subject of the predicate.

    c.   The Possessee NP (PE) is constructed in some oblique, adverbial case form.

For the most part I will follow this definition, with the additional restriction that the oblique adverbial case form referred to in (1c) must have comitative and/or instrumental functions. The rationale for this is that it restricts the discussion to constructions involving true correspondents of *with*, whereas Stassen's definition is designed to encompass other constructions that I argued in Chapter 2 should not be treated as part of the same phenomenon. Example (2), from the OVS language Hixkaryana, illustrates these properties (Stassen 2009, 56, his (46)), as does example (3) from Icelandic (Levinson 2011, 381, her (65)).

(2)   *Hixkaryana (Derbyshire 1979, 110)*

       Apaytara hyawo naha   biryekomo.
       chicken   with   be.3SG.PRES boy

       'The boy has chickens.'

(3)   Jón   er með gleraugu.
       John.NOM is with glasses.ACC

       'John has glasses.'

We have already seen that Freeze (1992) makes an unsuccessful attempt to assimilate WITH-Possessives to his locative paradigm. Levinson (2011) has recently criticized Freeze's account, and offers an alternative analysis of WITH-Possessives and their relationship to other possession constructions. We turn to this account now.

7.2   Levinson's (2011) Approach

Levinson (2011) shows that the *vera með* construction cannot have the same underlying syntax as Locational Possessives of the sort Freeze concentrates on. "Thus," as Levinson (2011, 383) puts it, "there must be at least two different sources of predicative possession structures cross-linguistically."

In the Icelandic *vera með* construction, the possessor surfaces as the nominative subject. The main verb is the copula *vera*, corresponding to BE, and the possessee is embedded in a prepositional phrase headed by *með* 'with'. The possessee surfaces in accusative case (but may also surface in the dative for some speakers in inanimate part-whole possession sentences–a point I will leave aside, as does Levinson 2011, 361, her fn 3). These facts are shown in (4), which also serves to give a sense of the semantic range of the construction (Levinson 2011, 360, her (14); see also Irie 1997).

(4)   *Vera með in Icelandic*

    a. Hún   er með bækurnar   fimm.
        She.NOM is with books-the.ACC five

        'She has five books (with her/at her disposal).'

    b. Jón   er með kvef.
        John.NOM is with cold.ACC

        'John has a cold.'

    c.   Jón   er með gleraugu.
           John.NOM is with glasses.ACC

           'John is wearing glasses/has glasses.'

    d.   Jón   er með blá augu.
           John.NOM is with blue eyes.ACC

           'John has blue eyes.'

We can see that *vera með* has the initially surprising semantic property of expressing both certain types of inalienable possession (body parts, illnesses) as well as alienable temporary possession. Note, however, that all of these subtypes of possession relation have in common that they concern possessees that accompany the possessor, in the sense of being in the same location as the possessor. This fact is plausibly connected to the lexical semantics of the preposition *með* 'with' itself, an observation I pursue below.

Levinson makes a number of observations about the syntax and semantics of this construction that make it implausible to label the relevant uses of *með* as locative, thus undermining any attempt to assimilate this construction to Freeze's locative paradigm.

First, Levinson (2011, 360-1) observes that *með* can have several interpretations in Icelandic more generally, and that there is a case difference that correlates with the different interpretations. In particular, *með* assigns accusative in some constructions, where it often implies that the subject is in control of *með*'s object; on the other hand, *með* assigns dative when it is used with a comitative meaning. This is shown in (5) (Levinson's (16)).

(5)   a.   Jón   er með barnið   sitt.
           John.NOM is with child-the.ACC his

           'John is with his child.' (holding baby, baby in a carriage, leading by the hand, etc.)

    b.   Jón   er með barninu   sínu.
           John.NOM is with child-the.DAT his

           'John is with his child.' (child is accompanying John by free will)

Importantly, it is the accusative-assigning variant that appears in the possession constructions involving *vera með*. Unlike what is normal with locative prepositions, "the complement of accusative-assigning *með* is never interpreted as a location" (Levinson 2011, 361). This is the first piece of evidence that the *vera með* construction cannot be assimilated to Freeze's Locative Paradigm.

Icelandic poses problems for Freeze's (1992, 587) proposed analysis of WITH-Possessives, according to which WITH is reanalyzed into a single complex head with BE. This predicts that BE and WITH should not be separable by adverbs and other constituents of the clause. I showed that this prediction is false for Portuguese (one of the WITH-Possessive languages discussed by Freeze) in Chapter 5. Levinson (2011, 367) shows that it is similarly false for Icelandic–witness the position of sentential negation in (6) (Levinson's (33), cited from Irie 1997).

(6)   *Vera and Með are not Reanalyzed as a Complex Head*

Skrímslið   er **ekki** með augu.

Monster-the.NOM is not   with eyes.ACC

'The monster doesn't have eyes.'

This poses a problem, for without this reanalysis there is no way to account for how *með* comes to precede the possessee given Freeze's D-structure:[1]

(7)   *Freeze's D-structure for the Locative Paradigm*

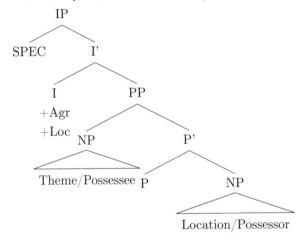

These problems do not arise in the same way for the approach in Kayne (1993/2000), because Kayne's D-structure has the possessor c-commanding the possessee before movement takes place:

---

1. Levinson (2011, 369-373) also points out problems for Den Dikken's (1995, 1998) extension of Freeze's approach in terms of generalized predicate inversion. I will not rehearse these criticisms here, for reasons of space.

(8)   *Kayne's D-Structure for Possession Sentences*

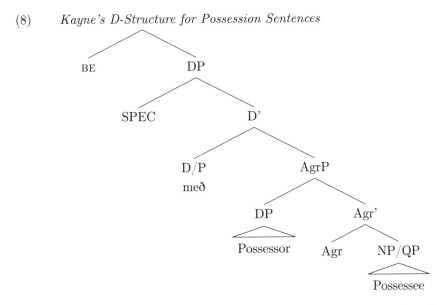

However, as Levinson (2011:374) points out, Kayne's theory cannot be adopted directly. This is because it relies on D/P Incorporation to allow the possessor to escape the possessed DP. Without this incorporation, the possessor cannot reach the subject position without violating the constraint on Improper Movement. The Icelandic *vera með* construction, since it is of the BE type rather than the HAVE type, cannot possibly involve such incorporation. Hence, there is no way to explain how the necessary movement of the possessor into subject position is permitted on Kayne's proposal.

For these reasons, Levinson (2011) concludes that *vera með* cannot be assimilated to either of the structures in (7) or (8). However, its properties follow straightforwardly if it is assumed that *vera með* is more or less what it looks like: a copula construction with a PP predicate, of which the possessor is the subject and the possessee is the complement. This is Levinson's analysis, and it is depicted in (9) (2011, 381, her (65)). In (9) $p_{control}$ is responsible simultaneously for the control semantics associated with temporary possession and for assinging accusative Case to the possessee.

(9)   Jón   er með gleraugu.
       John.NOM is with glasses.ACC

       'John has glasses.'

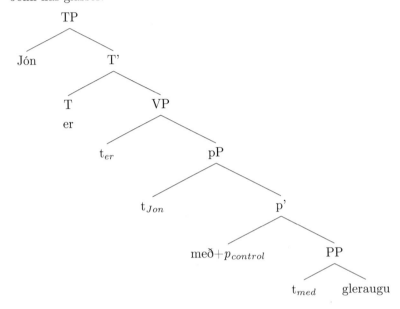

Since (9) cannot possibly serve as a structure for Locative Possessives of the Russian type or Adnominal Possessives of the Hungarian type, Levinson concludes that there must be more than one argument structure available for BE-based possession constructions in Universal Grammar.

I agree with the implications of Levinson's (2011) study with respect to BE constructions. Less persuasive, however, is her proposed extension of the approach to HAVE constructions in terms of P Incorporation.

Levinson (2011, 385-388) proposes that HAVE is derived by incorporating WITH into BE. Noting that the standard Agree approach to licensing that she adopts is not compatible with Baker's (1988) traditional explanation for Case-assignment in incorporation structures (Levinson 2011, 378), she puts forward a new way of implementing this idea. In particular, Levinson suggests that WITH is affix-like in that it must incorporate into a higher head. In the Icelandic derivation in (9), p serves as the host of WITH. She claims that, in English and German HAVE constructions, the p head responsible for assigning Case to the possessee in Icelandic is absent. Therefore, WITH is forced to incorporate into BE instead in these languages, and this is what derives HAVE. Since p is absent, Levinson assumes that the possessor is introduced in spec-vP. This makes the structure transitive, so v is able to assign Accusative to the possessee. This derivation is depicted in (10) (based on Levinson 2011, 388, her (83b), but with English morphemes substituted for Levinson's German ones).

Note that there are two important structural differences (apart from the landing site of incorporation) between the derivation in (10) and the derivation of *vera með*. One is that *p* is absent (which necessitates the incorporation step), and the other is that transitive v is present. Given this second difference, the suggestion that P Incorporation is what triggers the spell-out of BE as HAVE is not necessary. One could equally well claim that it is the presence of v (which is independently necessary for Case-assignment, on Levinson's assumptions) that triggers the realization of BE as HAVE. This would equate to the claim that HAVE is the transitive form of BE, the analysis adopted in this book.

(10)   Hans has a book.

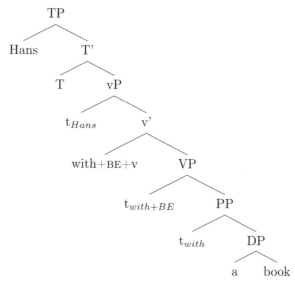

Levinson (2011, 385) claims that the incorporation assumption in (10) is not otiose, asserting that it plays a role in explaining why (11a) is not possible as a predicative possession construction in English. This contrasts sharply with the seemingly equivalent attributive possession construction in (11b), and the normal behavior of other PPs (including *with* itself in its comitative uses), as in (11c) (these are respectively Levinson's (75), (70a), and (77)).

(11)   a.   * The man is with a beard.

       b.   The man with the beard (is fun).

       c.   John is with the mayor this afternoon.

The idea is that (11a) is ungrammatical because the result of building the structure which would derive it involves failing to apply the obligatory incorporation step in a derivation like (10). Only if this incorporation step is applied can the derivation converge, but then the sentence is spelled out as *the man has a beard*. However, a closer inspection of how (11b) is ruled grammatical on Levinson's approach reveals that the real work is not being done by incorporation. For (11b), Levinson (2011, 390) assumes that p is present, and so *with* can incorporate into it. Unfortunately, no deeper explanation is provided for why p can be present in attributive contexts, but never in predicative contexts. Absent such an explanation, Levinson's account is no better than a stipulation barring possessive *with* from predicative contexts. Therefore, no real advantage inheres in keeping the P Incorporation approach to HAVE.

7.3   WITH-Possessives in Icelandic and Bantu

This section compares the WITH-Possessive in Icelandic with the WITH-Possessives found in Bantu languages. In Icelandic, the WITH-Possessive is semantically restricted in ways that are directly related to WITH's *accompaniment* uses. Bantu WITH-Possessives, on the other hand, are not semantically restricted in this way, and are usable for relations like ownership and kinship possession, where the accompaniment part of WITH's meaning is clearly absent. I will argue that this reflects grammaticalization as reformulated in a generative framework by Roberts and Rousseau (2003). The syntactic analysis will be based on Levinson's, but with a few necessary amendments.

7.3.1   *Vera Með* in Icelandic

We have already seen that the Icelandic *vera með* 'be with' construction involves the possessor surfacing as the nominative subject of a copular construction with a PP predicate. The possessee is the complement of this PP, which is headed by *með*. While *með* assigns dative case in its comitative uses, in this construction it assigns accusative case.

The examples in (4) demonstrated that *vera með* is compatible with a seemingly diverse set of possession relations, including temporary possession (4a), diseases

(4b), clothes that are being worn on the body (4c), and body parts (4d). As shown in the following examples (adapted from Myler, E.F. Sigurðsson, and Wood 2014, 12, their (37b) and (40b) respectively), *vera með* can also express abstract attributes.

(12)   *Abstract Attributes*

  a. Strákurinn var með óþekkt.
    boy.the.NOM was with disobedience.ACC

    'The boy was (acting) disobedient.'

  b. Uppistandarinn   var með skemmtilegheit.
    stand.up.commedian.the.NOM was with amusement.ACC

    'The stand-up comedian was amusing.'

However, it is not the case that *vera með* is free to express any subtype of possession relation. In particular, it is not able to express ownership, or kinship (Irie 1997; Myler, E.F. Sigurðsson, and Wood 2014). The following examples are adapted from Myler, E.F. Sigurðsson, and Wood (2014, 11-12, their (32) and (36) respectively).

(13)   *No Ownership or Kinship*

  a. Jafnvel þótt bókin mín sé týnd einhvers staðar í útlöndum...
    'even though my book is lost somewhere abroad...'

    * þá er ég með hana!
    then am I with it

    'it's still mine!'

  b. * Þeir   eru með systur.
    They.NOM are with sister.acc

    'They have a sister.'

It seems to me that the sets of possession relations with which *vera með* is and is not compatible fall under the following generalization.

(14)   *vera með* is compatible with possession relations in which the possessee accompanies the possessor.

This statement correctly unites temporary possession (in which a concrete object is 'with' the possessor), clothing, body parts, abstract attributes, and diseases (all of which go wherever the possessor goes). It also correctly excludes ownership and kinship, which do not share this accompaniment meaning.

Levinson (2011) does not note the generalization in (14), and concentrates on temporary possession. Nevertheless, the semantics that she attributes to *með* itself turn out to capture the intuition behind (14).

(15)   *Denotations Levinson (2011, 380, her (63))*

     a. $[\![\text{með}]\!] = \lambda x_e.\lambda e_s.\text{accompaniment}(e) \wedge \text{theme}(e,x)$

     b. $[\![p_{control}]\!] = \lambda P_{\langle s,t\rangle}.\lambda y_e.\lambda f_s.P(f) \wedge \text{controller}(f,y)$

The only alterations of Levinson's account that would be needed to fully accommodate (14) are (a) abandoning her assumption that control semantics are inherent to the little-*p* head that assigns accusative case in her system, and (b) changing the denotation of *með* so that it can take a relation as one of its arguments. Alteration (a) can be achieved either by postulating an expletive alloseme of *p* alongside Levinson's control meaning, or by abandoning that denotation altogether and accounting for the agentive aspects of temporary possession differently. I will not decide between these options here, but will adopt the first of them in the analyses below for concreteness. This is spelled out in the following set of allosemes for Levinson's *p_{control}* head.

(16)   *Allosemy of p_{control}*

     a. $[\![p_{control}]\!] = \lambda P_{\langle s,t\rangle}.\lambda y_e.\lambda e_s.P(e) \wedge \text{controller}(e,y)$ /___$\langle s,t\rangle$

     b. $[\![p_{control}]\!] = \lambda x.x$ /___ elsewhere

An attempt at alteration (b) is made in (17), which postulates conditioned allosemy of *með* depending on the type of its complement.

(17)   *Allosemy of Með*

     a. $[\![\text{með}]\!] = \lambda R.\lambda y_e.\lambda e_s.\exists x_e.\text{accompaniment}(e) \wedge \text{theme}(e,x)$
          $\wedge\ R(y)(x)(e)$ / ___ $\langle e\langle e\langle s,t\rangle\rangle\rangle$

     b. $[\![\text{með}]\!] = \lambda x_e.\lambda e_s.\text{accompaniment}(e) \wedge \text{theme}(e,x)$ / ___ elsewhere

Apart from this, however, little about Levinson's analysis seems to need to change in order to be compatible with the present system, and her syntax can be adopted wholesale, as follows (adapted from Levinson (2011, 381, her (65)). In the temporary possession case in (18), the alloseme in (17b) is chosen for *með*, and the alloseme in (16a) is chosen for *p_{control}*. In a case involving a relation-denoting noun, such as body-part possession, the alloseme in (17a) will be chosen for *með* instead, leading also to the selection of the alloseme of (16b) for *p_{control}*. This is shown in (19).

(18) Jón   er með gleraugu.
      John.NOM is with glasses.ACC
      'John has glasses.'

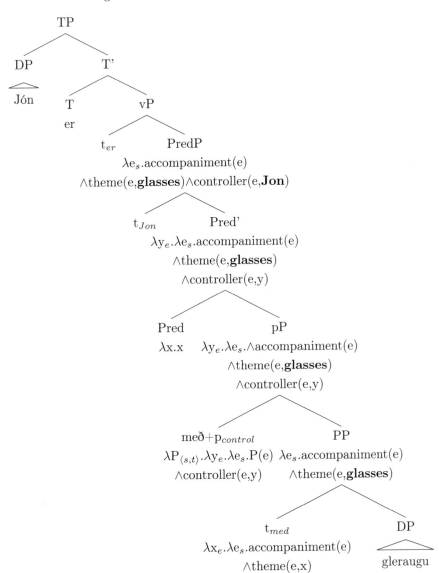

(19) Jón   er með blá augu.
     John.NOM is with blue eyes.ACC
     'John has blue eyes.'

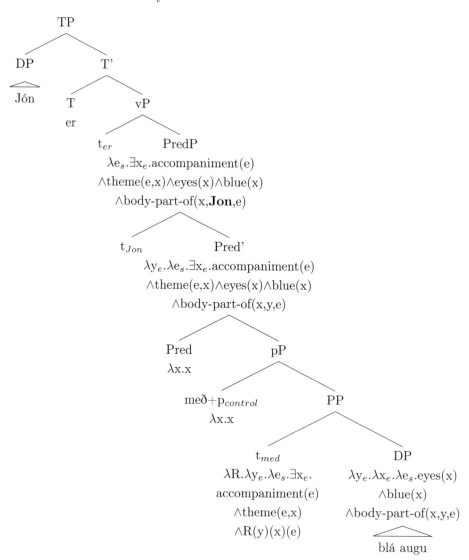

In this subsection, we have seen that the Icelandic *vera með* construction is a possession construction in which the lexical semantics of one of the components (namely *með* 'with') restricts the set of possession relations with which the overall construction is compatible. Not all WITH-Possessive constructions retain the accompaniment semantics of WITH in this fashion, however, as we will now see.

7.3.2 *Na* in Bantu

Bantu languages exhibit a WITH-Possessive construction as their main type of possession sentence (see Creissels 2013; Halpert & Diercks 2014). The WITH preposition in these languages is realized as *na*, or some cognate thereof. Importantly, this WITH-Possessive is capable of expressing the full gamut of possession relations, including ones that were shown to be ungrammatical with the Icelandic *vera með* construction. An example showing a comitative use of *na* is given from Zulu in (20). The remaining examples in (21)-(23) give examples of the construction being used in relational and ownership contexts, which clearly have nothing to do with the accompaniment sense of WITH (and, I argued in the previous section, are ungrammatical in the Icelandic *vera með* construction for this very reason). Numerals in the examples indicate noun classes. The gloss AUG refers to the augment prefix, whose status is much debated. I would like to thank William Bennett (pers. comm.) for sending me the Xhosa data.

(20) uXolani a-ka-dlal-i na-mfana. (Zulu)
AUG.1Xolani NEG-1S-play-NEG with-1boy
'Xolani isn't playing with any boy.' (Halpert 2012, 215)

(21) ngi-∅-na-bangane abaningi. (Zulu)
I-be-with-2friend 2REL.many
'I have many friends.' (Halpert 2012, 214)

(22) u-John u-funa uku-ba na-bantwana. (Xhosa)
AUG-1John 1S-want INF-be with-children
'John wants to have children'

(23) Ni-li-kuwa na nyumba. (Swahili)
I-PAST-be with 9house.
'I had a house.' (Diercks and Halpert 2014, 3)

Clearly, then, the *na* that appears in possession sentences in Bantu languages does not retain enough of its WITH-like lexical semantics to constrain the set of

possession relations that the structure as a whole can express. Plausibly, *na* itself
has been reanalyzed as a functional element in Bantu, and no longer corresponds to
WITH, but to *p*. This *p* must be restricted in its distribution so that it can surface
with a DP complement (as in (21)-(23)) or with a PP complement headed by a silent
P head which contributes the accompaniment semantics in an example like (20)–in
the latter case, the appearance is given that *na* means WITH, but the claim here is
that this appearance is misleading. That Bantu *na* might have been reanalyzed in
this way is consonant with the general pattern of grammaticalization revealed by
Roberts and Rousseau (2003). They point out (195-200) that many cases of grammaticalization involve reanalysis of a previous head-movement relation, in which a
lexical head moves to a functional head, so that the exponent of the lexical head
comes to be analyzed as an exponent of the higher functional head. Schematically,
while *na* was (presumably) once analyzed as in (24) (as Icelandic *með* still is–see
(18)), it is now analyzed as in (25).

(24)

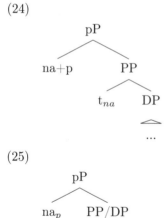

(25)

Semantically, I will take *na* to be like Levinson's p_{sym} (associated with dative
case and with neutrally comitative semantics in Icelandic) in one of its allosemes. Its
other alloseme will be expletive, meaning that *na* is compatible with any possession
relation.

(26)   *Allosemy of na*

   a. $[\![na]\!] = \lambda P_{\langle s,t\rangle}.\lambda y_e.\lambda e_s.P(e)\wedge companion(e,y)/\_\_\_\langle s,t\rangle$

   b. $[\![na]\!] = \lambda x.x$

To illustrate the analysis, on the next two pages I provide sample derivations for the Zulu examples in (20) and (21) (see (27) and (28)). Note that in (27) Voice composes with vP via Predicate Conjunction. For such comitative uses of *na*, the reanalysis illustrated in (24) vs. (25) entails that *na* itself is not the source of the comitative semantics. I will assume instead that na_p selects a PP headed by a silent comitative preposition COM in such examples. Notice also that the BE verb in structures like (28) is silent, causing the inflectional morphology associated with the clause to cluster around *na*. This gives the deceptive appearance that *na* is the verb in the structure.

This concludes this sketch of WITH-Possessives in Bantu.[2]

7.4   Conclusion: Syntax and Semantics in WITH-Possessives

This chapter has presented a preliminary analysis of WITH-Possessives from the perspective of the present framework. A comparison of Icelandic and Bantu revealed that WITH-Possessives vary in terms of whether any WITH-like semantics are retained by the adposition in question. If they are, then the possession construction as a whole will be constrained to expressing a subset of possession relations compatible with these semantics. In contrast, as Levinson (2011) shows, the Freeze/Kayne Tradition is unable to assimilate the WITH-Possessive.

---

2. In many languages, but by no means all, the comitative adposition is also used to mark instruments (see Seiler 1974; Stolz 2001, amongst many others). This is true, for instance, of Icelandic, but not of Bantu languages, which have a separate instrumental adposition. I have no insight to offer regarding this variation here.

(27)   uXolani   a-ka-dlal-i   na-mfana. (Zulu)
        AUG.1Xolani NEG-1S-play-NEG with-1boy
        'Xolani isn't playing with any boy.'

$$\textbf{VoiceP}$$
$$\lambda e_s.\text{accompaniment}(e) \wedge \text{theme}(e,\textbf{a-boy})$$
$$\wedge \text{companion}(e,\textbf{Xolani}) \wedge \text{play}(e)$$
$$\wedge \text{agent}(e,\textbf{Xolani})$$

DP

uXolani
Xolani

Voice'
$$\lambda y_e.\lambda e_s.\text{accompaniment}(e)$$
$$\wedge \text{theme}(e,\textbf{a-boy}) \wedge \text{companion}(e,y)$$
$$\wedge \text{play}(e) \wedge \text{agent}(e,y)$$

$\text{Voice}_{\{D\}}$
$$\lambda x_e.\lambda e_s.\text{agent}(e,x)$$

vP
$$\lambda y_e.\lambda e_s.\text{accompaniment}(e)$$
$$\wedge \text{theme}(e,\textbf{a-boy})$$
$$\wedge \text{companion}(e,y) \wedge \text{play}(e)$$

vP
$$\lambda e_s.\text{play}(e)$$

$\sqrt{play}$ v
dlal

pP
$$\lambda y_e.\lambda e_s.\text{accompaniment}(e)$$
$$\wedge \text{theme}(e,\textbf{a-boy}) \wedge \text{companion}(e,y)$$

p
na
$$\lambda P_{\langle s,t \rangle}.\lambda y_e.\lambda e_s.P(e)$$
$$\wedge \text{companion}(e,y)$$

PP
$$\lambda e_s.\text{accompaniment}(e)$$
$$\wedge \text{theme}(e,\textbf{a-boy})$$

COM
$$\lambda x_e.\lambda e_s.\text{accompaniment}(e)$$
$$\wedge \text{theme}(e,x)$$

DP

mfana
a boy

(28)   ngi-∅-na-bangane abaningi.   (Zulu)
       I-be-with-2friend 2REL.many
       'I have many friends.'

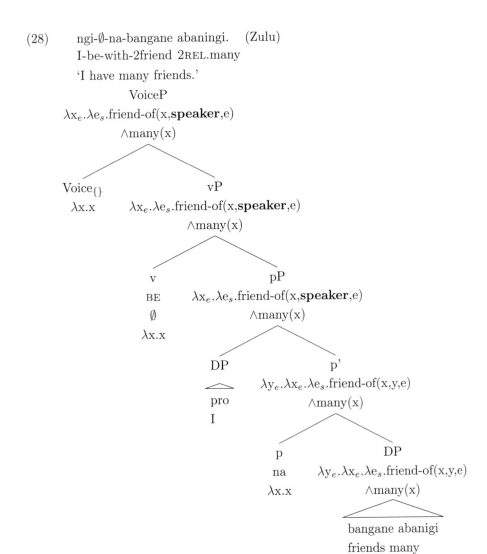

Conclusions and Prospects

This book has been an extended argument for a theory of the architecture of the grammar in which the syntactic component operates autonomously from the morphophonological component on the one hand, and the semantic component on the other. Morphophonology and semantics are interpretational components; they convert the output of syntax (which is written in an alphabet of formal features) into representations legible to language-external systems (phonetic implementation and the Conceptual-Intensional system, respectively). This view of the role of morphophonology and semantics in the architecture of grammar entails that these components can place conditions on the output of syntax, but cannot dictate syntactic operations themselves.

In any theory with this basic architecture, the question arises of what information relevant to the interfaces is present in the syntax itself, and what information is the property of the interface components only. The focus of the present work has been the place of thematic roles in the architecture of the grammar. I have argued that thematic roles are not part of the syntax, and that therefore they are not "assigned" to particular positions. Instead, thematic roles are (parts of) the meanings of particular functional heads in the thematic domain, which are introduced at the LF interface in a process analogous to Vocabulary Insertion.

In this concluding chapter, I summarize in section 8.1 how the previous chapters develop this argument. In 8.2, I describe some directions in which this work should be extended, focussing on aspectual auxiliary uses of HAVE and BE, and existential uses of HAVE. This section ends with a list of questions which the present work has left open–some of these are old questions concerning predicative possession that the present approach has failed to address, others are new questions that have been brought into relief by the proposal. Section 8.3 is a general conclusion.

8.1   Summary of the Proposal and Arguments

Chapter 1 began by laying out why the topic of predicative possession has received so much attention in the syntactic and semantic literature. I argued that much of this literature revolves around two main puzzles, which I dubbed the too-many-meanings puzzle and the too-many-(surface)-structures puzzle.

(1)   *The Too-Many-Meanings Puzzle*

        How can one possession structure have so many different meanings in a given language?

(2)   *The Too-Many-(Surface)-Structures Puzzle*

        How can it be that the same set of possessive meanings is realized on the surface in so many syntactically different ways across languages?

I claimed that these puzzles can both be solved by the following theoretical ideas:

(3)   *Theoretical Claims*

        a.   Thematic roles are not syntactic features; instead they are (parts of) the meanings of functional heads, relevant only in the semantic component.

        b.   Functional heads can vary within and across languages with respect to whether they require a specifier or not.

        c.   Heads can be semantically null or contentful at the LF interface (that is, they may or may not introduce additional entailments of their own), just as they can be phonologically covert or overt at the PF interface.

Of these, only (3c) is relatively unfamiliar, but it has been motivated in numerous recent works on argument structure, including Alexiadou, Anagnostopoulou, and Schäfer (2014); Schäfer (2008); and Wood (2015). The analyses developed in this book strengthen this idea. As Wood (2015) discusses, an important result of combining the claims in (3) is that they make the notions "syntactic argument of head X", and "semantic argument of head X" independent of each other. This is so because a meaningful head X might occur in a derivation, and yet fail to take a specifier in the syntax. If this occurs, then a DP merged higher up in the structure might end up "going in" as the missing argument of the function contributed by X, despite that DP not being in XP's specifier. This possibility, which I have referred to as *delayed gratification*, is depicted in (4). Here, the DP is *syntactically* an argument of Y, since it is merged in spec-YP; yet *semantically* it is an argument of head X.

(4)   *Delayed Gratification*

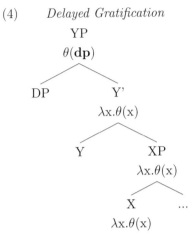

Of course, if XP did happen to take a specifier in the syntactic derivation, the semantic composition would have had the same result but would have occurred in a more familiar fashion. I referred to this more familiar situation, in which a thematic role is satiated by an argument in the specifier of the head that introduced it, as *instant gratification*. This is depicted in (5).

(5)   *Instant Gratification*

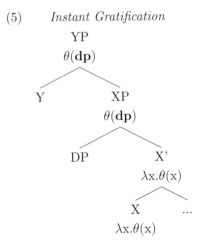

Mechanisms very like delayed gratification have been a feature of LFG (Alsina 1996; Bresnan 2001), HPSG (Sag, Wasow, and Bender 2003), and other non-movement-based theories (Jacobson 1990) for some time, where they are used to analyze raising and control constructions. This does not mean that delayed gratification is redundant with raising and control, however. While similar in its thematic

consequences, delayed gratification has very different syntactic consequences than
raising or control in the context of the present theory. This is because raising and
control entail that there is a syntactically present occurrence of an argument in the
lower A-position. This is not the case in delayed gratification, as can be seen by
comparing (4) with (6).

(6)   *Raising and Control*

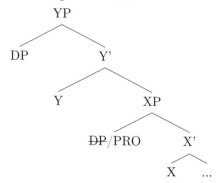

Hence, delayed gratification makes different predictions than raising and control,
and this book (especially Chapters 3 and 4) has presented evidence that all three
are necessary.

Having introduced delayed gratification and how its existence follows from the
claims in (3), I showed how its existence yields instant answers to both the too-
many-meanings puzzle and the too-many-(surface)-structures puzzle, once we adopt
four long-standing and well-motivated claims concerning the syntactic and semantic
properties of copulas and of possession relations.

(7)   *Syntax and Semantics of Possession Relations and Copulas*

   a. Possession is fundamentally a relationship between two DPs–the posses-
      sor and the possessee. (Szabolcsi 1981, 1994; Kayne 1993; Partee 1999).

   b. To link such a relation to tense, clause type, etc., one needs a copula–a
      dummy verb.

   c. Copulas exist to "sentencify" fundamentally non-sentence meanings
      (Pustet 2003; Tham 2013).

   d. The copula is realized as HAVE if the rest of the structure is transitive
      (Hoekstra 1994); it will be realized as BE otherwise. A structure is tran-
      sitive if and only if it contains a Voice head that both introduces an
      external argument and bears phi-features with which it licenses some
      DP in its complement domain.

As mentioned, all of (7a)-(7d) have appeared in many guises in previous literature. My contribution is to show that putting them together with (3) yields novel and promising solutions to both of the puzzles that have made predicative possession such a vexed topic.

(8)   *Solution to the Too-Many-Meanings Puzzle*

Possession constructions can mean so many things because they involve "sentencifying" a meaning that comes from inside DP. There are many subtypes of such meaning, and they do not form a semantic natural class. These meanings pattern together because they are a *syntactic* natural class: they are all introduced by syntactic heads inside DP.

(9)   *Solution to the Too-Many-(Surface)-Structures Puzzle*

Possession sentences involve a meaningless v head. Since it lacks a root and introduces no eventuality variable, this head makes no semantic demands on the surrounding structure. This means that syntax alone gets to decide where the possessor is introduced. Possession relations originate inside a DP (embedded) in the complement of this v. Since the possession relation originates low, Universal Grammar can choose from any position in the VoiceP as the first-merge position of the possessor.

The solution to the too-many-(surface)-structures puzzle in (9) makes rather different predictions about what the typology of possession sentences should look like than the standard solution to this puzzle in the generative literature–the Freeze/Kayne tradition. Two expectations that my approach gives rise to, but are incompatible with the Freeze/Kayne tradition, are as follows:

(10)   *Predictions of the Present Approach*

a.   Possession constructions can vary in the place in the structure where the possessor is introduced.

b.   The different ways of building possession sentences permitted by (a.) could have somewhat different (albeit potentially overlapping) meanings, depending on the semantic contributions of the pieces that make them up.

Chapter 2 reviews recent literature on the too-many-meanings and the too-many-(surface)-structures puzzles, focussing on developments from the 1990s onward. With respect to the too-many-(surface)-structures puzzle, I noted a general trend in the recent syntax literature in favor of the idea that different possession constructions at least sometimes have different underlying argument structures, a trend the present work carries to its logical conclusion. I also examined various approaches to the too-many-meanings puzzle, arguing that the most successful ones are those that take HAVE and BE to make no thematic contribution, a position adopted in this book, albeit in a more extreme form than has been previously entertained.

After the literature review in Chapter 2, I proceeded in Chapter 3 to a series of existence proofs that the predictions in (10) are correct. The existence proofs come from a series of very different BE constructions in two Quechua languages, with the data coming from novel fieldwork on Cochabamba Quechua (Bolivia) and Santiago del Estero Quechua (Argentina). As well as its theoretical import, this chapter provides the most detailed description of predicative possession in these (or any other) Quechua languages to date. I showed that Cochabamba Quechua exhibits an alternation between a BE-based possession construction very much like the Hungarian construction made famous by Szabolcsi (1981), and another construction involving the same existential verb plus an applicative head. These constructions, referred to respectively as the BE construction and the BE-APPL construction, turn out to be identical in terms of the subtypes of possession relation that they can and cannot express. Despite this, I showed that certain morphosyntactic differences between the two constructions are best accounted for if the possessor is introduced inside the possessed DP in the BE construction, but in the specifier of ApplP in the BE-APPL construction, thus providing an existence proof for (10a). Next, I compared the BE-APPL construction in Cochabamba Quechua to a identical-looking possession construction in its near relative, Santiago del Estero Quechua. Despite the superficial similarities, the two constructions turn out to differ widely across the two dialects in the types of possession relation they can express. I traced this difference partly to differences in the copula system of the two dialects, which initially conceals the fact that the BE-APPL construction is a predicate locative construction in Santiago del Estero Quechua, as opposed to an existential construction as it is in Cochabamba Quechua. The two constructions thus involve somewhat different (but overlapping) sets of syntactic pieces being put together in slightly different ways, yielding striking semantic differences–whence the existence proof for (10b). Finally, the chapter closed by showing that Santiago del Estero Quechua is a HAVE language whereas Cochabamba Quechua is not, and speculated, in the spirit of micro-comparative syntax, on what other syntactic properties might go along with this difference.

Chapter 4 turned away from the domain of BE and towards HAVE, in particular *have* in English, showing how the present proposal allows much of the main verb *have* paradigm to be unified under a single analysis. The properties of both possessive and non-possessive uses of HAVE follow straightforwardly–HAVE simply

passes the denotation of its complement up the tree, and Voice is interpreted either
expletively (if its complement denotes an unsaturated relation) or as introducing
an external role (agent, holder, or engineer) if its complement denotes a predicate
of eventualities. This accounts for a number of properties of causative, experiencer,
and light-verb *have* sentences, including Belvin's (1996) observation that *have*'s
status as stative or eventive is inherited from its complement. English *have* has
eventive experiencer and engineer uses involving an embedded bare infinitive, which
are absent from other HAVE languages, and I considered some reasons why English
might differ from other languages in these respects. Finally, I sketched an account
of languages that exhibit more than one transitive HAVE verb, drawing heavily on
joint work with Einar Freyr Sigurðsson and Jim Wood (Myler, E.F. Sigurðsson, and
Wood 2014, in progress).

   In Chapter 5, I discussed the consequences of the analysis of HAVE presented
in Chapter 4. I pointed out two phenomena with respect to which my analysis
makes very different predictions than the Freeze/Kayne tradition on HAVE. The
Freeze/Kayne tradition predicts that the definiteness effects found in certain types
of HAVE sentence should match up with the definiteness effects found in existential
sentences within and across languages, because it reduces HAVE to the same syntax
and semantics as existential sentences. The Freeze/Kayne tradition also predicts
that HAVE should pattern like an unaccusative verb, rather than a transitive one.
In both cases, the data come down against the Freeze/Kayne tradition. I argued
that definiteness effects in HAVE sentences are a species of composition problem:
definite determiners and strong quantifiers bind off the variables in an open relation, stopping delayed gratification of a possessor role from inside DP. On the other
hand, definiteness effects in existentials involving definite articles, demonstratives,
and proper names seem to be caused by information structural problems, to judge
by a growing consensus in the recent literature on them. With respect to the prediction that HAVE should pattern like an unaccusative, I showed that the traditional
argument for this latter position (that HAVE verbs passivize poorly) turns out not
to be true across the board. Moreover, certain other expectations that the unaccusative analysis of HAVE gives rise to (with respect to auxiliary selection and the
preservation of DP-internal idioms in HAVE sentences) are simply not met upon
close investigation.

   In Chapter 6, I turned to a set of constructions that Stassen (2009) has called
Predicativization, which involves the possessee being marked by a derivational morpheme appearing as the predicate in a copular construction of which the possessor
is the subject. In order to show that this phenomenon cannot be reduced to other,
more familiar subtypes of BE construction, I took a close look at a phenomenon

found in all Quechua dialects (although my discussion of it focussed on Cochabamba Quechua), namely, the *-yoq* construction. I argued, updating and defending a traditional analysis in the Quechua literature, that this construction involved the eponymous suffix merging with the possessee to create a predicate nominal, which could then be predicated of the possessor in a copular construction to yield a possession sentence. I further claimed, following Nevins and Myler (2014, submitted), that the *-ed* of English *Sarah is brown-eyed* is a variant of the same phenomenon, which is also found in Dutch, German, and Hungarian. I identified several parameters of variation in Predicativization, and pointed out a generalization that correlates the size of the DP substructure selected by the Predicativizing morpheme with the semantic subtypes of possession relation that they can express. This chapter thus validates both predictions in (10) simultaneously.

Chapter 7 aims to sketch how the present approach might extend to the class of WITH-Possessives. I adopted a syntactic approach along the lines of Levinson (2011), according to which WITH-Possessives are not related to other BE-based possession constructions by movement, but are instead what they look like: a predicative copular construction with a PP predicate. Via a comparison of the Icelandic WITH-Possessive with those found in Bantu, I showed that such constructions vary as to whether the WITH piece retains its lexical semantics of accompaniment. If it does, as in Icelandic, then the set of possession relations that the structure as a whole can express will be restricted to those compatible with these semantics. WITH-Possessives of this sort therefore constitute another case showing that possession sentences can have different meanings determined by the pieces that make them up.

8.2   Areas for Extension

Insofar as the analyses in the previous chapters are successful, they constitute a strong empirical argument that expelling thematic roles from the syntax yields a more successful theory of argument structure. However, many important questions concerning two of the main players, HAVE and BE, have been left open. Two prominent ones are what the present perspective has to say about the use of HAVE and BE as auxiliary verbs, and the use of HAVE as an existential verb. Some programmatic remarks on these topics are made in the next two subsections. There are, in addition, many other questions I had hoped to address before embarking on the present work, or which arose during the preparation of it, which I have been forced to set aside for lack of space, or time, or insight. The final subsection simply lays out these questions, which constitute a gauntlet thrown down to my future self and to others.

8.2.1   Prospects for an Extension to BE and HAVE as Aspectual Auxiliaries

The most widely-adopted approach to auxiliary HAVE and BE in the generative literature goes back to Kayne (1993/2000), and exploits his proposal that HAVE results from the incorporation of an adpositional element into BE. Since I have proposed the abandonment of this P Incorporation account in the domain of predicative possession, it is fair to ask what I intend to replace it with in the domain of aspectual auxiliaries.

I agree with Kayne (1993/2000) that it is desirable to maintain a unified analysis of HAVE and BE across the auxiliary and the possession domains. If this is to be achieved from the perspective of my proposal, then it will be necessary to find some way to motivate the idea that there is in fact a transitive Voice head local to auxiliary v when HAVE is used as an auxiliary. For languages that have a HAVE/BE alternation dictated by the argument structure of the verb, one might suggest structures of the sort seen below in (11) and (12).[1] Since the rule of Vocabulary Insertion that selects HAVE merely requires the local presence of a transitive Voice head, it will apply to v_{AUX} in (11) by virtue of the fact that its complement is a transitive VoiceP. On the other hand, BE will be spelled out for v_{AUX} in (12), because the VoiceP below it is not transitive. Problems arise, however, from the fact that unergative verbs also select HAVE in languages like French. Recall that in the domain of copulas BE clearly is insertable in unergative contexts (Cinque 1990a; Harves 2002), and for this reason I have claimed that both an external argument *and* the presence of phi-features on Voice is necessary for the insertion of HAVE rather than BE. The selection of HAVE in unergative auxiliary contexts would remain a mystery on this approach, therefore.[2]

---

1. For present purposes it does not matter whether the v_{AUX}s in the structures to come are part of the numeration, or are inserted in the derivation to PF in order to rescue stranded features, as on Bjorkman's (2011) analysis of auxiliaries. So long as this PF insertion precedes Vocabulary Insertion, and it is clear that this is what Bjorkman intends, the same issues will arise.

2. A reviewer points out that this problem disappears if unergatives are, following Hale and Keyser (1993), hidden transitives. However, there are various arguments against this approach–see Rimel (2012); Preminger (2009). In addition, this solution is incompatible with my analysis of main verb HAVE and BE; recall that unergative configurations (including ones involving predicate nominals and a subset of adjectives) trigger BE.

(11)   Jean a   mangé le pain. (French)
        Jean has eaten   the bread
        'John ate the bread.'

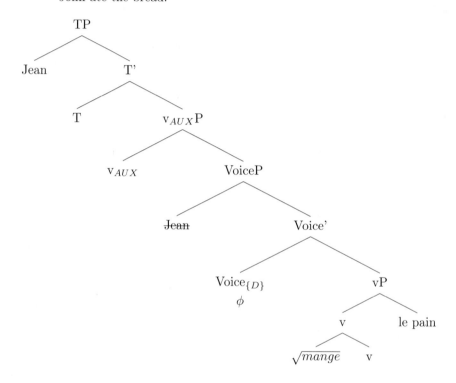

(12)   Jean est mort. (French)
         Jean is   died

         'John died.'

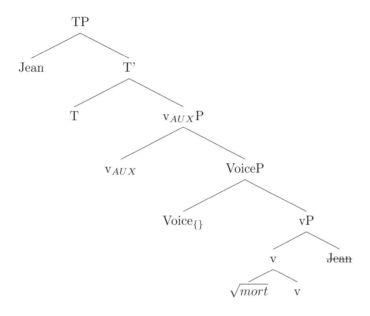

(13)   Jean {a/*est} dansé. (French)
         Jean has/is   danced

         'John danced.'

Another problem for the above approach is what to do about languages that
exhibit only HAVE in the auxiliary system, despite the existence of both HAVE and
BE elsewhere in the language. English and Spanish are familiar languages of this very
sort. The present approach will have to assume that the perfect in languages like
English and Spanish has a somewhat different structure than it does in languages of
the French kind. While this might seem undesirable, it seems more plausible in light
of my conclusion that there are many ways in which possession sentences can be
built and interpreted across languages. If this is true in the domain of possession,
then it is at least possible that it will turn out to be true in the domain of the

perfect also.[3] Hence, it could be the case that the perfect in languages like English and Spanish is structured as in (14).

The SOMETHING in (14) will have to be of some category other than DP, so that it does not intervene between the subject and spec-TP for the purposes of minimality. It will also have to be assumed in consequence that Voice's specifier requirement is not always for something of category D. It may ultimately be possible to make a plausible hypothesis about the identity of this SOMETHING. For instance, Demirdache and Uribe-Etxebarria (2000) claim that the perfect involves relating the reference time to the event time in some way. While these authors claim that an adpositional element is responsible for mediating this relation, one could imagine instead postulating that Voice is capable of mediating this relation–in which case, the SOMETHING in (14) would be a syntactic reification of the reference time.

(14)   The vase has broken.

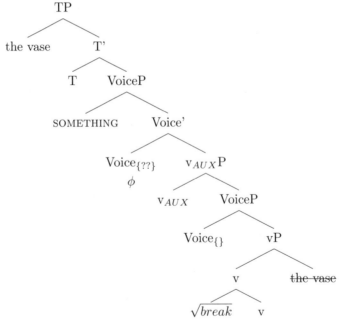

Finally, either one of the structures in (14) or (11) could feed into an account of Romance languages in which auxiliary selection is dependent upon the phi-features

---

3. I will also note that there is precedent for assigning slightly different structures to the perfect in different languages in Kayne's (1993/2000) approach, in which one parameter of variation is the size of the clausal substructure embedded inside the participle.

of the subject. Coon and Preminger (2012), building on Kayne's (1993/2000) P Incorporation analysis, make a proposal for the most common system of this sort, in which 1st and 2nd person subjects require BE and the 3rd person requires HAVE. They suggest that such systems are caused by the presence of a probe π, specified for [+Participant] features, which occurs inbetween v_{AUX} and a lower adposition, blocking incorporation of P into v_{AUX}. This idea can be adapted into the present approach–the same probe could break the locality between Voice and v_{AUX}, preventing its being spelled out as HAVE.

The foregoing is inadequate on a number of counts, but I will have to leave the development of a more satisfying account of auxiliary HAVE and BE for the future.

8.2.2   A Sketch of an Extension to HAVE in Existential Constructions

The structure of existential BE sentences has been alluded to at various points in this work. Throughout, I have adopted the approach of Tremblay (1991), Williams (1994), and Hazout (2004), with inconsequential notational differences.

(15)   There is no tea.

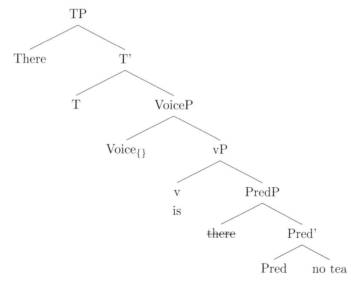

However, many languages that exhibit HAVE in possession contexts and BE in predicative copula contexts use HAVE rather than BE as their existential verb.

(16)   *HAVE in Existentials*

    a.   Na masa-ta ima sirene. (Bulgarian)
        On table-the has cheese
        'There is cheese on the table.'   (Błaszczak 2007, 326)

    b.   Il y   a   du   fromage sur la   table. (French)
        It there has of.the cheese   on the table
        'There is cheese on the table.'

What I would like to claim here is that French is wearing UG on its sleeve when it comes to the structure of HAVE existentials. As well as the clitic *y*, which I will follow Kayne (2008) in taking to be parallel to English *there* (and hence in spec-PredP in my approach), it displays a subject clitic *il*. My claim is that this clitic is first-merged in the specifier of transitive VoiceP, and that this is why French displays HAVE in its existentials. Languages like Bulgarian presumably have the same structure, except that the correspondent of *il* (and of *y*) is silent.[4] (Note that the surface position of *y* will be derived via clitic movement, not depicted in (17).) The usual comparative syntactic questions arise, all of which will be left unanswered here. Of particular interest is why only some languages apparently require the additional expletive in (17), whereas others do not. It will also be important to grapple with the intricate micro-comparative facts revealed by recent work on existentials and possession sentences in Romance (Bentley, Ciconte and, Cruschina 2015; Kayne 2008). Kayne (2008, 204), for example, notes an implicational relationship between having a "locative" pronoun in possession sentences and having BE (rather than HAVE) in existentials.

---

4. A question arises here regarding whether the expletive in spec-VoiceP has to be *it*-like in being fully specified for phi-features, and whether the expletive in spec-PredP always has to be *there*-like in not being fully specified. It has occasionally been indirectly claimed that the answer to these questions is yes–in particular, by Schoorlemmer (2007), who suggests that verb agreement with the associate happens only in BE existentials, and that lack of such agreement happens only in HAVE existentials. As Schoorlemmer acknowledges, however, there are counter-examples in both directions. African American Vernacular English famously uses the *it* expletive along with BE in its existentials. A counter-example from the other direction comes from some Spanish varieties, which have number agreement in existential HAVE sentences (in some such dialects, this agreement is restricted to non-present tenses).

(i)   Había-n   dos hombres. (Some Spanish)
    have.IMPF-PL two men
    'There were two men.'

(17)   *Existential HAVE*

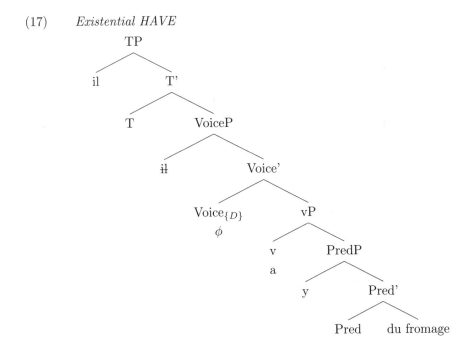

8.2.3   Some Open Questions

In this work, I have made a detailed case for the idea that possession sentences vary in their argument structure. This variation seems to mirror the variation in possible copular constructions more generally (Tham 2013), and I have shown how a particular theory of the architecture of the grammar is able to account for this fact. However, it is still unclear why particular languages "choose" to build their possession sentences in the way that they do. In other words, I have not alighted upon a satisfying characterization of what other syntactic properties of a language interact with the structures of their possession sentences. While I continue to hope that micro-comparative work within the Quechua family (and in other families) will shed light on this issue, up to now I have only been able to identify a tentative link, discussed in Chapter 3, between a particular subtype of psych construction and the presence of HAVE. The broader question of the relationship between predicative possession and experiencer predicates, cross-linguistically (Harley 2002; Harves and Kayne 2012; Isačenko 1974; Noonan 1993) remains complicated. So too does the relationship between predicative possession and ditransitives, which I have not been able to discuss in detail here. In Chapter 3, I discussed Richard Kayne's conjecture that all HAVE languages possess at least one preposition. The question of whether this generalization is correct was left open, as was the question of what the correct account is, if so.

In Chapter 4, I offered analyses of engineer *have* sentences like *I had someone wash my car* and of eventive experiencer *have* sentences like *I had someone total my car (on me)*. Noting that HAVE verbs in related languages lack these uses, I offered partially different explanations in each case. For engineer HAVE, I suggested that nearby languages can build the same structures, but happen to spell them out using some light-verb other than HAVE (such as MAKE or LET). On the other hand, I related the availability of eventive experiencer HAVE to the absence of free datives in a language. This predicts that a language could potentially have one but not the other. In contrast, recent work by Richard Kayne argues that the availability both engineer HAVE and eventive experiencer HAVE is tied to the structure of infinitives (in particular, the lack of infinitival morphology in English). In comparing these predictions, we are hampered by the fact that ECM uses of HAVE are not well studied beyond English and nearby languages. Work on HAVE languages beyond Romance and Germanic should be undertaken to address this question. While I have begun this process with the HAVE language Santiago del Estero Quechua, I have insufficient data to present any firm conclusions here (although early indications are that it lacks engineer HAVE and eventive experiencer HAVE). Diachronic work could also potentially be used to investigate the predictions of Kayne's account, since English lost its infinitive morphology during its recorded history.

Chapter 6 developed an account of Predicativization structures that involves four different parameters of variation: (i) the grammatical category of the predicativizing morpheme itself; (ii) whether the complement of that morpheme is an nP or a full DP; (iii) whether a modifier is required; and (iv) whether that modifier can be a whole phrase or is restricted to a single head. Combining these yields a parameter space consisting of 12 distinct types of Predicativization morpheme. In this preliminary study involving Quechua, Hungarian, and three West Germanic languages, four of those predicted morpheme types were attested. Future research should try to establish whether the other predicted types really exist. My approach also predicts a correlation between the size of the DP substructure embedded under the relevant categorizing morpheme and the sorts of possession relation that the structure can express–in particular, if a predicativizing morpheme selects nP, it should be restricted to expressing a subset of the inalienable possession relations (and this subset is predicted to exclude kinship). This prediction should be tested in future work as well.

Many corners of the HAVE/BE domain have been left relatively unexplored in this book. For instance, what sort of variation do we find in modal HAVE/BE constructions, and how is their interpretation derived (see Bjorkman and Cowper 2013, 2014 for recent discussion)? Beyond the discussion of perfect auxiliaries earlier in this chapter, we can also wonder about auxiliary constructions beyond the perfect. One observation to be made here is that, while BE and HAVE are used as perfect auxiliaries in many languages, the progressive auxiliary is almost always BE, with the partial exception of Basque (which has HAVE with progressives with verbs that otherwise take HAVE as an auxiliary, as Richard Kayne points out to me). Is HAVE the sole progressive auxiliary in any language? If not, why not?

An even broader question concerns the relationship of HAVE and BE to other light verbs. The set of v heads entertained in this book–one that introduces an eventuality variable and another (the copula) that does not–radically underdetermines the set of light verbs we can detect. This means that *give, take, make, do, get*, and brethren must be realizations of v in somewhat different structural environments. The question is, what are those environments? While some discussion of this matter as it pertains to GET in Germanic has been carried out in work from the same general perspective as the present work (Sigurðsson and Wood 2013), much of this domain remains to be explored (though see also van Urk 2012; Richards 2001). The complexity of these questions is thrown into sharp relief by the fact that even closely related languages can differ markedly in the "choice" of light verb employed in particular contexts (British English has *have* in many light-verb constructions that require *take* in American English, for example).

An important syntactico-semantic issue that arises for any theory in which predicative possession is held to "build on top of" attributive possession is how to deal with mismatches between available DP-internal relations and what is possible in HAVE/BE sentences. I addressed a corner of this question during the discussion of complex event nominals in Chapter 4, but much remains to be understood. For example, the relations that can be conveyed by a DP like *John's car* go significantly beyond ownership (*the car that John made, the car that John can't stop talking about*, etc.). Not all of these relations are equally available for a sentence like *John has a car*, however. It might be that those relations that cannot be expressed in predicative possession involve a syntax which forces projection of the possessor inside DP (thereby forbidding delayed gratification). This entails abandoning the widespread notion, that I have implicitly rejected throughout this work, that the multiple interpretations of phrases like *John's car* are a matter of a single vague semantic possession relation whose exact nature is filled in by pragmatics (see Adger 2013 for independent criticisms of this idea). If this were the case, there would be no way to explain why predicative possession and attributive possession differ in the observed way. Instead, the multiple interpretations of *John's car* must come from massive structural ambiguity, involving different syntactic structures, only some of which are able to feed the sort of delayed gratification that gives rise to predicative possession sentences. The question of what these structures are is another crucial question for the future.

8.3   General Conclusion

In this book, I have argued for a particular view on the place of thematic roles in the architecture of the grammar. I have shown that two major puzzles posed by possession sentences, the too-many-meanings puzzle and the too-many-(surface)-structures puzzle, can be solved if the view expressed in (18) is embraced.

(18)   *Thematic Roles are not "Assigned" Syntactically to Particular Positions*

   Thematic roles, while directly associated with particular terminal nodes in syntax, are not themselves features assigned by syntax (contra Hornstein (1999) et seq.). Instead, thematic-roles are (part of) the meaning of syntactic terminal nodes. Therefore, there is a certain amount of independence between the notion "syntactic argument of head X" and "semantic argument of head X."

Several theories of grammar are already able to accommodate (18). The central conclusion of this book is that all grammatical theories must.

Appendix: Existential BE-based Possession Constructions in the System of Francez (2009)

The main body of this book assumes, as a theory of convenience, an analysis of existentials adapted from Williams (1994). As a reviewer points out, this analysis is at variance with many of the semantic conclusions of Francez (2007, 2009, 2010). Francez (2009), in particular, points out a number of facts concerning the scope of quantifiers in codas which are not readily explained on earlier analyses. The reader might therefore wonder whether the analyses of existential BE-based possession constructions put forth in this book are already fatally undermined. The question is particularly pressing with respect to the analyses of the Cochabamba Quechua constructions of Chapter 3, which are crucial existence proofs of some of the predictions of my approach.

   It is the purpose of this appendix to show that the syntactic analyses of these constructions in Chapter 3 are, in fact, compatible with Francez's semantics, given certain non-crucial changes to my assumptions about the semantic contributions of the relevant pieces. First, though, a summary of Francez's analysis is called for.

Francez (2009)

Amongst the core explananda of Francez's (2009) analysis are some observations concerning the scopal interaction of quantified pivots and quantified codas, and of quantified codas with each other. Quantifiers inside codas invariably outscope quantifiers in the pivot, as shown in (1a). In addition, when multiple codas containing quantifiers are present, outer codas always scope over inner ones, as seen in (1b). The examples are from Francez (2009, 2, his (2)).

   (1)   a.   There was exactly one mutiny on most ships.
         b.   There was exactly one mutiny on most ships in every fleet.

   Francez's explanation for (1a) begins with the idea that the pivot itself provides the core meaning of an existential construction, so that neither the copula nor the expletive (in languages that have these overtly) make any contribution. In particular, the pivot in an existential construction is a second-order predicate, as follows (Francez 2009, 8, his (13)). The variable τ here stands for any simple type. $\mathbf{Q}$ is a relation between sets, filled in by the determiner inside the pivot. N represents the denotation of the head noun in the pivot. Finally, P represents the context set with respect to which the existential claim is evaluated. It is ultimately filled in by the coda if there is one, and if not by an implicit argument C whose content is determined pragmatically (see Francez 2010 for an explicit account of this pragmatic determination). The schema in (2) is given a specific instantiation in (3) (Francez 2009, 8, his (14)). Following the inclusion of the implicit argument C, the result is (4), which is true if the intersection of the set of things that are bread and the set of things that are in the current discourse context is null. Note that C is not present in syntax for Francez, but is rather introduced by a special semantic rule called *contextualization* (Francez 2009, 9, his (16)).

   (2) $[\![\text{there be NP}]\!] = [\![\text{NP}]\!] = \lambda P_{\langle \tau, t \rangle}.[\mathbf{Q}_{\langle \langle \tau, t \rangle, \langle \langle \tau, t \rangle, t \rangle \rangle}(N_{\tau, t}, P)]$

   (3) $[\![\text{there is no bread}]\!] = \lambda P_{\langle e, t \rangle}.[\mathbf{no}_{\langle \langle e, t \rangle, \langle \langle e, t \rangle, t \rangle \rangle}(\lambda \text{x}.[\text{bread(x)}], P)]$

   (4) $[\![\text{there is no bread}]\!]_{contextualized}$
         $= \lambda P_{\langle e, t \rangle}.[\mathbf{no}_{\langle \langle e, t \rangle, \langle \langle e, t \rangle, t \rangle \rangle}(\lambda \text{x}.[\text{bread(x)}], P)](C)$
         $= \mathbf{no}(\lambda \text{x}[\text{bread(x)}], C)$

For codas, Francez proposes that they semantically take a second-order predicate of the sort schematized in (2) as their argument, and end up supplying the argument that in (4) is saturated by C. Through particular assumptions about the prepositions that head codas, Francez is able to derive the fact that quantified codas always outscope quantified pivots. This works as follows. Take the sentence in (5).

(5)   There is a drummer in every punk band.

The core existential predication in this sentence, in accordance with the schema in (2), has the following interpretation (Francez 2009, 12, his (23)):

(6) $[\![\text{there is a drummer}]\!]=[\![\text{a drummer}]\!]=\lambda P_{\langle e,t\rangle}.[\mathbf{a}(\lambda \text{x}.[\text{drummer(x)}], P)]$.

The DP *every punk band* has an analogous denotation (Francez 2009, 12, from his (29)).

(7) $[\![\text{every punk band}]\!]=\lambda P_{\langle e,t\rangle}.[\mathbf{every}(\lambda \text{x}.[\mathbf{PB}(\text{x})], P)]$.

These two denotations are related by a preposition, *in* in this case, which Francez (2009, 12, from his (29)) assigns a polymorphic denotation.

(8) $[\![\text{in}]\!]=\lambda P_{\langle\langle\tau,t\rangle,t\rangle}\lambda Q_{\langle\langle\tau,t\rangle,t\rangle}\lambda C.[P^{c}(\lambda y\tau[Q(\lambda \text{x}\tau[\text{in(x,y)}])])]$

In first composes with *every punk band*, yielding the result in (9).

(9) $[\![\text{in every punk band}]\!]=\lambda Q_{\langle\langle e,t\rangle,t\rangle}\lambda C.[\mathbf{every}^{c}(\lambda x_{e}.[\mathbf{PB}(x)],\lambda y[Q(\lambda \text{x}[\text{in(x,y)}])])]$

Notice that, crucially, *every* itself ends up scoping over the variable Q here. When the denotation in (9) takes that in (6), *every* therefore inevitably ends up taking scope over the quantifier in the pivot, as desired.

(10) $[\![\text{There is a drummer in every punk band}]\!]=$
         $[\![\text{in every punk band}]\!]([\![\text{there is a drummer}]\!])=$
         $\lambda Q_{\langle\langle e,t\rangle,t\rangle}\lambda C.[\mathbf{every}^{c}(\lambda x_{e}[\mathbf{PB}(x)],\lambda y[Q(\lambda u[in(u,y)])])](\lambda P_{\langle e,t\rangle}.[\mathbf{a}(\lambda \text{z}.[\text{drummer(z)}],$
         $P)])$
         $=\lambda C[\mathbf{every}^{c}(\lambda x[\mathbf{PB}(\text{x})],\lambda y[\mathbf{a}(\lambda \text{z}[\text{drummer(z)}],\lambda u[\text{in(u,y)}])])]$

The remaining variable C can either itself undergo contextualization, or else end up being saturated after the addition of another coda. Any such additional coda will inevitably end up outscoping all of the quantifiers in the structure so far, and it is in this way that Francez accounts for the scopal interaction of stacked codas exemplified in (1b). The result of applying contextualization to (10) is shown in (11).

(11) $\mathbf{every}(\lambda \text{x}[\mathbf{PB}(\text{x}) \ \& \ C^{*}(\text{x})],\lambda y[\mathbf{a}(\lambda \text{z}[\text{drummer(z)}],\lambda u[\text{in(u,y)}])])$

This correctly predicts that sentence (5) is true if and only if every punk band in the contextually relevant domain is such that it has a drummer in it.

With this background in hand, we are now in a position to understand how my analyses of the BE construction and the BE-APPL construction in Cochabamba Quechua might be reconciled with Francez's account of existential sentences.

Cochabamba Quechua BE and BE-APPL Constructions in a Francez-style System

Recall the syntax assigned to these two constructions in Chapter 3, partially inspired by Hastings (2004):

(12)

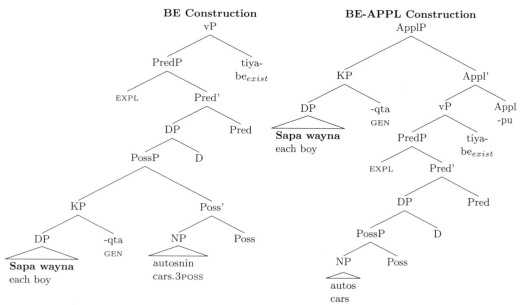

The intuition I would like to pursue here is that the possessor in existential BE-based possession constructions, in Quechua and more generally, semantically ends up taking on the same role as a coda. This involves assuming the following denotations for the pieces involved:

(13)   a. $[\![\text{autos}]\!]=\lambda P_{\langle e,t\rangle}.[\exists x.car(x)\wedge P(x)]$

       b. $[\![\text{Poss}]\!]=\lambda P_{\langle\langle e,t\rangle t\rangle}\lambda u.P(\lambda x.Poss(u,z,e))$

       c. $[\![\text{GEN}]\!]=\lambda P_{\langle\langle e,t\rangle t\rangle}.\lambda R_{\langle e\langle s,t\rangle\rangle}.\lambda C.P^{C}(\lambda z.\exists e.R(z)(e))$

       d. $[\![\text{sapa wayna}]\!]=\lambda P_{\langle e,t\rangle}.[\forall y.boy(y)\rightarrow P(y)]$

       e. $[\![\text{Pred}]\!]=\lambda x.x$

       f. $[\![\text{EXPL}]\!]=\lambda x.x$

       g. $[\![\text{tiya-}]\!]=\lambda x.x$

       h. $[\![\text{-pu}]\!]=\lambda x.x$

Since the material in (13e)-(13h) is all expletive, the interpretation of both constructions will involve applying GEN to *sapa wayna*, applying Poss to *autos*, and then applying the output of the first combination to the output of the second combination, as follows:

(14)   〚sapa wayna-GEN〛(〚autos-Poss〛)
=$\lambda R_{\langle e \langle s,t \rangle \rangle}.\lambda C.\mathbf{every}^C(\lambda z.\text{boy}(z))(\lambda z.\exists e.R(z)(e))(\lambda u.\lambda e.\exists x.\text{car}(x) \wedge \text{Poss}(u,x,e))$

=$\lambda C.\mathbf{every}^C(\lambda z.\text{boy}(z))(\lambda z.\exists e.\lambda u.\lambda e.\exists x.\text{car}(x) \wedge \text{Poss}(u,x,e))(z)(e))$

= $\lambda C.\mathbf{every}^C(\lambda z.\text{boy}(z))(\lambda z.\exists e.\exists x.\text{car}(x) \wedge \text{Poss}(z,x,e))$

Expanding the denotation of **every** and applying contextualization yields the following result, the last line of which says "for all boys in the discourse context, there is a possession state and a car such that the boy stands in that state to that car." This is the desired interpretation.

(15) $\forall y.[\lambda z.[\text{boy}(z) \wedge C^*](y) \rightarrow \lambda z.[\exists e.\exists x.\text{car}(x) \wedge \text{Poss}(z,x,e)]\ (y)]$
= $\forall y.[\text{boy}(y) \wedge C^* \rightarrow \exists e.\exists x.\text{car}(x) \wedge \text{Poss}(y,x,e)]$

An interesting consequence of this implementation is that a quantified possessor will always take scope over a quantifier in the possessee, even if the possessor is merged inside the Possessee DP (as it is, by hypothesis, in the BE construction). This thus resolves an important problem left open in the main text–namely, how to explain why quantifiers in the possessee can never outscope a quantifier in the possessor of the BE construction (a similar issue arises in the Hungarian equivalent of the BE construction–see Szabolcsi 1981, 1983, 1994 for discussion).

Bibliography

[1] Abbott, Barbara. 1997. Definiteness and Existentials. *Language* 73:103-108.

[2] Abbott, Miriam. 1991. Macushi. In Derbyshire, Desmond C., and Geoffrey K. Pullum (eds.). *Handbook of Amazonian Languages, Vol. 3.* 23-160. New York: Mouton de Gruyter.

[3] Ackerman, Farrell, and Adele E. Goldberg. 1996. Constraints on Adjectival Past Participles. In Adele E. Goldberg (ed.). *Conceptual Structure, Discourse and Language.* Stanford, CA: CSLI Publications.

[4] Adelaar, Willem F.H. 1994. Review of *A Grammar of Huallaga (Huánuco) Quechua, by David John Weber.* International Journal of American Linguistics 60(1):83-87.

[5] Adelaar, Willem F.H with Pieter Muysken. 2004. *The Languages of the Andes.* Cambridge: Cambridge University Press.

[6] Adger, David. 2013. *A Syntax of Substance.* Cambridge, MA: MIT Press.

[7] Adger, David, and Gillian Ramchand. 2003. Predication and Equation. *Linguistic Inquiry* 34.3:325-359.

[8] Adger, David, and Gillian Ramchand. 2006. Psych nouns and the structure of predication. In C. Davis, A. Deal, and Y. Zabbal (eds.). *Proceedings of NELS 36:* 89-102.

[9] Aikhenvald, Alexandra Y. and R. M. W. Dixon. 2012. *Possession and Ownership.* Oxford: Oxford University Press.

[10] Albarracín, Lelia Inés. 2011. *La Quichua: Gramática, Ejercicios y Diccionario Quichua-Castellano. Volumen 2.* Buenos Aires: Editorial Dunken.

[11] Albarracín, Lelia Inés, and Jorge R. Alderetes. 2013. El sufijo *-pu* en el quichua de Santiago del Estero. Talk given at *III Encuentro de Lenguas Indígenas Americanas*, San Carlos de Bariloche, May 2013.

[12] Alderetes, Jorge R. 2001. *El Quichua de Santiago del Estero. Gramática y Vocabulario.* (ucumán: Universidad Nacional de Tucumán, Facultad de Filosofía y Letras.

[13] Alexiadou, Artemis, and Elena Anagnostopoulou. 1998. Parametrizing AGR: Word order, verb-movement and EPP checking. *Natural Language & Linguistic Theory* 16:491-539.

[14] Alexiadou, Artemis, and Jane Grimshaw. 2008. Verbs, nouns and affixation. In Schäfer, Florian (ed.). *Working Papers of the SFB 732 Incremental Specification in Context 01,* 1-16.

[15] Alexiadou, Artemis, and Edit Doron. 2012. The syntactic construction of two non-active Voices: passive and middle. *Journal of Linguistics* 48, 1-34.

[16] Alexiadou, Artemis, Elena Anagnostopoulou, and Florian Schäfer. 2014. *External Arguments in Transitivity Alternations: A Layering Approach.* Oxford: Oxford University Press.

[17] Allen, W. Sidney. 1964. Transitivity and Possession. *Language* 40.3:337-343.

[18] Alsina, Alex. 1996. *The Role of Argument Structure in Grammar: Evidence from Romance.* Stanford: CSLI Publications.

[19] Anagnostopoulou, Elena. 2003. *The Syntax of Ditransitives: Evidence from Clitics.* Mouton: Walter de Gruyter.

[20] Antonov, Anton, and Guillaume Jacques. 2014. Transitive NEED does not imply transitive HAVE: Response to Harves and Kayne 2012. *Linguistic Inquiry* 45:147-158

[21] Aristotle. *Categories.* Available online at http://classics.mit.edu/Aristotle/categories.html.

[22] Aristotle. *Metaphysics.* Available online at http://classics.mit.edu/Aristotle/metaphysics.html.

[23] Arregi, Karlos, Neil Myler, and Bert Vaux. 2013. Number marking in Western Armenian: A non-argument for outwardly-sensitive phonologically conditioned allomorphy. Talk given at *the 87th Annual Meeting of the Linguistic Society of America*, Boston, MA.

[24] Arregi, Karlos, and Andrew Nevins. 2012. *Morphotactics: Basque Auxiliaries and the Structure of Spellout.* Dordrecht: Springer.

[25] Bach, Emmon. 1967. *Have* and *be* in English syntax. *Language* 43.2:462-85.

[26] Baker, Mark. 1985. The Mirror Principle and Morphosyntactic Explanation. *Linguistic Inquiry* 16.3:373-415.

[27] Baker, Mark. 1988a. *Incorporation: A Theory of Grammatical Function Changing.* London: University of Chicago Press.

[28] Baker, Mark. 1988b. Theta theory and the syntax of applicatives in Chichewa. *Natural Language and Linguistic Theory* 6, 353-389.

[29] Baker, Mark. 1997. Thematic Roles and Syntactic Structure. In L. Haegeman (ed.). *Elements of Grammar. Handbook of Generative Syntax.* Dordrecht, Kluwer.

[30] Baker, Mark. 2003. *Lexical Categories: Verbs, Nouns, and Adjectives.* Cambridge: Cambridge University Press.

[31] Baker, Mark. 2008. *The Syntax of Agreement and Concord.* Cambridge: Cambridge University Press.

[32] Baker, Mark, and Ruth Kramer. 2014. Applicative Markers as Agreement with PP in Amharic. Talk given at *NELS 45*, MIT.

[33] Baltin, Mark, and Paul M. Postal. 1996. More on Reanalysis Hypotheses. *Linguistic Inquiry* 27.1:127-145.

[34] Balusu, Rahul. 2014. The overt predicator -*gaa* in Telugu. Talk given at the NYU Syntax Brown Bag.

[35] Barker, Chris. 1995. *Possessive Descriptions.* Stanford, CA: CSLI Publications.

[36] Beavers, John, Elias Ponvert, and Stephen Wechsler. 2009. Possession of a Controlled Substantive: Light 'have' and Other Verbs of Possession. Ms, UT Austin.

[37] Beard, Robert. 1976. Once More on the Analysis of *Ed*-Adjectives. *Journal of Linguistics* 12.1:155-157.

[38] Becker, Misha. 2004. *Is* isn't *be. Lingua* 114:399-418.

[39] Béjar, Susana, and Milan Rezac. 2009. Cyclic Agree. *Linguistic Inquiry* 40:35-73.

[40] Belvin, Robert S. 1996. *Inside Events: The Non-Possessive Meanings of Possession Predicates and the Semantic Conceptualization of Events.* PhD Thesis, University of Southern California.

[41] Belvin, Robert S., and A. Arnaiz. 1994. Imperfective complements of possessive causatives. *LSRL* 24.

[42] Belvin, Robert S., and Marcel den Dikken. 1997. There, happens, to, be, have. *Lingua* 101:151-183.

[43] Bentley, Delia. 2006. *Split Intransitivity in Italian. Empirical Approaches to Language Typology.* Berlin: Mouton de Gruyter.

[44] Bentley, Delia, Francesco Maria Ciconte, and Silvio Cruschina. 2015. *Existentials and Locatives in Romance Dialects of Italy.* Oxford: Oxford University Press.

[45] Benveniste, Emile. 1959. 'Etre' et 'avoir' dans leurs fonctions linguistiques. *Bulletin de la Société Linguistique* 5.

[46] Benveniste, Emile. 1966. *Problèmes de linguistique générale.* Paris: Gallimard.

[47] Berman, Ruth. 1978. *Modern Hebrew Structure.* Tel Aviv: University Publishing Projects.

[48] Bhatt, Rajesh. 1997. Obligation and possession. In *The Proceedings of the UPenn/MIT Workshop on Argument Structure and Aspect, number 32 in MIT Working Papers in Linguistics.*

[49] Bills, Garland D., Bernardo Vallejo C., and Rudolph C. Troike. 1969. *An Introduction to Spoken Bolivian Quechua*. Austin: University of Texas Press.

[50] Bjorkman, Bronwyn. 2011. *BE-ing Default: The Morphosyntax of Auxiliaries*. PhD Thesis: MIT.

[51] Bjorkman, Bronwyn, and Elizabeth Cowper. 2013. Possession and Necessity: From individuals to Worlds. Talk given at *Ling Lunch*, MIT.

[52] Bjorkman, Bronwyn, and Elizabeth Cowper. 2014. Possession and Necessity: From individuals to Worlds. Talk given at the *GLOW 37 Semantics Workshop on Possession*.

[53] Błaszczak, Joanna. 2007. *Phase Syntax: The Polish Genitive of Negation*. Habilitationsschrift: Universität Potsdam.

[54] Bloomfield, Leonard. 1933. *Language*. New York: Halt.

[55] Bobaljik, Jonathan David. 2000. The ins and outs of contextual allomorphy. *University of Maryland Working Papers in Linguistics* 10, 35-71.

[56] Bobaljik, Jonathan David. 2012. *Universals in Comparative Morphology: Suppletion, Superlatives and the Structure of Words*. Cambridge, MA: MIT Press.

[57] Bobaljik, Jonathan David, and Heidi Harley. 2013. Suppletion is local: Evidence from Hiaki. *lingbuzz/001982*.

[58] Bochnak, Ryan, and Lisa Matthewson. (eds.) 2015. *Methodologies in Semantic Fieldwork*. Oxford: Oxford University Press.

[59] Boneh, Nora, and Ivy Sichel. 2010. Deconstructing Possession. *Natural Language & Linguistic Theory* 28:1-40.

[60] Bonet, Eulalia. 1991. *Morphology after Syntax: Pronominal Clitics in Romance*. PhD Dissertation: MIT.

[61] Borer, Hagit. 1984. *Parametric Syntax*. Dordrecht: Foris.

[62] Borer, Hagit. 1996. The Construct in Review. In Jacqueline Lecarme, Jean Lowenstamm, and Ur Shlonsky (eds.). *Studies in Afroasiatic Languages*. The Hague: Holland Academic Graphics.

[63] Borer, Hagit. 2005a. *Structuring Sense Volume 1: In Name Only*. Oxford: Oxford University Press.

[64] Borer, Hagit. 2005b. *Structuring Sense Volume 2: The Normal Course of Events*. Oxford: Oxford University Press.

[65] Borer, Hagit. 2013. *Structuring Sense Volume 3: Taking Form*. Oxford: Oxford University Press.

[66] Bowers, John. 1993. The syntax of predication. *Linguistic Inquiry* 24.4:591-656.

[67] Bowers, John. 2001. Predication. In Christopher Collins and Mark Baltin (eds.). *The Handbook of Contemporary Syntactic Theory*. 299-333. Oxford: Blackwell.

[68] Bowers, John. 2002. Transitivity. *Linguistic Inquiry* 33.2:183-224.

[69] Bravo, Domingo A. 1956. *El quichua santiagueño. Reducto idiomático argentino*. Tucumán: Universidad Nacional de Tucumán.

[70] Bresnan, Joan. 2001. *Lexical-Functional Syntax*. Oxford: Blackwell.

[71] Brillman, Ruth. 2012. Variants: a phi-feature account of lexical, auxiliary and modal alternations. Senior Honors Thesis: NYU.

[72] Brillman, Ruth. 2014.Too tough to see: null operators and hidden movement chains. Generals Paper: MIT.

[73] Bruening, Benjamin. 2010. Double object constructions disguised as prepositional datives. *Linguistic Inquiry* 41: 287-305.

[74] Bruening, Benjamin. 2013. *By* Phrases in Passives and Nominals. *Syntax* 16.1:1-41.

[75] Brugman, Claudia Marlea. 1988. *The syntax and semantics of HAVE and its complements.* Ph.D. Thesis, University of California, Berkeley.

[76] Buck, Carl Darling. 1949. *A Dictionary of Selected Synonyms in the Principal Indo-European Languages: A Contribution to the History of Ideas.* Chicago: University of Chicago Press.

[77] Burzio, Luigi. 1986. *Italian Syntax: A Government and Binding Approach.* Dordrecht: D. Reidel.

[78] Caha, Pavel. 2009. *The nanosyntax of case.* PhD Thesis: University of Tromsø.

[79] Carstens, Vicki, and Michael Diercks. 2010. Paramaterizing Case and Activity: Hyper-raising in Bantu. In *Proceedings of the 40th Annual Meeting of the North East Linguistic Society,* Seda Kan, Claire Moore-Cantwell, Robert Staubs (eds.), 99-118. Amherst: University of Massachusetts Graduate Linguistic Student Association.

[80] Cathcart, MaryEllen. 2011. *Impulsatives: The Syntax and Semantics of Involuntary Desire.* PhD Thesis, University of Delaware.

[81] Cattaneo, Andrea. 2009. *It is All about Clitics: The Case of a Northern Italian Dialect like Bellinzonese.* PhD Thesis, NYU.

[82] Cerrón-Palomino, Rodolfo. 1976. *Gramática Quechua: Junin-Huanca.* Lima: Ministerio de Educación.

[83] Cerrón-Palomino, Rodolfo. 1987. *Lingüística Quechua.* Cuzco, Perú: Centro de Estudios rurales andinos "Bartolomé de las Casas".

[84] Cerrón-Palomino, Rodolfo. 2008. *Quechumara: Estructuras paralelas del quechua y del aimara.* La Paz: Plural editores.

[85] Choi, Incheol, and Stephen Wechsler. 2002. Mixed Categories and Argument Transfer in the Korean light-verb Construction. In Frank van Eynde, Lars Hellan, and Dorothee Beermann (eds.). *Proceedings of the 8th International HPSG Conference, Norwegian University of Science and Technology.* 103-120. Stanford, CA: CSLI Publications.

[86] Chomsky, Noam. 1986. *Barriers.* Cambridge, MA: MIT Press.

[87] Chomsky, Noam. 1994. Bare Phrase Structure. (Cambridge, MA: *MIT Occasional Papers in Linguistics 5.* (MITWPL, Department of Linguistics and Philosophy, MIT)[Published in G. Webelhuth (ed.). 1995. *Government and Binding Theory and the Minimalist Program.* Oxford: Blackwell.]

[88] Chomsky, Noam. 1995. *The Minimalist Program.* Cambridge, MA: MIT Press.

[89] Chomsky, Noam. 2000. Minimalist Inquiries: The Framework. In Roger Martin, David Michaels, and, Juan Uriagareka (eds.). *Step by Step: Essays on minimalist syntax in honor of Howard Lasnik.* 89-153. Cambridge, MA: MIT Press.

[90] Chomsky, Noam. 2001. Derivation by phase. In Kenstowicz, Michael (ed.). *Ken Hale: a Life in Language.* 1-52. Cambridge MA: MIT Press.

[91] Chomsky, Noam. 2008. On Phases. In R. Freidin, C. Otero, and M.L. Zubizarreta (eds.). *Foundational Issues in Linguistic Theory.* 133-166. Cambridge, MA: MIT Press.

[92] Chomsky, Noam. 2013. Problems of Projection. *Lingua* 130:33-49.

[93] Cinque, Guglielmo. 1990a. Ergative adjectives and the lexicalist hypothesis. *Natural Language and Linguistic Theory* 8:1-39.

[94] Cinque, Guglielmo. 1990b. *Types of A-bar Dependencies.* Cambridge MA: MIT Press.

[95] Cinque, Guglielmo. 1999. *Adverbs and Functional Heads: A Cross-linguistic Perspective.* Oxford: Oxford University Press.

[96]   Cinque, Guglielmo. 2006. *Restructuring and Functional Heads*. Oxford: Oxford University Press.

[97]   Citko, Barbara. 2008. Small clauses reconsidered: Not so small and not all alike. *Lingua* 118:261-295.

[98]   Clark, Eve V. 1970. Locationals: A study of 'existential,' 'locative', and 'possessive' sentences. *Stanford University Working Papers in Language Universals* 3:1-36.

[99]   Clark, Eve V. 1978. Locationals: Existential, Locative and Possessive Constructions. In Greenberg, Joseph H. (ed.). *Universals of Human Language Volume 4: Syntax*. 85-126. Stanford, CA: Stanford University Press.

[100] Clark, T. W. 1966. *An Introduction to Nepali*. Cambridge: W. Heffers and Sons.

[101] Cole, Peter. 1982. *Imbabura Quechua*. Amsterdam: North Holland Publishing Company.

[102] Collins, Christopher. 2002. Eliminating Labels. In Samuel Epstein and Daniel Seely (eds.). *Derivation and Explanation in the Minimalist Program*. Oxford: Blackwell.

[103] Collins, Christopher. 2005. A Smuggling Approach to the Passive in English. *Syntax* 8.2:81-120.

[104] Collins, Christopher. 2006. A note on Derivational Morphology. Ms. NYU.

[105] Comrie, Bernard. 1989. *Language Universals and Linguistic Typology, 2nd edn*. Oxford: Basil Blackwell.

[106] Coombs Lynch, David, Heidi Carlson de Coombs, and Blanca Ortiz Chamán. 2003. *Rimashun Kichwapi. Una introducción al quechua cajamarquino*. Lima: Atares artes y letras.

[107] Coon, Jessica, and Omer Preminger. 2012. Taking 'ergativity' out of split ergativity: A structural account of aspect and person splits. *lingbuzz/001556*.

[108] Copley, Bridget, and Heidi Harley. 2009. Futurates, directors and *have* causatives. *Snippets* 19:5-6.

[109] Cornips, L. 1990. Possessive object constructions in Heerlens. In F. Drijkoningen, A. van Kemenade (eds.). *Linguistics in the Netherlands 1991*. 21-30. Amsterdam: John Benjamins.

[110] Coronel-Molina, S., and Rodríguez-Mondoñedo, M. 2012. Language contact in the Andes and Universal Grammar. *Lingua* 122:447-460.

[111] Cowper, Elizabeth. 1989. Thematic underspecification: the case of *have*. *Toronto Working Papers in Linguistics* 10. 85-94.

[112] Craenenbroeck, Jeroen van (ed.). 2009. *Alternatives to Cartography*. Berlin: Mouton de Gruyter.

[113] Creissels, Denis. 2013. Control and the evolution of possessive and existential constructions. In Elly van Gelderen, Jóhanna Barðal, and Michela Cennamo (eds.). *Argument Structure in Flux: The Naples-Capri Papers*. 461-476. Amsterdam: John Benjamins Publishing Company.

[114] Cuervo, Maria Cristina. 2003. *Datives at Large*. PhD Thesis: MIT.

[115] D'Alessandro, Roberta. 2012. Merging Probes. A typology of person splits and person-driven differential object marking. *lingbuzz/001771*.

[116] D'Alessandro, Roberta, and Adam Ledgeway. 2010. The Abruzzese T-v system: feature spreading and the double-auxiliary construction. In D'Alessandro, Roberta, Adam Ledgeway, and Ian Roberts (eds.). *Syntactic Variation*. 201-209. Cambridge: Cambridge University Press.

[117] D'Alessandro, Roberta, and Ian Roberts. 2008. Movement and agreement in Italian past participles and defective phases. *Linguistic Inquiry* 39.3:477-491.

[118] D'Alessandro, Roberta, and Ian Roberts. 2010. Past participle agreement in Abruzzese: Split auxiliary selection and the null subject parameter. *Natural Language and Linguistic Theory* 28.1:41-72.

[119] Davis, Henry, Carrie Gillon, and Lisa Matthewson. 2014. How to Investigate Linguistic Diversity: Lessons from the Pacific Northwest. *Language* 90.4:180-226.

[120] Deal, Amy Rose. 2013. Possessor raising. *Linguistic Inquiry* 44.3: 391-432.

[121] Demeke, Girma. 2003. *The Clausal Syntax of Ethio-Semitic*. PhD Thesis: U. of Tromsø.

[122] Demirdache, Hamida, and Miryam Uribe-Etxebarria. 2000. The primitives of temporal relations. In Roger Martin, David Michaels, and Juan Uriagereka (eds.). *Step by Step: Essays on Minimalist Syntax in Honor of Howard Lasnik*. Cambridge, MA: MIT Press.

[123] Den Besten, Hans. 1983. On the interaction of root transformations and lexical deletive rules. In Werner Abraham (ed.). *On the Formal Nature of the Westgermania*. 47-131. Amsterdam: John Benjamins.

[124] Den Dikken, Marcel. 1995. *Particles*. Oxford: Oxford University Press.

[125] Den Dikken, Marcel. 1997. Introduction: The syntax of possession and the verb 'have'. *Lingua* 101:129-150.

[126] Den Dikken, Marcel. 1998. Predicate inversion in DP. In A. Alexiadou and C. Wilder (eds.). *Possessors, Predicates, and Movement in the Determiner Phrase*. 177-214. Amsterdam: John Benjamins.

[127] Den Dikken, Marcel. 1999. On the structural representation of possession and agreement: The case of (anti-)agreement in Hungarian possessed nominal phrases. In Kenesei, István (ed.). *Crossing Boundaries*. 137-178. Amsterdam: John Benjamins.

[128] Den Dikken, Marcel. 2003. On the syntax of locative and directional adpositional phrases. Ms. Graduate Center, City University of New York.

[129] Den Dikken, Marcel. 2010. Directions from the GET-GO. *Catalan Journal of Linguistics* 9:23-53.

[130] Derbyshire, D. C. 1979. *Hixkaryana*. Amsterdam: North-Holland.

[131] Diesing, Molly. 1992. *Indefinites*. Cambridge, MA: MIT Press.

[132] Dixon, R. M. W. (ed.). 1976. *Grammatical Categories in Australian Languages*. Canberra: Australian Institute of Aboriginal Studies.

[133] Donati, C. 2006. On wh-head movement. In L.L.-S. Cheng and N. Corver. (eds.). *Wh-Movement: Moving on*. 21-46. Cambridge, MA: MIT Press.

[134] Dowty, David. 1979. *Word Meaning and Montague Grammar: The Semantics of Verbs and Times in Generative Semantics and in Montague's PTQ*. Dordrecht: Springer.

[135] Embick, David. 2004. On the Structure of Resultative Participles in English. *Linguistic Inquiry* 35:355-392.

[136] Embick, David. 2010. *Localism vs Globalism in Morphology and Phonology*. Cambridge, MA: MIT Press.

[137] Embick, David, and Alec Marantz. 2008. Architecture and Blocking. *Linguistic Inquiry* 39.1:1-53.

[138] Embick, David, and Rolf Noyer. 2001. Movement operations after syntax. *Linguistic Inquiry* 32:555-595.

[139] Embick, David, and Rolf Noyer. 2007. Distributed Morphology and the Syntax-Morphology Interface. In Ramchand, Gillian, and Charles Reiss. (eds.) *Oxford Handbook of Linguistic Interfaces*. 289-324. Oxford: Oxford University Press.

[140] Emonds, J. 1976. *A Transformational Approach to English Syntax*. New York: New York Academic Press.

[141] Francez, Itamar. 2007. *Existential propositions*. PhD Thesis, Stanford University.

[142] Francez, Itamar. 2009. Existentials, predication, and modification. *Linguistics and Philosophy* 32.1:1-50.

[143] Francez, Itamar. 2010. Context dependence and implicit arguments in existentials. *Linguistics and Philosophy* 33.1:11-30.

[144] Francez, Itamar, and Andrew Koontz-Garboden. 2015. Semantic variation and the grammar of property concepts. *Language* 91.3:533-563.

[145] Francez, Itamar, and Andrew Koontz-Garboden. 2016. A note on possession and mereology in Ulwa property concept constructions. *Natural Language and Linguistic Theory* 34.1:93-106.

[146] Freeze, Ray. 1992. Existentials and other locatives. *Language* 68: 553-595.

[147] Gehrke, Berit. 2008. *Ps in motion: On the semantics and syntax of P elements and motion verbs*. PhD Thesis: Utrecht University.

[148] Georgala, Effi. 2012. *Applicatives in their structural and thematic function: a minimalist account of multitransitivity*. (PhD Thesis: Cornell University)

[149] Georgala, Effi, Waltraud Paul, and John Whitman. 2008. Expletive and thematic applicatives. In Charles B. Chang and Hannah J Haynie, (eds.) *Proceedings of WCCFL 26*.181-189. Sommerville, MA: Cascadilla Press.

[150] Givon, T. 1984. *Syntax: A Functional-Typological Introduction, Volume I*. Amsterdam: John Benjamins.

[151] Grierson, G.A. (ed.). 1909. *Linguistic Survey of India. Vol. III. Tibeto-Burman Family. Part I. General Introduction. Specimens of the Tibetan Dialects, the Himalayan Dialects and the North Assam Group*. Calcutta: Superintendent Government Printing Office.

[152] Grimshaw, Jane. 1990. *Argument Structure*. Cambridge, MA: MIT Press.

[153] Grimshaw, Jane, and Mester, Armin. 1988. Light Verbs and Theta-Marking. *Linguistic Inquiry* 19:205-232.

[154] Grondin, Marcelo. 1980. *Método de Quechua*. La Paz: Los Amigos del Libro.

[155] Guéron, Jacqueline. 1985. Inalienable Possession, PRO-Inclusion, and Lexical Chains. In Jacqueline Guéron, Hans Georg Obenauer, and Jeans-Yves Pollock (eds.). *Grammatical Representation*. 43-86. Dordrecht: Foris.

[156] Guéron, Jacqueline. 1986. Le Verbe Avoir. In P. Coopmans, I. Bordelois, and B. Dotson Smith (eds.). *Forma Parameters of Generative Grammar II, Going Romance*. 83-105. Utrecht University.

[157] Gutiérrez-Rexach, Javier. 2012. *Have*, An Essentialist Semantics. *UCLA Working Papers in Linguistics: Theories of Everything*: 91-102.

[158] Hagège, Claude. 1993. *The Language Builder: An Essay on the Human Signature in Linguistic Morphogenesis*. Amsterdam: John Benjamins.

[159] Hale, Kenneth, and Samuel Jay Keyser. 1993. On Argument Structure and the lexical expression of grammatical relations. In Kenneth Hale and Samuel Jay Keyser (eds.). *The View from Building 20: Essays in Linguistics in Honor of Sylvain Bromberger*. 53-109. Cambridge, MA: MIT Press.

[160] Hale, Kenneth, and Samuel Jay Keyser. 2002. *Prolegomenon to a Theory of Argument Structure*. Cambridge, MA: MIT Press.

[161] Halle, Morris. 1997. Fission and Impoverishment. *MIT Working Papers in Linguistics* 30, 425-449.

[162] Halle, Morris, and Marantz, Alec. 1993. Distributed Morphology and the Pieces of Inflection. In Kenneth Hale and Samuel Jay Keyser (eds.). *The View from Building 20: Essays in Linguistics in Honor of Sylvain Bromberger*. 111-176. Cambridge, MA: MIT Press.

[163] Halle, Morris, and Marantz, Alec. 1994. Some key features of Distributed Morphology. *MIT Working Papers in Linguistics* 21:275-288.

[164] Halpert, Claire. 2012. *Argument licensing and agreement in Zulu.* PhD Thesis: MIT.

[165] Halpert, Claire, and Michael Diercks. 2014. More on *have* and *need.* Ms. University of Minnesota and Pomona College.

[166] Harbour, Daniel. 2003. The Kiowa Case for Feature Insertion. *Natural Language & Linguistic Theory* 21:543-578.

[167] Harley, Heidi. 1995. *Subjects, events and licensing.* PhD Thesis: MIT.

[168] Harley, Heidi. 1997. Logophors, variable binding, and the interpretation of *have. Lingua* 103:75-84.

[169] Harley, Heidi. 1998. You're having me on!: aspects of *have. semanticsArchive/TY3M2M5O.*

[170] Harley, Heidi. 2002. Possession and the double object construction. *Yearbook of Linguistic Variation* 2:29-68.

[171] Harley, Heidi. 2008. When is a Syncretism more than a Syncretism. In Daniel Harbour, David Adger, and Susana Béjar (eds.). *Phi Theory: Phi-Features across Modules and Interfaces.* 251-294. Oxford: Oxford University Press.

[172] Harley, Heidi. 2010. Affixation and the Mirror Principle. In Folli, Raffaella, and Christiane Ullbricht (eds.). *Interfaces in Linguistics.* 166-186. Oxford: Oxford University Press.

[173] Harley, Heidi. 2013. External arguments and the Mirror Principle: On the distinctness of Voice and v. *Lingua* 125, 34-57.

[174] Harley, Heidi. 2014. On the identity of roots. *Theoretical Linguistics* 40.3, 225-276.

[175] Hartmann, Jutta M., and Milićević, Nataša. 2008. The syntax of existential sentences in Serbian. In Gerhild Zybatow, Uwe Junghanns, Denisa Lenertova, and Petr Biskup (eds.). *Studies in Formal Slavic Phonology, Morphology, Syntax, Semantics and Information Structure. Proceedings of FDSL 7, Leipzig 2007 (= Linguistik International; 21).* 131-142. Frankfurt am Main: Peter Lang,

[176] Hartman, J. 2009. Intervention in tough constructions. In Suzi Lima, Kevin Mullin, and Brian Smith (eds.). *Proceedings of the 39th Meeting of the North East Linguistics Society.* 387-398. Amherst, MA: GLSA.

[177] Hartman, J. 2012. (Non-)Intervention in A-movement: some cross-constructional and cross-linguistic consequences. *Linguistic Variation* 1.2:121-148.

[178] Harves, Stephanie. 2002. *Unaccusative Syntax in Russian.* PhD Thesis, Princeton University.

[179] Harves, Stephanie. 2009. Class Handouts. Handouts from the seminar on *needing, wanting, having, and being.* New York University.

[180] Harves, S., and Kayne, R. 2012. Having 'need' and needing 'have'. *Linguistic Inquiry* 43.1:120-132.

[181] Haspelmath, Martin. 1993. More on the typology of inchoative/causative verb alternations. In Bernard Comrie, and Maria Polinsky (eds.). *Causatives and Transitivity. (Studies in Language Companion Series, 23.)* 87-120. Amsterdam: Benjamins.

[182] Haspelmath, Martin. 2011. The indeterminacy of word segmentation and the nature of morphology and syntax. *Folia Linguistica* 45.1:31-80.

[183] Hastings, Rachel. 2003. The semantics of discontinuous noun phrases in Quechua. In J. Anderssen, P. Menéndez-Benito, and A. Werle (eds.). *Proceedings of SULA 2, UMWPL.* 35-56. Amherst, MA: GLSA Publications.

[184] Hastings, Rachel. 2004. *The Syntax and Semantics of Relativization and Quantification: The Case of Quechua.* PhD Thesis: Cornell University.

[185] Hazout, Ilan. 1991. *Verbal Nouns: θ-theoretic Studies in Hebrew and Arabic*. Doctoral Dissertation, University of Massachusetts, Amherst.

[186] Hazout, Ilan. 2000. Adjectival genitive constructions in Modern Hebrew: A case study in coanalysis. *The Linguistic Review* 17:29-52.

[187] Hazout, Ilan. 2004. The syntax of existential constructions. *Linguistic Inquiry* 35:3, 393-430.

[188] Heim, Irene, and Angelika Kratzer. 1998. *Semantics in Generative Grammar*. Oxford: Blackwell.

[189] Heine, Bernd. 1997. *Possession*. Cambridge: Cambridge University Press.

[190] Hermon, Gabriella. 1985. *Syntactic Modularity*. Dordrecht: Foris.

[191] Hermon, Gabriella. 2001. Non-Canonically-Marked A/S in Imbabura Quechua. In A.Y. Aikenvald, R.M.W. Dixon, and M. Onishi (eds.). *Non-Canonical Marking of Subjects and Objects*. 149-176. Amsterdam: John Benjamins.

[192] Hewitt, B. G. 1989. *Abkhaz*. London: Croom Helm.

[193] Higginbotham, James. 1985. On semantics. *Linguistic Inquiry* 16:547-593.

[194] Hiraiwa, Ken. 2001. Multiple Agree and the defective intervention constraint in Japanese. In O. Matushansky (ed.). *The Proceedings of the MIT-Harvard Joint Conference (HUMIT 2000), MITWPL 40* 67-80. Cambridge, MA: MITWPL.

[195] Hiraiwa, Ken. 2005. *Dimensions of symmetry in syntax: Agreement and clausal architecture*. PhD Thesis: MIT.

[196] Hirtle, W. H. 1970. *-Ed* Adjectives like 'Verandahed' and 'Blue-Eyed'. *Journal of Linguistics* 6.1:19-36.

[197] Hockett, Charles F. 1958. *A Course in Modern Linguistics*. New York: MacMillan.

[198] Hoekstra, Teun. 1994. HAVE as BE Plus or minus. In Cinque, Guglielmo, Jan Koster, Jean-Yves Pollock, Luigi Rizzi, and Raffaella Zanuttini (eds.). *Paths Towards Universal Grammar; Studies in Honor of Richard S. Kayne*. 199-215. Washington DC: Georgetown University Press.

[199] Hoggarth, Leslie. 2004. *Contributions to Cuzco Quechua Grammar*. Bonn: Bonn Americanist Studies.

[200] Hornstein, Norbert. 1999. Movement and control. *Linguistic Inquiry* 30.1:69-96.

[201] Hornstein, Norbert. 2009. *A Theory of Syntax: Minimal Operations and Universal Grammar*. Cambridge: Cambridge University Press.

[202] Hornstein, Norbert, and Amy Weinberg. 1981. Case Theory and Preposition Stranding. *Linguistic Inquiry* 12.1:55-91.

[203] Hudson, R. A. 1975. Problems in the Analysis of *Ed*-Adjectives. *Journal of Linguistics* 11.1:69-72.

[204] Hyman, Larry M. 2003. Suffix ordering in Bantu: A morphocentric approach. *Yearbook of Morphology 2002* 245-281.

[205] Iatridou, Sabine. 1995. To Have and Have not: on the Deconstruction Approach. In J. Camacho, L. Choueiri, and M. Watanabe (eds.). *Proceedings of the 14h West Coast Conference in Formal Linguistics*. 185-201. Stanford, CA: CSLI Publications.

[206] Irie, Koji. 1997. Possessive verbs in modern Icelandic. *Tokyo University Linguistics Papers* 307-329.

[207] Irwin, Patricia. 2012. *Unaccusativity at the Interfaces*. PhD Thesis, NYU.

[208] Isačenko, Alexander V. 1974. On 'HAVE' and 'BE' Languages (A Typological Sketch). In Flier, Michael (ed.). *Slavic Forum: Essays in Linguistics and Literature* 43-77. The Hague: Mouton.

[209] Jacobson, Pauline. 1990. Raising as function composition. *Linguistics & Philosophy* 13.4:423-475.

[210] Jake, Janice. 1985. *Grammatical Relations in Imbabura Quechua*. New York: Garland.

[211] Jeong, Youngmi. 2007. *Applicatives: Structure and Interpretation from a Minimalist Perspective*. Amsterdam: John Benjamins.

[212] Jouitteau, Melanie, and Milan Rezac. 2008. From 'mihi est' to 'have' across Breton Dialects. In Paola Benincà, Federico Damonte, and Nicoletta Penello (eds.). *Selected Proceedings of the 34th Incontro di Grammatica Generativa: Special Issue of the Rivista di Grammatica Generativa, vol. 33.* 161-178. Padova: Unipress.

[213] Julien, Marit. 2002. *Syntactic Heads and Word Formation*. Oxford: Oxford University Press.

[214] Julien, Marit. 2005. *Nominal Phrases from a Scandinavian Perspective*. Amsterdam: John Benjamins.

[215] Jung, Hakyung. 2011. *The Syntax of the Be-Possessive*. Amsterdam: John Benjamins.

[216] Kahn, Charles H. 1966. The Greek verb 'to be' and the concept of being. *Foundations of Language* 2.3:245-265.

[217] Kalin, Laura. 2014. *Aspect and Argument Licensing in Neo-Aramaic*. Doctoral Dissertation: University of California, Los Angeles.

[218] Kastner, Itamar. 2016. *Form and meaning in the Hebrew Verb*. Doctoral Dissertation: New York University.

[219] Katz, Jerrold J., and Jerry Fodor. 1963. The structure of a semantic theory. *Language* 39:2, 170-210.

[220] Katz, Jerrold J., and Paul M. Postal. 1964. *An Integrated Theory of Linguistic Descriptions*. Cambridge, MA: MIT Press.

[221] Kayne, Richard S. 1984. *Connectedness and Binary Branching*. Dordrecht: Foris.

[222] Kayne, Richard S. 1985. Notes on English Agreement. Reprinted in Kayne, Richard S. 2000 *Parameters and Universals*. 187-205. Oxford: Oxford University Press.

[223] Kayne, Richard S. 1989. Facets of Romance Past Participle Agreement. Reprinted in Kayne, Richard S. (2000) *Parameters and Universals*. 25-39. Oxford: Oxford University Press.

[224] Kayne, Richard S. 1993. Toward a Modular Theory of Auxiliary Selection. Reprinted in Kayne, Richard S. 2000. *Parameters and Universals*. 107-130. Oxford: Oxford University Press.

[225] Kayne, Richard S. 1994. *The Antisymmetry of Syntax*. Cambridge, MA: MIT Press.

[226] Kayne, Richard S. 1996. Microparametric Syntax. Some Introductory Remarks. Reprinted in Richard S. Kayne. 2000. *Parameters and Universals*. 3-39. Oxford: Oxford University Press.

[227] Kayne, Richard S. 2000. *Parameters and Universals*. Oxford: Oxford University Press.

[228] Kayne, Richard S. 2005. *Movement and Silence*. Oxford: Oxford University Press.

[229] Kayne, Richard S. 2008. Expletives, datives, and the tension between morphology and syntax. In M. Theresa Biberauer (ed.). *The Limits of Syntactic Variation*. 175-218. Amsterdam: John Benjamins.

[230] Kayne, Richard S. 2008/2010. Antisymmetry and the Lexicon. Reprinted in Kayne, Richard S. 2010. *Comparisons and Contrasts*. 165-189. Oxford: Oxford University Press.

[231] Kayne, Richard S. 2009. The English indefinite article 'one'. Talk handout, June 2009, University of Cambridge.

[232] Kayne, Richard S. 2010a. Towards a syntactic reinterpretation of Harris and Halle (2005) In R. Bok-Bennema, B. Kampers-Manhe B. Hollebrandse (eds.) *Romance Languages and*

Linguistic Theory 2008, Selected Papers from 'Going Romance' Groningen 2008. 145-170. Amsterdam: John Benjamins.

[233] Kayne, Richard S. 2010b. *Comparisons and Contrasts.* Oxford: Oxford University Press.

[234] Keenan, Edward L. 1987. A semantic definition of "Indefinite NP". In Eric J. Reuland and Alice G.B. ter Meulen (eds.). *The Representation of (In)definiteness.* 286-317. Cambridge, MA: MIT Press.

[235] Kenesei, István. 1996. On bracketing paradoxes in Hungarian. *Acta Linguistica Hungarica* 43:153-173.

[236] Kerke, Simon C. van de. 1996. *Affix Order and Interpretation in Bolivian Quechua.* PhD Dissertation: University of Amsterdam.

[237] Kilian-Hatz, Christa, and Thomas Stolz. 1992. Comitative, concomitance, and beyond: On the interdependence of grammaticalization and conceptualization. Paper presented at the *Annual Conference of the Linguistic Society of Belgium,* November 26-28, 1992, University of Antwerp.

[238] Kim, Kyumin. 2010. High Applicatives in Korean causatives and passives. *Lingua* 121:487-510.

[239] Kim, Kyumin. 2012. Argument structure licensing and English *have. Journal of Linguistics* 48, 71-105.

[240] Kiparsky, Paul. 1973. 'Elsewhere' in Phonology. In Kiparsky, Paul, and S. Anderson, (eds.). *A Festschrift for Morris Halle.* New York: Holt, Rinehart and Winston.

[241] Koeneman, Olaf, Marika Lekakou, and Sjef Barbiers. 2011. Perfect Doubling. *Linguistic Variation* 11.1:35-75.

[242] Koontz-Garboden, Andrew, and Itamar Francez. 2010. Possessed properties in Ulwa. *Natural Language Semantics* 18.2:197-240.

[243] Koopman, Hilda. 1997. Prepositions, postpositions, circumpositions and particles: The structure of Dutch PPs. *Ms. UCLA.*

[244] Koopman, Hilda. 2002. Derivations and complexity filters. In Artemis Alexiadou, Elena Anagnostopoulou, Sjef Barbiers, and Hans-Martin Gärtner. (eds.). *Dimensions of Movement: From Features to Remnants.* 155-188. Amsterdam: John Benjamins.

[245] Koopman, Hilda. 2005. Korean (and Japanese) Morphology from a Syntactic Perspective. *Linguistic Inquiry* 38.4:601-633.

[246] Koopman, Hilda. 2006. Agreement: in defense of the 'Spec-head configuration'. In C. Boeckx (ed.). *Agreement Systems.* Amsterdam: John Benjamins.

[247] Koopman, Hilda. 2012. Samoan ergatives as double passives. In L. Brugé, A. Cardinaletti, G. Giusti, N. Monera, and C. Poletto. (eds.). *Functional Heads.* Oxford: Oxford University Press.)

[248] Koopman, Hilda, and Anna Szabolcsi. 2000. *Verbal Complexes.* Cambridge, MA: MIT Press.

[249] Kratzer, Angelika. 1981. The notional category of modality. *Words, Worlds, and Contexts:*38-74.

[250] Kratzer, Angelika. 1991. Modality. In Stechow, Arnim v., and Dieter Wunderlich. (eds.). *Semantics: An International Handbook of Contemporary Research.* 639-650. Berlin: de Gruyter.

[251] Kratzer, Angelika. 1996. Severing the external argument from its verb. In Rooryck, Johan, and Laurie Zaring. (eds.). 1996. *Phrase Structure and the Lexicon.* Dordrecht: Kluwer.

[252] Kratzer, Angelika. 2009. Making a pronoun: Fake indexicals as windows into the properties of pronouns. *Linguistic Inquiry* 40.2:187-237.

[253] Krejci, Bonnie. 2014. What Is Raining? English Weather *it* Revisited. Talk given at *the 88th Annual Meeting of the Linguistic Society of America,* Minneapolis, MN.

[254] Kusters, Wouter. 2003. *Linguistic Complexity: The Influence of Social Change on Verbal Inflection*. Utrecht: LOT.

[255] Laime Ajacopa, Teofilo. 2007. *Diccionario Bilingüe/Iskay simipi yuyayk'ancha Quechua-Castellano Castellano-Quechua*. La Paz.

[256] Landman, Fred. 2004. *Indefinites and the Type of Sets*. Oxford: Blackwell.

[257] Landman, Fred, and Barbara H. Partee. 1987. Weak NPs in HAVE sentences. Unpublished Abstract, UMass Amherst.

[258] Langacker, Ronald W. 1968. Observations on French possessives. *Language* 44.1:51-75.

[259] Langacker, Ronald W. 1987. *Foundations of Cognitive Grammar. Vol. 1: Theoretical Perspectives*. Stanford University Press.

[260] Langacker, Ronald W. 1993. Reference-point constructions. *Cognitive Linguistics* 4:1-38.

[261] LaPolla, R., and C. Huang. 2003. *A Grammar of Qiang, with Annotated Texts and Glossary*. Berlin: Mouton De Gruyter.

[262] Larson, Richard. 1988. On the double object construction. *Linguistic Inquiry* 19:335-391.

[263] Larson, Richard. 1990. Double objects revisited: Reply to Jackendoff. *Linguistic Inquiry* 21:589-632.

[264] Larson, Richard. 1998. Events and modification in nominals. In Strolovitch, D., and A. Lawson (eds.). *Proceedings from Semantics and Linguistic Theory (SALT) VIII*. Ithaca, NY: Cornell University.

[265] Lastra, Yolanda. 1968. *Cochabamba Quechua Syntax*. The Hague: Mouton.

[266] Le Bruyn, Bert, Henriette de Swart, and Joost Zwarts. 2013. Relational Nouns and Existential *have*. Talk given at SALT 23, UC Santa Cruz.

[267] Ledgeway, Adam. 2000. *A Comparative Syntax of the Dialects of Southern Italy: A Minimalist Approach*. Oxford: Publications of the Philological Society.

[268] LeFebvre, Claire, and Pieter Muysken. 1988. *Mixed Categories: Nominalizations in Quechua*. Dordrecht: Kluwer.

[269] Lehmann, Christian. 2002. *Possession in Yucatec Maya*. Erfurt: Universität.

[270] Leu, Thomas. 2008. *The internal syntax of determiners*. PhD Thesis, NYU.

[271] Leu, Thomas. 2012. The indefinite article–Indefinite?–Article? Talk given at *the 35th Penn Linguistics Colloquium*.

[272] Leu, Thomas. 2015. *The Architecture of Determiners*. Oxford: Oxford University Press.

[273] Levin, Beth, and Malka Rappaport Hovav. 2005. *Argument Realization*. Cambridge: Cambridge University Press.

[274] Levinson, Lisa. 2011. Possessive WITH in Germanic: HAVE and the Role of P. *Syntax* 14.4:355-393.

[275] Li, C. N., and S. A. Thompson. 1981. *Mandarin Chinese: A Functional Reference Grammar*. Berkeley: University of California Press.

[276] Lichtenberk, Frantisek. 1985. Possessive constructions in Oceanic languages and in Proto-Oceanic. In *Austronesian linguistics at the 15th Pacific Science Congress*. 93-140. Pacific Linguistics, C-88.

[277] Ljung, Magnus. 1976. *-Ed* Adjectives Revisited. *Journal of Linguistics* 12.1:159-168.

[278] Locker, E. 1954. Être et avoir. Leurs expressions dans les langues. *Anthropos* 49:481-510.

[279] Lohndal, Terje. 2012. *Without Specifiers: Phrase Structure and Events*. PhD Thesis: University of Maryland.

[280] Lohndal, Terje. 2014. *Phrase Structure and Argument Structure: A Case Study of the Syntax-Semantics Interface*. Oxford: Oxford University Press.

[281] Lomashvili, Leila. 2011. *Complex Predicates: The Syntax-Morphology Interface.* Amsterdam: John Benjamins.

[282] Longobardi, Giuseppe. 1994. Reference and proper names: A theory of N-Movement in syntax and logical form. *Linguistic Inquiry* 25.4:609-665.

[283] Loporcaro, Michele. 2007. On triple auxiliation in Romance. *Linguistics* 45.1:173-222.

[284] Lynch, John. 1973. Verbal aspects of possession in Melanesian languages. *Working Papers in Linguistics (Honolulu)* 5.9:1-29.

[285] Lyons, John. 1968. *Introduction to Theoretical Linguistics.* Cambridge: Cambridge University Press.

[286] Mahajan, Anoop. 1994. The Ergativity Parameter: Have-be Alternation, Word Order and Split Ergativity. In M. Gonzalez (ed.). *Proceedings of NELS 24.* 317-331. GLSA, Amherst.

[287] Marantz, Alec. 1991/2000. Case and licensing. In Reuland, Eric (ed.). *Arguments and Case: Explaining Burzio's Generalization.* 11-30. Philadelphia: John Benjamins.

[288] Marantz, Alec. 1993. Implications of asymmetries in double object constructions. In Sam A. Mchombo (ed.). *Theoretical Aspects of Bantu Grammar.* 113-151. Standford, CA: CSLI Publications.

[289] Marantz, Alec. 1997. No Escape from Syntax: Don't Try Morphological Analysis in the Privacy of your own Lexicon. *UPenn Working Papers in Linguistics, Volume 4.2, Proceedings of the Penn Linguistics Colloquium.* 201-225.

[290] Marantz, Alec. 2009a. Resultatives and re-resultatives: Direct objects may construct events by themselves. Paper presented at *Penn Linguistics Colloquium.*

[291] Marantz, Alec. 2009b. Roots, re-, and affected agents: Can roots pull the agent under little v? Talk given at *Roots* workshop, Universität Stuttgart.

[292] Marantz, Alec. 2013a. Verbal argument structure: Events and participants. *Lingua*: 152-168.

[293] Marantz, Alec. 2013b. Class lectures: Handouts from the Seminar on Argument Structure, Fall 2013. New York University.

[294] Markman, Vita G. 2008. Argument small clauses. *Journal of Slavic Linguistics*, Vol. 16, No. 2: 187-246.

[295] Martin, S. E. 1975. *A Reference Grammar of Japanese.* New Haven: Yale University Press.

[296] Maslova, E. 2003. *Tundra Yukaghir.* Munich: LINCOM Europa.

[297] Matthewson, Lisa. 2004. On the methodology of semantic fieldwork. *International Journal of American Linguistics* 70:369-415.

[298] McCarthy, John. 2002. *A Thematic Guide to Optimality Theory.* Cambridge: Cambridge University Press.

[299] McCarthy, John. 2007. *Hidden Generalizations: Phonological Opacity in Optimality Theory.* London: Equinox.

[300] McCarthy, John. 2008. *Doing Optimality Theory: Applying Theory to Data.* Oxford: Blackwell.

[301] McCloskey, James. 2014. Irish existentials in context. *Syntax* 17.4:343-384.

[302] McNally, Louise. 1992. *An Interpretation for the English Existential Construction.* New York: Garland.

[303] McNally, Louise. 1998. Existential sentences without existential quantification. *Linguistics and Philosophy* 21: 353-392.

[304] Mel'čuk, I. 1973. On the possessive forms of the Hungarian noun. In F. Kiefer and N. Ruwet (eds.). *Generative Grammar in Europe.* Dordrecht: Reidel.

[305] Merchant, Jason. 2015. How much context is enough? Two cases of span-conditioned stem allomorphy. *Linguistic Inquiry* 46.2:273-303.

[306] Meyers, Scott P. 1990. *Tone and the Structure of Words in Shona*. Garland Press: New York.

[307] Michael, Lev. 2012. Possession in Nanti. In Alexandra Aikhenvald and R.M.W Dixon (eds.). *Possession and Ownership*. 149-166. Oxford: Oxford University Press.

[308] Miller, George A., and Philip N. Johnson-Laird. 1976. *Language and Perception*. Cambridge, MA: Harvard University Press.

[309] Milsark, Gary. 1977. Toward an explanation of certain peculiarities of the existential construction in English. *Linguistic Analysis* 3:1-29.

[310] Muysken, Pieter. 1977. *Syntactic Developments in the Verb Phrase of Ecuadorian Quechua*. Lisse: the Peter de Ridder Press.

[311] Muysken, Pieter. 1995. Focus in Quechua. In K. Kiss (ed.). *Discourse Configurational Languages*. Oxford: Oxford University Press.

[312] Myler, Neil. 2009. *Form, Function and Explanation at the Syntax-Morphology Interface: Agreement, Agglutination and Post-Syntactic Operations*. MPhil Thesis, University of Cambridge.

[313] Myler, Neil. 2010. A Phrasal Derivational Affix: The Case of -yoq in Quechua. Talk given at the *Georgetown Linguistic Society Conference*, Georgetown University, February 2010.

[314] Myler, Neil. Forthcoming. Cliticization feeds agreement: A view from Quechua (Accepted for Publication in *Natural Language and Linguistic Theory*)

[315] Myler, Neil. In Press. Exceptions to the Mirror Principle and Morphophonological "action at a distance": The role of "word"-internal Phrasal Movement and Spell Out. In Heather Newell, Maire Noonan, Glyne Piggott, and Lisa Travis (eds.). *The Structure of Words at the Interfaces*. Oxford: Oxford University Press.

[316] Myler, Neil, Einar Freyr Sigurðsson, and Jim Wood. 2014. Predicative Possession Builds on top of Attributive Possession: Evidence From Icelandic. Talk given at the *GLOW 37 Semantics Workshop on Possession*, Brussels.

[317] Nardi, Ricardo L. J. 2002. *Introducción al quichua santiagueño*. San Miguel de Tucumán: Editorial Dunken.

[318] Nevins, Andrew. 2011. Multiple agree with clitics: Person complementarity vs. omnivorous number. *Natural Language & Linguistic Theory* 29.4: 939-971.

[319] Nevins, Andrew, and Neil Myler. 2014. A brown-eyed girl. *UCLA Working Papers in Linguistics, Papers in Honor of Sarah van Wagenen* Los Angeles, CA. Also available on Ling-Buzz: lingbuzz/002021.

[320] Nevins, Andrew, and Neil Myler. Submitted. A Relation-Headed Approach to Participialized Inalienable Possession. Ms., University College London and Boston University.

[321] Nichols, Johanna. 1988. On alienable and inalienable possesion. In William Shipley (ed.). *In Honor of Mary Haas: From the Haas Festival Conference on Native American Linguistics*. 557-609. Berlin: Mouton de Gruyter.

[322] Nichols, Johanna. 1992. *Linguistic Diversity in Space and Time*. Chicago: University of Chicago Press.

[323] Noonan, Máire. 1993. Statives, perfectives and accusativity: The importance of being HAVE. In Jonathan Mead (ed.). *Proceedings of the Eleventh West Coast Conference on Formal Linguistics*. 354-370. Stanford, CA: CSLI Publications.

[324] Oehrle, Richard T. 1976. *The Grammatical Status of the English Dative Alternation*. PhD Thesis: MIT.

[325] Oltra-Massuet, Isabel. 2010. *On the Morphology of Complex Adjectives*. PhD Thesis, Universitat Autònoma de Barcelona.

[326] Pak, Marjorie. 2014. *A/an* and *the*: allomorphy or phonology? Talk given at the *88th Annual Meeting of the Linguistic Society of America*, Minneapolis, MN.

[327] Paul, Waltraud, and John Whitman. 2010. Applicative structure and Mandarin ditransitives. In M. Duguine, S. Huidobro, and N. Madariaga (eds.). *Argument Structure and Syntactic Relations from a Cross-Linguistic Perspective*. 261-282. Amsterdam-Philadelphia: John Benjamins.

[328] Partee, Barbara H. 1999. Weak NPs in HAVE Sentences. In J. Gerbrandy, M. Marx, M. de Rijke, and Y. Venema (eds.). *JFAK, a Liber Amicorum for Johan van Benthen on the occasion of his 50th Birthday*. 39-57. Amsterdam: University of Amsterdam, Amsterdam.

[329] Partee, Barbara H., and Vladimir Borschev. 2001/2004. Some Puzzles of Predicate Possessives. In István Kenesei and Robert M. Harnish (eds.). *Perspectives on Semantics, Pragmatics, and Discourse: A Festschrift for Ferenc Kiefer*. 91-117. Amsterdam: John Benjamins. Reprinted in Partee, Barbara H. 2004. *Compositionality in Formal Semantics: Selected Papers by Barbara H. Partee*. Oxford: Wiley.

[330] Partee, Barbara H., and Vladimir Borschev. 2002. Genitive of negation and scope of negation in Russian existential sentences. Talk given at the Annual Workshop on *Formal Approaches to Slavic Linguistics*.

[331] Paster, Mary. 2006. *Phonological conditions on affixation*. PhD Thesis: University of California at Berkeley.

[332] Pensalfini, Robert J. 1997. *Jingulu Grammar, Dictionary, and Texts*. Doctoral Dissertation: MIT Press.

[333] Perlmutter, David. 1970. On the Article in English. In Bierwisch, Manfred, and Karl E. Heidolph (eds.). *Progress in linguistics*. 233-248. Mouton.

[334] Perlmutter, David, and Paul M. Postal. 1984. The I-advancement Exclusiveness Law. In D. Perlmutter and C. Rosen (eds.). *Studies in Relational Grammar, 2*. 81-125. Chicago: University of Chicago Press.

[335] Pesetsky, David. 1982. *Paths and Categories*. Ph.D. Thesis: MIT.

[336] Pesetsky, David. 1995. *Zero Syntax: Experiencers and Cascades*. Cambridge, MA: MIT Press.

[337] Pesetsky, David, and Esther Torrego. 2004. The Syntax of Valuation and the Interpretability of Features. In Simin Karimi, Vida Samiian, and Wendy K. Wilkins. (eds.). *Phrasal and Clausal Architecture: Syntactic Derivation and Interpretation: in Honor of Joseph E. Emonds*. Amsterdam: Benjamins.

[338] Pesetsky, David, and Esther Torrego. 2011. Case. In Cedric Boeckx (ed.). *The Oxford Handbook of Linguistic Minimalism*. Oxford: Oxford University Press.

[339] Pfaff, Alexander. 2015. *Adjectival and Genitival Modification in Definite Noun Phrases in Icelandic: A Tale of Outsiders and Inside Jobs*. Doctoral Dissertation: University of Tromsø.

[340] Pike, Kenneth L. 1967. *Language in Relation to a Unified Theory of Human Behavior*. The Hague: Mouton.

[341] Popjes, J., and Popjes, J. 1986. Canela-Kraho. In D. C. Derbyshire, and G. K. Pullum, (eds.). *Handbook of Amazonian Languages, Vol. I*. 128-99. Berlin: Mouton de Gruyter.

[342] Postal, Paul M. 1970. On the surface verb 'remind'. *Linguistic Inquiry* 1:37-120.

[343] Postma, Gertjan. 1993. The Syntax of the Morphological Defectivity of BE. 31-67. HIL manuscripts 3.

[344] Preminger, Omer. 2009. Breaking agreements: Distinguishing agreement and clitic-doubling by their failures. *Linguistic Inquiry* 40:619-666.

[345] Preminger, Omer. 2011. *Agreement as a Fallible Operation*. PhD Thesis, MIT.

[346] Preminger, Omer. 2013. That's not how you agree: A reply to Zeijlstra. *The Linguistic Review* 30.3:491-500.

[347] Press, Ian. 1986. *A Grammar of Modern Breton*. Berlin: Mouton de Gruyter.

[348] Prezioso, Mabel, and Rubén Torres. 2006. *Quechua Tukuypaj*. Buenos Aires: Nuestra América.

[349] Pustet, Regina. 2003. *Copulas: Universals in the Categorization of the Lexicon*. Oxford: Oxford University Press.

[350] Pylkkänen, Liina. 1998. The 'Be' of possession in Finnish. Ms. MIT.

[351] Pylkkänen, Liina. 2002/2008. *Introducing Arguments*. Cambridge, MA: MIT Press.

[352] Quesada, Félix. 1976. *Gramática Quechua-Cañaris*. Lima: Ministerio de Educación.

[353] Rando, E., and D.J. Napoli. 1978. Definites in *there*-sentences. *Language* 54.300-313.

[354] Ramchand, Gillian. 2008. *Verb Meaning and the Lexicon: A First Phase Syntax*. Cambridge: Oxford University Press.

[355] Richards, Norvin. 2001. An idiomatic argument for lexical decomposition. *Linguistic Inquiry* 32.1:183-192.

[356] Riemsdijk, Henk van. 1990. Functional prepositions. In Harm Pinkster and Inge Genee (eds.). *Unity in Diversity: Papers Presented to Simon C Dik on His 50th Birthday*. Dordrecht: Foris.

[357] Rimell, Laura D. 2012. *Nominal Roots as Event Predicates in English Denominal Conversion Verbs*. PhD Thesis: NYU.

[358] Ritter, Elizabeth, and Sara Thomas Rosen. 1993. Deriving causation. *Natural Language & Linguistic Theory*11, 519-555.

[359] Ritter, Elizabeth, and Sara Thomas Rosen. 1997. The function of *have*. *Lingua* 101:295-321.

[360] Rizzi, Luigi. 1997. The fine structure of the left periphery. In L. Haegeman (ed.). *Elements of Grammar: Handbook of Generative Syntax*. 281-337. Dordrecht: Kluwer.

[361] Roberts, Ian, and Anna Rousseau. 2003. *Syntactic Change: A Minimalist Approach to Grammaticalization*. Cambridge: Cambridge University Press.

[362] Rooryck, Johan. 1996. Prepositions and minimalist case marking. In Höskuldur Thráinsson, Samuel Epstein, and Steve Peter (eds.). *Studies in Comparative Germanic Syntax, Vol. 2*. 226-256. Dordrecht: Kluwer.

[363] Ross, John Robert. 1972. Act. In Donald Davidson and Gilbert Harman (eds.). *Semantics of Natural Language*. 70-126. Dordrecht: Reidel.

[364] Rothstein, Susan. 1999. Fine-Grained Structure in the Eventuality Domain: The Semantics of Predicative Adjective Phrases and BE. *Natural Language Semantics* 7:347-420.

[365] Roy, Isabelle. 2013. *Nonverbal Predication: Copular Sentences at the Syntax-Semantics Interface*. Oxford: Oxford University Press.

[366] Sæbø, Kjell. 2009. Possession and Pertinence: The meaning of *have*. *Natural Language Semantics* 17:369-397.

[367] Sag, Ivan, Thomas Wasow, and Emily Bender. 2003. *Syntactic Theory: A Formal Introduction*. Stanford, CA: CSLI Publications.

[368] Sánchez, Liliana. 1996. *Syntactic Structures in Nominals: A Comparative Study of Spanish and Southern Quechua*. PhD Thesis: University of Southern California.

[369] Sánchez, Liliana. 2010. *The Morphology and Syntax of Topic and Focus: Minimalist Inquiries in the Quechua Periphery*. Amsterdam: John Benjamins.

[370] Santo Tomás, Domingo de. 1560. *Grammatica o arte de la lengua general del Peru*. Valladolid: Francisco Fernández de Córdova.

[371] Schäfer, Florian. 2008. *The Syntax of (Anti-)Causatives*. Philadelphia: John Benjamins.

[372] Schäfer, Florian. 2012. The passive of reflexive verbs and its implications for theories of binding and case. *Journal of Comparative Germanic Linguistics* 15.3, 213-268.

[373] Schoorlemmer E. 2007. Agree and existential constructions. In J. Camacho, N. Flores-Férran, L. Sánchez, V. Déprez, M.J. Cabrera (eds.). *Romance Linguistics 2006: Selected Papers from the 36th Linguistic Symposium on the Romance Languages, New Brunswick, March-April 2006*. 275-295. Amsterdam: John Benjamins Publishing Company.

[374] Seiler, Hansjakob. 1974. The Principle of Concomitance: Instrumental, Comitative, and Collective. *Foundations of Language* 12.2:215-247.

[375] Selkirk, Elisabeth O. 1995. The prosodic structure of function words. In Jill N. Beckman, Laura Walsh Dickey, and Suzanne Urbanczyk (eds.). *Papers in Optimality Theory: University of Massachusetts Occasional Papers 18*. 439-469. Amherst, MA: UMass.

[376] Sigurðsson, Einar Freyr, and Jim Wood. 2013. 'Get'-passives and case alternations: the view from Icelandic. Talk given at the *31st West Coast Conference on Formal Linguistics*.

[377] Siloni, Tal. 2002. Adjectival constructs and inalienable constructions. In Jamal Ouhalla and Ur Shlonksy (eds.). *Themes in Arabic and Hebrew Syntax*. 161-187. Amsterdam: Kluwer Academic Publishers.

[378] Soto Ruiz, Clodoaldo. 2006. *Quechua: manual de enseñanza*. Lima: Instituto de Estudios Peruanos.

[379] Sorace, Antonella. 2004. Gradience at the Lexicon-Syntax Interface: Evidence from Auxiliary Selection and Implications for Unaccusativity. In A. Alexiadou, E. Anagnostopoulou, and M. Everaert (eds.). *The Unaccusativity Puzzle*. 243-268. Oxford: Oxford University Press.

[380] Starke, Michal. 2004. On the Inexistence of Specifiers and the Nature of Heads. In Adriana Belletti (ed.). *Structures Beyond: The Cartography of Syntactic Structures*. 252-268. Oxford: Oxford University Press.

[381] Starke, Michal. 2009. Nanosyntax–A short primer to a new approach to language. In Peter Svenonius, Gillian Ramchand, Michal Starke, and Knut Tarald Taraldsen (eds.). *Nordlyd 36.1*. 1-6. Tromsø: CASTL.

[382] Stassen, Leon. 1997. *Intransitive Predication*. Oxford: Oxford University Press.

[383] Stassen, Leon. 2009. *Predicative Possession*. Oxford: Oxford University Press.

[384] Stassen, Leon. 2013. Predicative Possession. In Matthew S. Dryer and Martin Haspelmath (eds.) *The World Atlas of Language Structures Online*. Leipzig: Max Planck Institute for Evolutionary Anthropology. (Available online at http://wals.info/chapter/117. Accessed on 2016-04-23.)

[385] Steddy, Sam, and Coppe van Urk. 2013. A Distributed Morphology View of Auxiliary Splits in Upper-Southern Italian. Talk given at *NELS 44*, UConn.

[386] Steele, S. 1990. Pass it on: A combinatorics-based approach to feature-passing. Unpublished ms. University of California, Los Angeles.

[387] Steriade, Donca. 2001/2009. The Phonology of Perceptibility Effects: The P-map and its Consequences for Constraint Organization. In Sharon Inkelas and Kristin Hanson (eds.). *On the Nature of the Word*. Cambridge, MA: MIT Press.

[388] Stolz, Thomas. 2001. To be with X is to have X: Comitatives, instrumentals, locative, and predicative possession. *Linguistics* 39.2:321-350.

[389] Stolz, Thomas, Sonja Kettler, Cornelia Stroh, and Aina Urdze. 2008. *Split Possession: An Areal Linguistic Study of the Alienability Correlation and Related Phenomena in the Languages of Europe*. Amsterdam: John Benjamins.

[390] Svenonius, Peter. 2003. Limits on P: Filling in holes vs. falling in holes. *Nordlyd* 31:431-445.

[391] Svenonius, Peter. 2010. Spatial P in English. In Cinque, Guglielmo, and Luigi Rizzi (eds.). *Mapping spatial PPs: The Cartography of syntactic structures, Volume 6.* 127-160. Oxford: Oxford University Press.

[392] Svenonius, Peter. 2012. Spanning. *lingbuzz/001501*.

[393] Svenonius, Peter, and Gillian Ramchand. 2014. Deriving the Functional Hierarchy. *Language Sciences* 46.b:152-174.

[394] Szabolcsi, Anna. 1981. The possessive construction in Hungarian: a configurational category in a non-configurational language. *Acta Linguistica Academiae Scientarum Hungaricae* 31:261-289.

[395] Szabolcsi, Anna. 1983. The possessor that ran away from home. *The Linguistic Review*, 3. 89-102.

[396] Szabolcsi, Anna. 1994. The noun phrase. In Ferenć Kiefer and Katalin E. Kiss (eds.). *The Syntactic Structure of Hungarian. Syntax and Semantics 27.* 179-274. San Diego, CA: Academic Press.

[397] Tham, Shiao Wei. 2004. *Representing Possessive Predication: Semantic Dimensions and Pragmatic Bases.* PhD Thesis: Stanford University.

[398] Tham, Shiao Wei. 2006. The Definiteness Effect in English *Have* Sentences. In Pascal Denis, Eric McCready, Alexis Palmer, and Brian Reese. (eds.). *Proceedings of the 2004 Texas Linguistic Society Conference.* 137-149. Somerville: MA: Cascadilla Proceedings Project.

[399] Tham, Shiao Wei. 2013. Possession as non-verbal predication. Handout from a talk given at the *39th Berkeley Linguistics Society Conference,* Feb 16-17, 2013.

[400] Thráinsson, Höskuldur. 2007. *The Syntax of Icelandic.* Cambridge: Cambridge University Press.

[401] Torero, Fernández de Córdova. 1964. Los dialectos quechuas. *Anales Científicos de la Universidad Agraria* 2.4:446-78.

[402] Torero, Fernández de Córdova. 1984. El comercio lejano y la difusión del quechua: El caso del Ecuador. *Revista Andina* 2.2. 367-402. Cuzco: Centro Bartolomé de las Casas.

[403] Torrego, Esther. 1992. Case and agreement structure. Ms., University of Massachusetts, Boston.

[404] Tremblay, Mireille. 1991. *Possession and datives: Binary branching from the lexicon to syntax.* PhD Thesis: McGill University.

[405] Trommer, Jochen. 2008. "Case suffixes," postpositions, and the phonological word in Hungarian. *Linguistics* 46.2:403-437.

[406] Tsujioka, Takae. 2002. *The Syntax of Possession in Japanese.* New York: Routledge.

[407] Tsunoda, Tasaku. 1996. The possession cline in Japanese and other languages. In Hilary Chappell and William McGregor. (eds.). *The Grammar of Inalienability: A Typological Perspective on Body Part Terms and the Part-Whole Relation.* 565-630. Mouton de Gruyter.

[408] Uriagereka, Juan. 1995. Aspects of the syntax of clitic placement in Western Romance. *Linguistic Inquiry* 25: 79-123.

[409] van Urk, Coppe. 2012. On idiomatic readings of *give, get,* and *have.* Talk given at Syntax Square, MIT, March 13, 2012.

[410] Vaux, Bert. 2008. Why the phonological component must be serial and rule-based. In Bert Vaux and Andrew Nevins (eds.). *Rules, Constraints and Phonological Phenomena.* Oxford: Oxford University Press.

[411] Verhaar, John W. M. (ed.). 1967. *The verb 'be' and its synonyms. Part 2. Foundations of Language, Supplementary Series, 6.* Dordrecht: Reidel.

[412] Weber, David. 1983. The relationship of morphology and syntax: evidence from Quechua. *Work Papers of the Summer Institute of Linguistics, University of North Dakota Session.* 161-181.

[413] Weber, David. 1989. *A Grammar of Huallaga (Huanuco) Quechua.* Los Angeles: University of California Press.

[414] Welch, Nicholas. 2012. *The Bearable Lightness of Being: the Encoding of Coincidence in Two-Copula Languages.* Doctoral Dissertation, University of Calgary.

[415] Willgohs, Beatriz, and Patrick Farrell. 2009. Case and Grammatical Functions in Imbabura Quechua: an LFG Approach. In Miriam Butt and Tracy Holloway King. (eds.). *Proceedings of the LFG09 Conference.* Stanford, CA: CSLI Publications.

[416] Williams, Edwin. 1980. Predication. *Linguistic Inquiry* 11:203-238.

[417] Williams, Edwin. 1994. *Thematic Structure in Syntax.* Cambridge, MA: MIT Press.

[418] Wolf, Matthew. 2008. *Optimal Interleaving: Serial Phonology-Morphology Interaction in a Constraint-based Model.* PhD Thesis: UMass Amherst.

[419] Wolf, Matthew. 2011. Candidate chains, unfaithful spell-out, and outwards-looking phonologically-conditioned allomorphy. *lingbuzz/001318.*

[420] Wood, Jim. 2009. Icelandic 'have' and 'need'. Seminar Handout, New York University.

[421] Wood, Jim. 2010. The Unintentional Causer in Icelandic. Talk given at NELS 41, UPenn.

[422] Wood, Jim. 2012. *Icelandic Morphosyntax and Argument Structure.* PhD Thesis: NYU.

[423] Wood, Jim. 2013. The unintentional causer in Icelandic. In Yelena Fainleib, Nicholas LaCara, and Yangsook Park (eds.). *Proceedings of the 41st Annual Meeting of the North East Linguistic Society.* 273-286. Amherst, MA: GLSA Publications.

[424] Wood, Jim. 2014a. Reflexive -*st* verbs in Icelandic. *Natural Language & Linguistic Theory* 32.4:1387-1425.

[425] Wood, Jim. 2014b. On Improper Movement of Accusative Subjects. Talk given at *NELS* 45, MIT.

[426] Wood, Jim. 2015. *Icelandic Morphosyntax and Argument Structure.* Dordrecht: Springer.

[427] Wood, Jim and Alec Marantz. 2015/To appear. The interpretation of external arguments. In Roberta D?Alessandro, Irene Franco, and Ángel Gallego. (eds.) *The Verbal Domain.* Oxford: Oxford University Press.

[428] Wood, Jim, and Einar Freyr Sigurðsson. 2014. Building deverbal ability adjectives in Icelandic. *University of Pennsylvania Working Papers in Linguistics 20 (1).* 351-360.

[429] Wurmbrand, Susi. 2001. *Infinitives: Restructuring and clause structure.* Berlin: Mouton de Gruyter.

[430] Zec, Draga. 1993. Rule domains and phonological change. In Sharon Hargus, and Ellen Kaisse (eds.). *Phonetics and Phonology, vol. 4: Studies in Lexical Phonology.* 365-405. San Diego: Academic Press.

[431] Zeijlstra, Hedde. 2012. There is only one way to agree. *The Linguistic Review* 29:491-539.

[432] 'Zeitoun, Elizabeth, Lillian M. Huang, Marie M. Yeh, and Anna H. Chang. 1999. Existential, Possessive, and Locative Constructions in Formosan Languages. *Oceanic Linguistics,* 38.1:1-42.

[433] Z'graggen, J.A. 1973. Possessor-possessed relationship in the Saker language, NE-New Guinea. *Oceanic Linguistics* 4:1/2:119-126.

Index

Abbott, Barbara, 335

Abbott, Miriam, 53

Abkhaz, 126

Accusative, 20, 116, 126, 133, 144, 179, 210-211, 224, 246-247, 249, 295, 314, 323-324, 340-341, 357-358, 363, 386-387, 389, 391-392, 394

Ackerman, Farrell, 369, 377

Adelaar, Willem F. H., 178-179, 352-353

Adger, David, 23, 43, 133-134, 234, 257-259, 419

Adnominal Possessive, 86-88, 117-118, 311, 325

Affix order, 53, 216

Agent, 1, 42-43, 92, 167, 207, 209, 212-214, 250-251, 255, 268-269, 271-272, 275-282, 286-287, 301, 303-305, 338, 400, 409

Agree (operation), 16, 20, 47, 156, 375-376, 390
  Definition, 16-17

Agreement, 17, 48-49, 85, 101, 104-105, 111, 115-116, 136, 138, 182-183, 190, 194-196, 198-201, 221, 247, 261, 313-315, 321-324, 328, 347, 363, 416

Aikhenvald, Alexandra Y., 53-54

Albarracín, Lelia Inés, 180, 210, 231

Alderetes, Jorge R., 180, 210

Alexiadou, Artemis, 10, 12, 19, 21, 46, 61, 254, 279, 320, 404

Alienator, 259

Allen, W. Sidney, 2

Allomorphy, 1, 12, 24, 31, 33-36, 44-45, 74-77, 114, 220, 233, 296, 319, 347
  conditioned allomorphy, 1, 31, 33-35, 77, 220, 233, 319
  restrictions on conditioned allomorphy, 34-36

Allosemy, 1, 40, 43, 45, 164, 219, 255, 265, 282-283, 301, 304, 394, 399

Alsina, Alex, 48, 405

Amharic, 216

Anagnostopoulou, Elena, 9-10, 12, 19, 21, 46, 61, 320, 404

Andoke, 345

Antonov, Anton, 132

Applicative, 24-25, 43, 49, 62, 81, 126, 138-140, 177-178, 182-198, 200-219, 221, 223-225, 227-233, 235-239, 267-268, 274, 346-347, 352, 364, 408, 422-423
  Low Applicative (functional head), 24, 210
  High Applicative (functional head), 21, 43, 192, 215-216

Arabic, 8-9, 85, 88, 124, 132, 135, 137-141, 253, 317
  Classical Arabic, 88
  Palestinian Arabic, 8-9, 85, 124, 135, 137-141, 253, 317

Arawakan, 50

Architecture of the Grammar, 1-2, 11-13, 15, 17, 19, 21, 23, 25, 27, 29, 31, 33-35, 37, 39, 41, 43, 45-46, 95-96, 403, 417, 420

Ariellese, 122-123

Aristotle, 3

Armenian, 36

Arnaiz, A., 152

Arregi, Karlos, 31-32, 36

Aspect, 18, 42, 44, 54, 121-122, 373

Athabaskan, 79

Austronesian, 109, 325
  See also Isbukun Bunun, Fijian, Samoan, Tagalog

Auxiliary, 8, 112-113, 119-123, 125, 171, 310-311, 320-321, 340, 403, 409-411, 413-415, 419
  auxiliary selection, 119-120, 122, 320-321, 340, 409, 414
  auxiliary uses of HAVE and BE, 112, 119, 123, 403

Bach, Emmon, 2, 4-5, 42, 150-151, 162

Baker, Mark, 7, 9-10, 15, 17-18, 23, 46, 120, 215-216, 321-324, 390

Baltin, Mark, 116

Balusu, Rahul, 23, 43-44, 234

Bantu languages, 66, 132, 215-216, 385, 392, 397, 399
  See also Swahili, Xhosa, Zulu

Barker, Chris, 50, 53, 172, 219, 256, 258, 364

Basque, 126, 419

BE-APPL construction (in Santiago del Estero Quechua) 178, 231-239, 408,

BE-APPL construction (in Cochabamba Quechua), 49, 81, 177-178, 183, 186, 189-198, 201-202, 215, 218-219, 221, 223-225, 230-232, 235, 237-238, 346, 408, 422-423

Beard, Robert, 369

Beavers, John, 2, 4, 163, 171-172, 255, 336, 340

Becker, Misha, 73

BE construction (in Cochabamba Quechua), 6, 49, 62, 81, 85-88, 106, 109-110, 124, 129, 131, 133, 177, 183, 189-202, 215, 218, 220-222, 224, 231, 311, 408-409, 422-424

Béjar, Susana, 17

BE languages, 6, 8, 115, 120, 124, 126, 128-129, 132-134, 143, 144, 146, 148, 161, 178, 248, 249, 309

BE-LV construction (in Isbukun Bunun), 110

Belvin, Robert, 2-4, 67, 119, 150-156, 162, 167, 255, 265-266, 273, 275, 280-281, 283, 289, 291, 315, 336, 409

Bender, Emily, 48, 405

Benefactive, 24, 192-193, 202-204, 206, 208, 210, 235

Bentley, Delia, 28, 119, 320, 416

Benveniste, Emile, 2, 5, 119

Yoruba, 74
Yukaghir (Tundra), 91

Zapotec
  Ixtlan Zapotec, 96
Zec, Draga, 39

Zeijlstra, Hedde, 17
Zeitoun, Elizabeth, 109
Z'graggen, J.A., 79
Zulu, 397, 399-401
Zwarts, Joost, 163